Artificial Intelligence with Microsoft Power BI
Simpler AI for the Enterprise

Jennifer Stirrup and Thomas J. Weinandy

Beijing · Boston · Farnham · Sebastopol · Tokyo

Artificial Intelligence with Microsoft Power BI

by Jennifer Stirrup and Thomas J. Weinandy

Published by O'Reilly Media, Inc., 1005 Gravenstein Highway North, Sebastopol, CA 95472.

O'Reilly books may be purchased for educational, business, or sales promotional use. Online editions are also available for most titles (*https://oreilly.com*). For more information, contact our corporate/institutional sales department: 800-998-9938 or *corporate@oreilly.com*.

Acquisitions Editor: Michelle Smith	**Indexer:** Sue Klefstad
Development Editor: Angela Rufino	**Interior Designer:** David Futato
Production Editor: Kristen Brown	**Cover Designer:** Karen Montgomery
Copyeditor: Paula L. Fleming	**Illustrator:** Kate Dullea
Proofreader: J.M. Olejarz	

April 2024:   First Edition

Revision History for the First Edition

2024-03-28:   First Release

See *https://oreilly.com/catalog/errata.csp?isbn=9781098112752* for release details.

978-1-098-11275-2

[LSI]

Table of Contents

Preface

The adoption of artificial intelligence (AI) in businesses has seen significant growth and is impacting various industries in diverse ways. As of 2023, the global AI market was valued at $136.6 billion, and it is anticipated to reach $1.8 trillion by 2030.[1] Further, the global acquisition rate of AI has increased in recent years, with a significant uptick in AI utilization across different business sectors. Regarding specific industry impacts, AI is expected to drive a substantial boost to gross domestic product (GDP) in various sectors. This widespread adoption emphasizes AI's versatility and potential with respect to data transformation, which is foundational to the success of all businesses. Due to the promise of AI, companies are keen to leverage AI as a Service (AIaaS) platforms to use sophisticated AI tools without needing vast in-house expertise. For example, AI will revolutionize customer interactions in the retail industry. Experts predict that 19 in every 20 customer interactions will be AI assisted by 2025, necessitating dependence on AI for enriching customer service and engagement.

What Is the Current State of AI Technology in Businesses?

At the time of this writing, businesses are increasingly using AI to streamline processes and increase productivity through automation. More and more, organizations use AI to automate tasks such as data entry, customer services like chatbots, and inventory management. This automation increases efficiency and allows employees to focus on the creative and innovative tasks that make us human. Humans cannot hold billions of data points simultaneously in our heads, so we develop tools such as AI and Power BI!

Businesses are increasingly using AI to analyze large datasets and extract insights, as well as to support data analytics via data exploration and data engineering. As of

---

1 Grand View Research, *Artificial Intelligence Market Size, Share & Trends Analysis Report by Solution (Hardware, Software, Services), by Technology (Deep Learning, Machine Learning, NLP), by End-use, by Region, and Segment Forecasts, 2023–2030*, https://oreil.ly/DYpAn.

2023, research shows that 48% of businesses use machine learning, data analysis, and AI tools to maintain the accuracy of their big data stores.[2] AI can be another friend at the analytics table, helping to forecast future trends and make data-driven decisions.

It applies to many spheres of business as well, such as customer behavior analysis, social media analytics, and operational inefficiencies. AI can support personalization by analyzing customer data, bringing insights to everything from how to engage new customers to how to retain customers and reduce churn. Businesses can use AI to craft recommendations, relevant content, and marketing messages for each customer lifecycle stage.

AI systems also assist leaders in strategic planning and risk assessment. However, for this to be effective, the data has to be appropriately presented so that its meaning is clear. Using AI and data visualization together gives decision makers the best tools to make optimal decisions. You can support this journey by providing business leaders with comprehensive analyses in Power BI powered by AI.

The Structure of This Book

We see the use of AI in Power BI as a journey that brings together many parts of a business, such as data, business goals, and cloud-computing infrastructure. The book's structure is designed to help you navigate this journey in a logical manner.

Every journey needs a map, so we start our journey by providing a roadmap in Chapter 1, "Getting Started with AI in the Enterprise: Your Data". Data modeling is a timeless skill that transcends technology—but is sometimes forgotten!

In Chapter 2, "A Great Foundation: AI and Data Modeling", we cover what you need to know so that your data is in great shape for your journey in AI and Power BI. Businesses usually want everything done in a manner that is good, fast, *and* cheap!

We show you how to get started with OpenAI and ChatGPT with Power BI in Chapter 3, "Blueprint for AI in the Enterprise". One blocker to getting started quickly is the data. If businesses think that their data is perfect, most likely they have not looked properly! In Chapter 4, "Automating Data Exploration and Editing", we help you to identify data quality issues before you start to go down the wrong path.

From Chapters 5 to 11, we take you through practical examples where you will use AI and Power BI to tackle real-world problems, learning how to help yourself and your business. In Chapter 5, "Working with Time Series Data", we will put our best foot forward with time series analysis, a tool that is important for analyzing business trends. Chapter 6, "Cluster Analysis and Segmentation", shows how to use cluster

---

2 Josh Howarth, "57 NEW AI Statistics," Exploding Topics, February 2, 2024, *https://explodingtopics.com/blog/ai-statistics*.

analysis and segmentation to support your business needs when grouping together similar entities. In Chapter 7, "Diving Deeper: Using Azure AI Services", you'll see how to use Azure AI Services, Microsoft's latest AI offering, to help you quickly get on board with AI.

AI and Power BI are not only for traditional data with a rectangular shape, such as spreadsheets or CSV files. Technologies like text processing are used in customer service to understand customer feedback, enhancing interaction and service quality. In Chapter 8, "Text Analytics", we will cover this topic in detail. Image data can be challenging in AI, and we will explore this type of data in Chapter 9, "Image Tagging".

What happens when you need to customize your AI? We cover this topic in Chapter 10, "Custom Machine Learning Models", so you can move further in your AI journey. In Chapter 11, "Data Science Languages: Python and R in Power BI", we dive into Python and R to support you as you develop your AI capabilities.

In Chapter 12, "Making Your AI Production-Ready with Power BI", we take the AI from your laptop and put it into production! We look at how you can iterate effectively in your AI development process.

We finish by looking at AI and beyond by discussing ethics in Chapter 13, "The AI Feedback Loop". There is a growing emphasis on ethical AI practices, mainly where AI interacts with customers. Businesses are becoming increasingly sensitive to the need to design and use AI in a way that is ethical, transparent, and compliant with privacy and data security guidelines.

Overall, the application of AI in business is diverse and rapidly evolving, with new use cases emerging as the technology advances. Businesses increasingly recognize AI's value in gaining a competitive advantage, improving customer experience, and streamlining operations.

Why Did We Write This Book?

AI is a significant and timely topic for businesses, and there is much interest in adopting it. Overall, the adoption of AI in businesses is on a robust upward trajectory, with its impact felt across every industry. AI technology enhances efficiency and productivity, drives innovation, and changes industry landscapes.

Who Is This Book For?

Understandably, people want to develop their careers to match the skill gap in AI. This book is aimed at reasonably data-savvy analysts and business intelligence users who are interested in rounding off their tool set by understanding how AI is used in

Power BI. Throughout the book, we provide practical examples so you can get started immediately in an actionable manner that is relevant to your business.

Despite its business benefits, AI faces challenges, including data quality issues, a lack of skilled personnel, and a technology mix that can be confusing. There is also a general need to learn more about AI ethics.

We are thrilled to take you on this journey of AI exploration, and we wrote this book to help you meet these challenges. We look forward to seeing how you can apply the knowledge in your business context.

Conventions Used in This Book

The following typographical conventions are used in this book:

Italic

> Indicates new terms, URLs, email addresses, filenames, and file extensions.

`Constant width`

> Used for program listings, as well as within paragraphs to refer to program elements such as variable or function names, databases, data types, environment variables, statements, and keywords.

`Constant width bold`

> Shows commands or other text that should be typed literally by the user.

`Constant width italic`

> Shows text that should be replaced with user-supplied values or by values determined by context.

 This element signifies a general note.

 This element indicates a warning or caution.

Using Code Examples

Supplemental material (code examples, exercises, etc.) is available for download at *https://github.com/tomweinandy/ai-with-power-bi*.

If you have a technical question or a problem using the code examples, please email *support@oreilly.com*.

This book is here to help you get your job done. In general, if example code is offered with this book, you may use it in your programs and documentation. You do not need to contact us for permission unless you're reproducing a significant portion of the code. For example, writing a program that uses several chunks of code from this book does not require permission. Selling or distributing examples from O'Reilly books does require permission. Answering a question by citing this book and quoting example code does not require permission. Incorporating a significant amount of example code from this book into your product's documentation does require permission.

We appreciate, but generally do not require, attribution. An attribution usually includes the title, author, publisher, and ISBN. For example: "*Artificial Intelligence with Microsoft Power BI* by Jennifer Stirrup and Thomas J. Weinandy (O'Reilly). Copyright 2024 Data Relish Ltd and Thomas J. Weinandy, 978-1-098-11275-2."

If you feel your use of code examples falls outside fair use or the permission given above, feel free to contact us at *permissions@oreilly.com*.

O'Reilly Online Learning

 For more than 40 years, *O'Reilly Media* has provided technology and business training, knowledge, and insight to help companies succeed.

Our unique network of experts and innovators share their knowledge and expertise through books, articles, and our online learning platform. O'Reilly's online learning platform gives you on-demand access to live training courses, in-depth learning paths, interactive coding environments, and a vast collection of text and video from O'Reilly and 200+ other publishers. For more information, visit *https://oreilly.com*.

How to Contact Us

Please address comments and questions concerning this book to the publisher:

O'Reilly Media, Inc.
1005 Gravenstein Highway North
Sebastopol, CA 95472
800-889-8969 (in the United States or Canada)
707-827-7019 (international or local)
707-829-0104 (fax)
support@oreilly.com
https://www.oreilly.com/about/contact.html

We have a web page for this book, where we list errata, examples, and any additional information. You can access this page at *https://oreil.ly/AI_microsoftPowerBI*.

For news and information about our books and courses, visit *https://oreilly.com*.

Find us on LinkedIn: *https://linkedin.com/company/oreilly-media*.

Watch us on YouTube: *https://youtube.com/oreillymedia*.

Acknowledgments

As I turn the final page of this remarkable journey, my heart brims with gratitude to and reverence for Lord Krishna, whose timeless wisdom and divine guidance have been the light in difficult times. Krishna's teachings, encapsulated in the *Bhagavad Gita*, have been a constant source of inspiration, strength, and solace. It is with humble acknowledgment of His grace and blessings that I present this work. As I reflect upon the journey of writing this book, my heart is filled with profound gratitude toward His Divine Grace A. C. Bhaktivedanta Swami Prabhupada. Through his example, I have learned the importance of living a life rooted in spiritual principles, and his teachings have guided me through both the challenges and joys encountered during the process of writing this book. Hare Krishna,

—Jennifer Stirrup

I wish to sincerely thank each of my former coworkers at BlueGranite. I learned so much from you about leveraging large datasets and solving real business problems for clients. Our time together affirmed my professional journey and enriched my personal life. This book would not have been possible without all of you, so it makes perfect sense that I dedicate this book to you as well.

—Thomas Weinandy

Getting Started with AI in the Enterprise: Your Data

Power BI is Microsoft's flagship business analytics service that provides interactive visualizations and business intelligence capabilities. Power BI is a business-focused technology with an easy-to-use interface that makes it easy to underestimate its power. In this chapter, let's explore the essential ingredient of getting the most out of Power BI: getting your data ready.

What problems are specific to the self-service data preparation domain? As anyone who has tried to merge data in Excel knows, cleaning data is a frustrating and lengthy process. It can be exacerbated by mistakes in formulas and human error, as well as having access only to a sample dataset. Moreover, the business analysts may not have straightforward access to the data in the first place. Business teams may have to procure data from across business silos, adding delays to an already frustrating process. Sometimes, they may even bend existing business processes or push boundaries to get the data they need. The frustration they feel gets in the way of exercising creativity when it comes to analyzing the data. Many organizations have a hidden industry of Excel spreadsheets that comprise the "little data" that runs the business. Often, IT cannot get any visibility into these data "puddles," so it cannot manage them or exercise its role as guardian of the data.

According to David Allen's Get Things Done methodology, there is clear strategic value in having bandwidth to be creative. To be creative, people need to be free of distractions and incomplete tasks. When people deal with data, they can gain insights by being playful, but to do so, they need to be free to focus their time and attention on the analysis. Having to spend a lot of time on cleaning up a data mess often interferes with the creative process. Instead of gaining insights from a lake of big data, they may have only a series of murky data puddles to work with. This situation leads to disappointment for the business leaders who expect astute observations and deep understanding from the business's data.

Overview of Power BI Data Ingestion Methods

Power BI provides several ways to bring data into your reports and dashboards. In this chapter, we will focus on dataflows and datasets. The method you choose depends largely on your use case's specific requirements and constraints and, in particular, on the nature of the data and the business needs. Let's begin by discussing one important differentiator: real-time data versus batch-processed data.

Real-time data is ingested and displayed as soon as it is acquired. The timeliness of the data is critical. Latency between data generation and data availability is minimal, often milliseconds to a few seconds. Real-time data allows decision makers or systems to act immediately based on current information, so it is critical in scenarios where immediate decisions or responses are needed. Real-time data is found in many areas, such as the Internet of Things (IoT), gaming, healthcare, and finance. The capability to promptly process and act on real-time data offers many benefits. It can give the business a competitive advantage, improve safety, enhance user experience, and even save lives in emergencies.

Batch processing involves collecting and processing large volumes of data in groups, or batches, rather than processing each piece of data as it arrives at the system. Batch processing is typically used when data doesn't need to be available in real time. The data can be stored temporarily and processed later, often during a period of lower system demand. For example, batch processing is appropriate when the data source has only intermittent network access and the data can be accessed only when the data source is available. Also, it can be more expensive to process data in real time, so when immediate access to the data is unnecessary, a business often determines that batch processing is sufficient.

Now that we've gotten an overview of the two basic data velocity options, let's take a look at the different methods of data ingestion in Power BI.

The *import data* method involves importing data from a source into Power BI. Once the data is imported, it is stored in a highly compressed, in-memory format within Power BI. With the import data method, report interaction is very fast and responsive to user clicks and ticks on the Power BI canvas.

The *direct query* method sets up a direct connection to the data source. When a user interacts with a report, queries are sent to the source system to retrieve and display the data on the Power BI dashboard. No data is copied to or stored inside Power BI.

The *live connection* method is similar to direct query, but it is explicitly intended for making connections to Analysis Services models.

Power BI dataflows are a Power BI service feature based in the Microsoft Azure cloud. Dataflows allow you to connect to, transform, and load data into Power BI. The transformed data can be used in both Import and DirectQuery modes. The process runs in the cloud independently from any Power BI reports and can feed data into different reports.

The *composite model* approach allows Power BI developers to create reports using either the direct query or import data methods. For example, real-time data could be set alongside reference data that does not need to be real-time, such as geographic data.

Using the *dataset method*, you can create reports based on existing Power BI datasets. A dataset can be reused many times for consistency across multiple reports.

This chapter will explore the potential of dataflows to resolve the previously mentioned data preparation issues.

Workflows in Power BI That Use AI

A *dataflow* is a collection of tables created and managed in workspaces in the Power BI service. A *table* is a set of columns used to store data, much like a table within a database. It is possible to add and edit tables in the dataflow. The workflow also permits the management and scheduling of data refreshes, which are set up directly from the workspace.

How Are Dataflows Created?

To create a dataflow, first go to *https://www.powerbi.com* to launch the Power BI service in a browser.

Next, create a *workspace* from the navigation pane on the left, as shown in Figure 1-1.

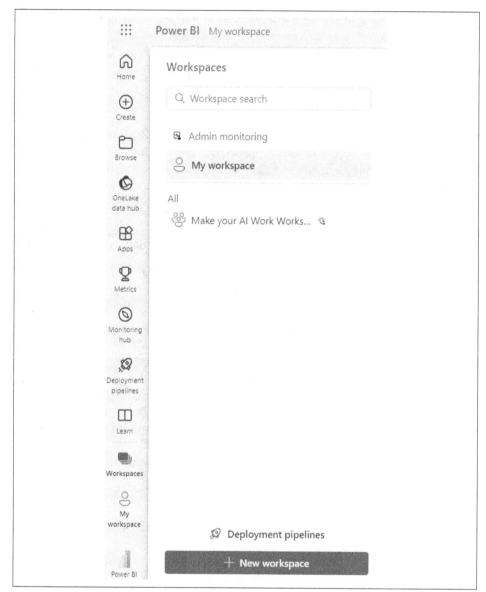

Figure 1-1. Creating a workspace

The workspace stores the dataflow. Creating a dataflow is straightforward, and here are a few ways to build one.

Creating a dataflow by importing a dataset

In the workspace, there is a drop-down list to create new resources, such as paginated reports or dashboards. Under New is an option to create a new dataflow, as shown in Figure 1-2.

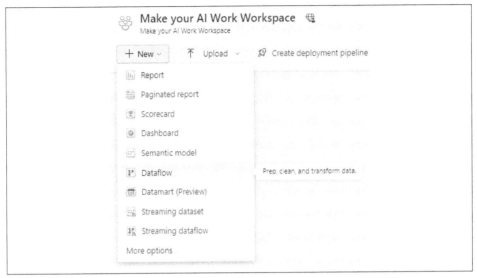

Figure 1-2. Creating a dataflow

Then, you are presented with the four options shown in Figure 1-3.

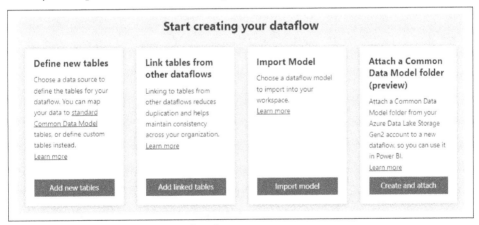

Figure 1-3. Options for creating a dataflow

For this example, choose the first option, "Define new tables." Then select "Add new tables" (Figure 1-4).

Figure 1-4. Using Define new tables

Next, you'll see a choice of many options for data ingestion. Figure 1-5 shows an example of the range of data sources for Power BI dataflows.

Figure 1-5. Example of possible data sources for a dataflow

For this example, ingest a CSV file that contains World Bank life expectancy data. To do this, select Text/CSV.

Then, in the text box labeled File path or URL, enter the following filepath:

```
https://raw.githubusercontent.com/tomweinandy/ai-with-power-bi/main/
Chapter1/WorldDevelopmentIndicators.csv
```

Next, you'll see options for selecting and accessing the file, as illustrated in Figure 1-6.

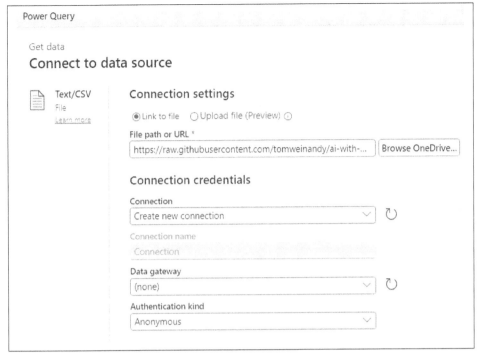

Figure 1-6. Entering connection settings for a text/CSV file

The dataflow will now display the data, as shown in Figure 1-7. To proceed, click "Transform data," which is located at the bottom righthand side of the Preview file data screen.

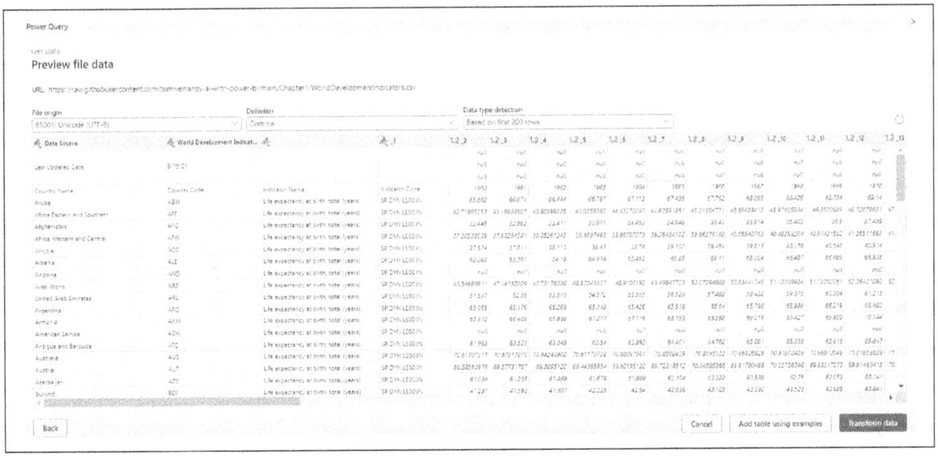

Figure 1-7. Viewing the data in the Preview file data screen

After choosing to transform the data, you need to do a few things:

1. Remove the first rows of data. Select "Reduce rows," then "Remove rows," and finally "Remove top rows" (Figure 1-8).

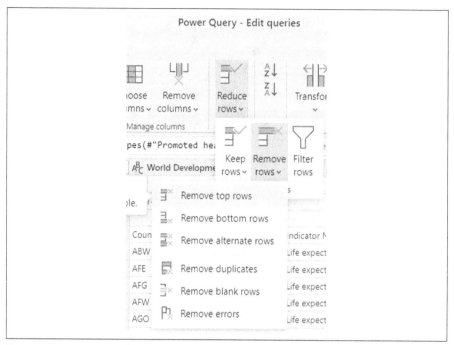

Figure 1-8. Removing the top rows from a dataflow

Type **3** into the text box and click OK (Figure 1-9).

Figure 1-9. Specifying the number of rows to remove

2. Set the first row of data as the column headers. In the Home tab, select Transform and then "Use first rows as headers." Figure 1-10 shows how these options appear in the Power Query Online tab.

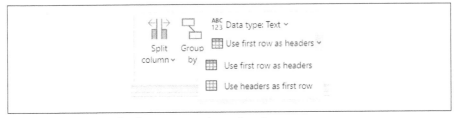

Figure 1-10. Setting the first row as column headers

3. Now remove unnecessary columns. Right-click on the Indicator Name column and select "Remove columns." Then right-click on the Indicator Code column and select "Remove columns." Figure 1-11 shows the "Remove columns" command in its drop-down list.

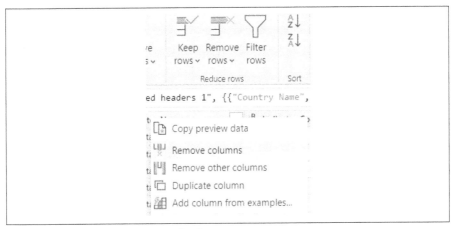

Figure 1-11. Removing unwanted columns

4. Shape the data. You want it in a long, narrow table format with many rows and few columns. In contrast, a wide table has many columns and fewer rows. Power BI will work better with data in a narrow format since the metric of interest, average life expectancy, will be contained in one column rather than being spread out over numerous columns.

   To unpivot the columns, select all the columns from 1960 onward. In the Transform tab, select "Unpivot columns" and then, from the drop-down list, "Unpivot columns." Figure 1-12 shows these options in the Power Query Online tab.

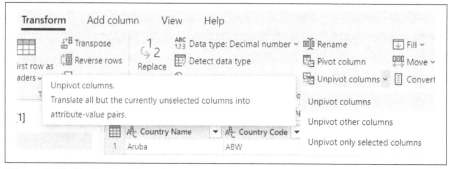

Figure 1-12. Unpivoting the columns

5. Make the columns easier to understand by renaming them. Rename the Attribute column to Year and rename the Value column to Average Life Expectancy.

6. Finally, amend the Year column so that it has a whole number datatype. Select the column and then open the Transform tab. Select "Data type: Text" and then "Whole number" from the drop-down list (Figure 1-13).

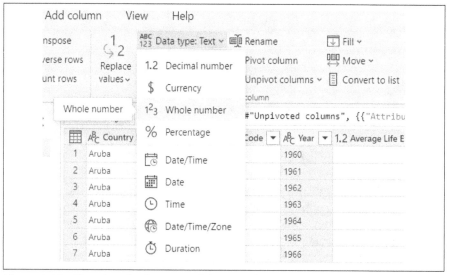

Figure 1-13. Changing the datatype of the year data

Once these steps are complete, the Power BI dataflow will appear as shown in Figure 1-14. Click "Save & close." We will use this dataflow in a later exercise.

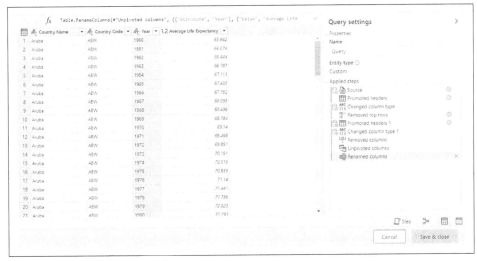

Figure 1-14. Completed dataflow

Creating a dataflow by importing/exporting a dataflow

You can create dataflows using the import/export option. This method is convenient since it lets you import a dataflow from a file. This process is helpful if you want to save a dataflow copy offline rather than online. It is also helpful if you need to move a dataflow from one workspace to another.

To export a dataflow, select the dataflow and then choose More (the ellipsis) to expand the options to export a dataflow. Next, select *export.json*. The dataflow will begin to download in CDM format.

To import a dataflow, select the import box and upload the file. Power BI then creates the dataflow. The dataflow can serves as the basis for additional transformations or remain as is.

Creating dataflows by defining new tables

You can also create a dataflow by defining a new table. The Define new tables option, shown in Figure 1-15, is straightforward to use. It asks you to connect to a new data source. Once the data source is connected, you will be prompted to provide details such as the connection settings and the account details.

Figure 1-15. Using "Define new tables"

Creating dataflows with linked tables

The Link tables option provides the ability to have a read-only reference to an existing table that is defined in another dataflow.

The linked table approach is helpful if there is a requirement to reuse a table across multiple dataflows. There are plenty of such use cases in analytics, such as when a date table or a static lookup table is reused. Data warehouses often have custom date tables that match the business need, such as varying custom date tables, and a static lookup table might contain country names and associated ISO codes, which do not change much over time. If the network is an issue, it is also helpful to use linked tables to act as a cache to prevent unnecessary refreshes. In turn, this reduces the pressure on the original data source.

In these situations, you create the table once, and it is then accessible to other dataflows as a reference. To promote reuse and testing, you can use the Link tables from other dataflows option (Figure 1-16).

Figure 1-16. Using "Link tables from other dataflows"

Creating dataflows with computed tables

You can take the idea of linked tables a step further by setting up a dataflow using a computed table while referencing a linked table. The output is a new table that constitutes part of the dataflow.

It is feasible to convert a linked table into a computed table; you can either create a new query from a merge operation, create a reference table, or reproduce it. The new transformation query will not execute using the newly imported data. Instead, the transformation uses the data that already resides in the dataflow storage.

Importing a dataflow model

Using Import Model, you can choose a dataflow model to import into your workspace (Figure 1-17).

Figure 1-17. Import Model

If a dataflow is exported to JSON format, for example, you can import this file into another workspace. To import a dataflow from a file, click "Import model" and navigate to the JSON file. Then the Power BI service will ingest the file to create the new dataflow.

Creating dataflows using a CDM folder

Business teams can make the most of the Common Data Model (CDM) format with dataflows that access tables created by another application in the CDM format. You can access the option when you create a new dataflow, as shown in Figure 1-18.

Figure 1-18. Attaching a Common Data Model folder (preview)

To access these tables, you will need to provide the complete path to the CDM format file stored in Azure Data Lake Store (ADLS) Gen2 and set up the correct permissions. The URL must be a direct path to the JSON file and use the ADLS Gen2 endpoint; note that Azure Blob storage (blob.core) is not supported.

The path is a link in HTTP format and will look similar to the example in the Common Data Model folder path box in Figure 1-19. The path is automatically generated when the developer configures the workspace dataflow storage, and it ends with *model.json*.

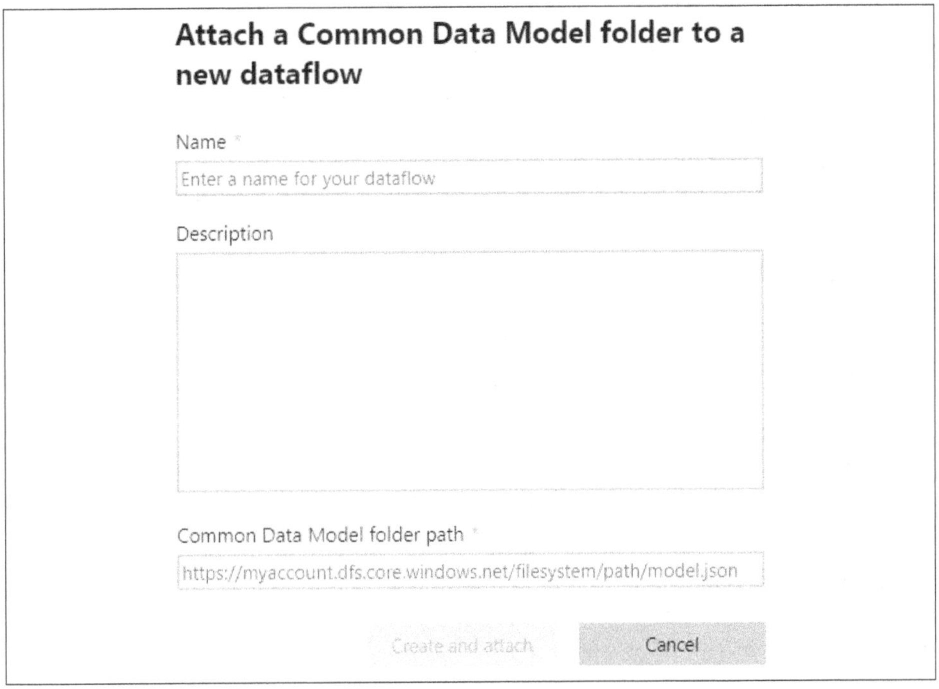

Attach a Common Data Model folder to a new dataflow

Name *

Enter a name for your dataflow

Description

Common Data Model folder path *

https://myaccount.dfs.core.windows.net/filesystem/path/model.json

Create and attach   Cancel

Figure 1-19. Specifying the Common Data Model folder path

In addition, the ADLS Gen2 account must have the appropriate permissions set up for Power BI to access the file. If the developer cannot access the ADLS Gen2 account, they cannot create the dataflow.

Most developers are now using the new workspace experience. For those who are not, the ability to create dataflows from CDM folders, which is available only in the new workspace experience, is an enticement to transition to it.

Things to Note Before Creating Workflows

Dataflows are not available in *my-workspace* in the Power BI service.

You can create dataflows only in a Premium workspace with either a Pro license or a Premium Per User (PPU) license. Computed tables are also available only in Premium.

You'll decide which data to use for the table once you're connected. Once you choose your data and a source, Power BI will reconnect to the data source to retain the refreshed data in the dataflow.

During the setup, you will also be asked how often you require data refreshes. This decision will partly be driven by your license, as it will determine the number of data refreshes available to your organization. Before starting to create the workflow, you should decide on the timing of the data refreshes. If you are not sure of the best times to schedule the data refreshes, it is a good idea to choose a time that will ensure the data will be ready for the business teams by the start of the business day.

The Dataflow Editor transforms data into the required format for use in the dataflow, as per the example given in the section "How Are Dataflows Created?" on page 3.

Streaming Dataflows and Automatic Aggregations

Power BI Premium now features streaming dataflows and automatic aggregation. These features will speed up report creation and consumption, and they will support projects with large datasets. For instance, streaming dataflows enable report creators to incorporate real-time data to make their reports more user-friendly and faster.

As the amount of data from new places grows every day, companies will need help to make it actionable. These features will play a critical role in allowing businesses to use data more efficiently to inform sound business decisions.

Getting Your Data Ready First

Artificial intelligence needs data; without data, there is no AI. Power BI Desktop uses dataflows to provide data to create datasets, reports, dashboards, and apps based on the data obtained from Power BI dataflows.

The ultimate goal is to derive insights into business activities, and the next step toward this goal is to get the data ready for Power BI dataflows.

Getting Data Ready for Dataflows

Data preparation is generally the most complicated, costly, and time-consuming task in analytics projects. Datasets may include shredded, missing, and incomplete data. Further, the data structures may be confusing and poorly documented. Power BI dataflows help organizations address all these challenges. They support the ingestion, transformation, cleaning, and integration of large volumes of data. Further, Power BI dataflows can structure data into a standardized form to facilitate reporting.

Dataflows help simplify and set up a self-service Power BI extract, transform, and load (ETL) pipeline. A dataflow follows the same pattern as a simple ETL pipeline that can connect to source data, transform the data by applying business rules, and prepare the data to be available to visualize. Power BI then connects to a data warehouse in business intelligence environments and visualizes the data from that point on.

Where Should the Data Be Cleaned and Prepared?

In many technical architectures, there are several options for data cleaning and preparation because a number of data sources are available—everything from Excel spreadsheets to big data systems to proprietary solutions such as Google Analytics. Consequently, you can choose from a myriad of data-processing pipelines to process data from different sources. It is worth looking at some of these options before diving into the question of why dataflows are essential for cleaning data for Power BI.

Option 1: Clean the data and aggregate it in the source system

The tool used for this option depends on the source system that stores the data. For example, if the technical architecture rests on a Microsoft SQL server, the solution could extract the data using stored procedures or views.

With this option, the overall architecture moves less data from the source system to Power BI. That is helpful if the business does not need low-level details and there is a desire to anonymize the data by aggregating it.

One disadvantage of this approach is that the raw source data is not available to Power BI, so the business needs to go back to the source system each time it needs the data. The data may not even still exist in the source system if it has undergone archiving or purging, so it is best for Power BI to import the data. Another issue is that data cleansing can strain the capacity of the source system, potentially slowing the system and affecting the business teams that use it. Further, the source system may not have fast performance due to business operations and thus not be able to provide fast reporting to business users. Power BI is an excellent option to circumvent these issues because it relieves the pressure on underlying source systems, pushing the workload to the cloud while supporting the business users who need their Power BI reports.

Option 2: Clean data from a source to a secondary store

Business users often don't understand why search engines such as Google or Bing can produce millions of results in seconds but IT departments take much longer to produce data. Some businesses work around IT, going off and purchasing their own datasets for their own analyses. This can lead to frustration when business staff find the technical aspects confusing. Data-warehousing experts create ETL packages that handle data transformation tasks on a schedule to prevent one-off data loads.

Repeatedly accessing operational systems can affect their performance. Pushing data into a secondary source solves this problem, as the original system is no longer affected by additional demand from business users.

However, ETL activity involves coordinating many different pieces of logic that need to interact in sequence. Many internal operational systems are simply not designed to work at the speed of the business, and they are not designed to work together. The reality is that people often export data to CSV or Excel and then mash it together. This means that businesses are running on operational data sources that can differ from the original data sources and each other in terms of structure, content, and freshness.

Microsoft is shifting its focus to services and devices rather than local, desktop-based, on-premise applications. Over time, this means that the proliferation of Excel throughout organizations may have to be addressed. Companies need help with new data challenges, such as an ever-growing variety of data sources, including social media data and big data. For some organizations, this will mean moving from a call center to a contact center methodology, for example—a huge process shift that will be reflected in the resulting data. If processes are not updated, business users will resort to mashing data together in Excel simply because there seems to be no clear way for them to combine data in a more robust manner. This does not always work well; for example, Excel tables may be overly decorated, or HTML tables may be interpreted as structural markup rather than actual markup. All this can be confusing for downstream frontend systems.

People need to be isolated from the need to write SQL as much as possible, since they do not always have the skill set to make changes correctly. Microsoft products that achieve this goal include SQL Server Integration Services (SSIS), Azure Data Factory, and Azure Databricks. These tools use complicated orchestration logic to guarantee that ETL packages run in sequence at the right time. ETL development requires a technical mindset to build routines that will import data correctly.

The business must recognize that data preparation is probably the most important aspect of strategic analytics, business intelligence, and, in fact, anything to do with data. Everyone has dirty data, and self-service data transformation is a necessity. If your organization thinks it doesn't have dirty data, it is not looking hard enough. Businesses must realize that the need for self-service data transformation to answer business questions is an operational fact of life if customer needs are to be satisfied. Fortunately, Power BI can help.

Real-Time Data Ingestion Versus Batch Processing

Building such an enterprise-grade data integration pipeline is time-consuming, and there are many design considerations and guidelines to take into account. Often, businesses move so fast that it becomes difficult for the IT team to keep up with the pace of change in the requirements. Microsoft has developed dataflows, a fully managed data preparation tool for Power BI, to overcome this challenge. There are two options: using dataflows to import data using real-time or batch data processing, or using streaming datasets to work with real-time data.

Real-Time Datasets in Power BI

Real time often means different things to different organizations. For example, in some organizations, data warehouse loads update once a day but are considered "realtime."

From the Power BI perspective, real-time streaming does happen in real time, often with updates happening more than once a second. Power BI lets you stream data and update dashboards in real time, and any Power BI visual or dashboard created in Power BI can represent and update real-time data and visuals.

What is the genesis of real-time data? Streaming data devices and sources can include manufacturing sensors, social media sources, or many other time-sensitive data collectors or transmitters. Thus, many scenarios involve real-time data, and Power BI offers various real-time data ingestion opportunities.

In Power BI, there are three types of real-time datasets to support the display of real-time data on dashboards:

- Push datasets
- Streaming datasets
- PubNub streaming datasets

This section will review how these datasets differ, and then we will discuss how real-time data gets into these datasets.

Setting up streaming datasets

The Power BI service allows you to set up streaming datasets. To do this, click the New button (+) in the upper-left corner of the Power BI service. Now, select Streaming dataset (Figure 1-20).

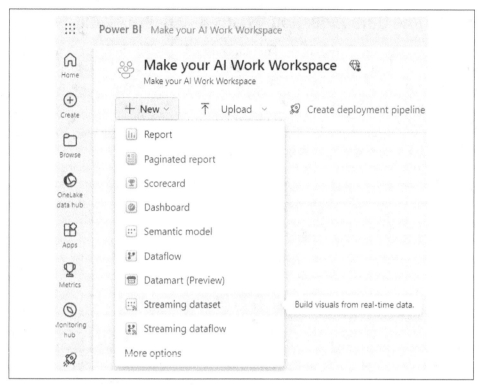

Figure 1-20. Setting up streaming datasets

When you click on the New button, you see the three options visible in Figure 1-21. From this point, there are three options to create a streaming dataset: one is to create a data stream using an API, the second is to create an Azure Analytics stream, and the third is to use PubNub as a dataset from the streaming data source.

API
   You can create a streaming dataset with the Power BI REST API. After you select API from the New streaming dataset window, you have several options to enable Power BI to connect to and use the endpoint, as shown in Figure 1-22.

Azure Stream
   To create an Azure Stream, you need to head to the Azure Stream Analytics help page to set up your streaming dataset. Microsoft will be surfacing this feature shortly on Power BI but it is not currently available in the Power BI portal (Figure 1-23).

PubNub

Azure Stream Analytics offers a way to aggregate the raw stream of PubNub data before it goes to Power BI, so that Power BI can optimally present the data. As PubNub is a third-party tool, we will not be covering it in this book.

Figure 1-21. Selecting the streaming dataset type

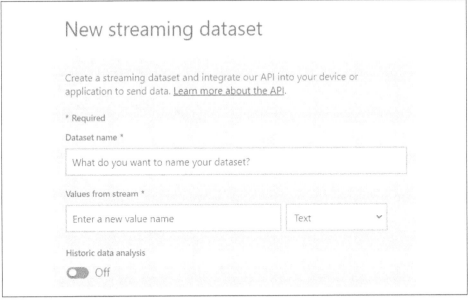

Figure 1-22. Configuring the Power BI API

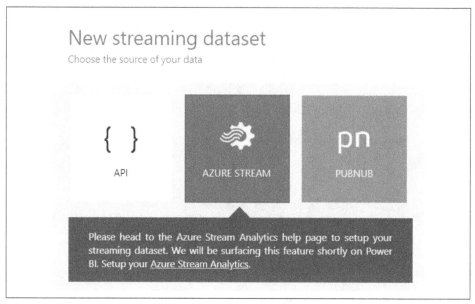

Figure 1-23. Selecting Azure Stream from Azure Stream Analytics

Ingesting data into Power BI: Push method versus streaming method

The push dataset and the streaming dataset methods receive data in a *push model*, in which the data is pushed into Power BI. Power BI creates an underlying database that forms the basis of the visualizations in Power BI reports and dashboards. In contrast, the streaming method does not store the data for more than an hour.

The push method allows the report developer to build reports using the data stored in the database, such as by filtering, using Power BI visuals, and using Power BI reporting features. On the other hand, the streaming method does not permit the use of standard Power BI reporting features; instead, it uses a custom streaming source that displays real-time data with very low latency.

Batch Processing Data Using Power BI

Power BI dataflows are perfect when there is a need for business-oriented, self-service data movement. Business users use dataflows to quickly connect to data sources and prepare the data for reporting and visualization. Power BI dataflows are similar to Excel worksheets, so users are already familiar with the skills needed to use this tool.

Even though Power BI dataflows are business-friendly, they work with the massive amounts of transactional and observational data stored in the ADLS Gen2. In addition, Power BI dataflows work with big data data stores and the little data that runs the business. Therefore, for cloud-first or cloud-friendly organizations, Power BI dataflows can access Azure data services.

For Microsoft customers, Power BI integrates neatly with the rest of the Power BI system. For example, Power BI dataflows support the CDM—a set of legal business entities such as Account, Product, Lead, and Opportunity. Dataflows enable easy mapping between any data in any shape and into CDM legal entities.

Power BI dataflows also have a rich set of capabilities that are useful for a variety of scenarios. Firstly, dataflows can connect to data sources and ingest data tables. They can merge and join tables together, as well as union tables. Further, dataflows can also perform the common practice of pivoting data. Dataflows enrich data by creating new computed columns in tables, and they can simplify data by filtering tables so that users can get what they need in a frictionless manner.

Another great advantage of dataflows is that they can automatically run on a schedule, allowing developers to set it and forget it! The "last-mile problem" of analytics is that businesses do not always understand how to realize value from an analytics project. Automation is a crucial way to gain value from these projects, helping businesses with the last-mile problem of putting their solutions into production environments.

Power BI dataflows can also interact with AI by training and applying AI models on the tables. Therefore, it is possible to use AI in dataflows.

Let's now understand some deeper concepts around dataflows.

Importing Batch Data with Power Query in Dataflows

Power Query, which helps create Power BI dataflows, is accessible from Power BI, Excel, and the Power Query online experience. This user-friendly tool for data transformation allows business analysts and data analysts to read data from an extensive range of sources.

The Power Query user interface (UI) offers dozens of ways to compute and transform data directly using the Power Query ribbon and dialogs. Besides being easy to use, Power Query can transform data in compelling and extensible ways. It supports more than 80 built-in data sources and a custom connector Software Development Kit (SDK) with a rich ecosystem. An SDK provides a collection of software tools, libraries, documentation, code samples, processes, and guides that allow developers to create software applications on a specific platform. When it comes to connecting to data, an SDK is used for connection management, security, and customization. The custom connector SDK streamlines the development process by abstracting complex details so it is simpler to connect and retrieve data from less common sources that are not part of the data sources available out of the box.

Everything in the Power Query UI gets automatically translated to code in a language called M. Although users do not need to write code, using M in Power Query is a great way to learn about coding and behind-the-scenes transformation activities. The M language is a topic in its own right and thus is outside the scope of this book.

The Dataflow Calculation Engine

Dataflows have a calculation engine that helps put all the columns together, making things easy. At some point, Excel users bump into an issue where there is a circular dependency involved in a formula. The dataflow calculation engine helps to clear up such issues by creating links to check out dependencies before implementation.

For many enterprises, it is necessary to produce multiple dataflows due to a variety of data sources, none of which is the source of truth. These multiple dataflows are created and managed in a single Power BI workspace, so they are easy to administer. Also, part of the process of ensuring high-quality data integrity involves examining the dependencies between the workflows for consistency.

Dataflow Options

Organizations can use Power BI dataflows in a few ways. Let's explore some of the options.

Option 1: Fully managed by Power BI

Power BI handles everything in the cloud, from data ingestion to data structuring and refresh to final data visualization. The data journey starts with use of the web-based Power Query online tool for structuring the data. An Azure data lake stores the data using Azure infrastructure, which is transparent to the organization. With this option, the organization cannot manage the data itself as Power BI is providing a comprehensive cloud service.

Option 2: Bring your own data lake

Option 2 is almost identical to Option 1 with one significant difference: the organization associates its own Azure data lake account with Power BI and manages it using tools such as Power Query and Power BI. This option is helpful for organizations that would like to access their data outside of Power BI.

Option 3: External dataflows

With this setup, a solution such as Azure Data Factory bears responsibility for managing the data. Power BI consumes the data but does not manage it.

Power BI dataflows in Power BI Desktop

Regardless of which option is used to manage Power BI dataflows, business users will extract the data using the Get Data option in Power BI Desktop or the online version of Power BI. The Get Data option is straightforward to use. There is no need for the Power BI developer to know where the data is stored, since the developer can select the relevant data tables. Another convenient feature is that it is possible to join tables that refresh on different schedules.

DirectQuery in Power BI

It is possible to connect to different data sources when using Power BI Desktop or the Power BI service and to make those data connections in different ways. The Power BI developer connects directly to data in the original source repository using a method known as DirectQuery.

Experience has found that users often say that they want the most up-to-date information right away. This does not mean that they want *real-time* data, however. In truth, *real-time* and *up-to-date* are not the same thing. Let's take an example. Say that the data is loaded every night using batch processing so it is ready for the business to view by 8:00 a.m. Since the data will not be refreshed until 8:00 a.m., using the Import method is perfect; the users will see the latest data as of 8:00 a.m.

Import Versus Direct Query: Practical Recommendations

You'll remember from earlier that the Import Data method stores the data in Power BI. The data is stored in memory, making visuals and reports more responsive. The data is transformed using Power BI dataflows or the Power Query Editor so that the developer can transform and shape data as required. The data is refreshed via specific schedules; the number of available schedules depends on the Power BI license that you have. You can use data from offline or sporadically available sources.

As you might expect, there are a few caveats, depending on your specific scenario. There are limits in terms of the data volume, with the limit depending on your license: the size limit per dataset is 2 GB for Power BI Pro and higher for Premium. Since the Import model pulls the data on a schedule, the data is only as fresh as the last refresh.

Direct Query is perfect if your scenario requires data updates on a higher frequency. Direct Query means that data is always up-to-date with the source. Since the data isn't stored in Power BI, there are no limitations on the data size. Also, the business logic remains centralized at the source.

However, since the data remains at the source, Power BI's reporting performance may be slower than with the Import method. With Direct Query, queries are sent to the source database, the data is retrieved from the source, and then the data is sent back to the Power BI dashboard. If the dashboard loses its connection, then Power BI will not be able to display any data. Therefore, Direct Query requires a constant connection to the data source.

The Import Data method is suitable when you have smaller datasets or datasets that fit within your capacity limitations. It is also appropriate for offline or data sources that are sporadically available. Direct Query is also useful if your scenario requires more data updates than are available with the Import Data method.

Premium, Pro, and Free Power BI

Different versions of Power BI each grant various levels of access to features within the software. The following is a broad overview of each followed by an explanation of which AI tools in this book require a paid Power BI subscription:

Free
> Unsurprisingly, the most popular version is the free Power BI Desktop, which lets users connect to data and create reports on their local machine.

Pro
> Power BI Pro includes all of the features within the free version and grants access to the browser-based version, the Power BI service, which lets a user create and share a live dashboard. Pro comes included in Office 365 E5 at no extra charge; otherwise, it costs $10 per user per month.

Premium Per User (PPU)
> PPU includes all of the Pro features as well as dedicated capacity on the Power BI tenant, meaning you will not have other users to compete with for cloud processing. It also unlocks more advanced AI, automation, and data preparation features while costing $20 per user per month.

Premium Per Capacity (PPC)
> Premium Per Capacity is an organization-wide subscription that includes all of the features available with the PPU license. Many organizations find it more cost-effective to register for Premium on a per-user basis, but those who want a single license will pay $4,995 per level of capacity units per month.

We will also refer to PPU and PPC collectively for the rest of the book simply as "Premium." There is no meaningful difference between the two when it comes to the AI features we discuss.

> All prices listed are current as of this writing, so check the Power BI site (*https://powerbi.microsoft.com/en-us/pricing*) for the latest rates. You can also follow the link to sign up for a 60-day free trial as well as to learn more about government and nonprofit pricing.

We discuss many different AI features of Power BI throughout this book, many of which require paid licensing to access. Table 1-1 breaks down the more significant items according to their corresponding chapter, as well as whether they require the Free, Pro, or Premium version of Power BI.

Table 1-1. Breaking down Power BI's AI features by chapter and required license[a]

Chapter	Free	Pro	Premium
1	✕	Creating dataflows in a Power BI workspace	Enhanced dataflow with AI features
2	Data modeling in Power BI Desktop	← and data modeling in Power BI service	←
3	Decomposition Tree, Key Influencers, Q&A, Insights	←	← and AutoML in Power BI
4	Get data from web by example, add column from examples, data profiling, table generation, fuzzy matching, smart narrative	← and Quick Insights, Report Creation	←
5	Line chart (forecasting and anomaly detection)	←	←
6	Scatter chart (clustering)	←	←
7	✕	Streaming dataset in Power BI, Azure AI services[b]	← with improved refresh frequency
8	✕	✕	Language detection, key phrase extraction, sentiment analysis
9	✕	✕	Image tagging
10	✕	✕	Consume a model trained in Azure Machine Learning[b]
11	Python and R for data ingestion, data transformation, data visualization, machine learning	←	←
12	✕	✕	Consuming a model trained in Azure Machine Learning[b] or AutoML

[a] The left arrow indicates it includes all features to the left, and the X indicates something not included with this license.
[b] Also requires paid Microsoft Azure credits. See "Azure Subscription and Free Trial" on page 330 for details.

Summary

The range of options in Power BI dataflows allows the organization to manage Power BI using the degree of "cloudiness" that it prefers. Ultimately, businesses are trying to find a balance between "silver platter" reports and self-service, and Power BI dataflows offer both methods of reporting while avoiding the Excel hell of data puddles that are unmonitored, unmanageable, and unruly pieces of data debt.

## CHAPTER 2

A Great Foundation: AI and Data Modeling

In Power BI, the objective overall is to produce dashboards and models to support business-oriented self-service. Unfortunately, data sources are often not documented from the analysts' perspective, so it is difficult to understand where to find the fields necessary to meet users' needs. However, business users are creative. They can create a lot of workarounds, resulting in "shadow" IT and "shadow" data sources such as Excel workbooks that are not under the guardianship of the IT department. Often, there is limited documentation. Sometimes, the business can supply a data dictionary or a database schema on request, but it is unclear what the tables and fields mean. Frequently, data sources contain many tables, so it is hard for report writers to find the information they need.

Further, database relationships, such as table joins, are not always apparent. Database tables and views can be challenging to relate to one another and subsequently to navigate. Often, tables are difficult to understand because they are broad with many columns. For business users, this is often a productivity issue because the team cannot do the analytics they would like. Instead, the team must build and rebuild datasets in Excel or Google Sheets to get the data they need. Due to time pressures and a lack of confidence in the data sources, the team cannot take time to ask questions about the requirements. Thus, they may produce what they think is required, only to have to redo parts of the reporting. For example, when someone asks for reports, the report writers don't have time to dig into the underlying purpose of the request, and there is no well-rounded data model in place; as a result, the business users waste time delivering incorrect reports.

In this chapter, we'll explore what a data model is and provide some practical take-aways to help you to get started developing your own data model. We will also provide definitions of some terms to help clear up confusion that can result when people talk about data models.

What Is a Data Model?

A *data model* is a conceptual representation of the data structures needed to build a database that supports a business need. The data model can be considered a canvas where the business and technical teams meet to define how pieces of data are connected to each other. The model becomes the target where the data will be stored and processed. The main goal is to ensure that data objects offered by the functional team are represented accurately.

In the realm of data warehousing and business intelligence, the data model often revolves around concepts like the fact table, the dimension table, and others. Before we get started, let's take a look at some key terminology.

What Is a Fact Table?

A central concept for data modeling is the fact table, which contains the lowest level of numerical facts, known as *measures*. In database terms, the fact table is a central table in a data warehouse with connections to other tables that help to describe the data. A fact table usually focuses on numeric performance measures that can be used for analytics and reporting. *Facts* are the result of a business process, such as a sale to a customer. Common examples of facts include invoices, transactions, sales, and refunds. For reporting, analytics, and data science, facts can be aggregated to provide a summary that is used to facilitate data-driven decisions. Thus, these measures contain the quantitative data for analysis, such as amount invoiced, profits, and quantities sold. A fact table has a time component, letting people know when the invoice was raised or the sale made, for example. The fact table also contains keys that correspond to primary keys in the dimension tables; these keys establish relationships between facts and dimensions.

What is a dimension table?

A *dimension table* contains descriptive attributes, or contextual information, to help the users slice and dice the data in a fact table, either aggregating it or separating it into its components. A dimension table generally has a *primary key* column that uniquely identifies each dimension record. This primary key is referenced by the corresponding *foreign key* in the fact table, establishing a relationship between facts and dimensions.

For example, you may want to see data by month, by location, or by customer. If you have a report called "Sales by Region," then the sales are the facts, and the regions are the dimensions. In other words, the terms before the "by" are the facts, and the terms after the "by" are the dimensional attributes you'll use to describe the facts.

Star and snowflake schemas

Star schemas and snowflake schemas are two main architectures for organizing fact and dimension tables. The *star schema* is the preferred design for Power BI. As shown in Figure 2-1, in the star schema methodology, each dimension table is directly linked to the fact table. The star schema is so named because a diagram of the schema looks like a star, with the fact table in the center.

The *snowflake schema* is an extension of the star schema. In this method, dimension tables are *normalized*, which means that the data is organized within the database to reduce *redundancy*, or data that is repeated unnecessarily. As a result, the snowflake schema adds more tables to a typical star schema, resulting in a structure that resembles a snowflake.

If you're using Power BI Desktop, you would import the needed tables. Then, you would create relationships between the fact table and dimension tables using the Relationships view. Once the relationships were set up, you would build your report.

In summary, a data model, especially in the realm of data warehousing, provides a structured way to organize and relate data, allowing businesses to create reports, gain insights, and make informed decisions based on their data. The use of fact tables, dimension tables, and schemas such as star and snowflake schemas are foundational concepts in this space.

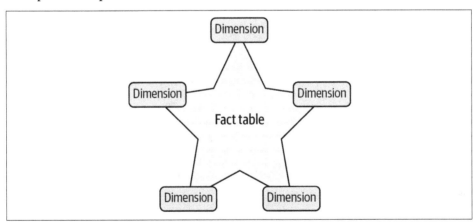

Figure 2-1. Example star schema

Why Is Data Modeling Important?

In the age of big data and AI, data modeling is often overlooked as part of the data lifecycle. However, it is a crucial part of delivering business requirements in a user-friendly fashion, and it can make significant contributions to the organization because it supports business intelligence, data science, and AI. *Data modeling* is the method of designing a data model to deliver business-focused data requirements for reporting, data science, and AI projects. As part of the data-modeling process, the designer formalizes data structures and entity types. However, data modeling is more than simply documentation for documentation's sake. Instead, the designer goes further by rewriting the documentation so that the business teams understand it. The data-modeling process could be said to involve a data translation component, in which the designer translates atomic data points into business-oriented models that help to serve up robust, accurate AI, data science, and business intelligence results. The output is a data model that provides a visual guide for designing and deploying databases with high-quality data sources as part of a more extensive business intelligence and AI data architecture.

Data modeling has been used for decades to help organizations distinguish and characterize their data, setting standards and rules to be applied and then used by information systems. If your data sources do not go through any data-modeling process, how can your business users be confident that their results are correct and trustworthy? Data modeling is a cost-effective and productive way to maintain and oversee massive data sources and align them to provide business-friendly data that users can recognize. Designers can automatically generate data models and database designs to boost efficiency and help other people in the process, such as analysts, become more productive.

Business leaders often find it hard to trust the results from AI systems, and their skepticism can prevent these systems from ever going into production. Therefore, understanding the benefits of data modeling is more important than ever, since the process can help the organization trust its data enough to put its data to work. Although data modeling isn't new, it is becoming increasingly important because of the large volume of data that organizations are processing and storing.

A good analogy is that of a carpenter creating a piece of furniture. The carpenter designs furniture with the end user in mind and considers the functionality of the various parts. The carpenter also has to consider the user's comfort; if the furniture isn't comfortable, the end user will not use it. If the carpenter is creating several pieces of furniture, then they will need to consider how they relate to one another.

Data modeling has to take the same approach; each component may interrelate with other elements, creating a multidimensional web of touchpoints that impact one another. If this structure is not well considered, the parts can negatively affect each other. At the scale of some data estates, this oversight can be catastrophic. On the other hand, humans are highly visual, and the visual representation provided by a data model gives organizations the trust to design their proposed systems and take them to a production environment.

Data modeling is a critical component of metadata management, data governance, and business intelligence. It provides a cohesive view of conceptual, logical, and physical data models to help business and IT stakeholders comprehend the data's foundation, interrelationships, and meaning.

Quite simply, you can't manage what you can't see. To paraphrase the legendary management guru Peter Drucker: what can't be measured, can't be managed. However, Drucker's sentiment was more subtle than people often think. He says that if we *care* about something, then we measure it. One should not assume that the business is measuring essential metrics. Data modeling allows business teams to mindfully consider what they want to measure. Ultimately, the business should not focus on measurements that fail to add value to the organization. What gets measured gets managed—even when it's pointless to measure and manage it and even if it harms the organization's purpose. The prevailing attitude seems to be this: measure, and then you'll get meaning. Instead, we need to consider measured measurement, considering what we want to measure and why. The data-modeling process can help the organization define and understand what is important to its success.

Why Are Data Models Important in Power BI?

Data models provide a framework for data to be used within information systems. In Power BI, the data model supports data integrity and optimizes performance. The fact table contains a timestamp, which allows for trend analysis. There may also be dedicated reporting tables that contain aggregated data such as monthly sales. In the age of big data, some data practitioners think that data modeling is not needed, often because data is being ingested as part of the big data philosophical approach. It is tempting to think there is no need for data modeling and to view it as overthinking. Why not just dive into the technology and get started?

The adage "fail to plan, plan to fail" is pertinent to many technology scenarios, and it is particularly relevant where business and technology meet. Data modeling is critical for a data project to be successful, especially where the data sources are big data. However, you still need to organize and understand the data. What makes sense from the technology perspective may not make sense from a business standpoint and vice versa. For example, a technical team member may be comfortable with 1s and 0s in a column of data, but this does not look good on a report. On the other hand, businesspeople may prefer the same data in the form of "Yes" and "No" because the words are immediately meaningful. The words are also clearly readable in the filters and slicers of a Power BI report.

Crucially, business teams or IT teams should not forget the data translation piece. If the data and subsequent analysis are essential, there is a need to share and communicate the analysis to others. Data modeling supports data translation by helping to facilitate and formalize the data translation process. For example, in a good data model, the model can assume that column types are homogeneous. As an aside, this contrasts with Excel, where any given cell in a spreadsheet can contain a different datatype than its neighbors. The data translation process will help to identify if there is a column match or mismatch. For example, the currency column could be treated as if it is in euros when it is thought to be US dollars, or sometimes it could be a mix of the two currencies. As a consequence, aggregations may be very confusing. In a well-constructed data model, the currency types would be split out into one column for euros and another column for dollars.

Data modeling is a timeless skill because it does not rely on a specific technology. In an age when technology moves very fast, it is appealing to learn a skill that does not go out-of-date while supporting business intelligence and AI projects alike. In addition, data modeling can adapt to meet new business requirements. Data is a "living" part of the business. As data moves to new, fluid, and dynamic business environments and interpretations, data modeling can adjust to the changes in business requirements. Data translation helps users to adapt and keep abreast of changes in the data, allowing them to understand the business environment better and more quickly.

You can design the data model without dependency on any particular technology application. Essentially, data modeling decouples the data from the technology. Moreover, the data model is reusable in other applications. In terms of technology, spreadsheets or proprietary data-modeling software can create and record visual depictions of data models. Every organization can use Microsoft Visio or even simple spreadsheets for data modeling since it does not require any special technical skills or niche, expensive software.

Why Do We Need a Data Model for AI?

A good data model improves comprehension of the data at a granular level. Since the data model helps comprehension, it improves the performance of dependent processes and systems, such as AI.

A good data model also increases resilience in an environment of change, and data should be expected to change over time. This benefit is particularly important for AI because businesses need to be able to trust the results of the AI process. If the AI algorithms are producing incorrect results due to unexpected changes in the data, then the data model must be flexible enough to identify what is happening and make the needed update.

The process of data modeling includes having important conversations that help the business to make crucial decisions about the data. One key issue concerns how current the information needs to be and the anticipated frequency of data changes. It is crucial to make decisions about latency early on, since this will drive decisions you may not have anticipated, such as which type of Power BI licensing is needed. In turn, data modeling can help to clarify issues that may not have been addressed earlier in the project, such as which method will be used to access the data. Data modeling helps to facilitate conversations about system availability, such as the amount of system downtime permitted to conduct updates. Data-modeling conversations can also reveal details about actual and predicted data volumes needed for storage. Often, these conversations can help management to understand the skills the organization has and any other required skill sets that the organization may need to implement the solution. In this way, management can identify what the organization can do on its own and where it may need to bring in external help. These factors can help determine the budget for training and external support.

To summarize, data modeling can help to facilitate conversations about user requirements, since requests will pop into users' heads when you go through the data-modeling process with them. Often, these unguarded requests can be gold, and they may even save you trouble in the longer term, so listen carefully!

Advice for Setting Up a Data Model for AI

How can we approach data modeling from the business perspective? Dimensional modeling is optimized for analytics, but often databases are optimized for supporting an application rather than a business reporting need. Transactional databases toil to track change over time, potentially delaying data retrieval. These databases do not effectively handle all the data accumulated from analytics because they are designed to *store* it rapidly rather than *retrieve and aggregate* it rapidly. Transactional databases can write the same record numerous times whenever there is a change event, adding more rows of data that make the database hard to traverse quickly. Also, the database structure may be confusing from the perspective of creating table joins because the columns may be named confusingly, rather than being set up in a business-oriented manner. Since these databases are designed to support transactions but not to answer analytical questions, there is a need for a separate datawarehousing or reporting database.

Analytics Center of Excellence

An organization could put in place an analytics center of excellence (ACE) to unify the business intelligence approaches within the organization.[1] As organizations move from knowledge to analytics, these teams are sometimes called analytics competency centers (ACCs), business intelligence competency centers, or analytics service centers. Your organization may have a different name for a similar team. On the other hand, if your organization does not have such a group, perhaps you should implement one. Let's take a closer look.

---

1 Gloria J. Miller, Dagmar Bräutigam, and Stefanie V. Gerlach, *Business Intelligence Competency Centers: A Team Approach to Competitive Advantage* (Hoboken, NJ: Wiley, 2006).

Translated into practical terms, an ACE is a virtual team that is responsible for establishing the business intelligence standards, processes, and central program management that is key to delivery and achievement. Technology choice is only one aspect of business intelligence expression within an organization. BI also involves enterprise requirements, data, and priorities from both internal and external sources.

Which factors enable an organization to lay the groundwork for an effective ACE, what are the main components of a successful ACE, and how can you maximize the likelihood of success if you invest in an ACE initiative?

With respect to the longer-term data strategy, the ACE can facilitate collaboration and cooperation between teams by:

- Resolving multiple development groups to contribute independently to this single framework
- Implementing decisions on how to present data for reporting, such as by using data from an application source system, operational data stores, data warehouses, or external data sources
- Securing architecture decisions to support an appropriate reporting architecture and a technical framework
- Providing a set of best practices and standardization for delivery and report consumption across all teams
- Resolving potential conflicts between groups on business definitions and rules

Earning Trust Through Data Transactions

The organization can start small by demonstrating analysis of a subset of transactions to show that insights can be gained. This is achieved by combining datasets to tell a story at the individual level. People who use Excel are often tasked with combining data sources to make tables for further analysis. Joining data together can be complex because the joins are not always obvious. The benefit of adding new datasets is that access will expand from restrictive data models to more flexible data sources that provide insights. The flexible data sources can be further improved by providing data more frequently than the overnight schedule provided by batch jobs.

Agile Data Warehousing: The BEAM Framework

A methodology such as Business Event Analysis and Modeling (BEAM) could be used to introduce a user-oriented, business focus to the data warehousing solution.[2] BEAM can be used in redesigning data stores to achieve provable, repeatable, small

---

2 Lawrence Corr (with Jim Stagnitto), *Agile Data Warehouse Design: Collaborative Dimensional Modeling, from Whiteboard to Star Schema* (Leeds, UK: DecisionOne Press, 2011).

---

successes that build up over time. In BEAM modeling, user stories are constructed from examples in a format known as the 7Ws (who, what, when, where, how many, why, and how). The resulting data model follows the user stories closely. This facilitates user adoption while helping developers to understand the business process better from end to end. The Agile Manifesto is normally applied to software, but it can also be applied to data warehouse design.

The method is considered Agile as long as it adheres to the four principles of the Agile Manifesto, which values:

- Individuals and interactions over processes and tools
- Working software over comprehensive documentation
- Customer collaboration over contract negotiation
- Responding to change over following a plan

The objective of Agile is to provide customer satisfaction by rapid, continuous delivery of useful data products. Through the iterative cycle, working data assets are delivered frequently, in weeks rather than months, and this is the principal measure of progress. Late changes in requirements are welcomed because the objective is user success, and this allows for flexibility in delivering results. The methodology requires close cooperation between business teams and developers. Agile produces continuous attention to technical excellence and good design, thereby building a lot of trust between developers and the end users, who feel that they have been heard. For the ACE, the simplicity and fluidity of self-organizing teams permit regular adaptation to changing circumstances, allowing the team to deliver urgent priorities and requirements.

In an Agile project, the team's composition is usually cross-functional and self-organizing, working around the barriers of corporate hierarchy or the corporate roles of team members. The team members normally take responsibility for the iterative tasks that deliver the desired functionality that iteration requires.

Agile relates to data warehouse development by facilitating the ability of end users and developers to drill down into understanding the data in an enterprise context. As the process proceeds, analyzing the data will allow more rules to be identified. In turn, this will lead to new requirements, which will necessitate changes ranging from minor to significant. As the developers' understanding deepens, end users get fast, ongoing delivery of value as they are still refining their needs.

During the development of a data warehouse, any number of small, independent projects can be executed to load the warehouse from different sources. The overall structure of development is loose, handling multiple interdependent data warehouse projects under one business intelligence program.

It is a big challenge to understand the dependencies during the development cycle, especially when there are dependencies among different systems at different levels. However, an Agile approach avoids the current situation, where the team is developing datasets and data assets on an ad hoc basis without considering a proper data model design.

Data Modeling Disciplines to Support AI

There are a range of patterns to use for arranging data into models. In this section, we will cover a few common methodologies for working with data to make it business-friendly.

Dimensional modeling is a perfect fit for analytics. It is straightforward for business users to operate and understand. It supports performance using large sets of data, and it works well with Power BI. Dimensional modeling's resilience when changes are needed, or "graceful extensibility," is one advantage of this approach. As concerns grow over topics such as data governance, the dimensional-modeling technique can be supported by using a data vault.

Data vault is a business-focused methodology that comprises data modeling and management.[3] Version 2.1, an update to the original data vault methodology, is currently being developed by Dan Linstedt; you can find out more at the Data Vault Alliance website (*https://datavaultalliance.com*). It is developed for building enterprise data warehouses and business intelligence platforms. The data vault methodology is designed to meet the requirements of today's need for real-time data as well as historical data, so it has flexibility, scalability, and adaptability built in right from the start. It meets complex business needs for governance as well as for managing large volumes of data from diverse sources. Let's look at the ways in which the data vault methodology seeks to address some of the limitations of traditional modeling techniques.

The data vault technique models several objects, such as:

- *Hubs*, which integrate data from different source systems. Hubs reliably list key business identifiers, including the business key, so you can uniquely and reliably identify a given entity over time. A valid business key has real business meaning, and it provides a sense of continuity from one source system to another. At the lowest level of the fact table, or *grain*, the data is consistent across source systems and thus easier to track.

---

3 Daniel Linstedt and Michael Olschimke, *Building a Scalable Data Warehouse with Data Vault 2.0* (Waltham, MA: Morgan Kaufmann, 2015).

- *Links*, which are tables that instantiate all the relationships between business entities.
- *Satellites*, which are tables that store descriptive attributes related to either a hub or a link.

The data vault methodology helps integrate data from various source systems into a data model that changes at different rates in the source tables. The data vault is first and foremost about the business; the business rules are both derived from the raw data and stored separately from the raw data, producing a separation of responsibility. As a result, it is easier to manage business rule changes over time, and overall system complexity is reduced. This is in contrast to tracking changes through snapshot dates, which demands complex queries that grow in complexity when obtaining a result at a "single point in time" view of the data (e.g., the previous week). Additionally, there is a risk that the source table may change the structure, such as by the addition of new columns.

The data vault methodology also addresses a standard limitation related to the dimensional model approach, specifically the limitation of having a "fixed" model. Dimensional modeling's resilience to change is one of the main advantages of the method because it can handle changing data relationships without affecting existing business intelligence applications such as Power BI. For example, adding facts consistent with the grain of an existing fact table can be accomplished by creating new columns. Moreover, developers can add new dimensions to a current fact table by creating new foreign key columns, presuming they don't alter the grain.

It is helpful to explain this scenario with an example. Let's take the case of a customer dimension, which is a table with 10 attributes. There is a fact table linked to the customer dimension, and four other dimensions all come from a single source system. As the business changes over time, it needs to integrate a second source system to have a richer unified data source for reporting. Now, the customer dimension table has 20 attributes. In the dimensional approach, the developer would need to refactor the dimension by revising the data load process to ingest the new attributes. In addition, if each source system contained the same attribute, the developer would have to decide which attribute is correct. This situation may be acceptable if you have to add only one feature. However, the development becomes more complex if there are many changes over time, such as in requirements or the number of attributes from source systems.

The data vault methodology is a business-aligned, resilient model that eliminates this refactoring activity. In addition, the methodology provides the ability to integrate new sources more quickly than traditional models. The advantage of this approach lies in its use of business keys that maintain their meaning across systems, providing a common set of attributes for aligning the systems horizontally.

Data vault also requires creating more tables than business users might expect to see in a dimensional model. From the reporting and analytics perspective, arranging the data into a simple star schema is a recommended starting point to give the business users some experience with a dimensional model format. With a star schema, the metrics are located in a fact table that is related to dimension tables.

Data vault is a very useful methodology when users have multiple source systems and relationships that change frequently. It works well because it makes adding attributes straightforward. If there is a change to only one source system, then the change doesn't have to appear for all of the other source systems. Similarly, limiting the number of places where changes are made is possible because attributes are stored separately from structural data in satellites. Further, it is easier to account for new and changing relationships by closing one link and creating another link; the developer doesn't have to amend the historical data to account for a new relationship or update an existing schema. Data vault simplifies this situation because the developer only needs to account for the changes going forward.

This methodology also helps users to be able to track and audit data easily. It enables auditing because the methodology stipulates that it is necessary to record load times and record sources, and this recording happens for every row. Data vault also tracks a history of all changes because the satellites include the load time as part of the primary key. Furthermore, when an attribute is updated, the methodology stipulates that the database system create a new record to reflect the change. Thus, the organization can quickly provide auditability for data governance purposes. Indeed, the organization stores all historical changes and can access data from any point in time.

In addition, data vault supports faster data loading because the methodology enables many of the tables to be loaded simultaneously in parallel. The model decreases dependencies between tables during the load process, thereby simplifying the data ingestion process. Data vault methodology leverages inserts only, thereby loading more quickly than merging data, for example.

Furthermore, a data vault model should never directly feed into your reporting tool. Due to the need to have three types of tables, your reporting tool would have to marry all related tables to report on one subject area. These joins would adversely impact report performance, which is unacceptable for business users. It would also increase the likelihood of error, because while reporting tools are fantastic at data visualization, they are not great at number-crunching data manipulation. Instead, the data vault would act as a data source to serve data into a dimensional model. Power BI can pick up the data from the data source with a dimensional model structure. If you plan to implement a data model using data vault for Power BI, then it is recommended that you create a dimensional model. The data vault will give you the necessary auditing, flexibility, and adaptability required for AI systems now and in the future, and dimensional modeling in Power BI will deliver a performant data structure that makes the most of Power BI.

Data-modeling decisions are often nuanced, and mistakes can become more impactful over time.

Data Modeling Versus AI Models

For many businesses, AI is a sophisticated way of solving complex problems using enormous datasets with high accuracy and reduced costs. An AI model is a tool or algorithm that is based on a certain dataset through which it can arrive at a decision—all without the need for human interference in the decision-making process. The AI model searches a dataset for patterns with the objective of arriving at a decision or making a prediction based on the data. It is important to understand the terminology associated with AI because some terms that mean the same thing can be used interchangeably.

AI models are hugely important in a range of applications. For example, they are very good at *pattern matching*, which involves identifying specific patterns within data based on certain rules or examples. In the context of AI, pattern matching refers to the ability of AI algorithms to recognize patterns within datasets, typically with the goal of making decisions, predictions, or classifications. The "last mile" of AI is to produce an automated model that makes decisions based on the data. In some ways, the last mile of AI is actually a "first-mile" problem; once the model is in production, it needs to be continually honed to ensure that it is making appropriate decisions.

So far in this chapter, we have focused on data models. We can also represent data in Power BI, so let's explore this topic next.

Data Modeling in Power BI

The data model is built in the Power BI Desktop. The data is ingested using Power Query, and Power BI builds a model of the data that is accessible from the Model view. Then, the tables are joined using relationships to enhance the model. It is possible to see the data in the Power BI workbook using the Data tab. It is also possible to see it from the Report tab, which rests on the data and the data model.

Figure 2-2 illustrates the dataflow, with the data ingestion going from left to right.

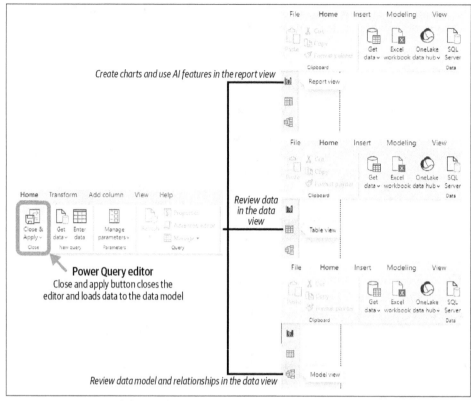

Figure 2-2. Ingesting data and building a model

Fact tables and dimension tables

Central to the Power BI model is the *fact table*, which contains measures. This is based on the Kimball methodology.[4] As a reminder, facts are the result of business processes, and they can be aggregated to provide a summary. Examples of facts include financial transactions, refunds, and costs.

As discussed at the start of the chapter, a *dimension table* contains information to help the users to slice and dice the data. For example, dimension tables include descriptive attributes, such as a customer, that define how business users would like to see the data. For instance, we may want to see the data by the customer so we better understand how much the customer spends with our organization. If we have a report called "Sales by Customer," then sales are the measured amounts, and

---

4 Ralph Kimball and Margy Ross, *The Data Warehouse Toolkit: The Definitive Guide to Dimensional Modeling*, 3rd ed. (Hoboken, NJ: John Wiley & Sons, 2011).

they come from the fact table. Words that come after the "by" are known as the dimensions—in this case, the customer is the dimension.

In Power BI, the fact table can be found in the Model view, and the dimension tables complement the fact table. In Figure 2-3, the fact table is the Sales table, and the dimension tables contain information about campaigns, customers, products, and dates.

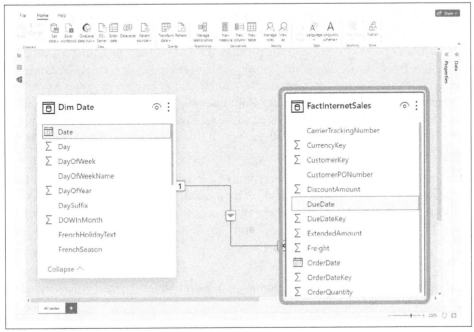

Figure 2-3. Viewing a fact table and its associated dimension tables in Model view

The fact and dimension tables need to be associated with each other, and this is where modeling relationships come in. Let's explore relationships in more detail.

Modeling relationships in the data model

At the most basic level, a relationship is a connection between two tables using columns from each table. The data model brings facts and dimensions together, providing a richer reporting and analytics experience for the business user. In data models, relationships can be challenging to understand, so let's look at how to use a technology that we all know and love—Microsoft Excel—to interpret relationships.

Let's consider the well-known Excel formula VLOOKUP, a function that brings two tables together. In Excel, we use VLOOKUP when finding things in a table or a range by row. For example, a VLOOKUP could tell us a product name based on product ID.

The syntax of VLOOKUP takes four arguments:

=VLOOKUP(what to look up, where to look for it, the column number in the range containing the value to return, whether to return an approximate or exact match)

Columns are numbered from left to right starting with 1. To tell VLOOKUP to look for an exact match, use FALSE or 0; to tell it to look for an approximate match, use TRUE or 1.

Let's say that we want to look up a product name based on the product ID in a table that has product transactions in it. There is one table of product information and another table of transactions with the product ID, and we want to return the product name. The transaction table is the "many" table because it has multiple instances of products; we assume that each product could be sold once or more than once. The product table is the "one" table; things would be very confusing if a product ID were associated with more than one product, so we will assume that each product is listed just once. Using a VLOOKUP, we can see which side is the many (*) and which is the one (1).

The *cardinality* is defined as the direction of the relationship, and it specifies how the tables are similar through their related columns. In Power BI, each model relationship needs a cardinality type. There are four cardinality type options representing the data characteristics of the "from" and "to" related columns. For example, the "one" side means the column contains unique values, and the "many" side means the column can contain duplicate values.

Relationships are set up between columns of different tables. There are three types of relationships between tables:

One-to-one
Each row in one table is connected to another row in another table. This is the most basic type of relationship.

One-to-many
One table has the (1) column and the other table has the (*) column. For example, a product dimension table and a sales transaction table are connected by a ProductID column that exists in both tables. In the product table, each product has a unique ID. In the sales table, each product listed has been sold at least once and possibly on multiple occasions. Therefore, the relationship between product and sales is one to many. Figure 2-4 shows an example of a one-to-many relationship in the Edit relationship window.

Many-to-many
Using Power BI composite models, it is possible to establish relationships with many-to-many cardinality between tables. This approach removes unique values

in tables, as we saw in the one-to-many relationship types. The many-to-many relationship type indicates that neither table contains unique values.

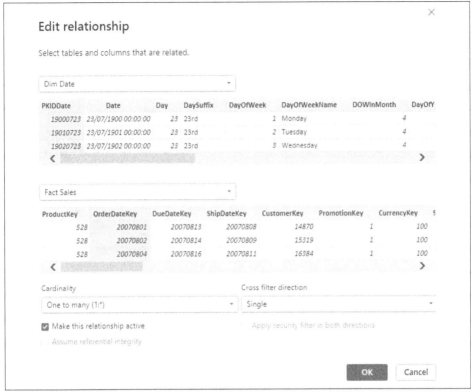

Figure 2-4. A one-to-many relationship in the Edit relationship window

There are different types of relationships that form the basis of getting the data right for AI, business intelligence, and data science.

What Do Relationships Mean for AI?

Relationships in a data model are key for AI. If the connection is not set up correctly, then there is a risk that data will be omitted from the analysis because the relationship type is not configured properly.

Also, if the data is not set up properly, the result may be a Cartesian product. A *Cartesian product* is a cross-join that returns all the rows in all the tables listed in a query. In other words, each row in the first table is paired with all the rows in the second table. This happens when there is no relationship defined between the two tables. The Cartesian product between two tables, Table 1 and Table 2, consists of all the possible combinations of Table 1 rows and Table 2 rows. The number of rows will be equal to the number of rows of Table 1 multiplied by the number of rows of Table 2. In this scenario, the volume of data balloons, resulting in incorrect datasets.

For AI, there is a crucial need for the underlying datasets to be correct. If data is missing, or if there is duplicate or extraneous data, the result is a faulty dataset.

The adage "garbage in, garbage out" is just as true for AI as it is for data warehousing. Both disciplines require correct data and depend on all other variables to be correct before reasonable conclusions can be drawn. It can be difficult for people to trust the results of AI due to misconceptions about what AI is, and using incorrect data will only breed further mistrust and confusion. To summarize, relationships between tables are one area where an insufficient underlying dataset may throw AI reasoning into disarray. Therefore, it is essential to ensure these dependencies are correct before thinking about AI.

Power BI relationships support filtering, so they have to be set up correctly because relationships impact what the users see at the frontend. When the users select filter options, filters on the columns of tables will be propagated to other model tables, filtering data from the users' view. The filters will propagate correctly as long as the relationships are correct. Ultimately, this means that the data in one table will display the visibility of the data of another table, since the user's selection will traverse the relationships between different tables. It is possible to disable relationships between tables. It is also possible to use Data Analysis Expressions (DAX) to change model calculations to prefer one relationship between table columns over another relationship.

When the Power BI developer creates a one-to-many relationship, Desktop will check that one side of the relationship is the "one" and the other is the "many." Note that, if a data refresh operation tries to load duplicate values into a column on the "one" side, the entire data refresh will fail because it will not be clear which row is the correct one. For example, if the "one" table contained multiple duplicate rows referring to the same product, it would not be clear which row should be considered the source of truth. In this example, Power BI would not be able to load the data correctly, and the load would fail.

Power BI defaults to a unidirectional relationship, based on the assumption that the relationship should allow filters to pass from the dimension attribute table to the fact table. A bidirectional relationship means that the filter is passed in both directions. In other words, the filter is passed from the dimension table to the fact table, and it is also possible for the fact table to filter the dimension table. With a bidirectional relationship, if you select an option in a slicer in Power BI, a related table will be filtered by your selection. Furthermore, if you select a specific row in a table, then the associated slicer will also be filtered.

Optimizing data storage and data retrieval

In Power BI, the data is stored in a columnar format in which each column is stored separately. You can think of Power BI storage as saving each column as if it is a separate file. This storage mechanism means it is faster to retrieve multiple rows from a single column, but it is slower to retrieve multiple columns from a single row.

This may seem like a disadvantage, but columnar databases are well suited for business intelligence and analytics. In contrast, a row-based data store is structured so that each row is stored separately. In the case of the row-based scenario, retrieving multiple columns from a single row is fast, and retrieving multiple rows from a single column is slower.

A good data model optimizes Power BI because it offers better performance. People do not like to wait for their data! Therefore, from the user perspective, it is better to have reports that return data faster. Power BI performs better when it is not handling a lot of text, so numeric columns will perform better.

To cope with text, Power BI uses a technique called *dictionary encoding* to further increase performance. With dictionary encoding, Power BI creates an integer value to represent a text string, and since computers find it faster to match numbers than text, data retrieval is quicker. So, for example, when Power BI is creating a model behind the scenes, it will create a dictionary of the distinct values within one column. In the example in Table 2-1, Power BI identifies the distinct values within the Department column and creates a dictionary by assigning indexes to those values. Then the stored index values serve as pointers to the real values.

Table 2-1. Power BI assigning index values to text values

Index	Department
0	Sales
1	Marketing
2	Operations
3	Finance

When Power BI displays the data, it replaces the actual values with index values from the dictionary. Dictionary encoding is powerful when there are few unique values in a column, as in the Department example in Table 2-1. However, it does not work well for ID fields, for example.

Once the data is compressed, Power BI automatically detects relationships in the data. Note, however, that it may not always do so correctly. Say, for example, that two columns have the same name and datatype, but they do not refer to the same business concept. Therefore, it is important to double-check the relationships between tables, preferably by creating a data dictionary to record the metadata and the context of the data itself.

Tips for improving performance in the data model

A better Power BI report model will result in faster performance—and happier users! Here are some tips to help you to improve the Power BI model's performance.

Sort columns before bringing them into a Power BI data model. Essentially, this activity will give Power BI less to do, since sorting data can be computationally expensive for many technologies.

Only bring the data that you need. For example, the datetime datatype is usually not required unless you are specifically using the Time component. For example, if you are storing someone's birthday, then there is no need to include the time of birth as well. If you really need Time, try splitting the information about date and time into two columns to reduce the number of unique values, thereby increasing the opportunity for compression.

Be mindful of bidirectional and many-to-many relationships. Avoid bidirectional and many-to-many relationships against columns that have a lot of unique values (i.e., high-cardinality columns). These relationships navigate more pathways and check more data points. As a result of navigating the additional search space, bidirectional relationships against high-cardinality columns will adversely impact report performance.

Use your own custom date table. It is recommended that you create your own custom date table rather than use the autogenerated date table in Power BI. The autogenerated date table creates a table for each date column, increasing the model size. It is possible to use a single custom date table to reduce the model size, connecting it with the fact table. As recommended previously, split the date and time to improve data compression.

Reduce data load on each page. Reduce the amount of data loaded on the page by using bookmarks, drill-through pages, and tool tips. This will increase the speed of the report.

Reduce the number of visuals on the page. You can also improve performance by reducing the number of visuals on the page. In addition, your colleagues will find it easier to understand the dashboards if the screen is not too cluttered. Sometimes, users ask for many charts all on the same page. In this case, you can encourage them to use drill-downs and navigation features such as bookmarks to understand the data better.

Avoid iterator functions (e.g., SUMX, RANKX). Iterator functions will go through the data in an RBAR fashion—that is, "row by agonizing row." As you might have guessed, this is not ideal for a columnar data store like DAX and will reduce performance.

There are two ways to identify iterator functions. The aggregation functions generally end in an X: SUMX, MAXX, CONCATENATEX, etc. Additionally, many iterators take in a table as the first parameter and then an expression as the second parameter. Iterators with simple logic are generally fine and in fact are sometimes secretly converted to more efficient forms.

Optimize the data source.   Power BI will be impacted by the performance of any source system. It is generally good to take the pressure off the source system by importing the data into Power BI, however. Say, for example, that Power BI is accessing data from a SQL Server database. If the SQL Server database is not performing well, then Power BI will take longer to ingest the data. Therefore, sometimes the best approach is not to optimize Power BI; sometimes you need to ask the data source owners to support you by optimizing the data source instead.

Why don't we just have one huge table?

Business users sometimes request that a single table hold all their information, rather than splitting the data out into dimensions and facts. What is wrong with this approach?

Although this approach can appear attractive, the wide table approach is highly inefficient because the model has duplicate copies of data. This results in slow performance because the system needs to traverse more data in order to get the result. The size of a flat table can expand quickly as the data model becomes increasingly complicated. It can also be slow to load data into tables that are wide and deep, adversely affecting performance of the technical system. Also, the table will not be flexible enough to be responsive to change; instead of changing just one part of the system, any changes impact the whole system.

Poor system performance will negatively affect user adoption. Business users hate reports that are slow. Ultimately, if they do not like the system, then they will not use it—even if they find it easier to navigate.

In contrast, you can easily meet business needs, such as adding or refactoring attributes in your model, if you use dimensional modeling. In addition, dimensions are very cheap to manage computationally, so it is possible to add many attributes to meet the business needs. Data vault supports the process by offering proper auditing and data governance as part of an overall architecture. It is better to use a dimensional structure with Power BI, such as a star schema model, to improve performance. These advantages can smooth the production of an enterprise solution that uses AI as part of an overall data strategy.

To pull off these concepts together, let's go through an example of using Power BI to create a simple data model that reduces redundancy while structuring the data in a way that is useful for Power BI.

Flat File Structure Versus Dimensional Model Structure in Power BI

Let's take a look at how Power BI works with a flat file structure versus a very small star schema. Using the World Bank example data from the previous chapter, we see that the data is all contained in one table. What happens when we try to break the wide table into smaller chunks?

Reimport the data from the World Bank as detailed in the previous chapter:

1. Download the file as an Excel format.

2. Open Power BI Desktop and select the Get Data button. Navigate to the Excel file of World Data Bank data.

Now, in the Power BI Navigator window, select the Metadata - Countries tab (Figure 2-5).

Figure 2-5. The Navigator tab with Metadata - Countries selected

Then, click the Transform Data button on the righthand side of the Navigator. The Power BI Desktop will appear (Figure 2-6).

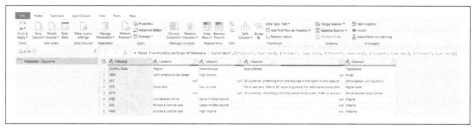

Figure 2-6. Power BI Desktop with World Bank data imported

On the Home tab, select "Use first row as headers"; the first row of data will be promoted to become the header of each column. On the right side of Power Query, you will see the Query Settings (Figure 2-7).

Figure 2-7. The Query Settings panel

The Region column contains null data. In our scenario, we would like to replace the null Region data with the data in the TableName column. To do this, navigate to the Add Column tab and select Conditional Column, shown in Figure 2-8, to create a new column called Full Region Name.

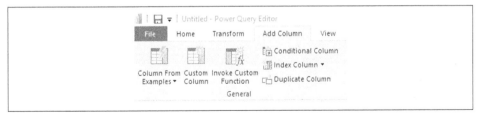

Figure 2-8. Selecting Conditional Column on the Add Column tab

Now, you can populate the Add Conditional Column screen as shown in Figure 2-9. Follow these steps:

1. In the "New column name" field, type Full Region Name.

2. In the If clause dropdown, select the Region column name.

3. In the Operator clause dropdown, select "equals."

4. Next to the Value text box, ensure that the Text option is selected. As you can see from the image, it is labeled ABC123.

5. Type "null" in the Value field.

6. In the Output dropdown, choose "Select a column" and then choose the column name "TableName."

Next, you want to instruct Power BI to use the Region Name by default. In other words, if it finds a null in the Region box, it will return the TableName. If it does not find a null, then by default it returns the contents of the Region column. To create this part of the rule, move on to the Else clause:

7. In the Else dropdown, choose "Select a column" and then choose the column name Region.

Once the steps are completed, click OK.

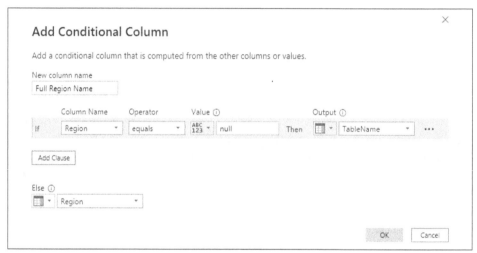

Figure 2-9. Adding a conditional column to replace null Region data with the data in the TableName column

To test the conditional rule, you can select the Region header and drag it to the righthand side so that it is next to the TableName column, as shown in Figure 2-10. The new calculated column called Full Region Name will display the results. You can see that when a region is not *null* in the Region column, the Full Region Name contains the content of the Region column. But if the region is *null*, Full Region Name picks up the value of TableName.

Figure 2-10. Testing that the conditional column Full Region Name is working as intended

Now, let's remove the original Region column. Don't panic! The Full Region Name column will continue to store the name from the original Region column when appropriate. To remove the column, right-click on it and select Remove (Figure 2-11).

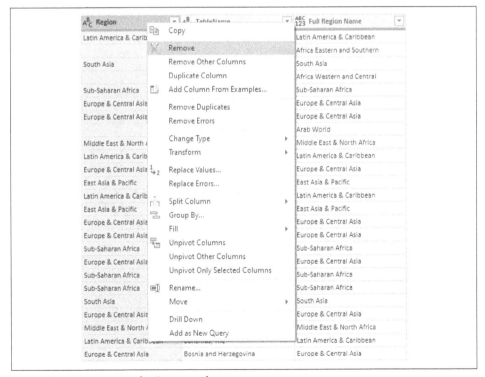

Figure 2-11. Removing the Region column

Now, rename the TableName column something more meaningful. Since the column name should convey that the column contains a mix of country and region information, let's call it Country / Region. To rename the TableName column, right-click on it and select Rename (Figure 2-12).

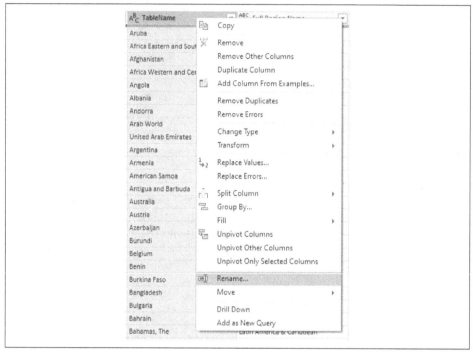

Figure 2-12. Renaming the TableName column

When you click Rename, the header will change at the top of the screen. Type in Country / Region and then click Enter. The column will appear as shown in Figure 2-13.

Figure 2-13. The TableName column renamed with the more descriptive heading Country / Region

You can repeat this exercise for the IncomeGroup column. If you examine this column, you will see that some of the rows are set to null; these are the same summary groupings that were handled in the last part of the exercise. Set up a new column called Income Group. (Note the space in the name! It will be easier for Power BI users to read.) The new Income Group column will display the IncomeGroup information if it is present; otherwise, it will display the Full Region Name.

To do this, navigate to the Add Column tab item and click on Conditional Column. Enter the details to create a new column that will display the original IncomeGroup data if it is present or the Full Region Name if the IncomeGroup value is null (Figure 2-14).

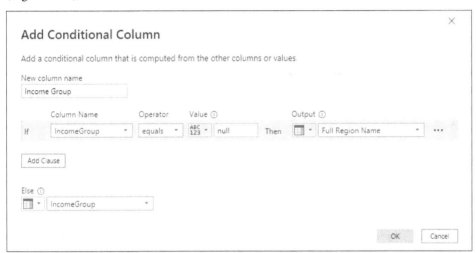

Figure 2-14. Adding a conditional column to replace null IncomeGroup data with the data in the Full Region Name column

Once the new conditional column is created, it will appear in the Power Query client as shown in Figure 2-15. As with the previous example, the columns have been moved so that they are easier to compare. You can see that when the value in the IncomeGroup column is null, the value of Full Region Name has been placed in the Income Group column; otherwise, the Income Group column contains the value from IncomeGroup.

Country / Region	IncomeGroup	Full Region Name	Income Group
Aruba	High income	Latin America & Caribbean	High income
Africa Eastern and Southern		null Africa Eastern and Southern	Africa Eastern and Southern
Afghanistan	Low income	South Asia	Low income
Africa Western and Central		null Africa Western and Central	Africa Western and Central
Angola	Lower middle income	Sub-Saharan Africa	Lower middle income
Albania	Upper middle income	Europe & Central Asia	Upper middle income
Andorra	High income	Europe & Central Asia	High income
Arab World		null Arab World	Arab World

Figure 2-15. Testing that the conditional column Income Group is working as intended

As before, you can remove the old IncomeGroup column by right-clicking on the column and selecting Remove.

To tidy up the table, you can remove the SpecialNotes column in the same way. In Power BI, the large data table now appears in Power Query as shown in Figure 2-16.

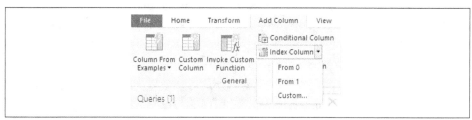

`= Table.RemoveColumns(#"Reordered Columns1",{"IncomeGroup", "SpecialNotes"})`

	Country Code	Country / Region	Full Region Name	Income Group
1	ABW	Aruba	Latin America & Caribbean	High income
2	AFE	Africa Eastern and Southern	Africa Eastern and Southern	Africa Eastern and Southern
3	AFG	Afghanistan	South Asia	Low income
4	AFW	Africa Western and Central	Africa Western and Central	Africa Western and Central
5	AGO	Angola	Sub-Saharan Africa	Lower middle income
6	ALB	Albania	Europe & Central Asia	Upper middle income
7	AND	Andorra	Europe & Central Asia	High income

Figure 2-16. Streamlined World Bank Data in Power Query

Now, you can add an index to this table. This will help you do a lookup later. Also, it will help the Power BI Desktop file stay as compressed as possible, since it will be working with integers rather than lots of repeated text. To add an index to the table, go to the Add Column tab (Figure 2-17).

Figure 2-17. Adding an index column

The new Index column will appear at the righthand side of the Power Query interface, but you can drag it to the lefthand side (Figure 2-18).

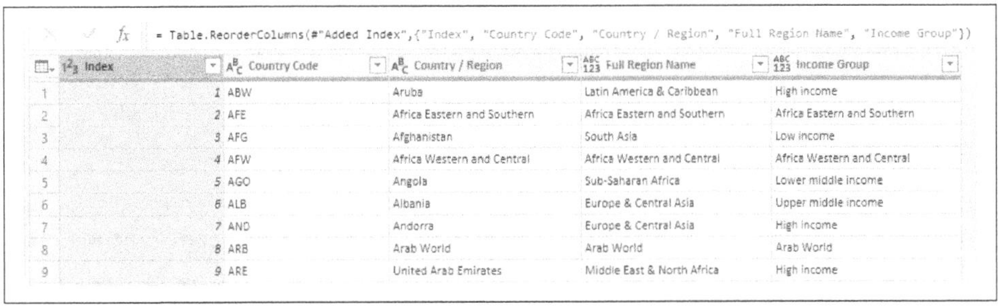

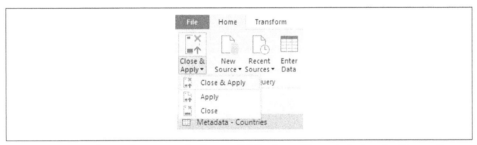

Figure 2-18. Index column after being dragged to the lefthand side

Then, apply your changes to the Power BI Desktop file from by Home tab by clicking on Close & Apply and then selecting Close & Apply (Figure 2-19).

Figure 2-19. Applying changes to the Power BI Desktop file and closing the Power Query Editor

The Power Query Editor will close, and you will be taken to the Power BI Desktop to save the file.

You can now check the file size by right-clicking on the file in Windows Explorer and selecting Properties. In the General tab, about halfway down, the file size can be seen (Figure 2-20).

Size:	32.3 KB (33,151 bytes)
Size on disk:	36.0 KB (36,864 bytes)

Figure 2-20. Displaying file size in Windows Explorer Properties

Now, you can add in the rest of the Life Expectancy data again. This time, simply load the data and replace the country information with the corresponding index number. For example, replace the Country Name and the Country Code columns with the contents of the Index column from your previous work. This will save some file space because the dataset will no longer be storing repeating text information. When there is less data for Power BI to traverse when it is searching, sorting, and filtering, its performance will be optimized, and users will be happier.

To reuse the same source, go to the Home tab and select Recent Sources. You may well find that the Excel file is already there, so you can select the file and then click OK to reimport it (Figure 2-21).

Figure 2-21. Selecting Recent Sources on the Home tab to quickly access a previously used file

Remove the unnecessary rows at the top by navigating to the Home tab and using Remove Rows to select the top two rows (Figure 2-22).

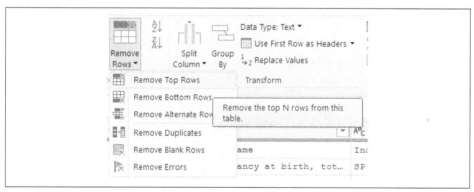

Figure 2-22. Using Remove Rows

The next step is to select the top two rows; in Figure 2-23, we are specifying that we want to remove the top two rows of data.

Figure 2-23. Removing the top two rows

You can then make the data clearer by using the correct column headers. To do this, in the Home tab, select "Use first row as headers" (Figure 2-24).

Figure 2-24. Selecting "Use first row as headers"

As in the earlier examples, remove the unnecessary columns Indicator Name and Indicator Code by right-clicking on these columns and selecting Remove.

As demonstrated previously, rename the Attribute column to Year and rename the Value column to Average Life Expectancy by right-clicking on each column in turn and selecting Rename.

You can then merge the Data query and the Countries query using the Merge option in Power Query. This will change the new Data query so that it produces a table that uses the Index key to match the countries information with the life expectancy data. You can then remove any surplus data to produce a streamlined data model that will support Power BI.

Let's get started by using "Merge queries" on the Home tab in the Power Query Editor (Figure 2-25).

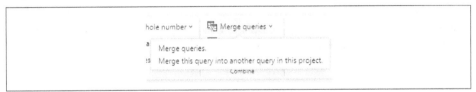

Figure 2-25. Selecting "Merge queries" on the Home tab

Click on "Merge queries," and the Merge editor will appear (Figure 2-26).

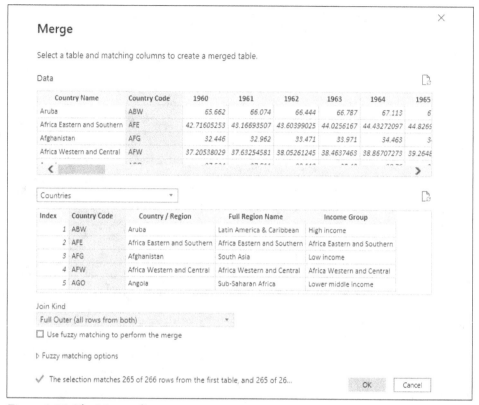

Figure 2-26. The Merge editor

The purpose here is to match the Data table with the Countries table using the Country Code column. Power BI will automatically try to work out relationships in the data by itself, using the column name. In this case, this automatic feature works well. However, you may find that sometimes it does not work for you, so let's walk through how we would accomplish merging the Data table with the Countries table using the Merge editor.

In the Data table at the top, select the Country Code column. In the Countries query result below it, select the Country Code column. In this example, for Join Kind, select Full Outer to return all rows from both tables. Click OK, and you will be presented with additional steps to merge the queries, visible in the Query Settings on the righthand side of the Power Query Editor (Figure 2-27).

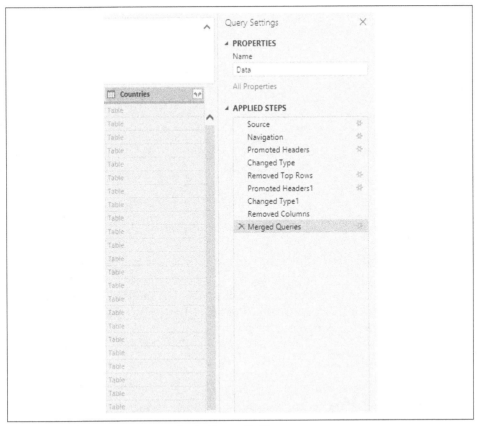

Figure 2-27. Steps to merge queries in Query Settings

Setting up the merge results in the Countries data appearing in a table format. In the interface, this is denoted by a yellow Table link in each cell. Next, choose which column you would like to include in the Data table. For this example, use the Index column so that the two tables are connected by one simple column rather than having duplicate data in both tables.

To include the Index column, select the icon on the righthand side of the Countries column. The list of columns will appear. Select the Index column and then click OK (Figure 2-28).

You will be able to see that the Applied Steps panel displays the steps that have just been completed.

Figure 2-28. Selecting the Countries Index column to include in the Data table

Let's go back into the Power Query Editor and tidy up the data model. One recommended practice is to keep index columns on the lefthand side of each table so they can be found easily and consistently throughout the data model. To move the Index column to the lefthand side of this table, right-click on the column, select Move, and then select To Beginning (Figure 2-29).

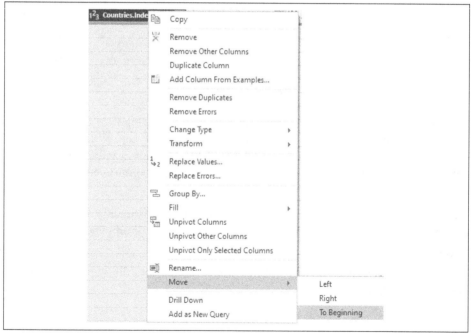

Figure 2-29. Moving the Index column

You can then unpivot the Average Life Expectancy data in the Data query by first selecting the columns that relate to years from 1960 onward and then selecting Unpivot Columns (Figure 2-30).

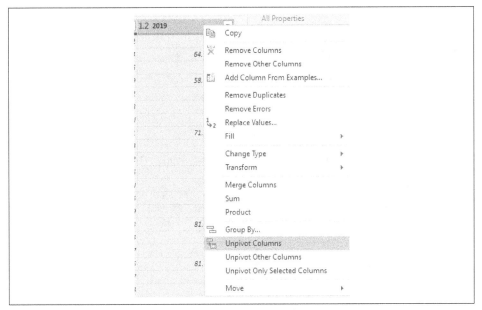

Figure 2-30. Unpivoting the Average Life Expectancy data

Now you can rename the Attribute column so that it becomes the Year column.

You can then rename the Value column to the Average Life Expectancy column. The Power Query Editor for the Data query is given in Figure 2-31.

Figure 2-31. Power Query Editor for the Data query

In the Applied Steps pane on the righthand side, shown in Figure 2-32, you should now be able to view the steps you have taken so far.

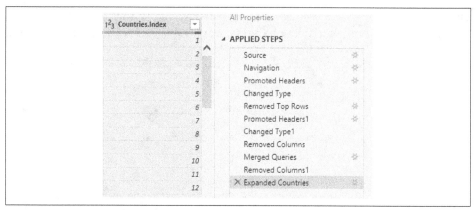

Figure 2-32. Viewing the steps taken so far in Applied Steps

Once the relationship is in place, you can remove the Country Name and Country Code columns by selecting them and right-clicking on each to choose Remove Columns (Figure 2-33).

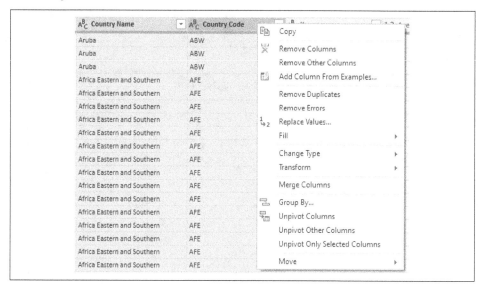

Figure 2-33. Removing the Country Name and Country Code columns

We can see that there are only three columns of data now. Power BI can use the relationship between the tables as a lookup to retrieve the country code or country name information as required (Figure 2-34).

1²₃ Countries.Index		A⁸_C Year		1.2 Average Life Expectancy	
1		1 1960		65.662	
2		1 1961		66.074	
3		1 1962		66.444	
4		1 1963		66.787	
5		1 1964		67.113	
6		1 1965		67.435	
7		1 1966		67.762	
8		1 1967		68.095	

Figure 2-34. Three columns of data, indexed by country

To commit the change to Power BI, click Close & Apply, as shown earlier in Figure 2-19.

It is crucial to check that the data model relationships are set up properly; if the relationships are incorrect, then Power BI will display incorrect data and aggregations. You can check that the data model relationships are set up properly. To do this, navigate to the Model canvas in Power BI. It can be reached by clicking the Model button on the lefthand side of the Power BI Desktop; it is the third button in the vertical pane on the left side of the screen (Figure 2-35).

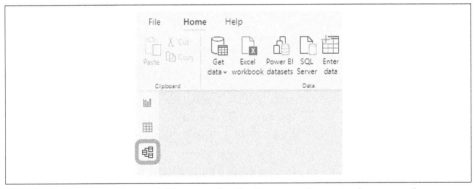

Figure 2-35. Finding the Model button, the third icon in the vertical pane on the lefthand side

In the Model pane, we can double-check the relationship between Data and the Countries tables to ensure that Power BI is using the index rather than the country code for matching up rows. Click on Manage Relationships on the Home tab to view the relationships. You will see that the Index columns are related to one another (Figure 2-36).

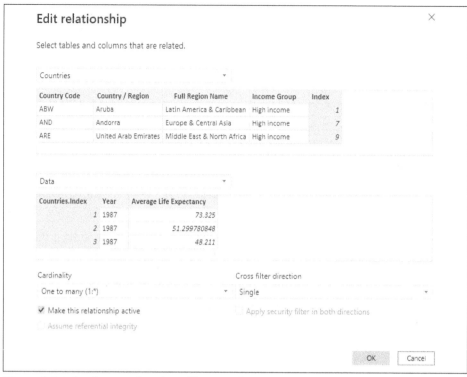

Figure 2-36. Confirming that the tables are relating to each other via the country index values

Now that the data is in place, you can create visualizations using the data in the streamlined data model. When the Power BI developer clicks on a field in the Data table, Power BI can use the relationship as a lookup in order to retrieve the correct data.

The datatype of the Year column will need to be changed from text to integer so that the Year data sorts correctly. To do this, go to the Data tab on the lefthand side of the Power BI Desktop. Select the Year column and go to the "Column tools" tab (Figure 2-37).

In the "Data type" dropdown, select "Whole number."

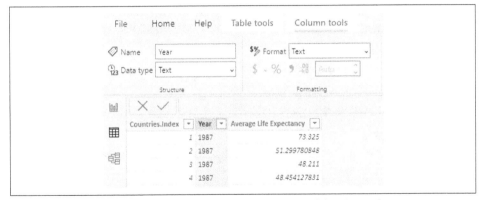

Figure 2-37. Using Column tools to change the datatype of the Year column

A warning dialog appears, but you can click OK to proceed since you do want to change the datatype (Figure 2-38).

Figure 2-38. The warning that appears when you enter a datatype change

When you click OK, the datatype and the format will be updated (Figure 2-39).

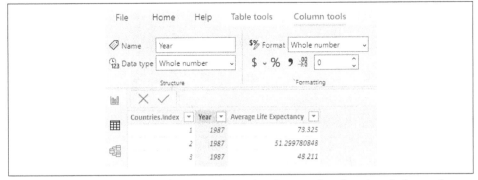

Figure 2-39. Confirming that the Year column has been updated to the whole number datatype

In the Fields pane on the righthand side of the Power BI Desktop, the Year column now has a sigma next to it, indicating that it is now a number (Figure 2-40).

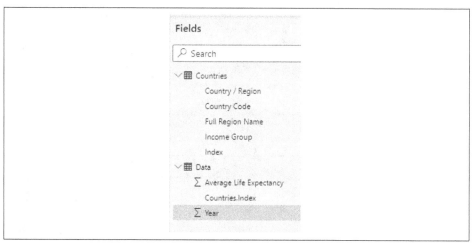

Figure 2-40. A sigma showing up next to Year in the Fields pane, indicating this is now a numeric field

Now, the hard work is over. Let's get to the fun part—creating the report!

Navigate to the Report tab in the Power BI Desktop. Go to the Visualizations pane and select the Line Chart option (Figure 2-41).

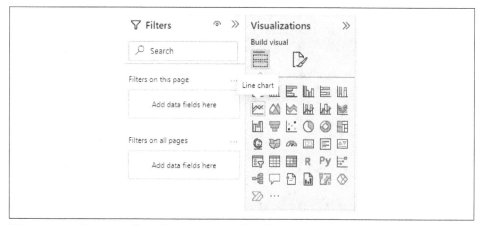

Figure 2-41. Selecting a line chart from the Visualizations pane

The Visualizations pane should be set up as follows:

1. Put Year in the Axis slot.

2. Put Income Group in the Legend slot.

3. Put Average Life Expectancy in the Values slot.

By default, Power BI will sum all of the averages. For our purposes, however, we need the average of the averages. To show the average life expectancy for each country, choose the dropdown under Values and select Average (Figure 2-42).

Figure 2-42. Averaging the average life expectancy data

Next, filter the Income Group data so the chart shows data by high income, low income, and medium income. To do this, click on the line chart first and then drag the Income Group field to the "Filters on this visual" section of the Filters pane (Figure 2-43).

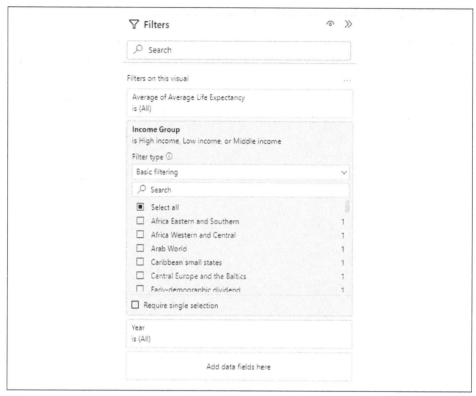

Figure 2-43. Filtering the Income Group field

To add some polish, let's add a title. Click on the Line Chart in the Power BI canvas and navigate to the Visualizations pane to select "Format visual." Next, go to the General tab where you will find the Title pane. In the Text field, enter "Average Life Expectancy by Year and Income Group." To make the title font larger, select 28 under Font (Figure 2-44).

Figure 2-44. Adding a title to the chart

The final Power BI Desktop report appears in the canvas (Figure 2-45).

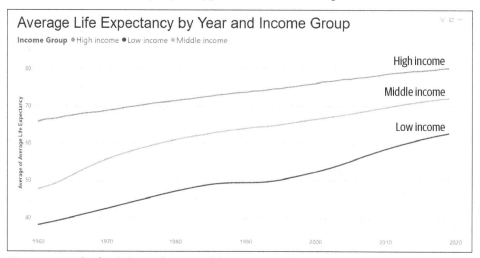

Figure 2-45. The final chart of average life expectancy by income group from 1960 to 2020

What did we learn from this demonstration?

We learned that Power BI can ingest data in various formats, and we determined the importance of a data model in providing a good foundation for further data analysis and data visualization.

In Power BI, as with most technologies, it takes some work to get the data model right. This effort involves a skill that is not always required in working with other technologies—data visualization and data modeling require empathy.

Empathy in business intelligence, AI, and data science is about humanizing data. It brings business insights to life, helping you to serve the users and, ultimately, your customer better. Doing so takes more than simply data or pieces of information. Empathy is about putting oneself in someone else's shoes as you search for useful insights and business-friendly processes that make it easier for other people to confidently make their business decisions.

The data model is created with the user in mind, regardless of the methodology that you choose. It makes the data easier to understand, purposeful, and relatable. It makes the data easier to adapt in an agile, dynamic, and fluid business environment. A good data model serves as a catalyst for helping your business to become truly data-driven and helps your organization to ensure that the data works for it and its customers.

Summary

In this chapter, we took a journey through data modeling and its impact on AI as well as on Power BI. We learned of ways to gather requirements using BEAM requirements capture. We also looked at the analytics competency center as a way of working through the people issues on the way to becoming insights-inspired and data-driven to improve business decisions.

Data modeling is a timeless skill that will lift up your data expertise in a technology-agnostic way. We have worked through a simple example that demonstrates a small data model with the result of enriching a small dataset with streamlined, easy-to-understand data.

In the next chapter, we will look at AI in the enterprise. We will review common models in AI, including when to use them and how to choose between models.

## CHAPTER 3

Blueprint for AI in the Enterprise

In technical architecture, a *blueprint* is a precise and structured plan that outlines the composition, structure, elements, and specifications of a system, software application, or technical solution. A blueprint is helpful because it provides a canvas that helps business teams, architects, engineers, and developers understand how the various parts of the AI solution will perform together to accomplish specific objectives.

The blueprint should speak to both the business audience and the technical audience, so using clear, concise language throughout is essential. Avoid unnecessary technical jargon. When it is necessary, clearly define technical terms, especially acronyms.

Since AI has many complex concepts and technical elements, it is a good idea to build a glossary of these terms as you go along. This approach will make the blueprint easier to understand for business leaders, nontechnical stakeholders, and team members. You can expect stakeholders to ask questions as they use the blueprint to better understand the proposed AI system's benefits and potential challenges.

All this may sound rather abstract, so let's look at a real-world example that illustrates how an AI architecture blueprint is necessary to develop an AI solution. Tesla's Autopilot system uses AI to facilitate semi-autonomous driving. The system incorporates AI-enabled features such as adaptive cruise control, lane centering, and cruise control sensitive to traffic conditions. Using data collected from Tesla vehicles worldwide, the Autopilot system continually learns and adjusts to different driving conditions and environments. A blueprint would be required to help pull all of these AI-enabled systems together in such a way that the data can be used effectively by the component parts. If no blueprint were in place, it would be difficult to develop and test the system effectively.

Although developing a blueprint can seem like a cost rather than an investment, it is worth considering the cost of *not* having an overall plan. That does not mean that there is no room for flexibility or an Agile approach. Instead, it means that the Agile approach should fit with the direction the project is going and what it should be delivering. The overall blueprint can bring efficiency, accuracy, and business understanding to the overall program.

In this chapter, we will look at some of the elements, such as a data strategy, essential to make AI work for an organization. Further, we will cover AI models in detail because this is an area that can cause confusion. We will look at the models themselves, their differences and similarities, and how to choose among them.

Stephen Hawking once commented that each equation in *A Brief History of Time* (1988)[1] would "halve the sales" because it would make the book much more difficult to understand. The opposite could be said about the aim of a data strategy, which is an important component of the foundation for a successful AI project. After all, AI is data-hungry, so it is crucial to get the data right. A strategy helps set the project up for success because it makes the data easier to understand.

What Is a Data Strategy?

One way of thinking about a data strategy is to consider what it gives the organization. At a high level, it provides a way to determine how the business will obtain value from its data. There are several ways a business can think about value, so without the guidance of a strategy, business leaders have no clear answers.

The business mission and vision statements should tell you about the organization's priorities. The vision statement tells you the why of the business and its future plans: Why does the organization exist? The mission statement tells you how the business will achieve its vision and is focused on the current state of the organization.

The data strategy will establish a roadmap to help the organization's decision makers make use of their data, from source to result, to reach optimal decisions. It should support the business vision and mission statement. If it does not fit the business strategy, it will need to be revised. It may be tempting to copy and paste a data strategy from one organization to another. However, a data strategy is not a one-size-fits-all solution.

Regarding data, the business can start with an area of focus that is aligned with the vision and mission. Often, this initiative will concern an area of specific interest to the business. For example, the business might be interested in cost reduction, meeting an unexpected challenge, or increasing customer satisfaction.

---

1 Stephen Hawking, *A Brief History of Time: From the Big Bang to Black Holes* (Toronto: Bantam Books, 1988).

Once the data strategy is in place, the business can determine an optimal business intelligence (BI) solution to deliver the data strategy. The BI and AI technology solutions blend strategy and technology in the service of the overall business vision and mission, helping the business to reach its goals. The organization may use different technologies as its data maturity progresses, from data ingestion to visualization. Technologies can support the overall business vision by providing information and analytics to help the business predict the future so decision makers can plan for it.

Often, it is tempting to jam as many charts onto a dashboard as possible. I was once asked to put two hundred different components onto a single dashboard—quite a feat if it could be delivered sensibly! However, the emphasis should be on helping decision makers get insights from the data without much effort. The purpose has to be clear and in line with the business strategy, or the customer will get confused. We want to reduce unnecessary clutter that interferes with the chart consumer's ability to understand the data. We also want to reduce the cognitive load for the chart consumer by making the chart easier and simpler to understand.

The purpose of a BI solution is to make everything as straightforward as possible for information consumers; if the users don't like it, they won't use the solution, and ultimately the lack of user adoption will cause the data strategy to fail. It is crucial to make user-friendliness a key success criterion of any project that involves data, regardless of whether it is AI or BI. This business-driven perspective provides guardrails and policies around how data is served up to the end user. The ultimate success criterion is whether the business adopts the design solution. Therefore, users need to be front and center.

How can we try to make data more user-friendly? Enter AI. A range of AI and machine learning (ML) capabilities are available in Power BI. There are plenty of useful Power BI integrations with AI capabilities for end users and data scientists. In this chapter, we will look at some key Power BI features that use AI, such as the key influencers visual and the decomposition tree visual, to demonstrate how people can discover new insights and inform their decision making with easy-to-use AI visuals. As a result, we can now bring AI into traditional BI use cases, powering up our abilities to make our data work for everyone in the organization.

New AI features are continually added, so Power BI is constantly evolving. The chapter aims to provide a comprehensive overview of AI and ML capabilities available across the Power BI platform. This chapter assumes no previous experience with AI; we will focus primarily on features developed with the analyst and end user in mind. Now that AI is included as part of Power BI, it is clear that Power BI is much more than simply a data visualization tool. Power BI is a mature, modern enterprise business intelligence platform built for everyone in the enterprise who touches data, from the inexperienced end user to the seasoned data scientist. To get started, let's focus on an overview of the specific areas of the platform where AI resides.

Artificial Intelligence in Power BI Data Visualization

Visualizations should honor and enhance the data. The objective is to make the data easy to understand, and AI can take this a step further by reducing the user's cognitive load while causing the data to "pop" for the user in a meaningful way. After all, if the visualization bores people, you are showing the wrong data. Developing an AI solution involves doing data exploration and visualization before selecting features and building models. It is crucial to understand the data before working with it.

Visualizations should encourage exploration by providing rich visual feedback. We can use visuals in Power BI to easily interpret and analyze our data. AI features already exist in Power BI default visuals, such as bar and column charts. AI can also help to deliver practical data visualization by highlighting the data and adding supporting elements, such as helpful explainers, to provide context.

Data is more than a by-product of an activity or process. It can be used as part of a process of continuous transformation to improve, inspire, and implement positive data-driven advancement and research. The purpose is to create centralized expertise that can be disseminated throughout the organization to produce decentralized expertise in data.

Understanding analytics will mean evolving an understanding of data, analytics, and digital transformation. Data validates the digital future, and organizations associate their data with having value. Being data-driven is not enough; the value of data is determined by how it can be used to create new sources of value. AI is part of this process. In this section, we will discuss some examples of how Power BI and AI can work together. It's an exciting area, and there will be further developments as time goes on.

The Power BI decomposition tree

The *decomposition tree* is a fantastic AI visualization that is very interactive and intuitive. Aimed at the ad hoc exploratory analysis of your data, the decomposition tree can be used to perform rootcause analysis, which is optimized by the AI functionality to help enhance your understanding of the dataset.

What is root cause analysis?

Root cause analysis (RCA) in AI refers to identifying and addressing the underlying reasons behind a particular problem or outcome. It involves investigating the factors contributing to a specific result and determining the primary cause of an issue.

Let's take a marketing example. If you were a marketing analyst, you might be required to investigate the factors influencing the success or failure of your marketing campaigns or strategies. Say you need to investigate conversion rates and sales that were lower than you expected. You have collected various online data, such as click-through rates, impressions, demographics, website traffic, and customer engagement metrics. You conducted a feature selection process analysis, focusing on key features such as pricing and the graphics used. You've undertaken BI and AI techniques on the data to see if you can analyze potential relationships between the key features and the campaign outcome. As a result, you've noted that some ads perform much better than others and some images perform poorly.

Now that you've understood the results, you can start to address the issue's root causes. You can recommend that the poorly performing images be removed altogether or reworked so that they are in line with those in better-performing ads. Once the root causes are addressed, you can rerun the campaign with the new ads to see if you achieve better sales and conversion rates.

You may have encountered root cause analysis in other spheres, such as software development or cloud computing. We can also use RCA in AI to identify the factors contributing to the marketing campaign's underperformance. Then, we can close the loop to take targeted actions to rectify the issues. This approach helps maximize the return on investment (ROI) by managing the root causes of the problem rather than simply making scattershot guesses regarding the solution.

The decomposition tree can play a valuable role in RCA by helping the user to drill down from the highest-level finding to the most fine-grained detail. In our marketing example, the analyst could drill down from the performance metrics to the ID of the ad image. This drill-down activity could help the analyst to conclude which ads are working.

The end user does not need to do any coding to use the decomposition tree visual. All the user needs to do is drag and drop their dimensions to the interface. If the user wants to drill into one of the dimensions, they can choose to display the high-value option or the low-value option. When the user selects one of these options, the visual performs an *AI split*, which is a heuristic that will identify the next field to drill into. Power BI will display the highest or lowest value depending on the user's selection.

Figure 3-1 shows an example of the decomposition tree. It uses the workbook from Chapter 2 that includes World Bank life expectancy data. It shows the maximum average life expectancy broken down by year and then further broken down by income group.

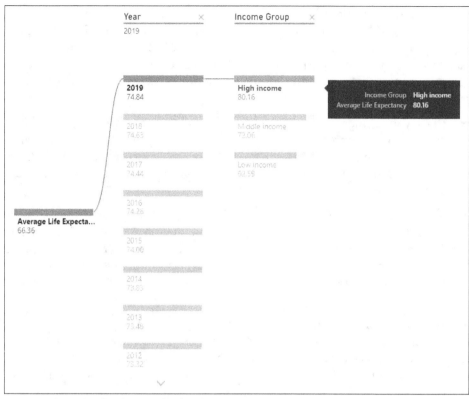

Figure 3-1. Example of using the decomposition tree in Power BI

To re-create the decomposition tree, you can copy the Power BI workbook from Chapter 2 and set up the canvas using the properties shown in Figure 3-2 in the Visualizations pane.

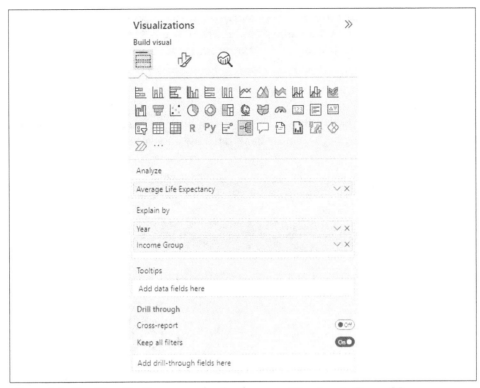

Figure 3-2. The Visualizations pane for the decomposition tree in Power BI

The fields used to generate the decomposition tree are indicated in the Fields pane, as shown in Figure 3-3.

Figure 3-3. Fields selected to create the decomposition tree

It is very straightforward to create a decomposition tree in Power BI, and it's a very powerful visualization option to understand the data better. It uses AI under the hood in order to analyze the data in a way that is easy for the user to understand.

Power BI key influencers visuals

Key influencers is a popular AI visualization in Power BI that is very useful when you want to understand the drivers behind a condition or metric. Let's take a look at a simple example using the World Bank data and the workbook from Chapter 2 (Figure 3-4).

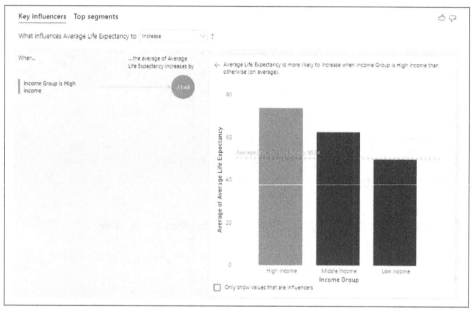

Figure 3-4. Example of using key influencers in Power BI

To re-create this key influencers visualization, you can make a copy of the Power BI workbook used in Chapter 2 and set up the key influencers in the Power BI canvas using the properties in the Visualizations pane (Figure 3-5).

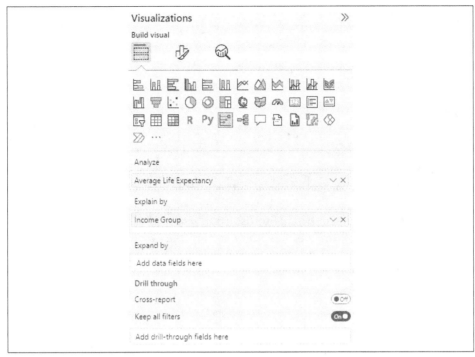

Figure 3-5. Visualizations pane for the key influencers visualization

The fields used to generate the key influencers visualization are configured in the Fields pane, as shown in Figure 3-6.

Figure 3-6. Field selection for the key influencers feature in Power BI

In this example, it is clear that income group is a driver of average life expectancy. The Power BI key influencers visual is laid out very simply and is a powerful tool to help you understand the data. Like the decomposition tree, the visual uses AI to help break down the dimensions to explain the data. The simplicity of the visualization means that the user finds it very intuitive to understand.

Q&A visual

In the 2002 film *Minority Report*, Tom Cruise's character interacts with data on a glass screen by simply swishing his fingers around in the air to get to the data that he wants to see. While interacting with our data is not yet as easy as that, the Q&A functionality allows us to create a visual in Power BI reports that responds to natural language requests for data via the Power BI service. This is an enhancement for business users who want to be able to use your report as a basis to ask their own questions. Furthermore, the business user can turn the Q&A result into a standard Power BI visual by clicking on the icon in the upper righthand corner. Figure 3-7 shows an example of the Q&A visual in Power BI using the World Bank dataset.

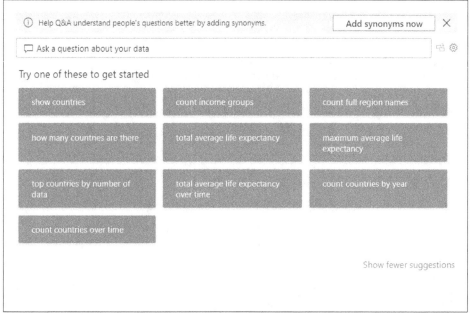

Figure 3-7. Q&A visual in Power BI using the World Bank dataset

The Q&A has offered some nice suggestions to help us start our analysis. For example, if we select the option "maximum average life expectancy," then we receive the result shown in Figure 3-8.

Figure 3-8. *The response to selecting maximum average life expectancy in the Q&A feature*

Even better, we can use this feature to create a visual. By clicking the option at the top righthand side of the Power BI canvas, we can add it to the canvas. The resulting visual is the same as if we had created a chart ourselves (Figure 3-9).

Figure 3-9. *Creating a visual in Power BI using the Q&A feature*

The Power BI service also includes the Q&A tooling interface, which allows you to review questions asked by users so that the feature becomes more user-friendly and customized to the business environment. This feature will help you to add synonyms and translations to make the Q&A functionality more accurate.

Insights Using AI

Have you ever seen a really busy pie chart where your eyes have to bounce back and forth between the legend and the chart as you try to understand the data? We have all seen an extremely cluttered chart at some point, and it can be very difficult to understand it without squinting and a lot of thought. This issue is known as *cognitive load*, and high cognitive load means that it takes significant effort for the viewer to understand the chart. Fortunately, it is possible to use AI and good data visualization techniques to make the data more digestible for users, leveraging the abilities of the human visual perception system in addition to alleviating cognitive effort.

In BI, we aim to reduce cognitive load as much as possible. Making the data easy to understand promotes user adoption and reduces the likelihood of people making errors in their calculations. In the case of Power BI, it is recommended to get Power BI to do the heavy lifting of the analytics work. This helps the business users viewing the report because they don't have to go through the process of working out the numbers for themselves, adding cognitive load to the process of understanding the data.

Using Power BI's AI Insights feature is one way to reduce cognitive load. Power BI developers can create visualizations to help users understand the reasons for differences in Power BI numbers. Power BI can also identify and explain the increase or decrease between two data points, helping to reduce cognitive load for the people consuming the dashboards and reports. Let's say, for example, that you notice a large increase in sales after the pandemic years. Rather than performing an analysis manually to explain the increase in sales, say in Excel, you can have Power BI perform that analysis for you!

Often, we need to do something more advanced when we want to analyze data more deeply. For instance, in a use case that involves data drift, you may need to analyze datasets where the data distribution is different from that when the original analysis was conducted. You may have the objective of identifying subpopulations in datasets that have changed over time, or you may seek to understand better where the data distribution would be the same or different for different dimensions. For such scenarios, the Insights feature in Power BI can help you look at the data more deeply. Using Power BI Desktop, you can investigate where distribution is different in the dataset. Just right-click on a data point, select Analyze, and then choose one of the options. Power BI will then show where the distribution is different, and results are displayed in a window to help you to understand the data more deeply.

Figure 3-10 shows an example of using the Power BI report that we produced in Chapter 2. Right-clicking on a data point will bring up a menu; click Analyze and then "Explain the increase." Power BI will then produce some insights into the data. You can add the visualization to the Power BI canvas. Here, Power BI is using AI to make the analysis easier for you.

Now that we have seen the power of the AI features in Power BI, let's take a look at AI implementations that we can use in our reports and visualizations.

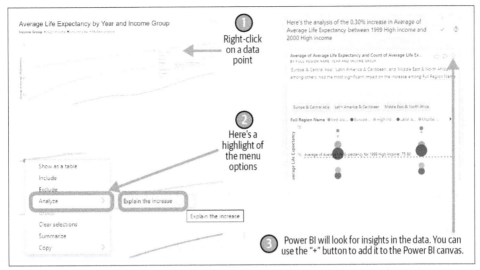

Figure 3-10. Using the AI Insights feature in Power BI

Automated Machine Learning (AutoML) in Power BI

Power BI invokes AutoML to create, train, and call machine learning models. You can consider this facility a low-code/no-code technology, meaning you don't have to worry about being an experienced data scientist to use it. Instead, you are more concerned with using the resulting model to make valuable predictions while also taking care to validate the model's accuracy.

 Please note that the features discussed here are only available in specific editions of Power BI. Power BI is leveraging Azure services, such as Azure Machine Learning (*https://oreil.ly/2PgrY*) and Azure Cognitive Services (*https://oreil.ly/OtpGg*), to use the AI workload enabled within your capacity. The Power BI subscription cost includes the use of these services. Since Microsoft licensing is a whole subject unto itself, it is recommended that the reader double-check the Microsoft website (*https://oreil.ly/nYqCm*) for accurate and up-to-date licensing details in their geographical location.

AutoML supports binary prediction, general classification, and regression models, and you can use these model types in Power BI (Figure 3-11). However, it can sometimes be hard for people to get started with their data. This option allows a data analyst to prototype functionality in Power BI in preparation for further, more advanced work by a data scientist.

Figure 3-11. Creating ML models fully within a Power BI dataflow

Cognitive Services

We can enrich our dataset with prebuilt AI functions from Cognitive Services within Power Query (Figure 3-12). The currently available functions are straightforward and can provide relevant insights. We can access these functions in Power Query within Power BI Desktop, but again, you'll need an account with access to Power BI Premium capacity to do so.

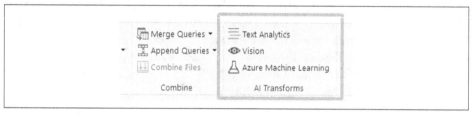

Figure 3-12. The AI Transforms section of the Power Query ribbon within Power BI Desktop

A great use case for these functions is to perform text analytics. You'll have a lot of fun with this technology in Chapter 8. For now, just be aware that you can leverage functions that enable sentiment scoring and key phrase extraction on text data, such as product reviews and comments and social media commentary.

Data Modeling

We covered data modeling in Chapter 2. A flexible, scalable data model allows users to create dashboards and reports. It also offers the foundation for using the data with AI. Here are some practical features that leverage a solid data model foundation.

Q&A

The "Q&A" in Power BI's Q&A functionality is short for "question and answer." It allows users to ask natural language questions in Power BI, which will then use the data model to produce results in reports and dashboards.

Quick Insights

Quick Insights is a very straightforward AI feature to leverage in Power BI. It involves clicking on your dataset and selecting the "Get quick insights" option in Power BI Desktop. Behind the scenes, Power BI will run various algorithms to identify trends in your data using the data model. Once Power BI has completed the Quick Insights process, you can click View Insights. Some of the results may be very interesting! If so, you can decide if you want to keep any resulting visuals by pinning them to a dashboard.

Real-World Problem Solving with Data

AI helps businesses to automate tasks by turning data into models. You can view a model as a recipe to support the automation process. The pieces of data serve as examples to help the algorithm work out the recipe.

We can use a variety of models with Power BI. Businesses want to serve customers better through better data-based insights and predictions. AI has become a valuable tool in helping companies put their data to work, but many businesses need to learn how to get started. One way to make a start is to obtain insights from these models through data visualization. Then, your reports, dashboards, and other analytics can disseminate these insights to the business users who need them the most. You'll be pleased to know that Power BI now makes it straightforward to incorporate the insights from models hosted on Azure Machine Learning, also known as Azure ML. Doing so just involves point-and-click gestures in an authentic low-code/no-code environment. When invoking the Azure ML model, Power BI will automatically batch the access requests for a set of rows so that the Azure ML model does not perform poorly due to processing large amounts of data at once. At the time of writing, Azure ML functionality is supported only for Power BI dataflows and Power Query online in the Power BI service.

Access to the Azure ML model is provided via the Azure portal. As long as the Power BI user has the appropriate access, Power Query locates all the Azure ML models and reveals them as dynamic Power Query functions. Then, using the Power Query Editor ribbon or the M function, the Power BI user can use those functions as if they are any other built-in functions.

Table 3-1 describes the main model types using the Power BI terminology.

Table 3-1. Model types available in Power BI

Model	Objective
Binary prediction	In Power BI, binary prediction is a supervised learning algorithm that categorizes new observations into one of two classes.
Classification	Classification categorizes the data depending on its similarities.
Regression	Regression predicts a numeric value.

Binary Prediction

Although Power BI uses the term *binary prediction models*, they are known as *binary classification models* by statisticians and data scientists. We will use *binary prediction* throughout the book to align with the Power BI interface.

Binary classification, at its simplest, is about sorting things into exactly two pots. It is as simple as saying, "This item belongs to either this group or that group." However, if you need to sort instances into more than two pots, this is known as *multiclass classification*—which is a bit of a mouthful!

Defined more formally, binary classification is a supervised learning algorithm that categorizes new observations into one of two classes—hence, binary. We use this algorithm to identify which class something belongs to, and we use a range of metrics to help us articulate the results clearly. For binary classification, standard metrics include accuracy, precision, recall, and F-score. Together, these metrics form a picture of how the classification model performs. Note that it is especially important not to examine a single metric in isolation when your data is unbalanced.

It may be challenging to understand some of the terminology associated with Azure ML. Therefore, in this section, we will discuss some of the terminology that is useful for understanding and describing your classification results. This will help you when you are evaluating your AzureML model.

Confusion matrix

The *confusion matrix* helps you understand how well the model predicts classes. It provides a tabular summary of the actual and predicted class labels. The potential results are as follows:

True positive
   The number of times a model predicts true when it is actually true

True negative
   The number of times a model predicts false when it is actually false

False negative

The number of times a model predicts false when it is actually true

False positive

The number of times a model predicts true when it is actually false

This is a simple explanation of classification. It becomes harder to understand when many classes are involved.

Accuracy

Overall classification *accuracy* is a crucial metric for understanding how well the classification model performs. Accuracy is defined as the fraction of instances that are classified correctly.

Per-class precision, recall, and F-1

The precision, recall, and F-1 score metrics are instrumental in understanding accuracy.

Using accuracy on its own could be deceiving. Looking at the metrics together is essential, especially when the class labels are not distributed uniformly. For example, if many of the instances belong to one class, then the algorithm could predict the dominant class most of the time. However, while it could acquire high overall accuracy for the dominant class, it may not achieve high accuracy for classes that appear less often.

Precision is the fraction of correct predictions for a specific class. In contrast, *recall* is the fraction of class instances that were forecasted accurately. These metrics, taken together, form the *F-1 score*, which is the harmonic mean (or a weighted average) of precision and recall. The weighted average takes class imbalance into account by finding a weighted average. In cases where there is an unbalanced dataset, the analysis could have very low precision or recall for other, less prevalent classes.

The metrics are judged by how well they identify an apparent trade-off between the precision and recall metrics. For example, when a classifier attempts to predict one class, it will achieve a high recall where most of the instances of the class will be identified. However, the classifier may mispredict examples of other classes, resulting in a lower precision. Therefore, the F-score is considered along with with precision and recall to provide useful context.[2]

---

2 The F-1 score is also known as the F-score or F-measure, and all of these terms mean the same thing.

Macro-averaged metrics

Macro average is concerned with aggregations or totals and gives equal weight to each class. The per-class metrics can be averaged over all the classes, resulting in macro-averaged precision, recall, and F-1. This calculation would involve taking the mean of precision, mean of recall, and mean of F-1 over all the classes.

One versus all
> Combining minority classes may be appropriate for some multi-class problems. Suppose you are in a situation where instances are not uniformly distributed over the classes. In that case, looking at the classifier's performance for one class at a time is helpful before averaging the metrics. For example, say you have one positive class, and the combination of all the other classes constitutes a negative class. In a way, this analysis could be considered to involve three separate binary classification tasks. In this example, you could first compute the one-versus-all confusion matrix for each class. Then, calculate the macro-averaged metrics. Together, these two steps will provide helpful information regarding the classifier's performance.

Average accuracy
> The *average accuracy* is the fraction of correctly classified instances in the sum of one-versus-all matrices. This metric is similar to the overall accuracy.

Micro-averaged metrics

If you have classes with many instances, then micro-averaged metrics can be beneficial. *Micro averages* involve studying individual classes and assigning equal weight to each sample. For example, if we have the same number of instances for each class, both macro averaging and micro averaging would provide the same score.

The micro-averaged precision, recall, and F-1 can also be computed from the matrix above. Using the micro-average method, we aggregate the contributions of all classes to calculate the average metric. This is a useful way to assess the implementation of a multi-class classifier, particularly in scenarios where the distribution of classes might be imbalanced. Because the sum of the one-versus-all matrices is a symmetric matrix, the micro-averaged precision, recall, and F-1 will be the same.

Evaluation of highly imbalanced datasets

Sometimes, your standard evaluation metrics suggest that a model is performing inadequately, possibly because data is not representative of all classes. Nonetheless, the predictions can add considerable value to your business. For example, if a model demonstrates a bias toward the majority class, its performance for the less frequently occurring class labels is ostensibly unacceptable. So how can you move forward? One suggestion is to compare them to those of baseline classifiers, revealing that they are still better than random chance predictions.

Majority class metrics

Here, we calculate precision for all classes individually and then average them. *Down-sampling* involves randomly removing observations from the majority class to prevent its signal from dominating the classifier model. When a class dominates a dataset, the classifier will predict the majority class for all instances in the test set. In addition, the classifier will predict labels correctly in most cases, demonstrating high overall accuracy.

If high accuracy is your sole objective, then a naive majority-class model may perform better than a learned model.

Random-guess metrics

What if the classifier can't learn anything? We could say that its results are random—basically, a lucky guess! Another baseline classifier predicts labels randomly, and no learning takes place. Understanding if the results of a model are better than chance is very helpful in evaluating the model.

If you were to make a random guess and predict any possible labels, the expected overall accuracy and recall for all classes would be the same as the probability of picking a specific class. The expected precision would be the same as the probability that a selected label is correct.

Classification

As noted above, binary classification refers to predicting one of two classes. On the other hand, multi-class classification involves predicting one of more than two classes. In the Power BI interface, multi-class classification is termed *classification*. Again, in line with the Power BI terminology, we will use classification to mean multi-class classification.

Being open-minded about what the data tells you is essential in a data-driven organization. Even if it makes you uncomfortable, it is worth uncovering any surprises before you investigate further. In business, we spend a lot of time classifying every day and don't think about it. For example, we might classify our customers based on their characteristics. If the customer characteristics show that they use Facebook but not X/Twitter and are within a particular age group, what customer group do they belong to? Classification is a great way to get started in understanding your data. You never know what might pop out of a classification investigation!

Classification is used when the data is categorical and categorizes the data depending on its similarities. In other words, if examples are similar to one another, then they are grouped. The foremost goal of classification is to correctly predict the target class for each example in the data. The classification technique categorizes the data, depending on its similarities, and identifies the class, with accuracy depending on encountering the class label accurately. The model used to classify the unknown value is known as a *classifier*. Figure 3-13 shows how classification works at a high level.

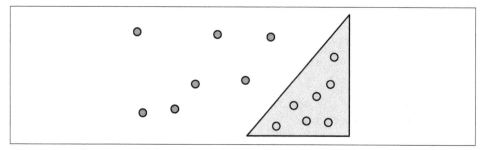

Figure 3-13. Illustration of the concept of classification

As Figure 3-13 shows, a classification model could find patterns in the data, categorizing items to belong either to the set on the white background on the lefthand side or on the darker background on the right.

Multi-class classification is an excellent way of understanding your data better. How well can you evaluate your Azure ML model, however? First, it's good to know that Azure ML prepares the data for you, making the output easier to understand. AutoML runs the input data through stratified sampling for classification models. The data preparation approach means that Azure ML will balance the classes to ensure that all row counts are equal for all classes.

As in the case of the binary prediction model, the output of an Azure ML classification model is a probability score. The score identifies the likelihood that a row will achieve the criteria for a given class.

Since binary classification and classification come from the same family of algorithms, for our purposes, the metrics used to measure the efficiency of the models are the same in Power BI. Here is a summary of the metrics for use to evaluate the classification models in Power BI:

- Accuracy measures the goodness of a classification model as the ratio of true results to total cases.
- Precision is the ratio of true results to all positive results.
- Recall is the ratio of correctly retrieved instances to all the instances.
- F-1 score is the weighted average of precision and recall. It is expressed as a probability between 0 and 1. The perfect F-1 score value is 1.
- *Area under curve* (AUC) measures the area under the curve plotted with true positives on the y-axis and false positives on the x-axis. This metric is helpful because it provides a single number, allowing you to compare models of different types easily.

Regression

What are businesses hoping to achieve with regression? *Regression* is an excellent place to start if you are trying to solve a business question that helps predict probabilities or scoring.

The primary purpose is to create a model we can use on future data. The output is a set of scores. In addition, regression produces an equation that defines the relationship between the thing we are trying to predict and the variables that might affect this thing. In other words, regression establishes the relationship between several predictor variables and the response variable.

The goal of regression is to use known data to create a model that makes predictions about future data as closely as possible. In contrast with classification, which focuses on separating data into classes, prediction focuses on finding a pattern among all the data points.

As an example, estimate the probability that a given customer earns above or below $50,000. Let's say the customer actually makes $40,000 a year, and the predicted value was $42,000 per year. The difference between the model's expected value and the true value is $2,000. The *residuals* are the difference between the actual values of the variable you're predicting and predicted values from your regression, and are expressed as $y - \hat{y}$.

Regression generates a *line of best fit* that gets as close as possible to all known data points. Future data points are predicted to fall close to this line. Figure 3-14 illustrates how a line of best fit might look.

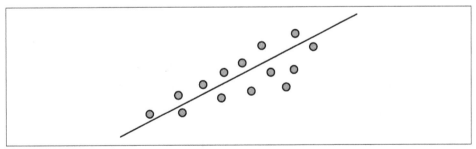

Figure 3-14. Illustration of a line of best fit

People frequently utilize classifiers instead of risk prediction models in AI and data science. Unfortunately, this means that people sometimes mislabel prediction as a classification method. Depending on the previous data, we need to predict the missing data for a new observation.

In Azure ML, the output of a regression model is the predicted value. This output contrasts with the binary prediction and classification models described earlier, which produce a probability score as an output. So, for example, if you were predicting someone's yearly salary in dollars, the predicted output would be a predicted yearly salary amount in dollars.

In an ideal world, the residuals will look like a normal distribution when the data is plotted on a chart in Power BI. So, a good model will hit the bull's-eye sometimes, but we can expect it to miss occasionally. If it doesn't hit the bull's-eye, then we can hope it is missing the mark in all areas equally.

R-squared

In statistics and data science, the *coefficient of determination*, sometimes known as *R-squared*, represents how well the model fits the data. In other words, it tells us the proportion of the variation explained by the model. You can think of the error as the difference between the predicted value and the actual value. The error is calculated by capturing the total magnitude of the error across all instances. We square the differences between the predicted and true values, as the differences can be in a positive or negative direction but squaring the differences generates uniformly positive values.

Let's take a simple marketing example: a marketing analyst could try to predict sales based on the amount spent on advertising. Let's say we have this linear regression model:

$$\text{Sales} = a_0 + a_1 \times \text{Advertising}$$

Where:

- Sales are what the analyst is trying to predict. This part of the equation is known as the *dependent variable*.
- Advertising is the predictor, sometimes known as the *independent variable*.
- a_0 and a_1 are parameters of the model; a_0 is the y-intercept, and a_1 is the slope.

We fit this model to our data and get estimates for a_0 and a_1.

The coefficient of determination tells us the proportion of the variance in the dependent variable that is predictable from the independent variable. It allows us to determine how certain one can feel about predictions made from a given model or graph. The marketing analyst can calculate the R^2 value using the following formula:

$$R^2 = 1 - (\text{SSR}/\text{SST})$$

Where:

- SSR is the sum of the squares of the residual errors. In our example, the residual errors are the differences between the actual and predicted sales numbers given the amounts spent on advertising.

- SST is the total sum of squares. This is the variance in the dependent variable—in this case, the sales amount.

This R^2 equation will give a value between 0 and 1. If the value is closer to 1, then the model explains a large portion of the variability in the outcome variable. A lower R^2 means the model explains less of the variability and is less helpful in making predictions.

In this example, if the marketing analyst finds that the R^2 value is 0.8, that would mean that 80% of the variance in sales can be predicted from the advertising budget.

Root mean square deviation

Another helpful measure is the *root mean square deviation* (RMSD), also known as the *root mean square error*, which measures the differences between values predicted by a model versus the actual values. In other words, it looks at the difference between an estimator and the observed values. RMSD is often used in predictive analytics to gauge the effectiveness of a model.

This is found by taking the square root of the mean square error (MSE). We take the square root of the squared error to get a value that matches the scale of the y-axis. In this way, the average error rate matches the scale on which we've measured our prediction assessment.

The general equation for RMSD is:

$$RMSD = sqrt((1/n) \times \Sigma(P_i - O_i)^2)$$

Where:

- n is the total number of observations.
- P_i is the predicted value for the ith observation.
- O_i is the observed (actual) value for the ith observation.
- sqrt() indicates the square root.
- Σ indicates summation (we sum up the quantity for all i from 1 to n).

Let's take another marketing example to illustrate the concept. As before, a marketing analyst has built a model to predict the amount of sales based on advertising spend. Using the model, the analyst makes predictions based on a test dataset of n

observations. After testing the model, the analyst must measure how competently it performed.

For each observation in the test dataset, we calculate the difference between the predicted sales (P_i) and the actual sales (O_i). We square each difference and sum them all up. Then, we divide this figure by the number of observations (n) and take the square root. The resulting value is the RMSD. Table 3-2 shows a worked example using a handful of sample data points. The predicted sales are derived from the regression model, which used advertising spend as the independent variable.

Table 3-2. Sample actual advertising and sales data with the sales predicted by the model

Day	Advertising spend ($)	Actual sales (units)	Predicted sales (units)
1	2,000	100	100
2	2,500	125	130
3	1,800	110	105
4	3,000	200	175
5	5,000	250	210

To calculate the RMSD, first calculate the squares of the differences between actual and predicted sales. Then we add up the squares of the differences. Table 3-3 shows these calculations.

Table 3-3. The squares of the differences between actual and predicted sales

Day	(Actual sales – predicted sales)	Result
1	$(100 - 100)^2$	0
2	$(125 - 130)^2$	25
3	$(110 - 105)^2$	25
4	$(200 - 175)^2$	625
5	$(250 - 210)^2$	1600
	Total	2,275

Summing the squares yields 2,275.

The total number of observations here is 5, so next, divide the sum by 5 to get the average squared error: $2,275 \div 5 = 455$.

Finally, take the square root of average squared error: sqrt(455) = ~21.33.

So, the RMSD of our model on this data is approximately 21.33 units, meaning that on average, our model's predictions are about 21.33 units away from the actual sales values. This finding gives a quantitative measure of the accuracy of the sales predictions from the advertising spend model. The lower the RMSD, the better a model's predictions match the observed values, while high values of RMSD indicate that a model's predictions tend to be far from the actual values. A high RMSD suggests that the model might need to be retrained to become more accurate. The ultimate decider is whether or not the business would be happy with the model's prediction rate.

To summarize, the error metrics measure a regression model's predictive performance by calculating its predictions' mean deviation from the true values. If the model makes predictions pretty accurately, it will return lower error values. If the model fits the data faultlessly, it will produce an overall error metric of 0.

The following additional metrics might be useful in helping to understand the output of the regression metrics:

- The *relative absolute error* (RAE) is the relative absolute difference between predicted and true values; it is relative because the mean difference is divided by the arithmetic mean.

- The *relative squared error* (RSE) divides the total squared error of the actual values, yielding a normalized total squared error of the predicted values.

- The *coefficient of determination* is helpful because it represents the predictive power of the model. It represents the resulting value between 0 and 1. If the model explains nothing, then it returns zero. If it is perfect, then it returns 1. However, as with anything to do with data, evaluating R^2 is more nuanced than that! We must look at the context, since low values may be completely expected and high values could actually indicate something is wrong with the data.

Practical Demonstration of Binary Prediction to Predict Income Levels

Now that we've discussed the models available in Power BI, let's explore how we can use the technology. This demo will give you a practical example of using binary prediction to predict people's income levels. Let's walk through a practical, end-to-end example of how we can build a binary prediction model to predict income levels.

The data is available from the UC Irvine Machine Learning Repository, and it was extracted by Barry Becker from the 1994 Census database (*https:// archive.ics.uci.edu*).[3]

We will go through the process of training, testing, and evaluating the model on the Adult dataset.

---

3 Barry Becker and Ronny Kohavi, Adult [dataset], UCI Machine Learning Repository, 1996. *https://doi.org/ 10.24432/C5XW20.*

AutoML in Power BI supports the creation of binary prediction, classification, and regression models. Power BI dataflows incorporate these models to make predictions for new data. These trained models use known observations labeled for training; hence, they are examples of supervised machine learning techniques. During training, the input dataset has known outcomes since these are marked with the results. Once the model is trained, it can be used in Power BI.

As we train a binary prediction model on the Adult dataset, the algorithm will predict whether an individual's income is greater or less than $50,000 based on their characteristics, such as education levels. In this example, we will use AutoML to demonstrate how you can perform basic data processing operations. As a first step, we will divide the dataset into training and test sets. Then, we will train the model on the training data. Once that process is completed, we will score the test dataset and evaluate the predictions that the model has made.

You will need to have the Premium version of Power BI to use AutoML. See the end of Chapter 1 for details, including how to sign up for a free trial.

Gather the Data

In order to proceed, you will need to download the CSV file containing the Adult data. You will need to do this for the test data (*https://oreil.ly/ch3_testcsv*) and for the training data (*https://oreil.ly/ch3_datacsv*).

Create a Workspace

Dataflows aren't available in the default workspace in the Power BI service, which is called myworkspace. If you have not created a separate Power BI workspace, you will need to do so.

- In the Power BI service, select Workspaces > "Create workspace."
- Give the workspace a unique name (in Power BI, the workspace has to have a unique name). If the name you try first isn't available, change it to come up with a name that is unique.

Create a Dataflow

To create a dataflow, launch the Power BI service in a browser and select a workspace from the nav pane on the left.

Navigate to your workflow by clicking New, and then select Dataflow (Figure 3-15).

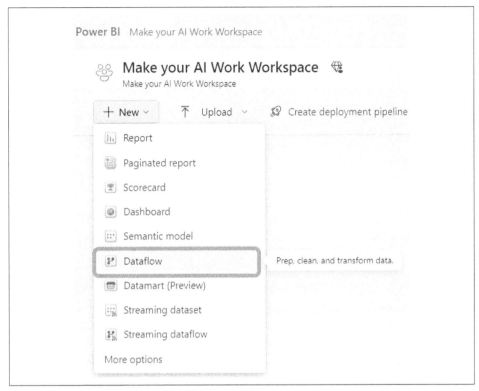

Figure 3-15. Creating a new dataflow

You may be asked if you want to build a datamart instead. At the time of writing, this is a preview feature and we will not be using it. If you see the screen in Figure 3-16, select "No, create a dataflow" to proceed.

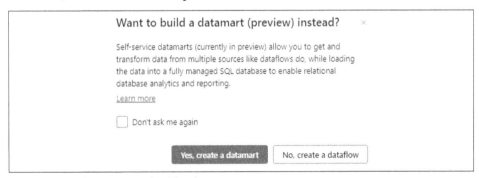

Figure 3-16. The option to build a datamart

Select "Add new tables" (Figure 3-17).

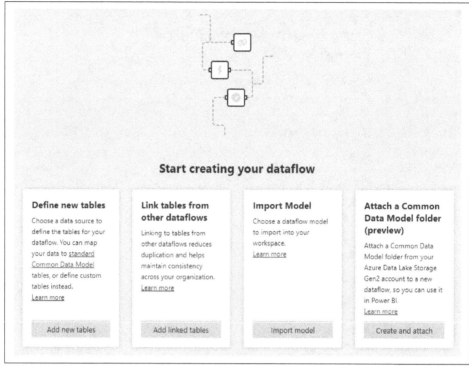

Figure 3-17. Starting to create your dataflow Power BI

Next, you will be asked to indicate the type of file that you want to use. Figure 3-18 shows the options available for file type. In our example, we will be using a Text/CSV file.

Figure 3-18. Choosing a Text/CSV data source

Next, you will be able to select your file (Figure 3-19). Then select the Next button.

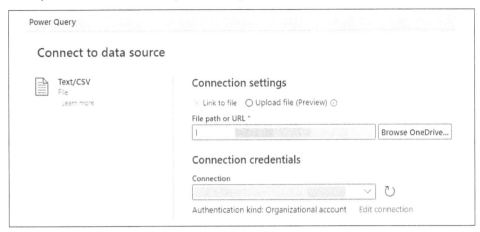

Figure 3-19. Connecting your Power BI dataflow to a data source

After you click Next, you can preview the data (Figure 3-20).

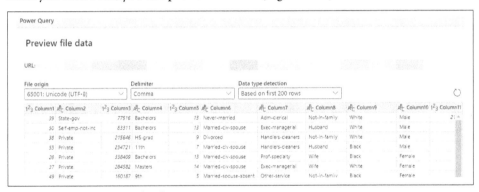

Figure 3-20. Previewing the data

Let's make the data more comprehensible by transforming it. To do this, click "Transform data" at the bottom righthand corner of the Power Query window. This will bring up the window shown in Figure 3-21.

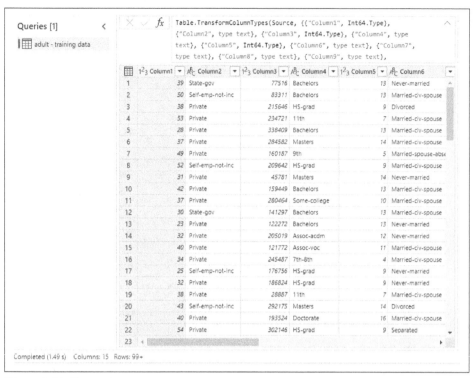

Figure 3-21. Example query

Let's rename the columns to make more sense to the human eye. Right-click Column1 and select Rename (Figure 3-22). One by one, rename the columns in order:

age
workclass
fnlwgt
education
education-num
marital-status
occupation
relationship
race
sex
capital-gain
capital-loss
hours-per-week
native-country
salary

Figure 3-22. Renaming a column in Power Query

Next, remove the fnlwgt column since you won't need it. To do this, right-click on the column and select "Remove columns" (Figure 3-23).

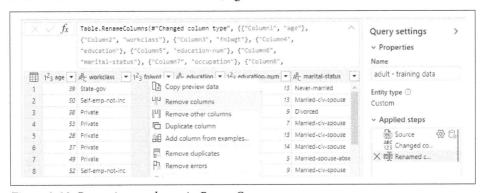

Figure 3-23. Removing a column in Power Query

After you click Next, you will be asked to "Save your dataflow" (Figure 3-24).

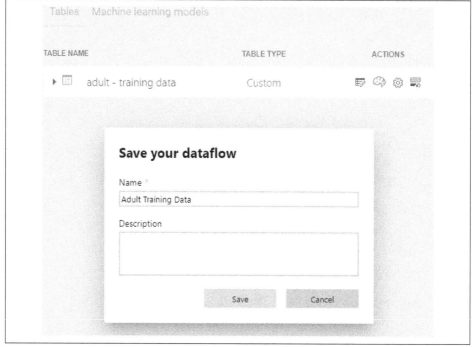

Figure 3-24. Saving your dataflow

Once the dataflow is saved, you will be able to see a few options at the righthand side of the screen (Figure 3-25). In this example, we are using the "salary" column as the outcome.

Now go to the "Choose a model" option (Figure 3-26).

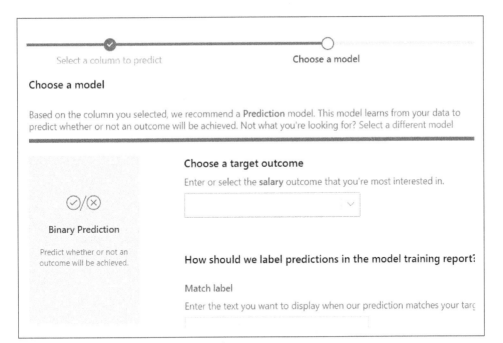

Figure 3-25. Selecting a column to predict

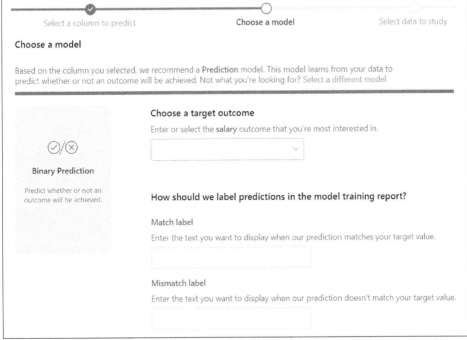

Figure 3-26. Choosing a model configuration pane in Power BI

For our analysis, we want to identify people who are in the higher earning bracket. To do this, choose the configuration as follows:

- From the dropdown under "Choose a target outcome", choose >50K.
- Under "Match label," choose >50K.
- Under "Mismatch label," choose <=50K.

Figure 3-27 shows an example of choosing a model with these options.

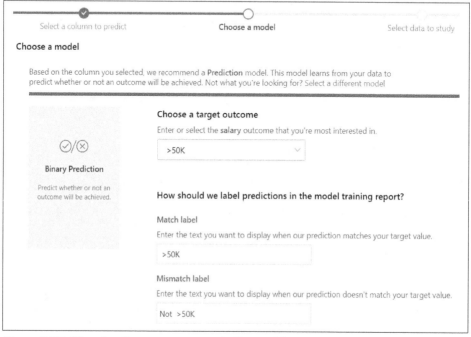

Figure 3-27. Choosing the target outcome in Power BI

Since this is a demo, we are starting small, so we will look only at the Age variable (Figure 3-28).

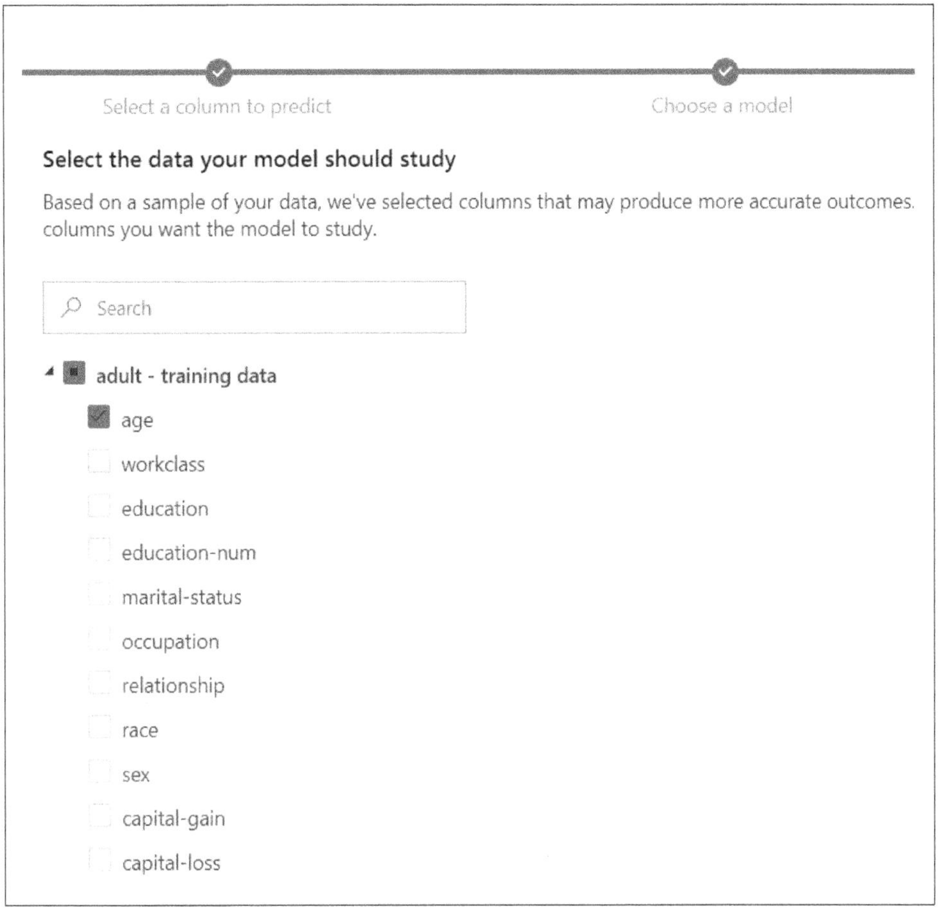

Figure 3-28. Selecting the data for the model to study

Finally, select the "Name and train" option and fill out the screen as shown in Figure 3-29.

Figure 3-29. Naming and training the model in Power BI

Click Save and Train to start the training process. The training process will begin by sampling and normalizing your training dataset. Then, it will divide the dataset into two new entities. In the example shown in Figure 3-30, the two entities are called Age and Salary Relationship Training and Age and Salary Relationship Testing.

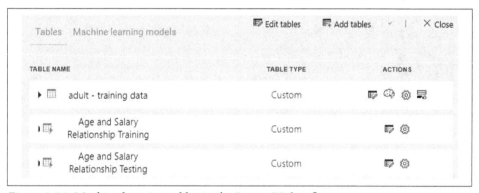

Figure 3-30. Machine learning tables in the Power BI dataflow

When you look at the model in the dataflow, you can see its status on the righthand side of the screen (Figure 3-31).

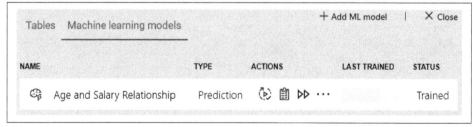

Figure 3-31. Checking the status of the machine learning model

Now that the model is trained, let's look at the results in more detail. Fortunately, Power BI offers a number of reports that will help you to understand the performance of the model.

Model Evaluation Reports in Power BI

You can find the prediction report in your workspace. Figure 3-32 shows how that might look in your environment.

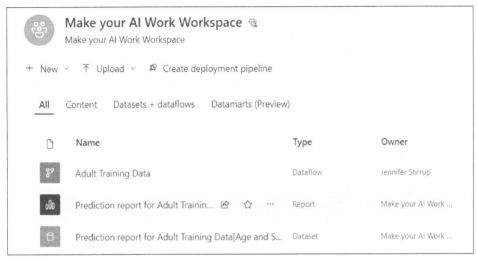

Figure 3-32. Power BI workspace showing the prediction report

Clicking on the report brings up the visualization in Figure 3-33.

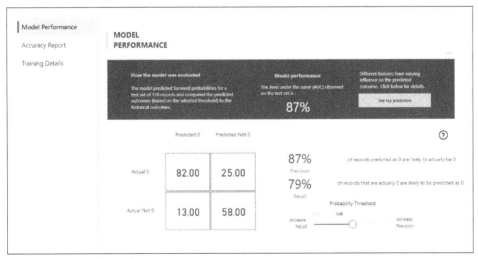

Figure 3-33. Model performance report

The model performance report provides helpful information. Earlier, you learned about the area-under-curve metric, which you can see in the report is 87% for this model. On the lefthand side is a confusion matrix. Precision and recall are also reported, as 87% and 79%, respectively. There is also a probability threshold slider; if you play around with this, you will see that the precision and recall values will change accordingly.

Accuracy report

A ROC curve (which stands for Receiver Operating Characteristic curve) is a graphical plot that illustrates the diagnostic ability of a binary classifier system as its discrimination threshold is varied. It is created by plotting the true positive rate (TPR, also known as sensitivity) against the false positive rate (FPR, also known as 1 – specificity) at various threshold settings. The true positive rate is plotted on the y-axis, and the false positive rate is plotted on the xX-axis. You can see an example in Figure 3-34.

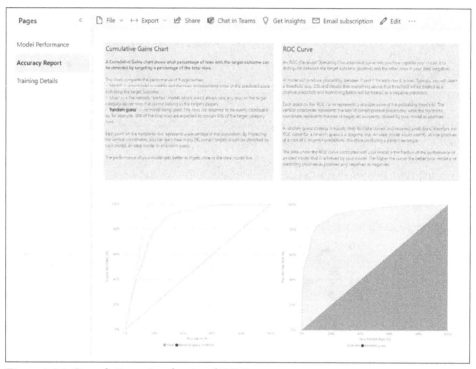

Figure 3-34. Cumulative gains chart and ROC curve

The ROC curve provides a comprehensive view of the trade-off between the true and false positive rates for different threshold values. This trade-off is crucial in many AI applications where the balance between detecting positives and avoiding false alarms is essential. In cases such as fraud detection or disease diagnosis in healthcare, it is important to reduce false alarms while endeavoring to detect the positive cases.

Training report

The training report is quite lengthy, so please scroll to the bottom. This report provides you with detailed information regarding the training process. Here, you can see the number of rows used for training.

The final model used in this training is also identified as the Pre-fitted Soft Voting Classifier. In this model, each classifier provides a probability value that a specific data point belongs to a particular target class (Figure 3-35).

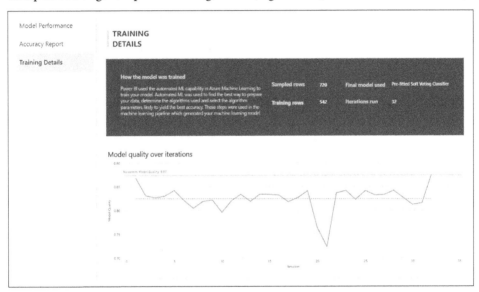

Figure 3-35. Training Details report

The features are laid out in a table, along with the column type (Figure 3-36).

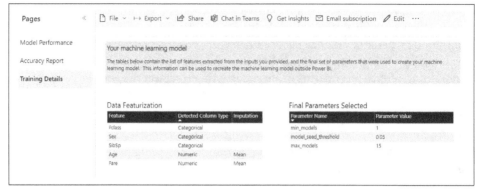

Figure 3-36. Machine learning model details

Power BI can create ensemble ML models. These models try to create more suitable predictive performance by converging the predictions from various models. If an ensemble ML model was used, it is displayed in the training details report. In this example, the ensemble model is shown in a donut chart (Figure 3-37).

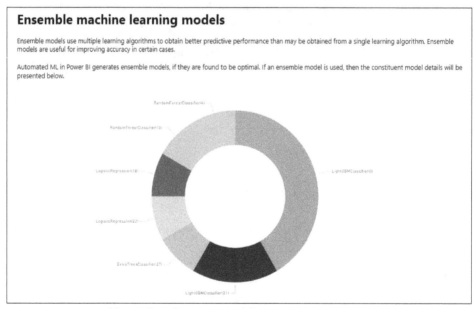

Figure 3-37. Ensemble machine learning models

Summary

We have covered a lot in this chapter. You'll be pleased to know that you've learned the difficult part. Congratulations! We have looked at ways that we can use AI in Power BI. We have also spent some time looking at how we can evaluate AI models. These terms will become very useful as we look at models throughout the remainder of the book.

You will see from the model that an AUC value of 87% would be considered excellent, but, as always, it would be prudent to continue testing the model. In the Adult dataset used in our worked example, a separate test file is provided. As a next step, you could test the model with the test file that was mentioned in the instructions.

## CHAPTER 4

Automating Data Exploration and Editing

Most of this book shows you how AI can do something new that could not have been done before, whether that is identifying key features and anomalies, building a machine learning model, or applying Azure AI Services to your data. This chapter, however, is about how AI can automate aspects of the data exploration and editing process. The first half of the chapter reviews the built-in AI components of Power Query Editor that automate data preprocessing steps. The second half explores the AI tools and features that help speed up the process of interpreting information and generating reports. Together, these automation features of Power BI allow the analyst to spend less time on tedious tasks and free up more time for more thoughtful work.

The Transformational Power of Automation

As a reader of this book, you are likely the kind of person who is excited to see advances in the technological landscape. The opposite kind of person, someone who rejects new technology, is often called a Luddite. But did you know this was the name of a labor movement in northern England in the early 1800s? The original Luddites were skilled textile workers who would break into factories and destroy the new looms that were competing with their labor. Their sabotage was serious enough that Parliament passed the Frame-Breaking Act in 1812, making such crimes punishable by death.[1] Notably, for the Luddites, it was never about being against technology per se—they were just trying to protect their livelihoods.

---

[1] Richard Conniff, "What the Luddites Really Fought Against" (*https://oreil.ly/Jd0bs*), *Smithsonian Magazine*, March 2021.

But not all progress is bad for all people. Sometimes automation substitutes for skills, work, or people, and other times it can serve as a complement. For example, you may have a job title that did not exist 20 years ago and was only made possible by recent advances in data collection and analysis. Two MIT researchers, Erik Brynjolfsson and Andrew McAfee, describe how modern innovations benefit some people but not everyone:

> Technological progress is going to leave behind some people, perhaps even a lot of people, as it races ahead. As we'll demonstrate, there's never been a better time to be a worker with special skills or the right education, because these people can use technology to create and capture value. However, there's never been a worse time to be a worker with only "ordinary" skills and abilities to offer, because computers, robots, and other digital technologies are acquiring these skills and abilities at an extraordinary rate.[2]

The same concept of disruptive technology applies to organizations as well. Take the example of how the introduction of automated teller machines (ATMs) changed the way bank branches operated.[3] This new technology allowed a branch bank to operate with one-third fewer workers; however, this made it cheaper for banks to open more locations. The net effect was that *more* tellers were hired. The ATMs also changed the kind of work done at the branches: they reduced the number of cash-handling tasks performed, allowing tellers to spend more time building customer relationships and selling other financial products.

Many companies have the choice of either embracing disruptive technology or becoming the victim of it. AI has already transformed society, business, and our own lives and shows no sign of stopping as it advances the technological frontier. So what's next? In 2018, the CEO of Google, Sundar Pichai, gave an answer: "I think of [AI] as something more profound than electricity or fire." This bold proclamation, in part, is because AI is a *general purpose technology*—that is, a type of technology that has broad applications across various products and industries. Electricity, as mentioned by Pichai, is also a general purpose technology. By itself, electricity is not able to do much, but it set the stage for a wide series of inventions: factories with electrical machines allowed for more precise control in manufacturing, incandescent illumination affordably extended days, and the refrigerator, the television, and (eventually) the personal computer revolutionized home life. AI will likewise change how we live and how we work by opening up a new era of technological development.

---

2 Erik Brynjolfsson and Andrew McAfee, *The Second Machine Age: Work, Progress, and Prosperity in a Time of Brilliant Technologies* (New York: W. W. Norton & Company, 2014), 11.

3 James Bessen, "Toil and Technology: Innovative Technology Is Displacing Workers to New Jobs Rather Than Replacing Them Entirely" (*https://oreil.ly/L6PyL*), *Finance & Development* 52, no. 1 (2015): 16.

Surviving (and Thriving with) Automation

The only constant in business is change, so it is important for individuals and organizations to navigate the changing technological landscape. Automation can dramatically change how work is done, but those who embrace it will fare much better than those who ignore automation. Let's discuss ways you and your company can best prepare for development in automation.

How a data analyst can prepare

Embrace broad learning.
> Studying a wide variety of topics makes you better able to pursue a specific field that is taking off (or step away from a field that is declining) due to automation. Generalists also tend to be more innovative and can succeed in a given field by utilizing a multidisciplinary mindset.

Embrace narrow learning.
> Another approach is to earn a degree or certification in a discipline that has dependable future demand. Quantitative and technical disciplines are still a good bet in the Age of AI. Note that this approach is not mutually exclusive with learning broadly; one can do both.

Become a domain expert.
> It's also important to learn the ins and outs of a business and the industry in which it operates. If a domain expert is in a role that can be automated away, they are more likely than other employees to be able to fulfill some other role within the same business.

Specialize in automation.
> If you can't beat 'em, join 'em! Automation can make some jobs obsolete but, in the process, will create new jobs. Recent advances in large language models will increase demand for machine learning engineers to train such models as well as prompt engineers trained in asking the best questions to produce high-quality outputs.

Enter an un-automatable role.
> Pursue a specialty within data and analytics that cannot be automated (or at least is harder to automate). Consider fields like data governance, privacy, or ethics.

Strengthen your data storytelling.
> Automation in Power BI makes it easier and faster to transform, analyze, and visualize data, increasing the number of reports generated. This in turn will make data storytellers more valuable, as they can create narratives from data and uncover new questions to ask.

Exercise those soft skills.

Humans will still want to work with other humans, and it's difficult to receive empathy from an algorithm. If AI becomes ubiquitous, then successful managers will be those with high emotional intelligence.

How a data-driven organization can prepare

Invest in professional development.

Dedicate meaningful time and resources to your employees' learning, especially in areas that complement advances in AI.

Embrace a growth mindset.

Promote a forward-thinking culture that strives to grow. This includes organizing your company in a way that makes it nimble enough to pivot in response to changing technologies and allows it to support execution on that growth.

Restructure job roles.

Be willing to move employees around within an organization if new forms of automation allow a team to operate with a smaller headcount. Also consider what new roles could better leverage the latest technology.

Prioritize delighting your customer.

If widespread automation is turning your previously differentiated product or service into a commodity, then you will have to find a way to stand out against rising competition. One way to do this is by taking a customer-first approach with personalization and superior service.

Explore new market opportunities.

Just as the internet led to the development of ecommerce, advances in AI and automation will allow for the creation of new products, markets, and industries.

Emphasize creativity and innovation.

Double down on aspects of your business that cannot be automated, such as human creativity and innovation.

Build the automation.

Don't passively wait for the future to happen; make it happen by leading the development of automation within your product or service.

AI Automation in Power BI

Business intelligence platforms as a whole are not easily automated because they do not perform just one task; rather, they are a suite of tools performing many functions. Additionally, BI dashboards are often used for data exploration where there is not always a clear objective or outcome to optimize. We can instead look at different components of a BI platform and see which parts are best suited for automation.

Consider the business intelligence cycle shown in Figure 4-1. Start the cycle at the upper right, where an analyst *identifies a business problem*. They next *define a data model* that will allow them to solve the business problem or answer a specific question. Next, they must *gather data* from within the organization that will allow them to build the specified data model. These first three steps, shown on the right in blue (darker gray in the print edition), are not good candidates for automation. There is no computer program that will tell you the most pressing problem at a company, what data is required to address that problem, or where the data can be accessed. These steps must be done by a human.

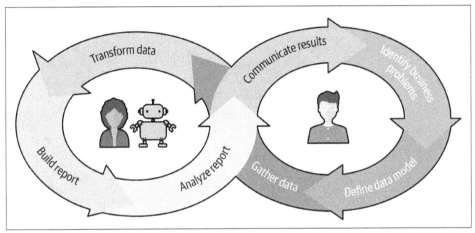

Figure 4-1. The business intelligence cycle

After the analyst has gathered the data, they *transform the data* to build a data model. Next, they use that processed data to *build a report* with summary data and/or data visualizations. The analyst will then *analyze the report* to solve the business problem or answer the question. These three steps, shown on the left in green (lighter gray in the print edition), have elements that can be automated to some degree. This means there are real opportunities for a data analyst to partner with some AI-based automation tools to speed up certain tasks or help with decision making.

For example, within Power BI there are many automated data transformation tools in Power Query that utilize AI, including get data from web by example, add column from examples, data profiling, table generation, and fuzzy matching. Additionally, there are automated report-building tools, such as Q&A and report creation. Also in Power BI, you have the report-analyzing features with built-in automation, like *smart narrative* and *quick insights* visualizations.

The last step of the business intelligence cycle is for the data analyst to *communicate results* to their organization. As seen in Figure 4-1, this is also represented in blue (darker gray in print edition) since it is not a good candidate for automation. The cycle returns to the initial step because business intelligence involves an iterative process of discovery.

AI in Power Query

 This book assumes the reader is already familiar with the fundamentals of Power BI and therefore knows that Power Query is where a developer can connect to one or more data sources and then transform the data into a desired format. If, however, you need to catch up or have a refresher, check out this Power Query overview (*https://oreil.ly/tt8OV*).

The next round of AI-based automation features within Power BI are part of Power Query. These tools leverage AI to more quickly perform a variety of data manipulations. This is beneficial for the data analyst because no one goes into their line of work saying, "I want to spend my career cleaning data." Indeed, some of the most underrated applications of AI involve dull or tedious tasks.

This is also important at the organizational level, where companies using AI have a clear advantage over those who are not. Recent developments in large language models, such as ChatGPT, discussed in Chapter 7, show how a new technology can increase an employee's capacity by essentially giving everyone their own personal assistant. Similarly, there are AI tools in Power BI that empower individuals to quickly complete mundane tasks.

In this section, we will review six such time-saving features that can make your job easier or unlock a new dataset for analysis. They include get data from web by example (web scraping), add column from examples, data profiling, table generation (from text, CSV, JSON, web API, or Excel), and fuzzy matching.

Get Data from Web by Example

Sometimes we know about the existence of some data of interest, but it is in a format that is not readily accessible. For example, one relatively common quip describes PDFs as "where data goes to die" due to their immutable design. Web pages are another such instance: incredible quantities of information live on them, but their format is optimized for browsing and not for large-scale data sharing.

This is where web scraping comes in. *Web scraping* is the automated process of extracting information from web pages. It parses the underlying hypertext markup language (HTML) of a website and stores it for later use. If you are using the Firefox or Chrome browser, then you can view a page's HTML by right-clicking on the page and selecting Inspect Figure 4-2 shows the underlying HTML on a page of O'Reilly resources (*https://www.oreilly.com/products/books-videos.html*). After clicking Inspect, you can go to the right-side panel and navigate through some drop-down sections to reveal the stored text that populates the page.

Figure 4-2. Revealing the underlying HTML of a web page

Power BI gives the option to load a web page and extract the HTML into a data table. The user provides a few examples of the desired output, and Power BI uses AI to automatically predict all of the desired entries from the website.

In our experience, AI is pretty good at identifying the pattern of HTML extraction after two or three examples but does not improve much after that. If you are not getting good results, try these tips:

- Check your previous entries for typos.
- Make sure you select an entry from the dropdown after typing the first few characters.
- Check if there is extra text at the end of an entry by double-clicking and using the right arrow key.
- Start over from the beginning.
- Try scraping a larger section than you initially wanted (e.g., in Demo 1, we extract "By [author name]" because extracting the author name alone was not consistently working).

Demo 4-1: Get Data from Web by Example

Let's walk through an example of web scraping with get data from web by example. Open a new Power BI report and select the "drop-down arrow" from "Get data." Then click Web, as shown in Figure 4-3.

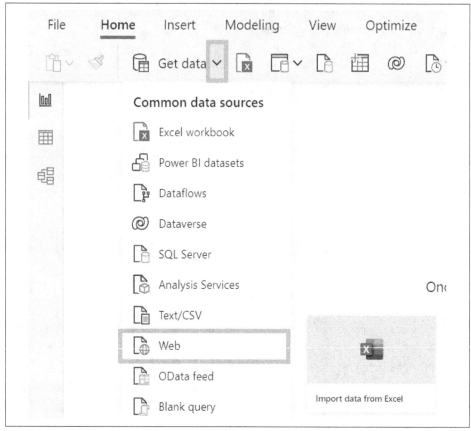

Figure 4-3. Getting data from a web source

Under URL, paste this:

> *https://web.archive.org/web/20231120092630/https://www.oreilly.com/products/*
> *books-videos.html*

Then, click OK (Figure 4-4). This will open a web page that lists O'Reilly products.

If asked which level to apply these settings to, select the full URL from the drop down and select Connect (not pictured). It may take a full minute to connect.

This opens the Navigator window, which provides several options for displaying the underlying data of the web page. By selecting Web View, you can see the original website as if you had opened it in a browser (Figure 4-5). Or you can select Table View and HTML Code to see the code that generates the page (Figure 4-6). Alternatively, you can click Table View and the Table 1 box to reveal a suggested table generated from the page's HTML (Figure 4-7).

Figure 4-4. Telling Power BI which website you want to scrape

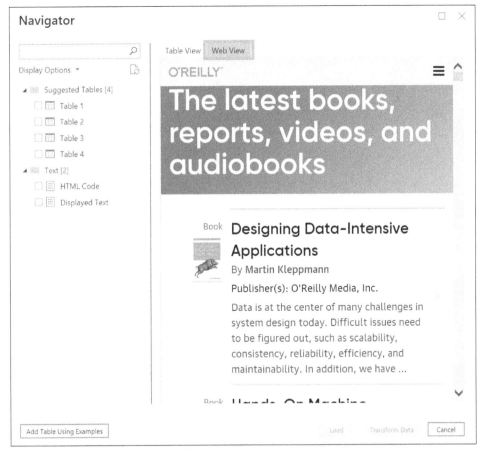

Figure 4-5. A rendered version of the website

Figure 4-6. Displaying the website's HTML

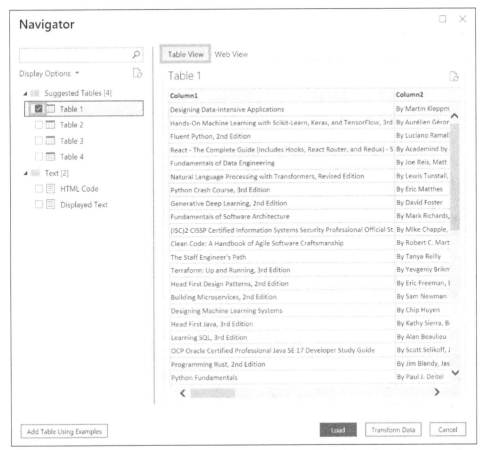

Figure 4-7. One of four suggested tables with data pulled from the website's source code

Instead of using one of the suggested tables, try building your own. Click Add Table Using Examples in the bottom-left corner. This opens a new window, shown in Figure 4-8.

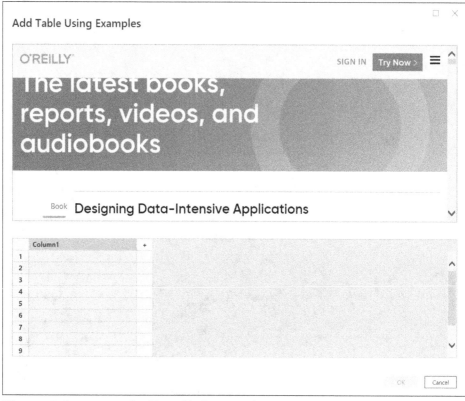

Figure 4-8. Beginning to build a table from a web page

The top box of the window displays the rendered web page, and the bottom box is where we will begin filling in the example data we wish to extract. Next, scroll down in the top box to reveal the first book. Then in the bottom box, name the headers Title, Authors, Publisher, and Description. Now input the information from the first book by adding the title, author, publisher, and book description (Figure 4-9). Include "By" before the author name (e.g., "By Martin Kleppmann") to help the AI find what you are looking for. We will shorten this later.

We find that it is best to begin typing an entry and then select the option that automatically fills in the correct input. This reduces the chance of an unnoticed typo confusing the AI into making predictions based on what you wrote and not what you meant.

Figure 4-9. Inputting information from the first book to create a table

Now scroll down in the first box to reveal the second book on the list. Input the title, author (including "By"), publisher, and description, remembering to begin typing and then select the option from the list. Your window should now look like Figure 4-10.

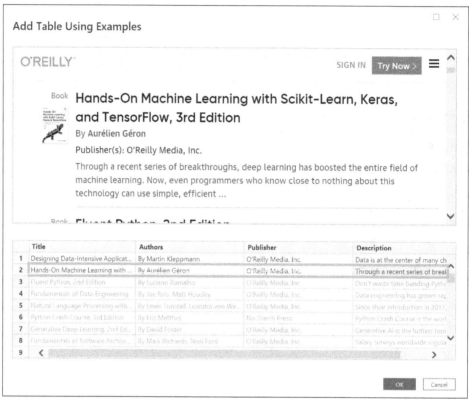

Figure 4-10. Adding a second example from the web page

Notice in Figure 4-10 that after two rows of examples, the AI in get data from web by example has populated the rest of the table. It uses gray text to indicate it is making a prediction. If you are not getting the same results, be sure to check out the tips for using web scraping immediately before this section.

When ready, click OK to continue. This will display the Navigator window, as shown in Figure 4-11. The results from the HTML extraction appear on the lefthand side as Table 6. Now we want to modify the list of authors using add column from examples, so click Transform Data. We will pick up from here in Demo 4-2.

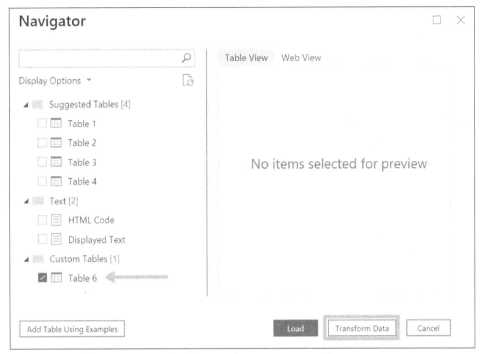

Figure 4-11. The newly created Table 6 in the Navigator window

Add Column from Examples

Here is another tool in the automation toolkit that empowers an analyst to quickly transform data. Add column from examples prompts a user to give sample inputs to show the AI what they want a new column to look like. Then an algorithm attempts to identify the Power Query M formula that produces the same results.

 We assume the reader already has a foundational knowledge of the Power Query Formula Language (referred to simply as M and discussed briefly in Chapter 1) that underlies all of Power BI's queries. We will not be working directly with M code in this book, but for those who want an overview or refresher, check out the Power Query M Introduction (*https://oreil.ly/abWJO*).

What's interesting here is that the AI model is predicting an intermediary step (the M formula), and we are evaluating the prediction based on how the final step (generating a new column) appears. Although there is no documentation stating how the add column from examples feature works, this is a similar function within large language models like ChatGPT where a user can give one or few prompts and the algorithm will generate an output as if it is "learning" in real time. See Chapter 7 for more details on that topic.

You can use add column from examples to combine, extract, transform, or enhance data into a new column of your choosing. The best situation for using this feature is if you already know the desired transformation exists within Power BI (either as in M expression or within the UI); however, it is also useful for testing out different manipulations to explore what is possible.

From our experience, we find that the AI is good at generating a new column based on two or three examples but does not improve much after that. If you are not getting good results, try out these tips:

- Check your previous entries for typos.
- Correct predictions that are incorrect.
- Provide examples that cover a breadth of examples.
- If all else fails, start over from the beginning.

Demo 4-2: Add Column from Examples

Let's go through an example of generating a new column from a dataset using examples. This picks up from Demo 4-1, where we scraped data of resources from the O'Reilly website. It is a natural follow-up because HTML extraction sometimes collects data that is not precisely what we want.

Open Power Query Editor if it is not already opened. Select the Authors column and then click the Add Column tab (Figure 4-12). Now select Column From Examples and from the dropdown choose From Selection. This means you are generating a new column based on information found in the Authors column.

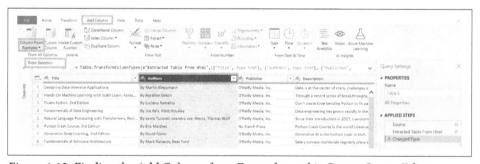

Figure 4-12. Finding the Add Column from Examples tool in Power Query Editor

The window will change, adding a new Column1, as shown in Figure 4-13. This is where you can add examples of the formatted data you want from Authors.

Figure 4-13. A new column before examples are added

Rename the column Authors2 and add the first example of Martin Kleppmann without the preceding "By." As you can see in Figure 4-14, from just one example the AI has predicted all entries are the list of authors without "By." Also note the predicted M formula appearing at the top for how the new column is generated. It states, *From the Authors column, take all text coming after the first whitespace.*

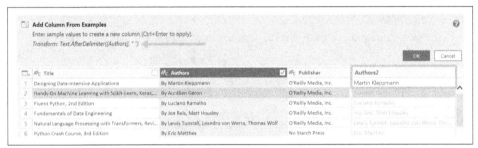

Figure 4-14. The predicted entries in gray based on just one input example

We also want to replace all commas from the lists of authors with semicolons. Let's skip ahead a few rows and replace those two authors with Joe Reis; Matt Housley. Now in Figure 4-15, we can see that all of the authors in a list are separated by a semicolon. The corresponding M formula for generating the column also appears above.

Figure 4-15. Adding a second example that replaces the comma with a semicolon

Click OK to complete the column generation. We will pick up from here in Demo 4-3, where we will see how to profile our new dataset.

Data Profiling

As you are transforming your data with Power Query Editor, at any point you are able to take a pause and review a profile of the data in its current state. *Data Profiling* allows you to catch errors and even automatically suggests specific transformations to assist with your query. These transformations include keeping, removing, replacing, filtering by, grouping by, and copying values.

Specifically, there are three features within Power Query Editor that make up a data profile:

Column quality
> This feature breaks down the share of entries in each column that are either valid, an error, or empty.

Column distribution
> This feature displays a frequency distribution of values within each column.

Column profile
> This feature shows descriptive statistics for each column as well as a more detailed frequency distribution.

Possibly the largest benefit of data profiling is the built-in suggestions about which transformation the analyst should consider based on the state of the data. For example, if a column includes empty values, hovering over the Column quality section will reveal an AI-powered recommendation (indicated with a light bulb icon) to remove those empty values.

There is no complicated deep learning algorithm powering this feature. Instead, this example reminds us that any algorithm replicating human intelligence still fits under the umbrella of artificial intelligence. We decided to include this feature in the book because it aligns with the chapter on automation and utilizes decision making by suggesting transformations.

> Power Query by default uses only the top 1,000 rows to build a profile. This can be changed in the bottom lefthand corner of the Power Query window by clicking "Column profiling based on top 1000 rows" and selecting "Column profiling based on entire data set."

Demo 4-3: Data Profiling

We pick up the data transformation that is a continuation of Demo 4-1 and Demo 4-2. Open Power Query Editor if it is not already open. Navigate to the View tab and check the "Column quality" box within the Data Preview section (Figure 4-16). This reveals new information under the column headers that profiles the share of data in each column that is either valid, an error, or empty. In this example, we see that our dataset is complete because each column has 100% of the data identified as "Valid."

You can also hover over this new section to reveal a pop-up. When you click on the ellipsis at the bottom-right of that pop-up, a dropdown lists some quick actions you can take based on the quality of the data. This is a good example of how Power BI allows you to quickly make data transformations with the assistance of AI.

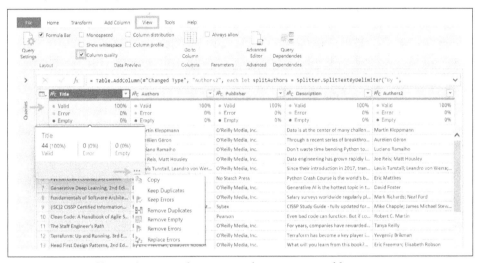

Figure 4-16. Profiling column quality using a shortcut to possible actions

Unselect Column quality and select "Column distribution" instead. This reveals a new section on the frequency distribution of values within each column, as shown in Figure 4-17. This shows that there are three authors with two books under their names. Hovering over the Authors section invokes a pop-up with a clickable suggested action to Remove Duplicates.

Figure 4-17. Profiling column distributions with a suggested action

Finally, we will learn the last automated way to profile our data. Unselect Column distribution and select "Column profile." Nothing will appear until a column is selected, so click on the Publisher column to reveal a new section at the bottom. On the left side are summary statistics for the column, and on the right is the value distribution. Figure 4-18 shows that O'Reilly is the most common publisher in this dataset, which makes sense given that we scraped the list of resources from O'Reilly's website.

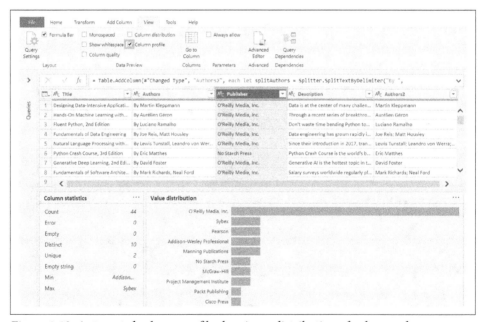

Figure 4-18. Automated column profile showing a distribution of values and summary statistics

---

Next, hover over the horizontal O'Reilly Media, Inc. bar to show the precise share of items published by the company (54% in this example). The pop-up also includes clickable suggested actions that will filter rows based on whether or not they have O'Reilly Media, Inc. as the publisher. Additionally, the ellipsis in the pop-up reveal more handy filtering options (Figure 4-19).

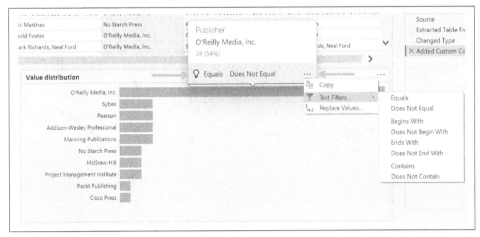

Figure 4-19. Additional actions for filtering the data

Table Generation

Another feature within Power Query that utilizes built-in AI is *Table Generation*. This is where Power BI is able to identify a table from either (1) a file type that is not natively a table structure or (2) a table-based file type with poorly organized data.

For the first situation, Power BI is able to automatically generate a table from nested data types, such as JSON and responses from web-based APIs. Figure 4-20 shows an example of nested data from a JSON file. Generating tables from data in this format is a real time-saver for data analysts, especially when integrating Power BI with APIs.

```
[
  {
    "title": "Designing Data-Intensive Applications",
    "author": "Martin Kleppmann",
    "publisher": "O'Reilly Media, Inc.",
    "description": "Data is at the center of many challenges in system design today. Difficult issues need to be figured out, such as scalability, consistency, reliability, efficiency, and maintainability. In addition, we have ...",
    "format": "book"
  },
  {
    "title": "Hands-On Machine Learning with Scikit-Learn, Keras, and TensorFlow",
    "edition": "3rd",
    "author": "Aurélien Géron",
    "publisher": "O'Reilly Media, Inc.",
    "description": "Through a recent series of breakthroughs, deep learning has boosted the entire field of machine learning. Now, even programmers who know close to nothing about this technology can use simple, efficient ...",
    "format": "book",
    "language": "English"
  },
  {
    "title": "Fluent Python",
```

Figure 4-20. A JSON file showing the first two items from the O'Reilly web page

The second category of file types that Power BI can use to generate tables includes Microsoft Excel, CSVs, and text files. Excel files, like JSON files, are automatically generated into a table, even if the data is messy and not perfectly formatted as a table. CSVs and text files have even more flexibility for the data analyst; Power BI generates a table based on several examples in a way nearly identical to that of get data from web by example and add column from examples.

From our experience, we find that the AI is rather sensitive to the quality of the data from which a user is providing examples. Like the other "by example" functions of Power Query, the AI prediction is not likely to improve after more than three examples. If you are not getting good results, try out these tips:

- Check your previous entries for typos.
- Correct predictions that are wrong.
- Provide a breadth of examples.
- Extract longer entries (these can always be transformed after the table is loaded).
- If all else fails, start over from the beginning.

Demo 4-4: Table Generation

The best way to understand how the table generation features work is by seeing them in action. Here we will begin with a new demo; however, we will use the data from the previous demos in this chapter about resources from O'Reilly Media's website. Although the *table generation* functionality works with JSON, web API, Excel, CSV, and text file types, here we will only demonstrate it with CSV and JSON.

Our first step is to import the CSV file we'll work with. Begin by clicking the "Get data drop-down arrow" and selecting Web, as previously shown in Figure 4-3.

Then under URL, copy the sample dataset (*https://raw.githubusercontent.com/tomwei nandy/ai-with-power-bi/main/Chapter4/oreilly.csv*) hosted on this book's GitHub page. Click OK (Figure 4-4).

This will open up a preview of the data. As you can see in Figure 4-21, there are some empty rows, a note about the price data being randomly generated, and the prices themselves combined in a column with the resource format. We want to extract a table using examples, so click the aptly named Extract Table Using Examples button.

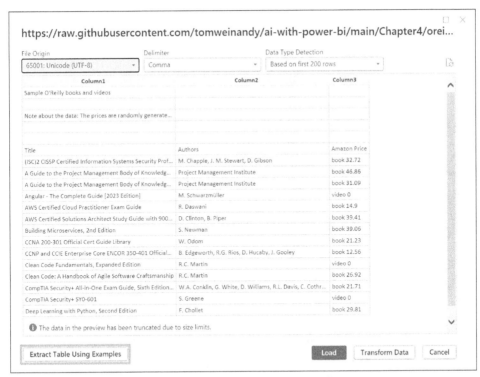

Figure 4-21. Extracting a table from a CSV file using examples

Next, you will want to make the window fullscreen and widen the first column to give more room for working. In the place of Column1, make Title the header of the first column. Then begin typing the name of the first example until the full name, (ISC)2 CISSP Certified Information Systems Security Professional Official Study Guide, 9th Edition, appears, as shown in Figure 4-22. Select it.

Recall that when giving examples, it is best to select an item from a dropdown instead of typing it out or copy-pasting the entry. This ensures that the actual value from the data is identified.

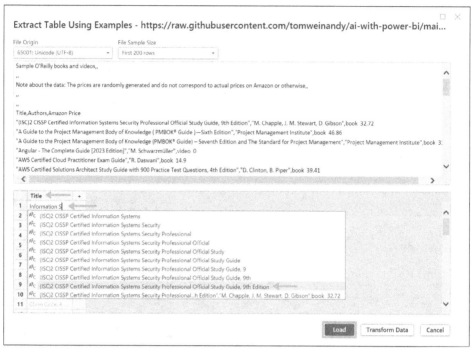

Figure 4-22. Adding the first entry of an example row

As you can see in Figure 4-23, the algorithm has already (correctly!) made predictions about the remaining titles in the CSV. The entries are gray to indicate they are merely predictions. Move on to the next column and replace Column1 with Author. Then begin typing the name of the authors until M. Chapple, J. M. Stewart, D. Gibson appears. Select it.

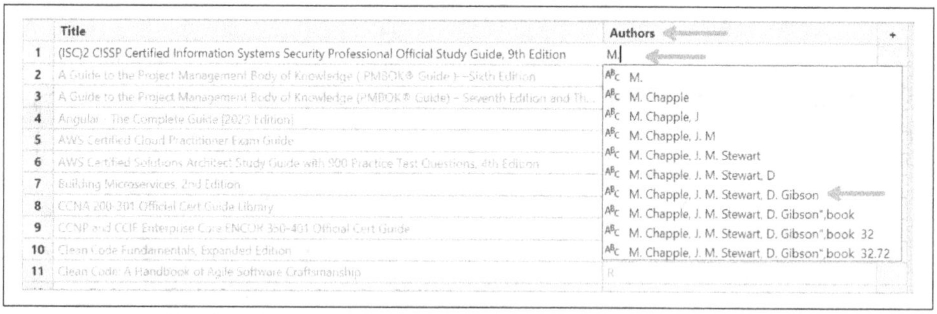

Figure 4-23. Adding the second entry of an example row

Repeat this by going to the next column, replacing Column1 with Price, searching for 32.72, and selecting it from the list (Figure 4-24). Press Enter when done.

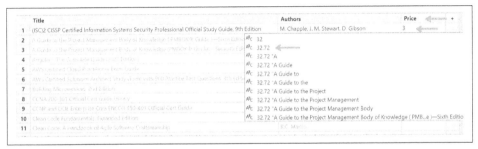

Figure 4-24. Adding the third entry of an example row

We see in Figure 4-25 that the top displayed rows of the raw CSV files correspond to the formatted rows of gray text. Just from this one example, the algorithm has correctly predicted what the rest of the table should look like. Click Load.

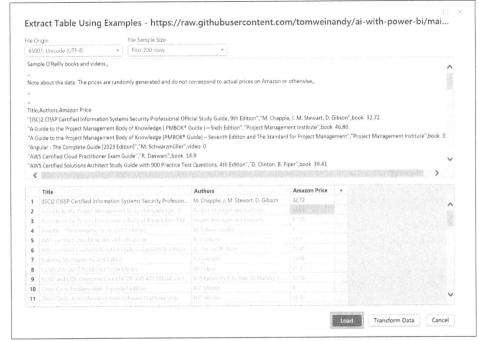

Figure 4-25. After just one example, the algorithm correctly predicted the remaining table rows

We will now move to a second example, this time with the file type JSON made from nested data. We already showed what this data looks like in its raw format in Figure 4-20, located at the beginning of this section. You can see two resources defined as a dictionary with pairs of entries representing a key (e.g., "title") and an associated value (e.g., "Designing Data-Intensive Applications").

As we did in Figure 4-3, click the "Get data drop-down" icon and select Web. Then, just like we did in Figure 4-4, paste our JSON file (*https://oreil.ly/hJJGO*) under URL. Click OK.

Power BI recognizes that we have added a JSON file and automatically converts it to a table format within Power Query Editor. Looking at Figure 4-26, you can see that the new table created from the JSON file (*oreilly2*) is listed on the lefthand side below the previous table based on the CSV file (*oreilly*).

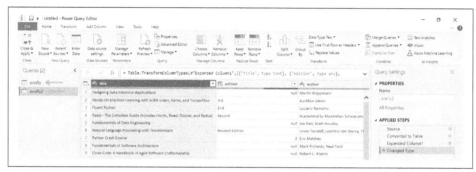

Figure 4-26. A JSON file automatically converted to a table, listed as one of two tables

We will pick up with this example later in Demo 4-5, where we will showcase a merge using fuzzy matching. But for now, take a moment to save the file, selecting Apply if prompted.

Fuzzy Matching

What is your name? Stop reading now and answer the question, preferably aloud.

Did you use a nickname or your legal name? Did you mention a middle name or initial? How about your last name(s)? What about any titles, honorifics, or suffixes? To a computer, each of these names is different. For example, `"Thomas J. Weinandy"` = `"Tom Weinandy"` will return `False` because those two strings (i.e., text data) do not match.

Now imagine a business has two datasets that each share a column of shipping addresses but lack the proper join keys. If the addresses in the two columns are slightly different, they cannot be joined through traditional means. This is where fuzzy matching enters the picture. *Fuzzy matching*, or *fuzzy logic*, is a statistical method for calculating a similarity score between two strings, and if the score passes a defined threshold, joining them. The similarities are based on factors such as character substitutions, deletions, and insertions.

Fuzzy matching is built into Power BI as part of Power Query Editor, allowing a user to combine datasets with similar columns of strings. It includes several configuration options, including:

Similarity threshold
> An optional parameter indicating how similar two strings need to be in order to match. A value of 0.0 will cause all values to match, and a value of 1.0 will join only perfect matches. The value is 0.8 by default.

Ignore case
> This parameter indicates whether matches should be case-insensitive (e.g., *internet* is matched with *Internet*). Case is ignored by default.

Match by combining text parts
> When this is selected (the default), spaces are ignored in matching; if this is unchecked, then spaces are considered.

Maximum number of matches
> This option returns either all matches (default) or a specified number of matches. For example, a value of 1 means that each row will return exactly one match.

Transformation table
> This option specifies whether there is a third, bridge table that allows for matches across a wider mapping. For example, a transformation table could contain country names with two-letter ISO country codes.

Demo 4-5: Fuzzy Matching

This demo picks up from where we were at the end of Demo 4-4. Open up Power Query Editor if it is not already open. On the Home ribbon, click the "Merge Queries drop-down arrow." Then select "Merge Queries as New" (Figure 4-27).

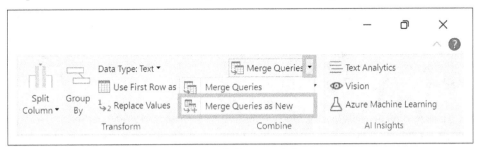

Figure 4-27. Accessing query merging with fuzzy matching

Now a new Merge window opens. The first table should already be populated with the *oreilly* query, but in the second table, select the "oreilly2" query from the drop-down. You now need to select which column(s) these two tables will be joined on.

In this case, you want to merge according to the title and author of the resources. Select Title and Author in the first query (using the Ctrl key for multi-selection) and "title" and "author" in the second query. Make sure the column numbers 1 and 2 correspond to each other, as shown in Figure 4-28, where *Title* and *title* are both 1 and *Author* and *author* are both 2.

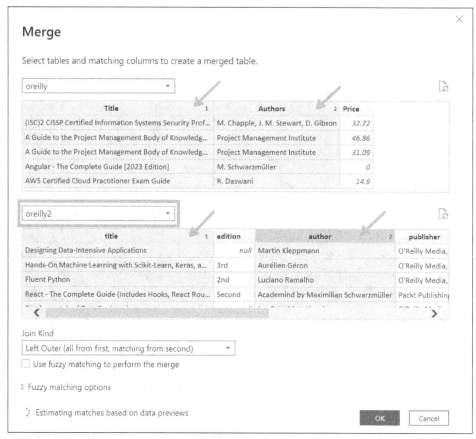

Figure 4-28. Selecting columns within queries to merge

After you select the columns from both tables, a pop-up window will appear warning you of privacy concerns related to the two datasets being merged. Since there are no privacy concerns with this data, check Ignore Privacy Levels and click Save to continue (Figure 4-29).

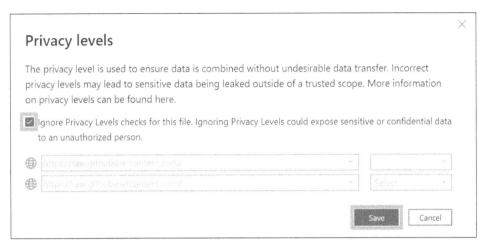

Figure 4-29. Confirming there are no privacy concerns in this case

At the bottom of the Merge window are additional options for what kind of merge we would like to perform. Select Full Outer from the dropdown to include all data. You also want to check "Use fuzzy matching to perform the merge." From here, you'll get a glimpse of how many matches occur according to the default similarity threshold for fuzzy matching of 0.8. As indicated by the arrow in Figure 4-30, only 12 out of 50 rows match.

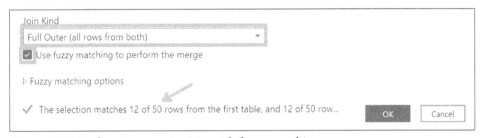

Figure 4-30. Performing an outer join with fuzzy matching

We want to improve the match rate of our data, even at the risk of creating more false positives. Click "Fuzzy matching options" to reveal additional ways to modify the join. Then, as shown in Figure 4-31, add 0.5 to "Similarity threshold" to allow for more matches. Once this is done, the message at the bottom of the window shows that all 50 rows out of 50 match at these settings. Click OK.

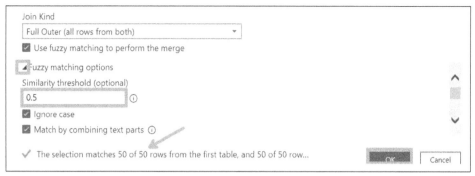

Figure 4-31. Setting a lower similarity threshold to increase the number of matches

We now have a combined query, called Table1, visible in Power Query Editor. The second query is currently shown as a column of tables. To expand this, select the split icon to the right of "oreilly2," as shown in Figure 4-32. Make sure Expand is selected and click OK.

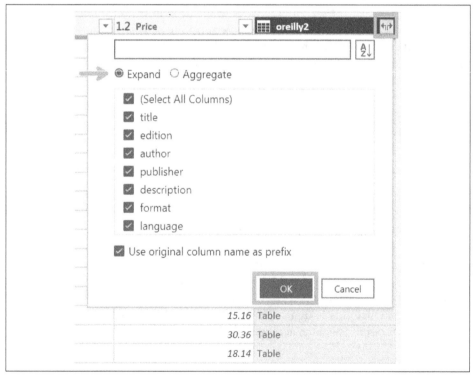

Figure 4-32. Expanding the second query in the merged table

If you look at the bottom-left corner of the window, you will see that the table has 10 columns and 54 rows. The 10 columns are good, because this means the merge was successful; however, the row count indicates that we now have 4 more rows than the 50 in each original table. To find out which rows are false positive matches, drag the Title column to the immediate left of the "oreilly2.title" column. Widen both of these columns until the edition is revealed, as shown in Figure 4-33.

Figure 4-33. Comparing titles to discover duplicate records after the match

When using fuzzy matching in Power BI, it is often better to match too many rows than too few rows because you can always remove the false positive matches. This, however, is not practical at larger scales. The trade-off of costs and benefits between having too few matches or too many matches will depend on the particulars of each use case.

Since four records is a small enough overlap, we can manually search for the rows we wish to remove and filter them out using an index column. To create one, select the Add Column ribbon, click on the "Index Column dropdown," and select From 0 (Figure 4-34).

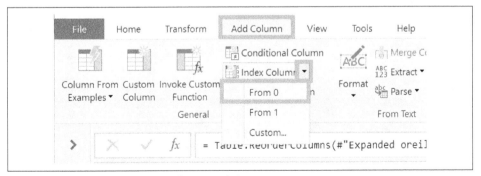

Figure 4-34. Adding an index column with base 0

Now drag the new Index column to the immediate left of the Title column, as shown in Figure 4-35. By comparing the two title columns, we identify the four resources with incongruent editions. Since these are all titles listed twice, we can safely drop them from our data model.

Figure 4-35. Identifying the mismatched rows to remove

To remove the rows, click the Index dropdown. Then unselect 1, 3, 11, and 15. Click OK (Figure 4-36).

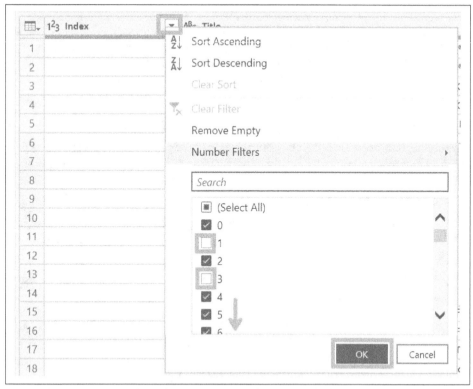

Figure 4-36. Using an index column to remove the mismatched rows

Now, as shown in Figure 4-37, we are left with the same 50 rows as in our original datasets. We thus conclude our demo on fuzzy matching. You are welcome to save the report, selecting Close & Apply if prompted.

Figure 4-37. The result of successfully merging two tables with fuzzy matching

This ends the section on how to use the AI-based automation tools within Power Query to better and more quickly transform your data. Now, we'll move on to look at ways in which AI can assist with report generation and data analysis.

Intelligent Data Exploration

One of the most impactful elements of Power BI is how rapidly it empowers a user to go from raw data to new insights. AI-based automation within Power BI takes this one step further by allowing for quick data exploration and report creation through a variety of tools. These tools leverage the power of AI to build rapid prototypes and insights but leave the developer to decide which is worth keeping.

The role of the human here is less that of a programmer and more akin to a museum curator who is building a narrative around a business situation with data. AI can make your work easier, but it does not tell you the right questions to ask or which answers are most meaningful. The algorithms can, however, complement the skills of a person who knows how to integrate their work with the AI.

This brings us back to the business intelligence cycle of Figure 4-1, where previously in the chapter we discussed the role of automation in data transformations. Now the rest of the chapter will consider how AI-based automation can support report building and analysis. We will highlight three features here: quick insights, report creation, and smart narrative. The Q&A visual could appropriately be included in this section, since it enables an end user to ask questions from the data to quickly generate visuals. However, we discussed Q&A in Chapter 3 and so will leave it to the reader to return there if interested.

In November 2023, Microsoft announced the public preview of Copilot (*https://oreil.ly/3QgHj*), a generative AI tool embedded in the Power BI service that can analyze data and create reports with a chat-based interface. This is a fast-changing feature, so we suggest searching online for the latest capabilities of Copilot in the Power BI service and Power BI Desktop. In the meantime, the rest of this chapter focuses on the tools for intelligent data exploration that are generally available at the time of writing.

Quick Insights

Quick insights automatically scans a dataset and performs a variety of analyses on pairs of variables within that dataset to uncover interesting patterns and relationships. This assists a user looking to better understand the dataset, identify an insight they might not have considered, quickly build a dashboard, come up with ideas to incorporate into a report, or simply get unstuck from being overwhelmed by a new dataset.

Using quick insights functionality on an entire dataset is possible on the browser-based Power BI service but not on Power BI Desktop, meaning it requires a Pro or Premium license. You can still use insights on a specific visual on Power BI Desktop, as discussed in Chapter 3. Quick insights is only available for data uploaded to Power BI and not DirectQuery or streaming data.

Quick insights performs many different automated analyses on your dataset. The following lists break them down by data types.

For numeric and categorical data:

Numeric outliers
One or more numeric data points meaningfully differ from others if sliced by a single category.

Category outliers
One or two categories have a disproportionately higher share of values than other categories.

Correlation
Multiple numeric data points within a category share a positive or negative relationship.

Low variance
Numeric data points are close to the mean across a category.

Majority factors
A majority of a total is from a single category.

For time series data:

Time series outliers
There are values that unexpectedly change at a point in time.

Trends in time series
There is a positive or negative trend over time.

Change points in time series
There are multiple meaningful changes in a trend.

Seasonality in times series
There is a cyclical pattern that persists over time.

Steady share
There is low variance (mentioned above) holding steady over time.

You are ready to begin exploring quick insights and saving time in the process. If, however, you run into issues, try these tips for organizing your data to get better results:

- Hide unimportant or duplicate columns in your dataset to exclude them from quick insights.

- Use a mix of numeric, categorical, and time series data.

- If you receive an error message saying your data is not statistically significant, it may be because your dataset is too simple, lacks sufficient data, or does not include numeric data or dates.

Demo 4-6: Quick Insights

Now we get to see quick insights in action. This demo uses data concerning taxis in New York City. We will use quick insights for an entire dataset, which means this demo must be performed on the browser-based Power BI service and will require a Pro or Premium subscription. Reference "Premium, Pro, and Free Power BI" on page 26 for details and information on how to sign up for a free trial.

First, download this completed report (*https://oreil.ly/timeseriescomplete*) about New York City taxis and save it locally. Then go to the Power BI service (*https://app.pow erbi.com/home*) and sign in.

We want a space to keep all of our assets together for this demonstration and the others in this chapter. On the lefthand side, select Workspaces and either go to "My workspace" or create a new one by selecting "New workspace" and following the prompts to set that up. This demo will use the workspace AI Demos (Figure 4-38).

Figure 4-38. Going to your home workspace or creating a new one

From here, click on Upload and select Browse (Figure 4-39).

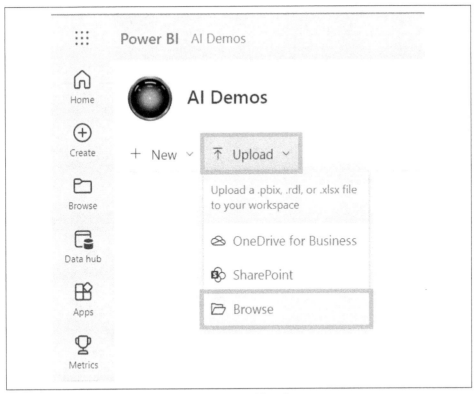

Figure 4-39. Uploading a Power BI report saved locally

Find the taxi report that you've downloaded from GitHub named TimeSeriesComplete and click Open (Figure 4-40).

Figure 4-40. Selecting the Power BI report

Now you will see the Power BI report saved in your workspace along with the underlying dataset. Click the ellipsis icon that corresponds to the dataset (where the arrow is pointing in Figure 4-41, under the drop-down menu) and then select "Get quick insights." Finally, click "View insights" (not pictured).

Figure 4-41. Accessing quick insights from a dataset

You can now review the entire list of insight cards, like the one pictured in Figure 4-42. Each card includes a visual along with an explanation of why the potential insight was identified as such. This insight card pictured here found day 359 (i.e., Christmas) was an outlier for the number of taxi trips taken on a particular day.

You can use the expand icon at the top-right corner to enter a focus mode with a larger version of the visual. You can also select the pin icon to pin the insight card to a dashboard of relevant insights.

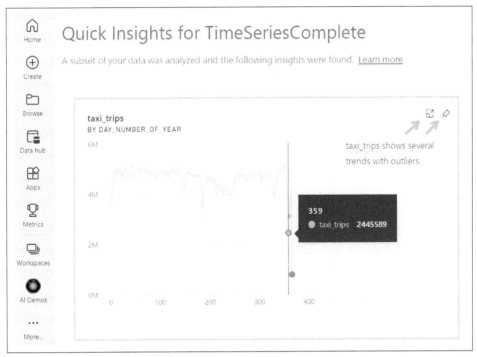

Figure 4-42. An insight card highlighting the number of taxi trips taken on Day 359 with the options to enlarge or pin to a dashboard

Let's explore some more examples of interesting findings, shown in Figure 4-43. The left insight card points out how the daily number of taxi trips includes both seasonality and an overall downward trend. The right insight card shows a positive correlation between daily tip amounts and daily total amounts spent on taxi trips.

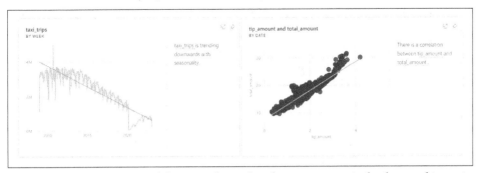

Figure 4-43. Cards generated from quick insights showing, respectively, the trend in taxi trips and the correlation of total fares and tip amounts

We continue to explore the wide variety of insights with the two examples in Figure 4-44. The left card shows that snowfall in New York City is highest in the months of January and February. The right card identifies two days of the year that were outliers for the amount of precipitation received.

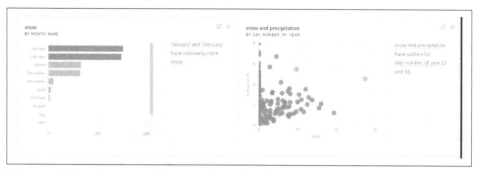

Figure 4-44. Cards generated from quick insights showing, respectively, snowfall by month and outlier days for precipitation

Not all of the findings from quick insights are meaningful or even interesting, and that is OK. This tool is meant to be used in concert with someone who knows the use case or has the right judgment to determine which insight cards are relevant.

Report Creation

We have made it to our penultimate profile of an automation feature in Power BI: report creation. *Report creation* automatically generates a fully developed Power BI report from a given dataset. This is consistent with the theme of AI tools that empower humans to more effectively and efficiently work through the business intelligence cycle.

Report creation is similar to quick insights in that it also must be done on the Power BI service, and accordingly, requires a Pro or Premium license. The two functions are also similar in that both take just a few clicks to create after a dataset is loaded into a workspace. There are differences, however; let's explore them by diving directly into a demonstration of how report creation works.

Demo 4-7: Report Creation

We pick up from the previous demo that generated insight cards from data on daily taxi trips in New York City. You do not need to have completed Demo 4-6 to follow this one; however, we will skip the steps on loading this Power BI report (*https://oreil.ly/timeseriescomplete*) into a workspace. Refer back to Demo 4-6 if you need guidance.

Once the report is loaded into a workspace in the Power BI service, locate the TimeSeriesComplete dataset (shown in Figure 4-45 within a workspace entitled "AI Demos"). Click the ellipsis icon and select "Auto-create report" from the list.

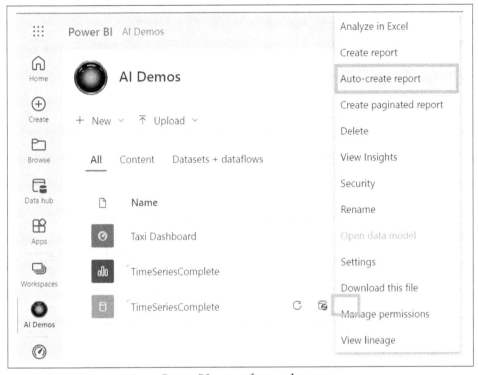

Figure 4-45. Auto-creating a Power BI report from a dataset

 There is another way to auto-create a report if you already have the desired dataset saved in the Data Hub. As Figure 4-45 shows, on the lefthand side of the Power BI Service, you can click the Create icon and then select "Pick a published dataset," choose a dataset within the Data Hub, and click "Auto-create report."

And violá, your report is made! This, unfortunately, does not mean you are done. The algorithm that generates the report attempts to identify which variables and visuals are most meaningful; however, it still requires someone to ensure it meets the business needs and to customize it accordingly.

For example, look at Figure 4-46, acknowledging that your results may be slightly different. Maybe we are not interested in the daily share of trips that go to the airport or the total passenger count. Some values displayed are also meaningless, such as "Sum of day_number_of_year by day_name" and "Sum of avg_wind_speed by day_name." Let's make a few changes.

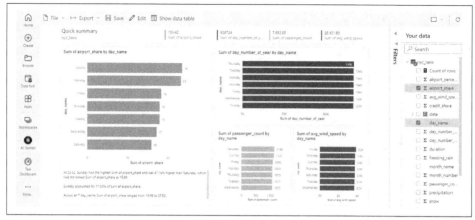

Figure 4-46. An automatically created report

First, we want to swap out the variables used in the report. Unselect all current variables and select credit_share, date, and tip_amount. This should match what you see in Figure 4-47.

Figure 4-47. Changing the report to include the selected variables

Next, change the numeric variables to be averages, not sums. On tip_amount, click the ellipsis icon and select Average. Repeat this for credit_share. The report should now show the same data labels as in Figure 4-48; however, the visuals may be slightly different in your version.

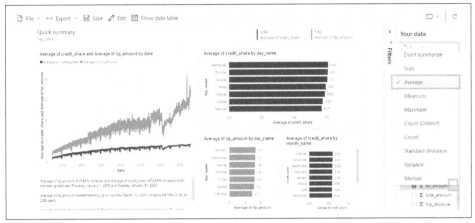

Figure 4-48. The same auto-generated report as in Figure 4-46 but with newly selected variables

Now the report is looking better! The bar charts on the right show some of the day-of-week and month-of-year differences in average daily tip amounts given to taxi drivers as well as how often passengers pay with a credit card.

The line plot on the left also tells an intriguing story. The darker line shows how the daily share of payments by credit card have been increasing over time and approaching 100%. The lighter line shows how the average daily amount tipped also has been increasing over time. The correlation between the two is actually just an artifact of the data, since tips from cash payments are not recorded (affecting the average). This means that people are not necessarily tipping more over time; however, around 2022 it does appear that the growth in tipping seems to outpace the growth in the rate of credit card use.

Did you notice the text in the bottom-left corner of the report in Figure 4-48? That is the smart narrative visual and the topic of the next section.

If you wish to make further changes to the visuals, simply hover over a visual and select the "Personalize this visual" icon (Figure 4-49).

Figure 4-49. Further personalizing a visual

Save your work when done. If you would like to continue editing the report in Power BI Desktop, at the top-left click File and then "Download this file" (not pictured).

Smart Narrative

Recall from Chapter 3 that the Q&A features allow a user to ask a question of the data by taking text as an input and producing a visual as an output. In that regard, smart narrative is simply a reverse version of Q&A. *Smart narrative* searches through visuals on a report and produces a text summary from the data.

Smart narrative can be used in Power BI Desktop or the Power BI service and can be applied in three ways:

- As a text box summarizing all of the visuals on a report
- As a text box summarizing a single visual
- As an icon on a visual that, when clicked, reveals a text summary of the visual

Figure 4-50 shows how to access the smart narrative feature through the icon in the Visualizations pane. Selecting the icon will provide a summary of all visuals in the report. In this case, the smart text appeared at the bottom of the canvas as three insights.

 Figure 4-50 shows the Power BI report on taxi trips in New York City used in Demo 4-6 (see Figure 4-41). Return to that demo for download instructions if you wish to follow along.

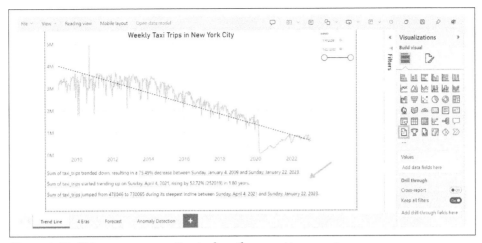

Figure 4-50. Using smart narrative to describe an entire report

To create a smart narrative of an individual visual, all you have to do is right-click the visual and select Summarize.

If you do not see the Summarize option for a visual, make sure you have edit access and are in edit mode.

Finally, you can add a smart narrative icon to a visual by selecting the visual, going to "Format visual" > General > Header icons > Icons and then toggling on "Smart narrative," as shown in Figure 4-51.

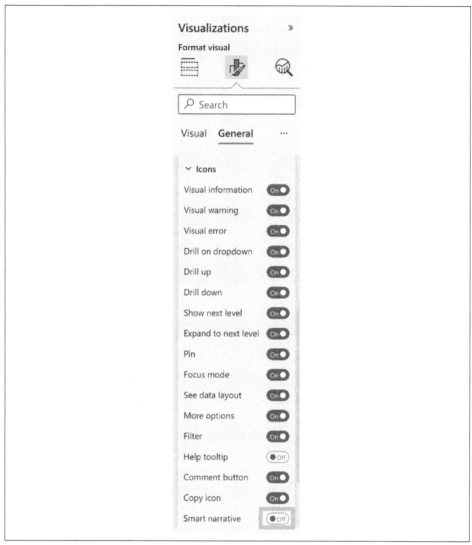

Figure 4-51. Adding a smart narrative icon to a visual

Not only does the smart narrative feature describe visuals when created, but it also automatically updates when slicers and filters are applied. Take the smart narrative in Figure 4-50 as an example. If a user changes the date range using the filter at the top-right, then the text will change in real time to new insights specific to data within the specified date range.

Additionally, a user is able to format the text as they see fit and even add their own text or values. Figure 4-52 shows the text "Cumulative Trips" and indicates how to add a dynamic value. A *dynamic value* is a field or measure tied to your data and displayed as regular text but updated with changes to the report.

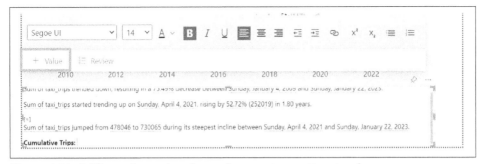

Figure 4-52. Adding a dynamic value to the smart narrative visual

Next, a prompt allows a user to search for a custom value. Figure 4-53 shows how the input "Sum of taxi trip" successfully identifies "taxi trip" as a dynamic value, as indicated by the blue line underneath. This value can also be further formatted, such as adding a comma. Click Save.

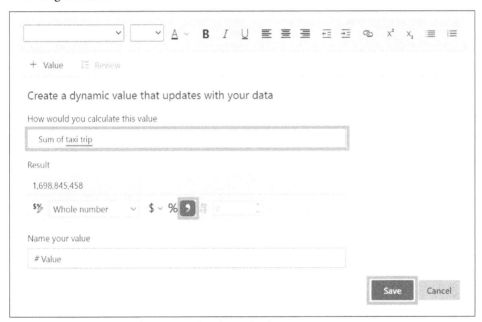

Figure 4-53. Defining a dynamic value from the data

You can see the resulting dynamic value in Figure 4-54, where smart narrative states there were nearly 1.7 billion taxi trips during the selected time period.

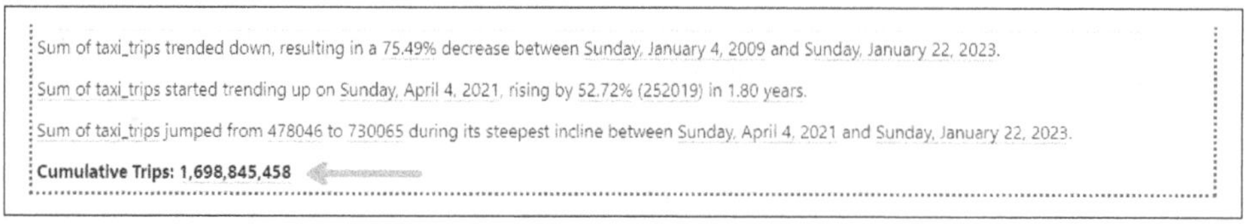

> Sum of taxi_trips trended down, resulting in a 75.49% decrease between Sunday, January 4, 2009 and Sunday, January 22, 2023.
>
> Sum of taxi_trips started trending up on Sunday, April 4, 2021, rising by 52.72% (252019) in 1.80 years.
>
> Sum of taxi_trips jumped from 478046 to 730065 during its steepest incline between Sunday, April 4, 2021 and Sunday, January 22, 2023.
>
> **Cumulative Trips: 1,698,845,458**

Figure 4-54. A dynamic value with custom formatting

Summary

We reviewed how to use the AI-based features in Power BI that help automate the process of transforming data as well as building and analyzing reports. These tools speed up your ability to go from business questions to answers, making you a more productive analyst. We also discussed the aspects of the business intelligence cycle that are not easily automated, at least in the near future.

Hopefully you are able to learn important skills that can help future-proof your job or organization. AI is already transforming the way we work, and the pace of disruption does not appear to be slowing. We believe that you should be less concerned about AI replacing your job and more concerned that you will be replaced by an analyst who better harnesses the power of AI.

Reading this book is a step in the right direction for becoming that AI-fluent developer and strengthening your work quality as well as your job security. As Elbert Hubbard said, "One machine can do the work of fifty ordinary men. No machine can do the work of one extraordinary man." So leverage the power of AI to become extraordinary and help your organization achieve the same, because the algorithms are not going anywhere. I, for one, welcome our new AI coworkers.

## CHAPTER 5

Working with Time Series Data

I (Thomas) remember the first time someone told me there is a hidden arrow within the FedEx logo. It blew my mind to realize that something I had known for as long as I could remember contained a deeper meaning hidden in plain sight. There are some features within Power BI that remind me of this same story. I had been using line charts in Power BI for a while before learning that with just a few more clicks, I could quickly generate more advanced analytics. This chapter is dedicated to some of the AI features seemingly hidden within common visualizations. After exploring these new abilities, it will be difficult to see these visualizations the same way again—just like the FedEx logo.

We continue the discussion from Chapter 3 about ways a business can use artificial intelligence for better decision making. Now we dive into more AI features included in the free Desktop version of Power BI. This chapter explores ways an organization can utilize the AI tools of trend lines, forecasting, and anomaly detection. Before we dive into those directly, it will be helpful to cover some fundamentals around how time series data is different from other datatypes.

More Than Just Timestamps

Time series data is a type of data that measures observations of the same variable across points of time and is dependent on previous observations.

Let's break apart that definition into some bite-size pieces. Importantly, time series data is measuring how the same object, process, or aggregation changes over time. The time itself is recorded along with the observation, whether that be by a timestamp (e.g., a reading from a factory sensor), an aggregation (e.g., daily store sales), or merely as a generic unit of time (e.g., period 1, period 2, etc.). These measures are often at equal intervals but do not need to be. For example, one could measure how a student performed on different tests throughout an academic year.

Finally, time series data is dependent on its previous observations. *Dependence* is a statistical term meaning that one observation is impacted by the value of past observations. Imagine you collect a data series on the temperature around you for each minute of the next hour. Those measures are dependent because the temperature right now influences what the temperature will be the next minute. Similarly, daily sales at a store are dependent because sales for one day indicate the level of demand for that store and can be used to predict how much traffic there will be the next day.

Time series data is fundamental to any organization. Figure 5-1 shows one of the very first uses of a line chart to visualize time series data. The 1786 graph displays England's trade balance with Denmark and Norway as the net difference between imports and exports over time. The elegant visual shows that gains in the trade balance are due to a rapid growth of exports starting around 1756 rather than the level of imports, which remains steady.

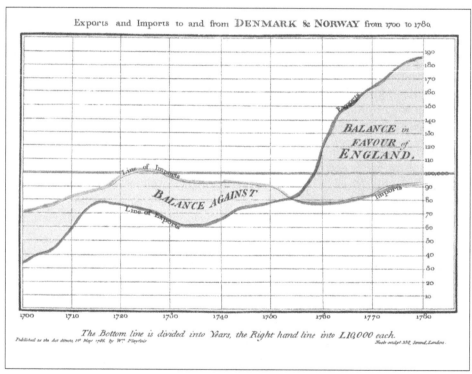

Figure 5-1. One of the earliest known examples of a line chart, from The Commercial and Political Atlas *by William Playfair (1786)*

William Playfair (1759–1823) of Scotland was not only one of the first users of the bar chart and line chart but also the inventor of the pie chart and area chart.[1] The *Encyclopedia of Mathematics* describes him best, saying, "William Playfair, engineer, political economist and scoundrel, was the most important developer of statistical graphics. In the two centuries since, there has been no appreciable improvement on his basic designs."[2] Not bad for a scoundrel!

Line charts are an ideal way to visualize data, especially when it is important for a business to see how a variable changes over time. However, line charts can be misused when a measure is independent or generally has no meaningful relationship with time or order. For example, rolling dice produces independent observations because the previous value on a die roll has no impact on the outcome of another die roll.

Consider an example where a pair of fair dice are rolled 100 times. The left graph in Figure 5-2 shows the rolls as a time series on a line chart, while the right graph in Figure 5-2 shows a histogram of outcomes. The line chart is less effective for this data because the time dimension does not provide additional insight into the pattern behind dice rolls. In other words, it's just noise. The histogram, however, is better because it readily shows the frequency distribution of outcomes. This illustrates that just because a dataset includes a time variable does not mean that it will help uncover insights.

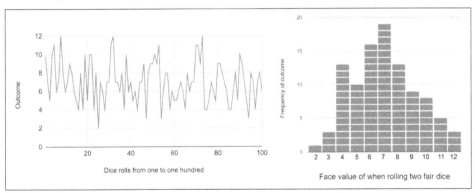

Figure 5-2. Graphing the outcome of 100 rolls of a pair of fair dice

1 Michael Friendly, *Milestones in the History of Thematic Cartography, Statistical Graphics, and Data Visualization* (*https://oreil.ly/cJrxU*) (August 24, 2009).

2 "Playfair, William" (*https://oreil.ly/j6-3l*), Encyclopedia of Mathematics, last modified September 22, 2016.

The Components of a Time Series

Let us tell you a story about the Timeseries Family. Grandma Trend decided she wanted to go to the park and invited her grandson, Seasonality, who requested they bring their dog, Noise. The three began walking in the same direction. Grandma Trend knew the straight bike path was the best route, and given her age, she stayed in the middle to reduce the number of steps to get to the park. Seasonality, on the other hand, was 10 and made a game of weaving between the stripes of the dashed dividing line down the middle of the path. He walked behind Grandma Trend as he predictably moved left and right, holding tight to their dog's leash. Noise was a small dog and never could pull Seasonality away from his weaving. But Noise was also a curious, energetic dog that ran all over without rhyme or reason. The Timeseries Family never could tell where the dog would go next, yet Noise kept being pulled back to Seasonality by the leash. The three of them enjoyed their walk together, with Noise never going too far from Seasonality and Seasonality never going too far from Grandma Trend.

Just as the story suggests, times series data can be decomposed into its component parts. This simple example shows one data-generating process that produces a data series with three components. A time series can include more or fewer, but we will focus on these three as they are the most common.

A *trend* is a persistent movement in one direction observed over a period of time. Trends can be linear or curvilinear and generally refer to patterns in the data that are not caused by random chance (more on that later). Recall that Grandma Trend in the story was guiding the family in the direction of the park, while the others were merely following. Her path can be represented as the dotted line in Figure 5-3.

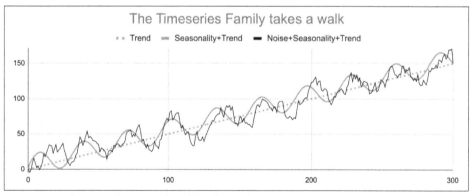

Figure 5-3. The cumulative paths of the three characters in our story, representing three components of a single time series

Seasonality is the regular variation in time series data that follows a predictable path based on some known timeframe. For example, a typical grocery store will see multiple different seasonal patterns in customer foot traffic, including patterns dependent on (1) the time of day (with a peak right after work), (2) the day of week (with surges of weekend shoppers), (3) the day of month (as many government benefits are dispersed early in the month), and (4) the day of year (with spikes before holidays like Thanksgiving and Christmas). The grandson Seasonality from the story is represented by the smooth bold line in Figure 5-3 that oscillates around the trend but does not dictate the long-term direction.

The third and final component of this time series is *noise*, or the random component that cannot be predicted or explained. Businesses rarely know with complete certainty why a past outcome or value occurred (let alone a future predicted outcome!). Noise is simply a catchall of "everything else" that remains beyond the known components. The dog from the story is called Noise because it's impossible to know where it will go next. The thin black line for Noise in Figure 5-3 shows the dog's behavior, which was erratic but still led by Seasonality and guided by Grandma Trend.

The story is helpful for understanding how a data-generating process (in this case, the family's walking habits) creates particular time series data; however, the real world works the opposite way. Usually an analyst like you is presented with time series data and is asked to make sense of it, sometimes without being given any context as to what would have influenced those values. Now consider Figure 5-4 and think about how you would describe the data. Can you estimate the trend's slope or the number of periods in its seasonality?

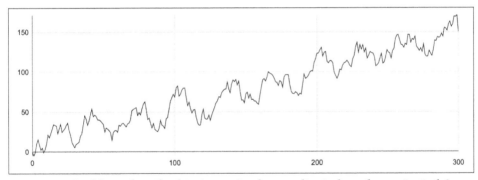

Figure 5-4. Could you describe this time series data qualitatively and quantitatively?

Changes to a Time Series

The data in the previous section was rather consistent over time, but the real world is seldom that simple. Businesses are always trying to influence specific outcomes and are subject to external influences and shocks. In this section, we will demonstrate three ways in which time series data can change: shifts, kinks, and structural breaks.

A *shift* is a sudden increase or decrease in a time series that changes the trend's level but not the trend's direction. In graphical terms, the *y*-intercept of a trend line changes but not its slope or shape. Imagine the y-axis in Figure 5-5 is money in a business's checking account. The account fluctuates each day based on revenue and expenses, but then at time period 150, the business has an expensive tax bill due. The balance immediately drops, but the business continues operating as it had before.

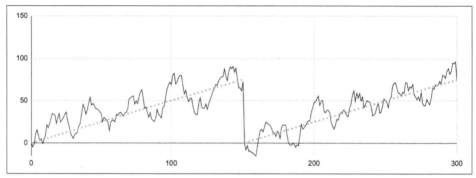

Figure 5-5. A shift in a time series trend

A *kink* is when the slope of a time series changes (in the positive or negative direction) without any level change. The example in Figure 5-6 would describe a business that was growing until time period 150, when maybe a competing store opened up nearby and the business's growth stopped.

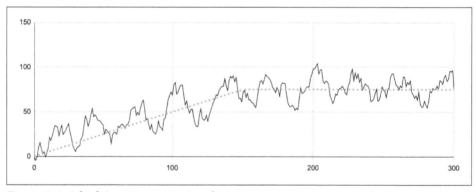

Figure 5-6. A kink in a time series trend

Finally, a *structural break* is when the underlying data-generating process changes in some fundamental way. We can see new dynamics in Figure 5-7 beginning at time period 150 when, in addition to a kink in the trend, there is wider oscillation and a new, curvilinear trend. A business can experience a change to its fundamentals when there are large disruptions in its organization, industry, market, or geography.

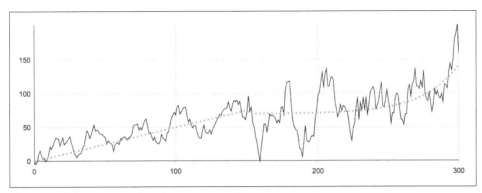

Figure 5-7. A structural break in a time series

All three of these changes to a time series have serious implications for machine learning models. Algorithms trained on past observations to make future predictions will deteriorate in performance when there are shifts, kinks, or structural breaks. This can sometimes be resolved by simply retraining a model; however, retraining requires a sufficient amount of new data since the change occurred.

How Trend Lines Work in Power BI

Trend lines are available across many visuals in Power BI but only if the dataset includes time series data. The visuals that can show trends include:

- Area chart
- Clustered column chart
- Line chart
- Line and clustered column chart
- Scatter chart

 Find the trend line within the analytics pane of these visuals. While there, you should explore other helpful additions, such as lines for a constant value, minimum, maximum, average, median, and percentiles. Also, scatter charts specifically have the additional features of a y-constant line, x-constant line, and symmetrical shading.

The math behind creating a trend line involves solving a simple linear regression problem, such as the one described in "Regression" on page 95. This creates a "line of best fit" that minimizes the squared error (i.e., the distance between an observation and the trend line).

Although regression is classically a machine learning problem, the computation is simple enough that a visual can quickly re-estimate the trend every time data is filtered. At the moment, only straight trend lines are supported within Power BI. This means that it may not make sense to include trend lines if your data is highly cyclical or curvilinear.

Limitations of Trend Lines

Trend lines within Power BI can only show the relationship between a date variable and a single other variable. They also fit only a straight-line trend, even if the true trend is curvilinear. This makes the tool rather simple and mostly just useful in drawing attention to a pattern rather than uncovering a new insight. Trend lines also cannot be used on line charts when there is a secondary y-axis.

Demo 5-1: Exploring Taxi Trip Data

We will now explore some real-world time series within Power BI to apply what we have learned so far. Our dataset includes daily measures of taxi trips, among other related variables, from January 2009 through January 2023, during which over 1.7 billion taxi rides took place (Figure 5-8). I (Thomas) even used this very data source in my dissertation to understand why gas prices impacted taxi drivers differently than Uber and Lyft drivers. Special thanks to the City of New York and all governments that make their data open and accessible! You can explore more open data at *https://opendata.cityofnewyork.us* and find the original trip-level files we used to create our dataset. We also merged weather data from *https://www.ncei.noaa.gov*.

Figure 5-8. The iconic New York City yellow taxicab

Open a new report in Power BI Desktop and click through the pop-up window. Now it is time to ingest the dataset. In the Home ribbon, select "Get data" and then Web as the source of the data (Figure 5-9).

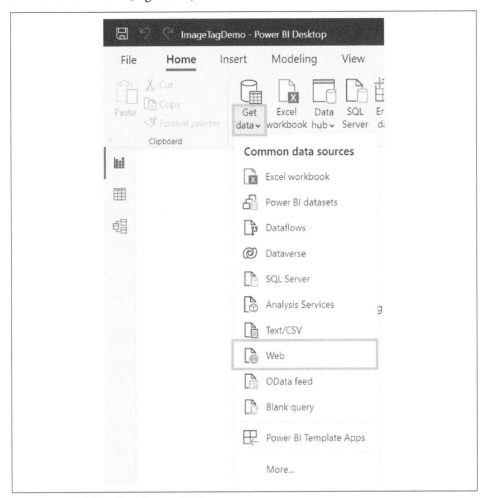

Figure 5-9. Adding data from a URL

 If you selected the "Get data" icon instead of the "Get data" text, you will instead see a different pop-up window. If this happens, type "web" in the Search bar, select Web, and then click Connect before proceeding to the next step.

In the new pop-up window, paste the link (*https://raw.githubusercontent.com/tomwei nandy/ai-with-power-bi/main/Chapter5/NYCTaxis.csv*) in the box under URL. This is a CSV of the New York City taxi data hosted on the book's GitHub repository. Click OK (Figure 5-10).

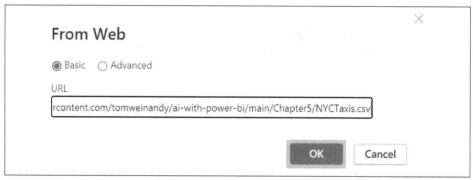

Figure 5-10. Pasting a URL of raw data from GitHub

We now see a preview of the data that shows the listing name and description. Change the Data Type Detection to "Based on entire dataset" to ensure the variables are properly encoded. Otherwise, this dataset does not need to be transformed, so select Load to bring it into the report (Figure 5-11).

https://raw.githubusercontent.com/tomweinandy/ai-with-power-bi/main/Chapter5/NY...

File Origin		Delimiter		Data Type Detection					
65001: Unicode (UTF-8)		Comma		Based on entire dataset					

date	taxi_trips	duration	passenger_count	trip_distance	tip_amount	total_amount	airport_share	credit_share	day_n:
1/1/2009	324225	10.11042291	null	2.907790495	0.329896375	10.377966	null	0.145649293	Thursc
1/2/2009	372059	10.52132256	null	2.706210569	0.339906293	10.35336558	null	0.154869001	Friday
1/3/2009	427312	10.67645581	null	2.748637428	0.366798988	10.27846819	null	0.168207307	Saturd.
1/4/2009	362132	10.66558874	null	3.101978478	0.452461955	11.06483839	null	0.19024257	Sunda
1/5/2009	365983	10.47673175	null	2.81638244	0.439258427	10.60549761	null	0.190239785	Mond
1/6/2009	421853	10.84393323	null	2.576320508	0.433328849	10.21985866	null	0.201593672	Tuesd
1/7/2009	366820	11.23827381	null	2.51595292	0.454904256	10.25791251	null	0.216806523	Wedne
1/8/2009	471510	11.20174818	null	2.527508059	0.461077022	10.2762152	null	0.214106857	Thursc
1/9/2009	514394	11.32859342	null	2.510175989	0.446458339	10.26943826	null	0.209504883	Friday
1/10/2009	476509	10.1316944	null	2.548152921	0.406663101	9.68177118	null	0.199800308	Saturd
1/11/2009	398391	10.01817465	null	2.864774837	0.47362644	10.3995111	null	0.214193142	Sunda
1/12/2009	409069	10.57531236	null	2.570557959	0.471311445	10.20653156	null	0.213434584	Mond
1/13/2009	436828	10.84825301	null	2.514573783	0.488093496	10.20132692	null	0.224014633	Tuesd
1/14/2009	482764	11.07319639	null	2.484790293	0.50467336	10.22765461	null	0.230630435	Wedne
1/15/2009	479938	11.38186141	null	1.951125163	0.516707801	10.34308498	null	0.236638262	Thursc
1/16/2009	528148	11.2529528	null	2.527864942	0.484807735	10.32943232	null	0.22296275	Friday
1/17/2009	504118	10.46675325	null	2.529803423	0.416432881	9.83568047	null	0.201814651	Saturd.
1/18/2009	413777	10.4270703	null	2.763891362	0.452049828	10.22283947	null	0.21556295	Sunda
1/19/2009	347171	10.45968231	null	2.773167125	0.491902398	10.29186833	null	0.221345955	Mond
1/20/2009	427773	10.77176961	null	2.575622608	0.499173391	10.31334665	null	0.226967909	Tuesd
1/21/2009	472311	11.60007234	null	2.494126154	0.507382346	10.39759773	null	0.23313429	Wedne

Extract Table Using Examples   Load   Transform Data   Cancel

Figure 5-11. Loading the data into a report (no transformation is needed)

Now we are ready to begin exploring our data. We'll use a cooking show trick and take out our already-baked desserts so we can dedicate more time to the AI components specifically.

You can use a column and line chart to consider how each day of the week is associated with taxi demand. As shown by the columns in Figure 5-12, taxis are busiest on Thursdays through Saturdays and least busy on Monday. The bold line also shows the shares of those trips going to the airport. It appears that Sundays and Mondays are the relatively most common days to fly. Note that the columns showing average number of trips use the y-axis on the left, and the bold line showing percent of airport trips uses the y-axis on the right. Together, these charts show us that the time series data has weekly fluctuations.

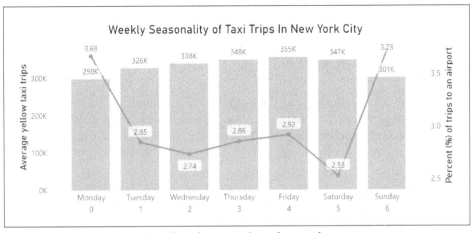

Figure 5-12. Showing the day-of-week seasonality of taxi rides

You can also consider the annual fluctuations in the time series, as shown in Figure 5-13. The depressed columns indicate that taxi demand is lowest in January after the holidays and in the summer months of July and August, when many New Yorkers leave the city on vacation. The overlaid line also reveals some very slight changes in average passenger counts, with more people sharing a taxi in July and December. Together, Figures 5-12 and 5-13 show how we should expect to see these repeated patterns across our time series data.

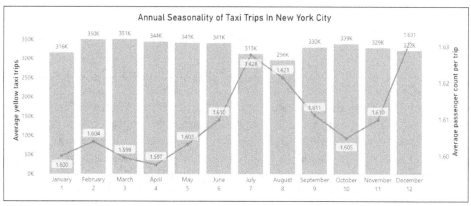

Figure 5-13. Showing the month-of-year differences in taxi rides

We pick up here with the step-by-step demo. Under the Visualizations pane, select the "line chart" visual, as shown in Figure 5-14. Then drag the taxi_trips variable into the Y-axis well.

Our plot would look too crowded if we plotted the thousands of daily observations, so try grouping the data by weeks. This has the added benefit of smoothing out the weekly fluctuations found in Figure 5-12.

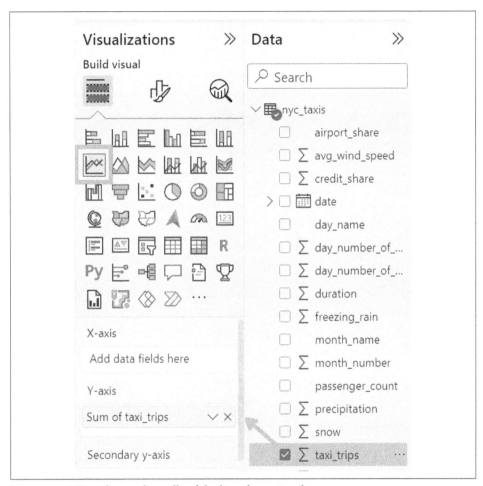

Figure 5-14. Populating the wells of the line chart visual

Within the Date pane, select the ellipsis to the right of the date variable. From the dropdown, select "New group" (Figure 5-15).

Figure 5-15. Creating a new group from the date variable

In the new Groups window (Figure 5-16), name the variable "week," add a bin size of 7, and select Days. Click OK, and you will see the new week variable appear in the Data pane.

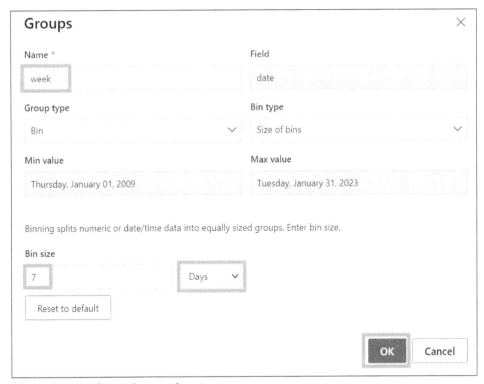

Figure 5-16. Defining the new date group

Drag the newly created week variable to the X-axis well to display the time series. Resize the line chart to better view the data, as shown in Figure 5-17. We also went ahead and formatted the chart for better viewing here, but that is an optional step for you.

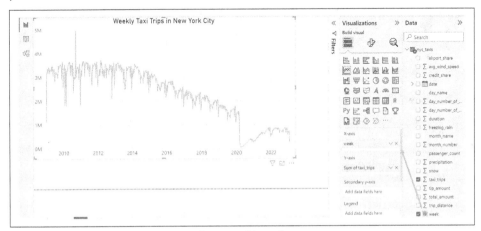

Figure 5-17. Adding the x-axis to a formatted line chart

Let's make one more addition before analyzing trends. If you hover over the first observation, you will notice the date is December 28, 2008; however, our dataset begins on January 1, 2009. It appears our weekly grouping did not create a complete first week or last week. Let's add a slicer to control which date ranges are displayed.

Click away from the line chart visual if you already have it selected, and add the Slicer visual to your canvas (Figure 5-18). Next, drag the week variable to the Field well. Now you can adjust the date range to be from 1/4/2009 to 1/23/2013.

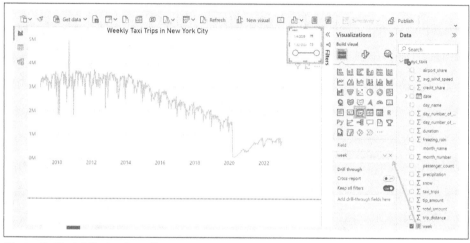

Figure 5-18. Adding a date slicer

You are now ready to add a trend line. Select the line chart and then, under the Visualizations pane, click the Analytics icon and toggle "Trend line" (Figure 5-19).

 If you get an error message saying "Analytics features are not available for this visual," it is because you do not have the line chart selected.

The resulting trend line is decent for this dataset, but its blunt approach does not capture how the underlying market dynamics of taxi trips have changed over time. Since we have a slicer included in the report, we can adjust the time frame to see if we can find intervals of time when there was a linear trend.

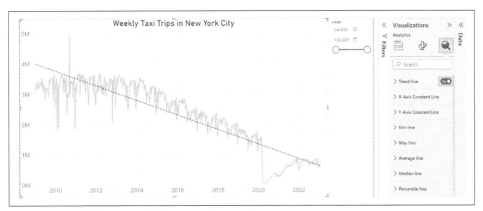

Figure 5-19. Adding a trend line to a time series

Sometimes the best way to evaluate a time series is to conduct an "eye analysis." This simply means looking at the data and roughly identifying the major changes. You can use the information in "Changes to a Time Series" on page 169 and your own domain knowledge about the data source to better describe the narrative around what happened. You can also use the slicer to adjust the date range of your time series.

For example, the number of daily taxi trips appears to have a flat trend until right after 2014, when there is a kink in the trend, which is thereafter marked by a steady decline. This reflects the rise of ride-hailing apps like Uber and Lyft, which proved to be serious competitors to the iconic yellow taxi. The decline continued until after 2020, when there was an abrupt downward shift of the trend line as well as a structural break that completely changed the time series. This of course was the COVID-19 pandemic, which triggered a nearly two-year recovery period for the industry. Then a new chapter for taxis began in 2022 with a period of flat or slightly negative growth.

Figure 5-20 summarizes four eras with what the trend line looks like in each. These four lines are merely a line object overlaid on the chart, since line charts currently do not support multiple trend lines for the same time series.

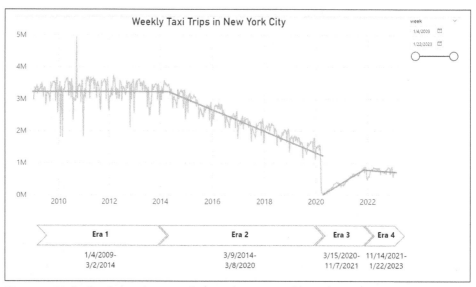

Figure 5-20. Stylized visualization showing how a trend line changes over four eras of the New York taxi time series data

Explore the results on your own by considering the following questions:

- If the trend in Figure 5-19 continues as shown, roughly how many weekly taxi trips will there be at the start of 2026?
- Approximately what are the slopes of the four trend lines in Figure 5-20?
- If you had to pick a week other than 3/2/2014 for when Era 1 ended, what week would it be and why?
- We described the transition from Era 1 to Era 2 as a kinked trend line. In what ways was this also a structural break?
- What would the trend line look like if Eras 3 and 4 were combined? Do you think this trend would support an accurate forecast for what happened in February 2023?

Be sure to save your work, as we will use this same dataset for more demos in the chapter. You can explore a completed report available for download on our GitHub page (*https://oreil.ly/timeseriescomplete*).

Forecasting

As discussed in "More Than Just Timestamps" on page 165, the observations in time series data are dependent on the order or timing of their occurrence. In other words, the past influences what happens next—just like how today's temperature partially determines whether it will rain tomorrow. Determining what will happen tomorrow is difficult, but fortunately for your own job security, it's possible to make an educated guess. Yogi Berra, former catcher for the New York Yankees, put it best when he said, "It's tough to make predictions, especially about the future."

Forecasting is a class of problems where, at the highest level, we are simply predicting what will happen next in time series data. This falls into the realm of machine learning because the best forecasts are trained from historical data to predict future observations. There are a plethora of different algorithms used in forecasting, from the more traditional ARIMA model developed by statisticians in the 1970s to Prophet, developed by researchers at Facebook and made open source in 2017. In this section, we will discuss how to leverage Power BI's built-in forecasting tools to provide better business insights.

Forecasting for Business

Imagine a business builds a reliable forecast model that projects future sales for the next two years. This single time series can be used across the organization to inform decisions in various areas, including:

- Production planning to determine how much of different products to make
- Supply chain optimization to know what materials need to be ordered and when
- Inventory management to estimate how much stock on hand is needed
- Human resource planning to conduct the right hiring and training
- Research and development to launch new products as old models are sunsetted
- Financial planning to maintain cash flow and optimize investments based on maturity dates
- Pricing and advertising strategy to adjust pricing and spending based on expected consumer demand

How Forecasting Works

Forecasting is built into Power BI line charts to enhance analysis of time series data. The results can also be downloaded for use outside of the platform. Microsoft does not describe what algorithm it uses to produce forecast results; however, some commentators online speculate it is based on exponential smoothing.

Exponential smoothing is a method of forecasting that puts greater weight on more recent observations and exponentially less weight on observations from further in the past. This method is computationally lightweight and is thus ideal for highly responsive reports that can quickly recalculate a forecast each time a cross-filtering changes the underlying data. It is also very effective in capturing seasonal patterns in data. The length of the seasonality can be automatically estimated or declared when enabled.

Forecasts also include confidence intervals on the predictions. This is shown visually as a gray shaded area around the predicted value, and the user can adjust the percentage of the interval.

Limitations of Forecasting

Among all of the AI features within Power BI, forecasting within line charts yields some of the least impressive results. As of this writing, the built-in forecast does not appear to incorporate trends into its predictions. This means that time series data with a clear upward trend when forecasted will appear to immediately flatten out (see the example in Demo 5-2 later in this chapter). The line chart forecast also only uses the time series being forecasted to predict future outcomes and does not allow for additional variables to improve the estimation.

Forecasts cannot be used with anomaly detection or when there are multiple time series on the same line chart. They can, however, be used with a trend line.

Finally, Microsoft does not provide transparent documentation about what algorithm it uses. This opaque approach makes it impossible to know how results are produced.

Despite these many limitations, forecasts tend to be reliable when times series data has a flat trend. Power BI also does an excellent job of incorporating seasonality into its estimates. If those conditions are met, we recommend using forecasts to monitor for unexpected behavior but not for business planning. Overall, we suggest that Microsoft improve the forecasting algorithm within Power BI due to the many robust options now available and its wide business applications.

Demo 5-2: Forecasting Taxi Trip Data

We are picking up from Demo 5-1, in which we (1) loaded our times series data, (2) created a new seven-day group appropriately called "week," (3) added a line chart visual, and (4) included a week slicer. You can either retrace those previous steps or simply download this report (*https://oreil.ly/timeseriescomplete*).

Now that the taxi trip data is loaded, modeled, and plotted, you are ready to create a forecast. Select the line chart visual on the canvas and, within the Visualizations pane, click the Analytics icon. Then scroll down and toggle the Forecast tab so it is on (Figure 5-21).

Figure 5-21. Enabling the forecast feature within a line chart

And with just a few clicks, we have a forecast! It does not tell us much as is, so let's imagine a new question: How many weekly taxi trips would there have been in New York City had the COVID-19 pandemic not occurred?

To consider this, click the chevron to open up the Forecast section (Figure 5-22). Under Options, add 150 to Forecast length and 150 to "Ignore the last." This indicates we want to forecast the next 150 periods (i.e., weeks) while ignoring the previous 150 periods (weeks). These values do not need to equal each other; however, when they do, we can compare the predictions with the actual values. This is useful for a what-if analysis like the question at hand or to evaluate how accurate a forecast is.

Next, change the seasonality from being automatically detected to 52 because we have weekly data and already know from Demo 5-1 that our time series has annual fluctuations. Click Apply.

Figure 5-22 reveals the previously discussed limitation of the forecast tool, which doesn't seem to take into account the negative trend in the data. We can, however, see the annual fluctuations in the forecast, which even include drops around Christmas.

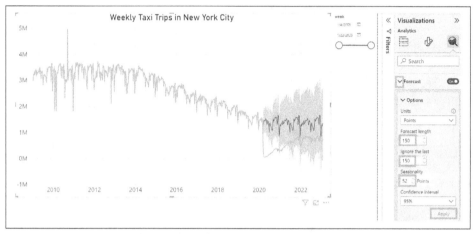

Figure 5-22. Forecasting the number of taxi trips had the COVID-19 pandemic not occurred

Let's try another forecast but this time for Era 1 (from Figure 5-20) when the trend was flat. Use the slicer to cross-filter a date range from 1/4/2009 to 3/2/2014. Then select the line chart visual and navigate to the Visualizations pane. From there, click the Analytics icon and open the Forecast section. You want to forecast taxi trips from the past year, so set 52 for the "Forecast length" and 52 for "Ignore the last." Make sure Seasonality is still 52 and click Apply.

The results in Figure 5-23 show the forecast of weekly taxi trips compared to the actual values over the same period. The prediction seems to be rather accurate, judging by how closely the two time series follow each other. This shows how forecasts can be a useful tool when a time series has a flat trend.

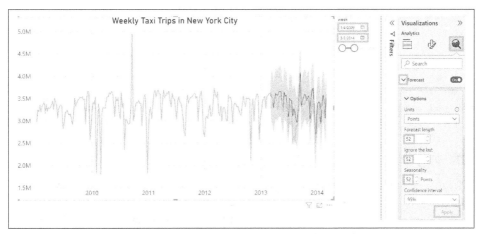

Figure 5-23. Forecasting the number of taxi trips when there is a flat trend line

Explore the results on your own by considering the following questions:

- What happens to the gray area when you decrease the confidence interval to 80%? What happens to the forecast (black line)?
- Why do you think the confidence interval fans out over time?
- Why is there a forecasted spike on 9/15/2013?
- How many more weekly trips would there have been at the start of 2020 if ride-hailing apps had not been invented?
- Test out ways to make the best prediction for what will happen in February 2023. What modifications did you change and why?

Forecasting broadly is important for business decision making. Data analysts should keep in mind that the feature is available within Power BI, even if it is only useful in scenarios where there is no moderate or large trend in the positive or negative direction. We suggest an organization use forecasting within line charts as a monitoring tool but not for decision making.

Anomaly Detection

Let's return to the Yogi Berra quote, "It's tough to make predictions, especially about the future." The line is humorous because we already know what happened in the past and predictions, therefore, must only apply to the unknown future. Right? Well, not quite.

It's true that forecasting is forward-looking, but often we are curious about what is happening at this very moment (sometimes called "nowcasting") or what we expected to happen in the past (sometimes called "hindcasting" or "backcasting"). *Anomaly detection* is a backward-looking approach that in essence is making predictions about historical data by asking, "Given the pattern of previous observations, what would we expect each of those past observations to be?" and then flagging any observations falling out of that range.

Anomaly detection, which is generally available in line charts within Power BI, provides a quick way to identify which observations within time series data merit further investigation.

Anomaly Detection for Business

The goal of any organization is to provide a good or service that is both consistent and valuable. What makes an organization exceptional though is that it has a system in place to monitor its operations to identify when they fall short, evaluate what went wrong, and change the process for the better. This philosophy of continuous improvement, known in the business management literature as *kaizen*, was made famous by the Toyota production system in mid-20th-century Japan.[3]

Although the philosophy of kaizen is not new, the problems of monitoring a large and high-frequency dataset have never been more prevalent. Anomaly detection is a way for businesses to ensure that their data is reliable or that their operations are running as expected. Here are some examples of use cases for monitoring for deviations:

- System health to ensure that a process or machinery has not degraded or broken
- Fraud and cybersecurity breaches to identify and forestall nefarious actions
- Spikes in demand that will have to be met with increased supply
- Anomalous events within a supply chain that can be better optimized
- Social media content and activity for brand management or new product opportunities
- Manufacturing quality control to minimize waste and maximize consumer protection

How Anomaly Detection Works

Anomaly detection broadly uses past data to identify when previous, current, or future observations fall outside of an expected range. Anomaly detection within Power BI line charts consists of two distinct functions: identification and explanation.

The *identification* component is when Power BI flags a data point from a time series that exceeds some defined confidence threshold. Outside of Power BI, confidence

---

3 "Toyota Production System" (*https://oreil.ly/_5GZd*), Toyota, accessed January 7, 2024.

bands for a dataset can be calculated in a way that is relatively simple (e.g., falling within 95% of the past observations, being three standard deviations from the mean) or more complex (e.g., training a machine learning algorithm to predict a variable of interest and flagging values observed to be more than two standard errors from their expected value). Power BI determines these bands from a measure of "sensitivity" that is adjustable from 1% to 100%. Higher values correspond to lower confidence bands, which means more outliers are likely to be detected.

Within Power BI, anomaly detection is determined from a spectral residual (SR) algorithm that identifies which small sections of a time series stand out as outliers and a convolutional neural network (CNN) algorithm that makes predictions from patterns in visual data. You can learn more about deep learning generally from "A Simple Neural Network" on page 296, and you can also read Microsoft's technical blog post on the SR-CNN model (*https://oreil.ly/MEkyF*).

The second component of anomaly detection is a root cause analysis that attempts to explain *why* an observation falls outside of an expected range. It compares the time series of interest against other candidate variables within the report, but most importantly, the user has to define which variables are included in this analysis. This is when a data analyst should use domain knowledge to discriminate between which other time series could plausibly impact the outcome and which time series are sufficiently unrelated that they would only add noise.

Limitations of Anomaly Detection

We have found anomaly detection to be seemingly accurate in identifying which observations are outliers. This is, of course, an imprecise science because there is no clear definition of what an outlier is. That said, the flagging component of anomaly detection is useful for considering which data points merit additional analysis.

The root cause analysis, however, has much more limited results. The output tends to produce many false positives as to which variables correspond to a specific anomaly. The biggest flaw of this method is how the dataset is not always complete enough to include the true reason for anomalous outcomes. This is not to discourage the use of anomaly detection—instead it is to emphasize that you should not make business decisions based on what you see in a root cause analysis.

From our experience, results of the root cause analysis that measure a strength at or near 50% tend to be the least reliable. Read those with an extra grain of salt. We also find that root cause analysis is most helpful when there is aggregated data, such as monthly sales coming from different stores in various regions based on distinct products. Such results are more useful because they suggest which store/region/product is underperforming.

Anomaly detection is only available in the line chart visual and only with time series data. It also does not function with multiple time series or with forecasts.

Demo 5-3: Anomaly Detection with Taxi Trip Data

This demo will show how a business can use anomaly detection to identify outliers and consider possible explanations for the anomalous outcome. We continue with the same dataset on taxi trips in New York City. Be sure to follow the steps in Demo 5-1 to prepare your report, or you can download it from our GitHub page (*https://oreil.ly/ timeseriesdemo*) with preloaded data.

If you are picking up from the previous demo, be sure to turn off the forecast since that prevents anomaly detection from working. We only want to consider the first era of data (as shown in Figure 5-20), so set the week slicer from 1/4/2009 to 3/2/2014.

First select the line chart visual and then click the Analytics icon. Scroll down to the bottom and toggle "Find anomalies" so that it is on. Within Options, increase the Sensitivity to 85% and click Apply.

Figure 5-24 shows the confidence intervals as the gray area surrounding the time series based on the level of sensitivity you input. All of the observations falling beyond that range are tagged with a gray circle.

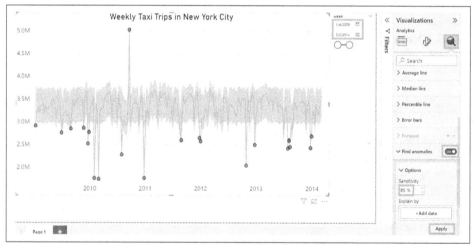

Figure 5-24. Using anomaly detection to identify outliers

These results would be incredibly useful for a taxi company wanting to understand what went well on days of unusually high demand and what went poorly on days of unusually low demand. You may have noticed that many tags correspond to a holiday week, such as Thanksgiving, Hanukkah, Christmas, and New Year's Day. These holiday weeks appear to the algorithm as anomalous because there is no variable indicating their presence. Adding such a variable would make those low-demand weeks expected and, thus, likely not identified as anomalous.

Next we will explore what could be causing the unexpected observations using a built-in root cause analysis. Select the anomaly marker on 8/28/2011 to reveal a new Anomalies pane on the right (Figure 5-25).

 If the anomaly marker on 8/28/2011 is not visible for you, make sure you are using the week group and the specified date range and that the sensitivity level matches the values from the previous step. If that still does not work, try increasing the sensitivity some more.

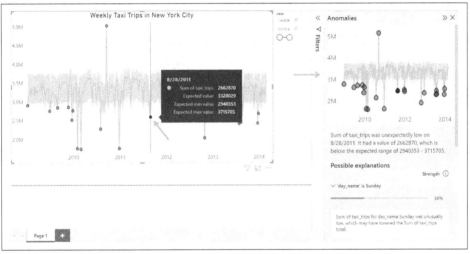

Figure 5-25. Selecting an anomaly marker opens an Anomalies pane on the right

The Anomalies pane explains why this observation was flagged as an outlier. Scrolling down reveals possible explanations, including new visuals that can be added to your report (Figure 5-26).

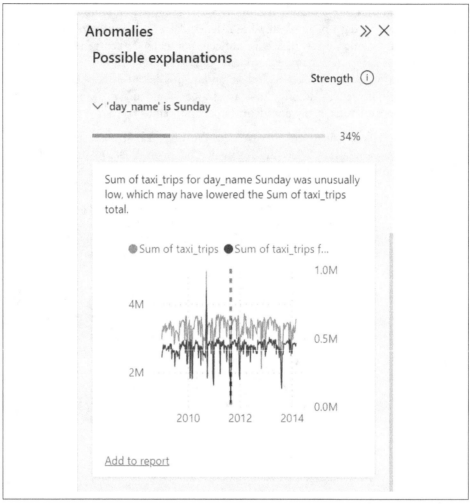

Figure 5-26. Listing of possible explanations for why a single observation was anomalous

The first possibility given is that Sunday was exceptionally low. The visual shows that Sundays (the bottom line) already have fewer taxi trips than non-Sundays (the top line). This aligns with what we already learned from Figure 5-12 in Demo 5-1. But the fact that this was flagged means this particular day was exceptionally low, even for a Sunday. Why? This is where the ability of anomaly detection stops and you, as a data analyst, have to use your domain knowledge to delve deeper.

In this case, we searched "8/28/2011 New York City" online and found on that day, the city was being hit by Hurricane Irene, which by then had become a tropical storm. No wonder the demand for taxis was low!

Explore the results on your own by considering the following questions:

- How many anomalies are there when you change the sensitivity from 85% to 80%?

- Why do you think there are more downward than upward spikes in this time series?

- When do most of the anomalies occur?

- What was the expected range of outcomes during the week of 9/19/2010? What was the actual outcome?

- Are the given reasons for what potentially caused the anomaly on 9/19/2010 satisfactory to you? Why or why not?

Summary

Data-driven companies do not ignore intuition; instead, they inform their experiences and instincts with the right insights. We focused on two ways to leverage the power of machine learning and artificial intelligence with times series data. First, we used trend lines and forecasting to identify what happened in the past and what could happen in the future. Next, we explored anomaly detection, which identifies instances in the past that contradict expectations as well as possible causes of the anomalies.

Power BI offers quick ways to use all these tools within existing visuals that do not require a paid plan. The solutions are optimized to allow a user to quickly go from data ingestion to data insights. In the next chapter, we pick up on another free AI tool hidden in plain sight: cluster analysis. However, users seeking more sophisticated or robust methods should look ahead to Chapter 10 on training a machine learning model with Azure or Chapter 11 on leveraging Python and R in Power BI.

## CHAPTER 6

Cluster Analysis and Segmentation

At this very moment, you may be one of many people reading this book. Maybe you are a college student assigned the book for class or a junior analyst in finance looking to advance your career. You could also be a Power BI developer who bought a digital copy with professional development funds or a data scientist wanting a faster way to visualize data. Those are all examples of marketing personas: semi-fictional characters used to describe groups of customers with similar qualities or behaviors. Marketers then use these customer segments to better meet demand with the best product at the best place at the best price with the best promotion.

Customer segmentation has a long history in business, but the rise of the digital age made it easier than ever to make data-driven decisions about customers. The right kind of data can reverse the way customer segments are designed. Instead of forcing customers into predefined groups, machine learning can leverage customer data to build a model that clusters similar customers together. This can uncover previously unseen patterns in data to help a business offer a better product or service.

Cluster Analysis for Business

Creating marketing personas is not the only application of cluster analysis; in fact, there are many ways an organization can leverage this machine learning algorithm, including:

- Clustering customer reviews to detect themes for new product development
- Detecting suspected financial fraud with unlabeled data
- Identifying patterns of churn to reduce attrition rates
- Grouping app users by browsing activity for better UX
- Clustering like-minded voters for more targeted political messaging

- Segmenting products to improve inventory or distribution
- Grouping geographic locations to define sales regions
- Identifying similar customers for cross-selling opportunities

What all of these examples have in common is how the groups are automatically determined from an algorithm instead of being predetermined from some rules-based criteria or heuristics. It is, however, still up to the developer to use their domain knowledge to determine which variables should be included in a cluster analysis.

Segmentation Meets Data Science

This chapter is about cluster analysis, or as it's sometimes known, clustering or segmentation. *Cluster analysis* is the class of methods that organizes data into their most similar groups. There are many types of algorithms that perform cluster analysis; however, here we will highlight one of the most popular: k-means.

K-means clustering is an unsupervised machine learning algorithm that separates data into *k*-many clusters based on their similarity. It is unsupervised because there is no objectively true answer for when a specific observation belongs in one cluster relative to another.

The best way to explain k-means clustering is with an example. Imagine you work in an IT department and are given a dataset of help desk tickets. The data includes one column with a numeric score of how important the task is and another column with a numeric score of the effort required to resolve the ticket. Your manager wants to create three different workflows depending on the importance of and effort required for each incoming ticket, and asks you to create a system that assigns tickets into one of the three workflows.

This, you realize, is a problem best solved with cluster analysis. Let's first plot out the data, shown in Figure 6-1. Now it is time to apply k-means clustering with $k = 3$ groups.

The first step of the k-means clustering algorithm is to randomly select *k*-many points (in this case, three) within the range of the dataset. We can neatly plot this on a scatter chart because we are clustering our dataset with only two numeric values. Each *centroid*, represented as a diamond in Figure 6-2, will become the center of its own cluster.

Next, each data point is assigned to a cluster based on whichever centroid is closest. Our first iteration of clustering is done (Figure 6-2), but we are not finished.

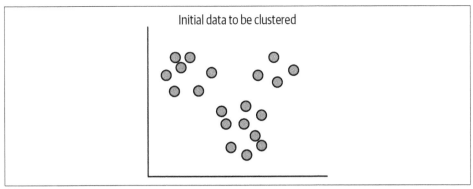

Figure 6-1. A scatter chart with two numeric axes: one for importance and another for effort

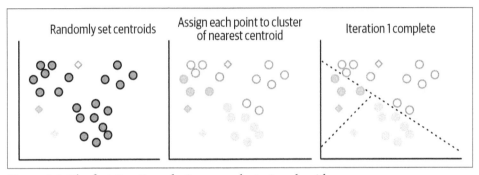

Figure 6-2. The first iteration of a 3-means clustering algorithm

Now that all observations are assigned an initial group, move the centroid to the average value of that group—thus the name *k-means*. Next, check if any observations are closer to a different centroid and reassign them if they are. This finishes the second iteration (Figure 6-3).

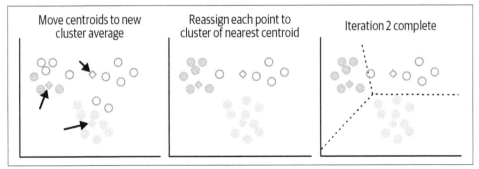

Figure 6-3. The second iteration of a 3-means clustering algorithm

Repeat the process again, as shown in Figure 6-4, by moving the centroids to the new mean values of their clusters. Next, check if any observations have changed groups. In this case, just one data point needs to be reassigned. The third iteration is done.

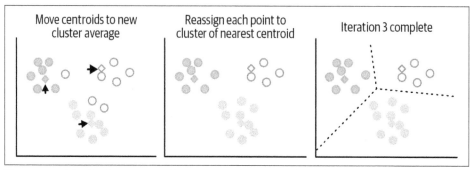

Figure 6-4. The final iteration of a 3-means clustering algorithm

You move the centroids again, but this time, all observations remain closest to the same centroid (not pictured). Since the solution is now stable, you are done. Not only do you have clusters for all observations in the dataset, but you also know how to assign future observations based on their values. These assignment areas are visualized in Figures 6-2 through 6-4 by the dotted lines.

There are many ways to expand on a k-means clustering algorithm. We leave that for the eager reader to explore on their own, but you now have a foundational understanding of how a popular clustering algorithm works.

Preprocessing Data for Cluster Analysis

One serious problem with k-means cluster analysis is its sensitivity to outliers. Consider the example above and imagine there was now an outlier far to the right of the other observations. This would move the centroid over toward that single point, making the outlier its own cluster and splitting the rest of the observations between just two clusters, as shown in Figure 6-5.

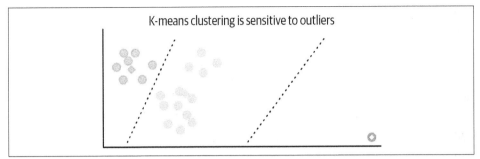

Figure 6-5. Introducing a single outlier can change the assignment of clusters in k-means clustering

Another problem with k-means clustering is that the results are sensitive to a variable's scale since the centroids are determined by the distance between points. For example, consider two points with a value of $1 and $2; they are one unit (dollar) apart. Now consider those same points measured in pennies as 100 cents and 200 cents; they are now 100 units (cents) apart. K-means clustering may assign a point to different clusters when different scales are used, as shown in Figure 6-6, even though the values are the same.

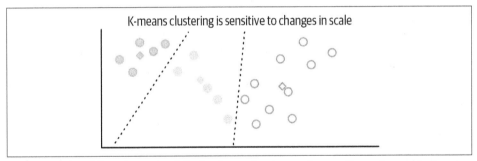

Figure 6-6. Doubling the scale of the horizontal axis can change the assignment of clusters in k-means clustering

One common way to reduce the impact of outliers and eliminate the impact of scale is to first normalize data before running it through a k-means clustering algorithm. *Normalization* is a preprocessing stop that scales a variable from 0 (its minimum value) to 1 (its maximum value). Normalization is sometimes used synonymously with the preprocessing step of standardization; however, *standardization* is often used specifically to mean that a variable is scaled to the number of standard deviations away from its mean of 0. All variables used in k-means clustering should first be normalized.

How Cluster Analysis Works in Power BI

There are two visuals within Power BI that include a built-in cluster analysis feature: table and scatter chart. Both produce results pretty quickly and allow the user to download the cluster variables once calculated. In each method, a user can set the number of clusters or let the algorithm select a value for k. We recommend the data analyst set this number themself based on what makes sense for the business use case.

Although scatter charts can be useful for visualizing data in two-dimensional space, you cannot cluster on more than three variables within a scatter chart (the third variable being the "size" dimension). Tables are preferred because clusters there are determined by more observations.

The results from a cluster analysis are stored within the data model. This means they can then be used throughout a report, such as in other visuals or as filters.

Under the hood, cluster analysis in Power BI uses *expectation maximization* (EM) *clustering*. This is a scalable, more efficient, and more robust algorithm than k-means; however, it takes a similar approach of iteratively trying to solve calculations until a solution converges. The first component (expectation) assumes every cluster has a different distribution and calculates the likelihood that each data point belongs to each cluster. The second component (maximization) updates the maximum likelihood estimation of each cluster's distribution based on the observations within the current iteration of the cluster. If you are looking for a light beach read on the subject, check out the original paper behind expectation maximization clustering (*https://oreil.ly/zKgGX*).

But Jennifer and Thomas, you ask, why did you spend so much of this chapter discussing k-means clustering when Power BI uses EM clustering? Good question! K-means clustering is easier to visualize for those who are new to cluster analysis, making it a better algorithm for exploring key concepts like convergence, normalization, and outliers. K-means clustering is also popular within the field of artificial intelligence and can be readily applied with Python and R. EM clustering, however, performs better than k-means clustering and is less sensitive to outliers and changes in scale. Just remember to normalize your data first if you use k-means clustering in the future.

Limitations of Cluster Analysis

There are several limitations to know about when using the built-in cluster analysis in Power BI, including the following:

- The clustering algorithm only works with numeric variables that are an aggregate in the data model.
- Category variables may be included but only if they have already been converted to 0s and 1s.
- It supports a maximum of 15 variables.
- Clusters do not update on data refresh, so new observations are added as a blank cluster.
- Like all unsupervised machine learning algorithms, there is no optimal answer for what the best number of clusters should be or for which observation should be in which cluster.

You can also perform cluster analysis using Python or R in Power BI. See Chapter 11 to learn more.

Demo 6-1: Cluster Analysis with AirBnB Data

Let's dive into a clear example of how a business can use cluster analysis to produce better results in a recommendation system. For this demo, we will be using data scraped from 100 AirBnB listings in the Italian province of Trentino (Figure 6-7). This dataset does not have extreme outliers, so we do not need to first normalize the data when using the EM clustering algorithm built into Power BI. We will use two such cluster analysis tools to segment the observations into groups of similar listings.

Figure 6-7. Sample AirBnB listing in northern Italy

The first step is to load in the dataset, found on this book's GitHub page. Open a new Power BI report and click the "Get data" drop-down arrow (not the "Get data" text!) and select Web (Figure 6-8).

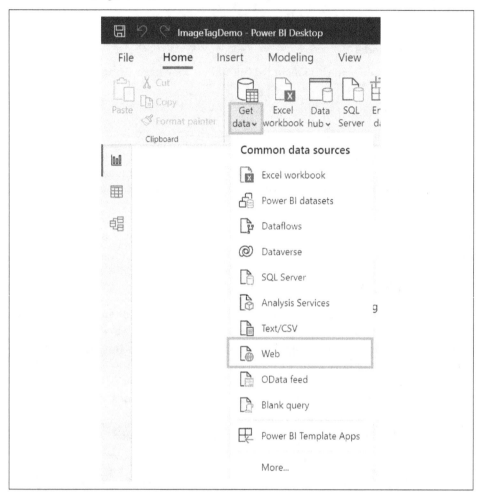

Figure 6-8. Adding data from a URL

Then paste this link (*https://raw.githubusercontent.com/tomweinandy/ai-with-power-bi/main/Chapter6/TrentinoListings.csv*) under URL and click OK (shown in Figure 6-9). We are not transforming the data, so click Load.

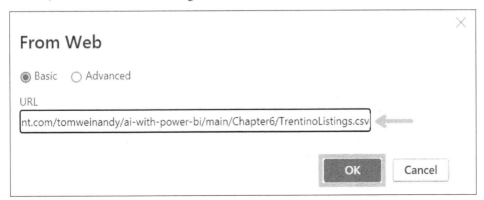

Figure 6-9. Pasting a URL of raw data from GitHub

Select the Scatter chart icon from the Visualizations pane (Figure 6-10). Place the name variable in the Values well, review_scores_rating under X Axis, and price under Y Axis. Note that the name variable is just being used as an ID and is not part of the clustering calculation.

 Not only must your variables be numeric, but they must be an aggregate, shown in Power BI with the Greek Σ (capital sigma). Your aggregate variables should begin with "Sum of…," and you should completely avoid the "Don't summarize" option.

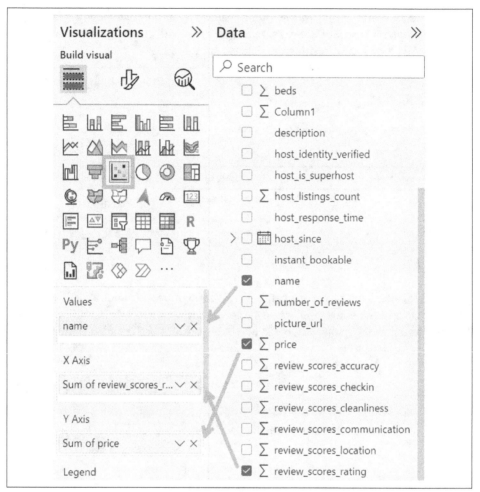

Figure 6-10. Finding the scatter chart icon

Resize your visual so that it takes up a majority of your canvas. We also increased the size of the markers and fonts for the screenshot in Figure 6-11, but that is optional for you. First select your visual and then click the three ellipsis icon, which will be in one of the corners. Then select "Automatically find clusters."

A Clusters window will pop up and give you the option of changing the name and description. For the sake of this example, add the arbitrary number 4 under "Number of clusters." Although we can leave this blank to let our algorithm automatically determine the number of groups, in this case we will require four (Figure 6-12). Click OK.

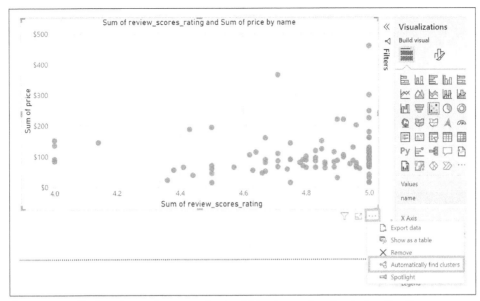

Figure 6-11. Performing a cluster analysis within the scatter chart visualization

Figure 6-12. Setting the number of clusters

You now have four clusters, shown in Figure 6-13. Most importantly though, you will see under the Data pane on the right that the clusters have been added to the data model. The same variable is then added under the Visualizations pane within the Legend well, which is how it shows up on the scatter chart on the canvas.

Remember that when clusters are added to the data model, they are visible throughout the report. You can always delete the variable if you change your mind about using it by right-clicking it within the Data pane and selecting "Delete from model." You can also keep it and use it on other visuals or other pages.

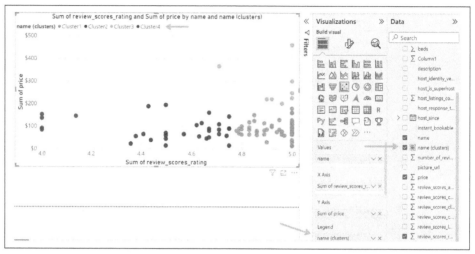

Figure 6-13. Running a cluster analysis, which creates a new variable in the data model

Nice work! Now save your report as a good practice. Next, we will perform another cluster analysis using a different visual: the table.

Open a new page and select the Table icon (Figure 6-14). Resize the visual on the canvas and make sure it is first selected. Then add "name" as the first column. This will be the unique field to which the clusters are assigned. Next, add all of the aggregate variables (those preceded with a Σ) except for Column1 (which we leave unsummarized because it is an index). Double-check that you have "name" selected and all other variables begin with "Sum of" or "Average of." You can always go back and add in more columns after the clusters are determined.

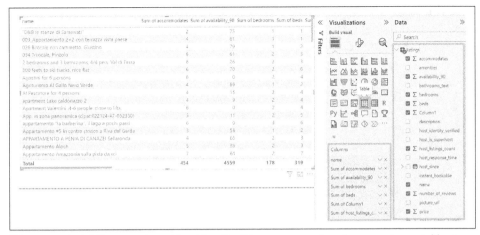

Figure 6-14. Adding a unique identifier (in this case, name) and aggregate variables to a table visualization

Next, select the ellipsis and then "Automatically find clusters," as shown previously in Figure 6-11.

Now change the name to avoid duplication. Under Name, type Clusters, and this time let the algorithm automatically determine the number of clusters. Click OK (Figure 6-15).

Figure 6-15. Allowing the algorithm to automatically determine the number of clusters

Notice in Figure 6-16 that "Clusters" now appears in the Data pane, the Visualizations pane, and as the rightmost column of the table visual. It appears that the algorithm selected $k = 3$ for the number of clusters.

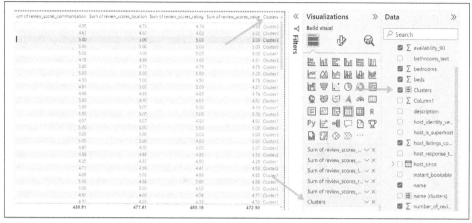

Figure 6-16. Adding clusters to the data model and visual

We can also visually see how these clusters are different from our first set. Return to the scatter chart and replace Legend with the new Clusters variable, as shown in Figure 6-17.

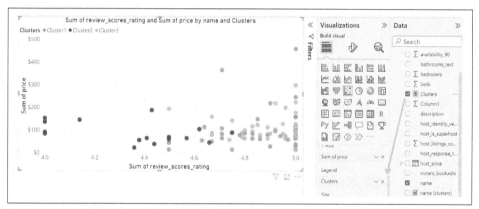

Figure 6-17. Adding the newly identified cluster to the previously used scatter chart

You'll see that the data points are not as cleanly separated. This makes sense because the cluster analysis performed within the table visual included more than just those two variables on the scatter chart.

As a final example of how to use clusters to build out an entire report for business decision making, download this one (*https://oreil.ly/ch6_pbix*) hosted on this book's GitHub. The solution provides three segments of AirBnB listings. The user can click on the slicer in the top-right box to cross-filter on each of the clusters and see how the descriptions of the three groups of listings change.

For example, Figure 6-18 shows the results for Cluster1. These AirBnB locations can be called "value listings" because they have high ratings but still affordable prices. If we work for AirBnB, we would want to prioritize these options for users who are more experienced travelers but tend to be price-sensitive.

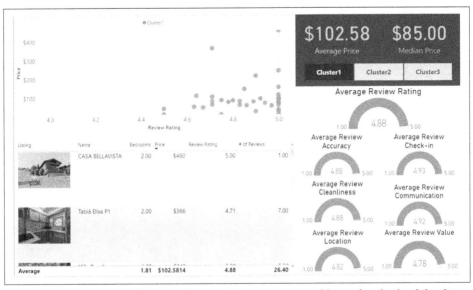

Figure 6-18. A segment of AirBnB listings that contains good bang-for-the-buck bookings

Next, Cluster2 offers even lower prices—and even lower ratings (Figure 6-19). These properties should be served to customers who in the past have booked budget locations.

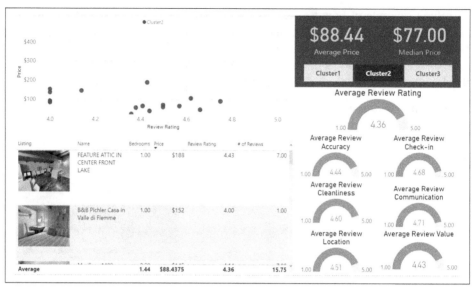

Figure 6-19. A segment of AirBnB listings that are ideal for travelers who seek the lowest-cost option

Finally, Cluster3, shown in Figure 6-20, has the highest ratings—but also the highest prices. These listings are best for travelers willing to pay for quality.

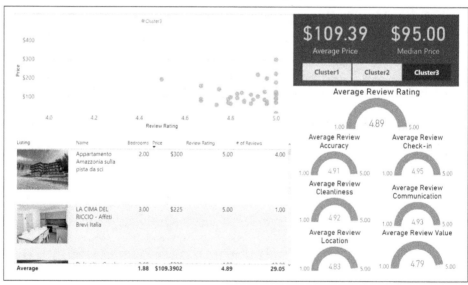

Figure 6-20. A segment of AirBnB listings that are ideal for high-income travelers looking for the best experience

Explore the results on your own by considering the following questions:

- Using a table chart, perform a cluster analysis with all of the numeric variables excluding Column1 and all reviews. How do the results compare to the example from the demo?

- Using a scatter chart, add a variable to the Size well and perform the cluster analysis. How do the results compare to the example from the demo?

- Theoretically speaking, what are the maximum and minimum number of clusters you can set for this dataset?

- From the table chart, which of the three clusters is most popular in terms of the number of stays? Explain how you came to this answer.

- Use any of the previous scatter charts with price and review score as the axes. Now add a trend line to the visual. Is there a positive or negative relationship between price and review score for all of the listings? Does this change when filtering only one cluster at a time?

Summary

Cluster analysis is a useful way to segment large amounts of data into a handful of groups for better analysis and decision making. The expectation maximization clustering built into Power BI provides an easy and efficient tool to cluster data with a few clicks. It is also more robust for outliers and scaling than the more popular k-means clustering.

Cluster analysis is also a core competency for anyone studying data science and artificial intelligence. Although much more attention is given to supervised machine learning algorithms that are trained with labeled datasets, there are many business applications for unsupervised machine learning models like cluster analysis. This chapter's demonstration gives a compelling example of how a data analyst can leverage this AI tool to build an actionable Power BI report with segmented products.

We hope you explore the cluster analysis feature built into the scatter chart and table visuals or train your own algorithm within Power BI using Python and R, as described in Chapter 11.

## CHAPTER 7

Diving Deeper: Using Azure AI Services

Microsoft is making considerable investments in artificial intelligence and business solutions. AI is one of the building blocks of the future, along with mixed reality, quantum computing, and blockchain.

All of these technologies, however, are data hungry. As a consequence, organizations are moving toward an intelligent data platform and therefore will need to consider better ways of handling their data. They may need to design and implement a data modernization strategy, which could mean upgrading on-premises estates, planning hybrid estates, or becoming cloud-first such that the organization prioritizes storing new data only in the cloud. As businesses expand to 24-hour global operations, they will need to consider how to manage and monitor globally distributed datasets while offering cloud-scale analytics to ensure that they are making the right decisions at the speed of the global customer.

Businesses also need to trust the results of these technologies, and data visualization is one crucial way of helping companies to make data-based and AI-based decisions. Power BI can build trust in the data and AI operations.

We can use AI tools, such as ChatGPT, for assistance from a business or personal perspective, using natural language to interact with them. For example, ChatGPT can help you create a data dictionary. In fact, we will do this in one of the chapter exercises. However, it's not enough to throw a few questions at ChatGPT and expect it to define your data dictionary (yet!).

This chapter will look at ways to use AI in Power BI. We will look at Azure AI Services in Power BI and how we can use ChatGPT. Azure AI Services offers pretrained machine learning models integrated directly into Power BI. It can obtain data from various sources such as documents, images, and social media feeds. We will look at importing ChatGPT content into a Power BI workbook as an exercise.

Supporting Data-Driven Decisions with a Data Dictionary

Before diving into AI tools, organizations should have a *data dictionary*. However, organizations often like to run before they can walk, so they may start using AI without establishing a good business intelligence estate first. Does your organization have a data dictionary? If not, it's a great way of standardizing data definitions. It can also help facilitate data sharing, which can be more complicated than it should be within organizations, and help to improve data quality.

How can you get started with a data dictionary? First, it is good to start broadly by identifying the data sources the dictionary should cover. It could include databases, spreadsheets, or other data repositories. These datasets could be internal or they could be external, such as open source or rented third-party datasets from research companies.

It is essential to discern the scope of the data dictionary. You can define its content by determining the specific data elements, attributes, or fields that should be incorporated. Be sure to consider both structured and unstructured data. For each element, define the name, description, datatype, size, and any other relevant attributes. You may also want to include additional information, such as the source system, owner, or data quality rules.

It is also important to determine relationships, such as dependencies or hierarchies. This will help ensure that the data dictionary is comprehensive and consistent enough to support your data initiatives.

The data dictionary can support data governance. If your organization finds it difficult to get started on data governance initiatives, the process of building the dictionary can help determine the roles and responsibilities for maintaining it. This activity could include defining a data stewardship program or establishing data quality metrics.

By following these steps, you can create an extensive data dictionary that will provide a workable understanding of the data within your organization and improve data management and governance. This initiative will help Power BI to be successful in AI and BI, particularly in the area of automation.

Power BI can support businesses in making data-driven decisions in many crucial business areas. AI automation can help to smooth out external as well as internal processes. For example, AI can help companies engage customers in various ways. AI can improve customer service by responding directly to customers who make more straightforward inquiries. The business could even consider completely automating communication. For instance, say a small business has a larger organization as a customer and wants to ask the larger organization when it will pay an invoice. The accountant could use an AI chatbot on the larger company's website to submit the inquiry. The AI chatbot could take the details about the invoice and interrogate the larger company's payment system to identify the payment date.

Power BI provides access to a set of functions from Azure AI Services to enrich your data in the self-service data prep for dataflows. Currently, the Azure AI Services supported in Power BI are Sentiment Analysis, Keyphrase Extraction, Language Detection, and Image Tag.

Azure AI Services is available to businesses with a Power BI Pro subscription. See the end of Chapter 1 for details, including how to sign up for a free trial.

What Is Azure AI Services?

Azure AI Services is an umbrella term covering a range of services in vision, speech, language, and Azure OpenAI, to name a few. In addition, Microsoft often adds new services and features. Starting in July 2023, Azure AI Services encompassed a range of services that were previously known as Cognitive Services and Azure Applied AI Services. You may continue to see these names in Azure billing, cost analyses, price lists, and price APIs. In line with the latest changes, we will use Azure AI Services in this text.

It is possible to use Azure OpenAI to access AI services, such as ChatGPT. Note, however, that Azure AI Services is a vast subject and could have its own book! Let's take a brief look at the topic.

Azure AI Services offers a wide range of AI-powered services that enable developers to add intelligent features to their applications without requiring machine learning or artificial intelligence expertise. Some services available in Azure AI Services include:

Vision
Services for image and video analysis, including Computer Vision, Face, Content Moderator, and Video Indexer

Speech
Services for speech-to-text and text-to-speech conversion, including Speech to Text, Text to Speech, and Speaker Recognition

Language
Services including natural language processing, Language Understanding (LUIS), Text Analytics, and Translator Text

Decisions
Services including automated help for decision making and recommendation systems, such as Personalizer and Anomaly Detector

Azure AI Services
Advanced coding and language models to support a variety of use cases

These services are aimed at both developers and data scientists. They are straightforward to use and integrate with other Azure services. In addition, Azure AI Services makes it uncomplicated for developers to add full AI powers to their applications.

Azure AI Services provides JSON data as an output and sophisticated pretrained models. It uses a range of popular data science frameworks, such as PyTorch, TensorFlow, and Keras, to democratize AI for businesses where developers and data scientists create applications in open source technology.

Since the technology is in the cloud, businesses can use Azure infrastructure to accelerate model development and deploy models on the cloud or even the edge.

As an aside, you may be familiar with the LUIS service. However, you should note that LUIS will be retired on October 1, 2025. Therefore, since April 1, 2023, you have not been able to create new LUIS resources, and this chapter will not cover LUIS. Instead, we will focus on the new conversational language-understanding service that will benefit from continued product support and multilingual capabilities.

Accessing Azure AI Services in Power BI

In Azure AI Services, the data undergoes a series of changes called *transformations*, which operate on the data to provide results. Power BI developers can create, maintain, and monitor Azure AI Services transformations using the self-service data preparation tools in Power BI dataflows.

The Azure AI Service data transformations run on the Power BI service behind the scenes, so you don't need to do anything to set them up. Power BI developers can integrate Azure AI Services with Power BI to add advanced analytics and machine learning capabilities to their data visualizations. For example, you can use Text Analytics to identify key phrases and sentiments in text data or Image Recognition to detect objects and faces in images.

Let's review the steps to use Azure AI Services with Power BI.

Creating an Azure AI Services Resource

There's no need to have a separate Azure AI Services subscription, but we have included the steps here for completeness's sake. This is an optional exercise if you want to know how to create an Azure AI Services resource in the Azure portal.

1. Sign in to the Azure portal (*https://portal.azure.com*).
2. At the top lefthand menu, you will see a "hamburger" menu (three horizontal lines). From this menu, select "Create a resource" (Figure 7-1).

Figure 7-1. Creating a resource in the Azure portal

3. In the search bar, type Azure AI Services.

4. Select AI Services from the drop-down menu.

5. On the AI Services page, click Create (Figure 7-2).

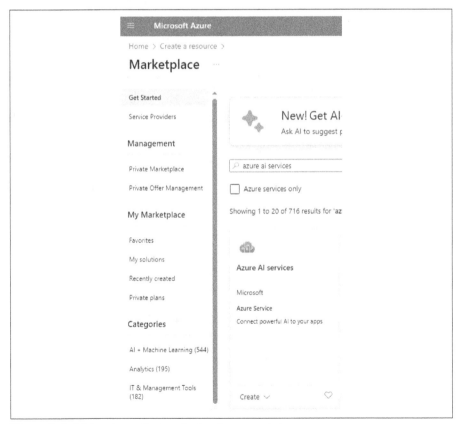

Figure 7-2. AI Services offerings in the Azure portal

6. Next, you will be taken to the Create AI Services page. Select the Create button (Figure 7-3).

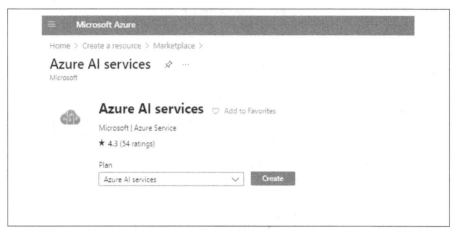

Figure 7-3. Next step to create Azure AI Services

7. On the next page, fill out the details there so that Azure can create the service (Figure 7-4).

8. Under the heading Project Details, choose your subscription, Resource Group, and the appropriate region for your resource. If you don't have a Resource Group, the portal will ask you to create one by specifying a Resource Group name.

9. Enter a unique name for your resource. In this example, the name is MakeYour-AIWork.

10. Choose the pricing tier. In this example, the pricing tier is Standard S0.

11. Review and accept the terms and conditions.

12. Click Create to create your Azure AI Services resource.

It will only take a moment to create the resource for you. Once it has been set up, you will receive an endpoint and subscription key. You will need both the endpoint and the subscription key to access the AI services APIs. You can also manage your Azure AI Services resource by monitoring billing and usage.

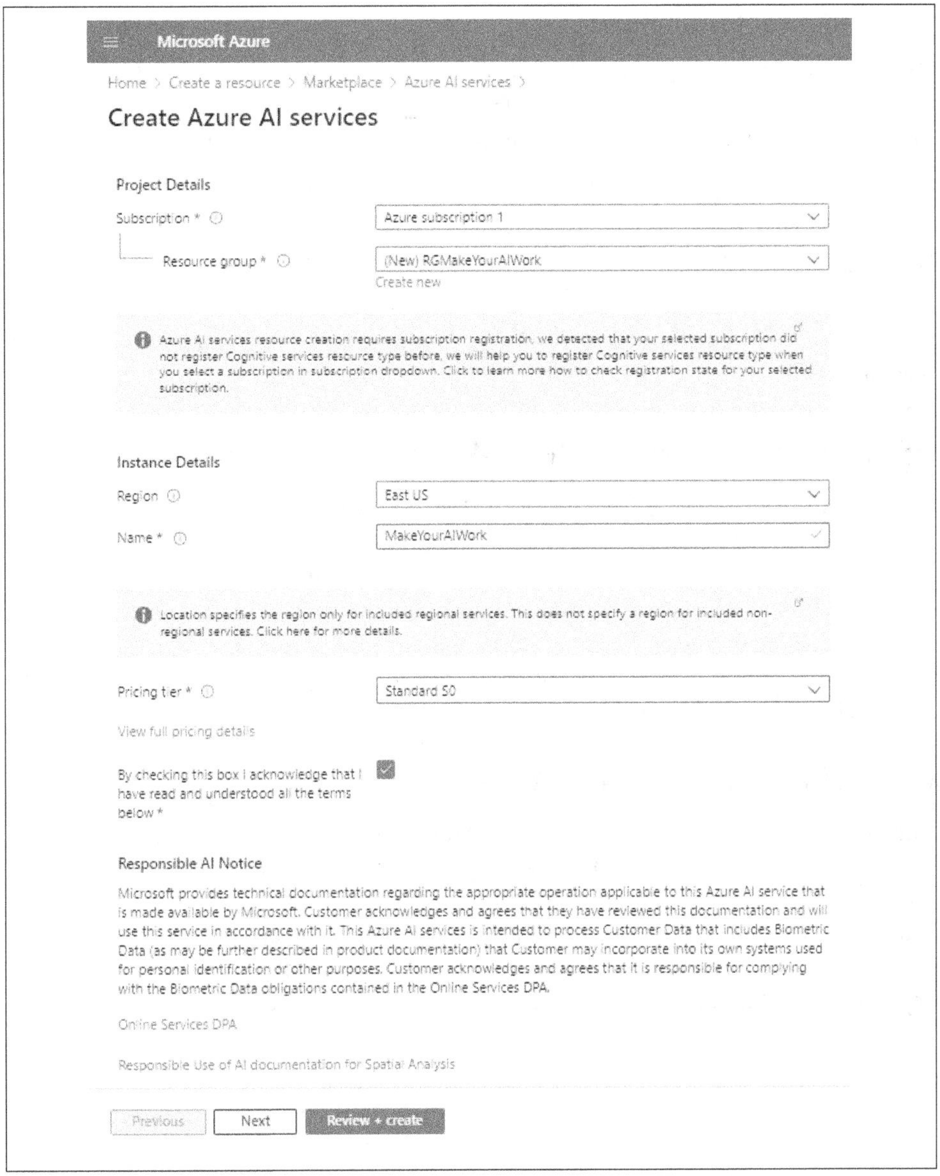

Figure 7-4. Providing the details that allow the creation of the Azure AI Services resource

Creating a Power BI Report

To use Azure AI Services with Power BI, you must create a Power BI report and connect it to the data source you want to analyze. If you have completed the previous tutorials in this book, you have made some Power BI reports already.

The next step is to add Azure AI Services to the Power BI report. From the business perspective, this will add advanced analytics and machine learning capabilities to your report, helping the organization make data-driven decisions using Power BI and AI.

This is covered in detail in Chapters 8 and 9, with relevant examples for you to walk through.

OpenAI ChatGPT and Power BI

One of the most exciting technological innovations of recent years is ChatGPT, which has demonstrated advanced language understanding and production. It can be used to create various AI-based applications that would not otherwise be possible without extensive AI expertise. These applications can work with humans to make us more productive or automate applications to make our lives easier. ChatGPT has the potential to revolutionize how we interact with technology and, even better, help us make our data storytelling so much easier.

What Is the Purpose of the Exercise?

This section will examine how we can use Power BI to access ChatGPT and display it on a Power BI dashboard next to data, helping users to place the data in context. The purpose is to demonstrate that we can use ChatGPT for a real-world purpose. Here, it is used to add up-to-date information about an online, publicly accessible data source and display it. If the organization uses external data sources, ChatGPT can help to keep the content updated if information about the data sources changes.

Exercise Prerequisites

In this exercise, you will connect the OpenAI API with Power BI. To do this, you will need the following subscriptions:

OpenAI ChatGPT API
> You will need the OpenAI ChatGPT API "pay as you go" subscription for this exercise. At the time of writing, using the API to access OpenAI ChatGPT is not free. Note that the OpenAI ChatGPT API and ChatGPT Plus subscriptions are billed separately. The API's pricing can be found at *https://openai.com/pricing*. The ChatGPT Plus subscription covers usage on *https://chat.openai.com* only and costs $20/month.

Power BI Pro
> At the time of writing, to create and run a streaming dataset, you need a workspace that's part of a Power BI Pro license (*https://oreil.ly/fgEuG*).

Azure OpenAI and Power BI Example

Let's start off with a copy of the workbook from Chapter 3. If you want to start with a fresh copy, please download a copy from this book's GitHub repository.

We'll begin with the first tab, which appears as shown in Figure 7-5.

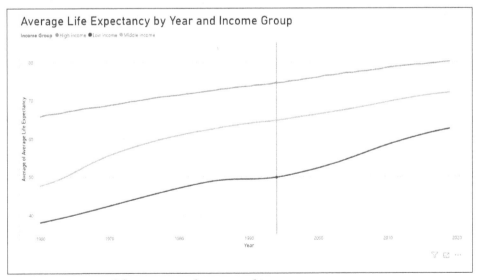

Figure 7-5. Average life expectancy by year and income group

Now, turn this data into a table in Power BI. Click on the visual and then go to the Visualizations pane on the righthand side (Figure 7-6).

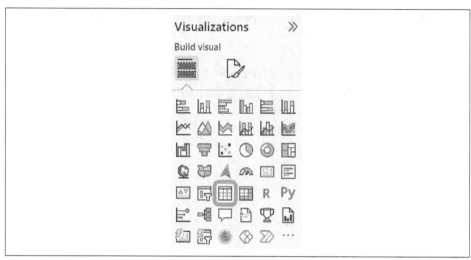

Figure 7-6. Visualizations pane with the table visual highlighted

When you click on the table icon, your Power BI canvas will appear as shown in Figure 7-7.

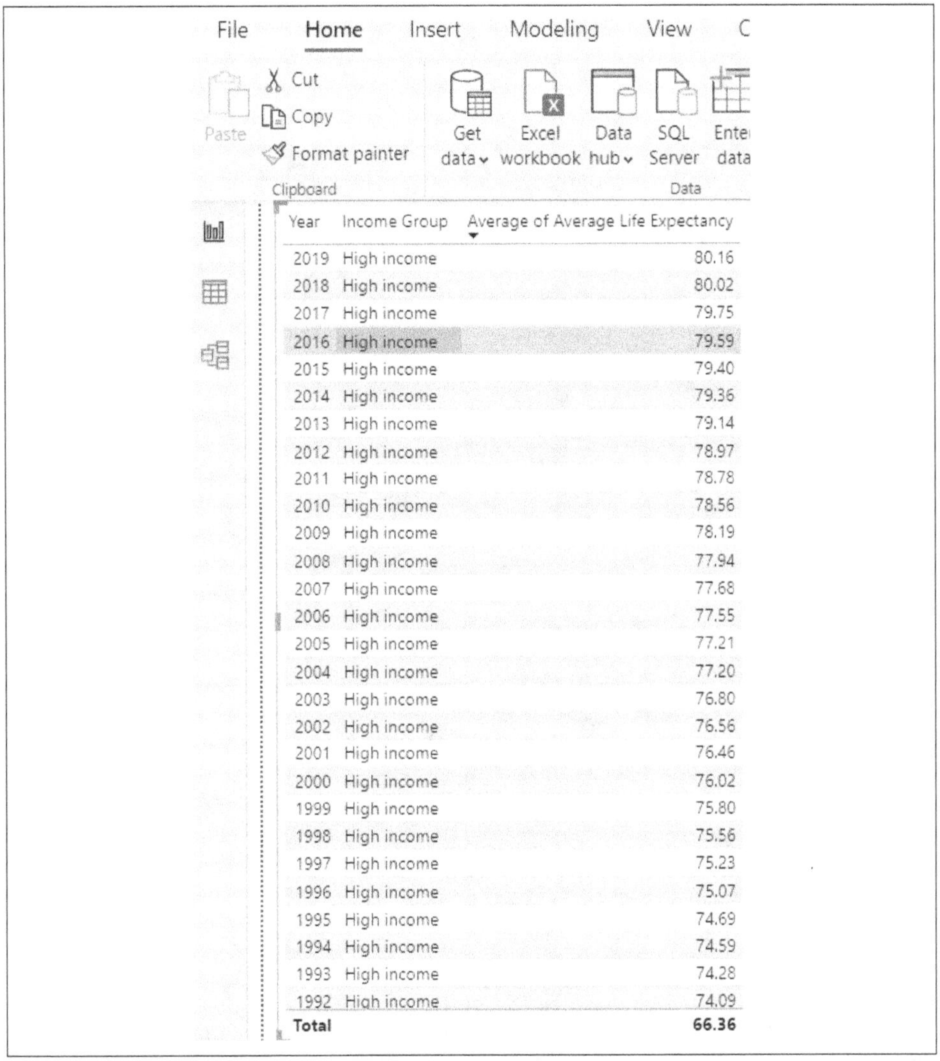

Figure 7-7. A table of life expectancy data in Power BI

The title "Average of Average Life Expectancy" doesn't read very well, does it? So let's change it to read "Average of Life Expectancy." To do this, click on the table and the Visualization pane again. Look for the column Average of Average Life Expectancy and right-click on it. Select Rename for this visual and rename the column (Figure 7-8).

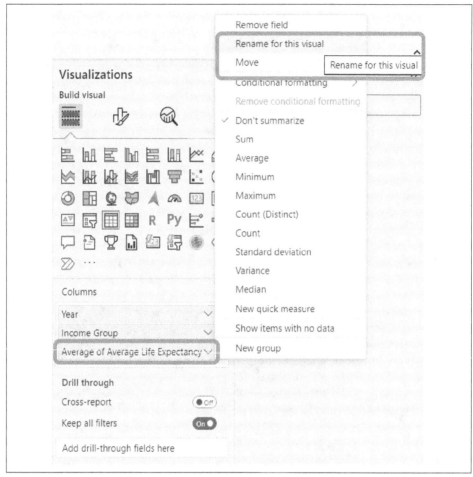

Figure 7-8. Renaming the column

Now that you have set up your workbook, save it as a new copy. In the next section, we will show you how to obtain the information you need from ChatGPT so it connects with Power Automate and Power BI.

Generating a Secret Key and Code from the OpenAI Website

Now for the fascinating part! In this section, we assume that you have a ChatGPT account already. Please head over to the ChatGPT website (*https://openai.com*) and log in. In the following steps, we want to get the API key from your profile.

To do this, go to the Documentation section (*https://oreil.ly/Rjmkd*) of the OpenAI website.

Once you head to the Documentation page, you may be required to log in again. After you are logged in, you can select "API keys" (Figure 7-9).

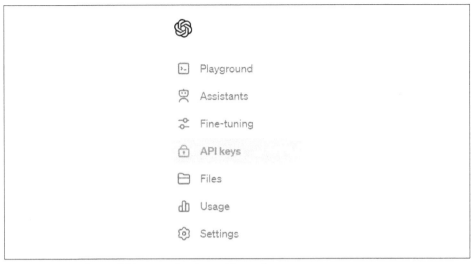

Figure 7-9. Finding API keys in the OpenAI panel

When you open the "API keys" page, you will be able to create a new API key. Click "Create new secret key" (Figure 7-10).

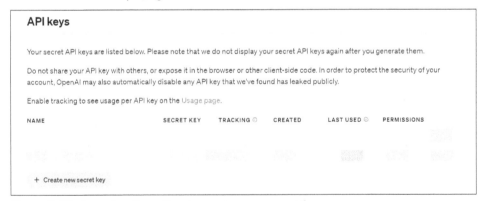

Figure 7-10. Accessing the option to create a new secret key

The area shown in Figure 7-11 will appear, and you can enter a name for your new secret API key.

Create new secret key

Name Optional

My Test Key

Permissions

All   Restricted   Read Only

Cancel   **Create secret key**

Figure 7-11. Naming your secret key

Click "Create secret key," and the OpenAI service will create a new API key for you (Figure 7-12).

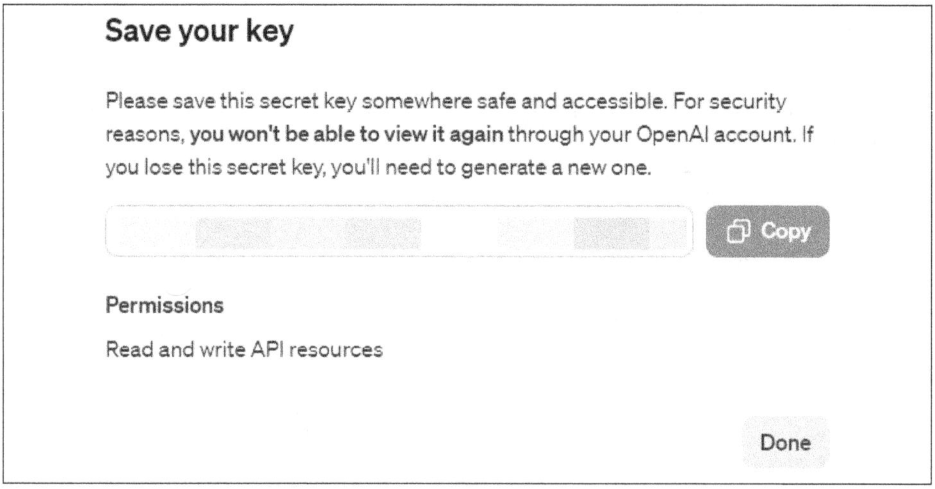

Save your key

Please save this secret key somewhere safe and accessible. For security reasons, **you won't be able to view it again** through your OpenAI account. If you lose this secret key, you'll need to generate a new one.

📋 Copy

Permissions

Read and write API resources

Done

Figure 7-12. Viewing the new API key

Copy the secret key by clicking on the green button with rectangles at the righthand side of the panel. Alternatively, use the keyboard shortcut Ctrl-C. Paste that information somewhere safe, such as a Notepad file, as you will need it later. Then, click Done.

We can now collect the information to connect ChatGPT with Power BI. From the OpenAI ChatGPT website, go to the Documents section and look for the "API reference" section (*https://oreil.ly/YMFUS*). Under the Getting Started section, open the "Making requests" section (Figure 7-13).

Figure 7-13. OpenAI ChatGPT API Reference

Scroll down the page until you find the black box with the heading "Making requests" and copy the URL in the first line (Figure 7-14). For safekeeping, you can paste the URL into your preferred text editor to hold in safekeeping while we progress through the exercise. Your link may appear different, but as of this writing, the link is *https://api.openai.com/v1/chat/completions*.

Making requests

You can paste the command below into your terminal to run your first API request. Make sure to replace $OPENAI_API_KEY with your secret API key.

```
1  curl https://api.openai.com/v1/chat/completions \
2    -H "Content-Type: application/json" \
3    -H "Authorization: Bearer $OPENAI_API_KEY" \
4    -d '{
5      "model": "gpt-3.5-turbo",
6      "messages": [{"role": "user", "content": "Say this is a test!"}],
7      "temperature": 0.7
8    }'
```

Figure 7-14. Create completion page

In a black box, you will see some code. You'll need to copy the code from the first curly bracket to the final curly bracket. For reference, Figure 7-15 shows the code with the irrelevant areas blurred out.

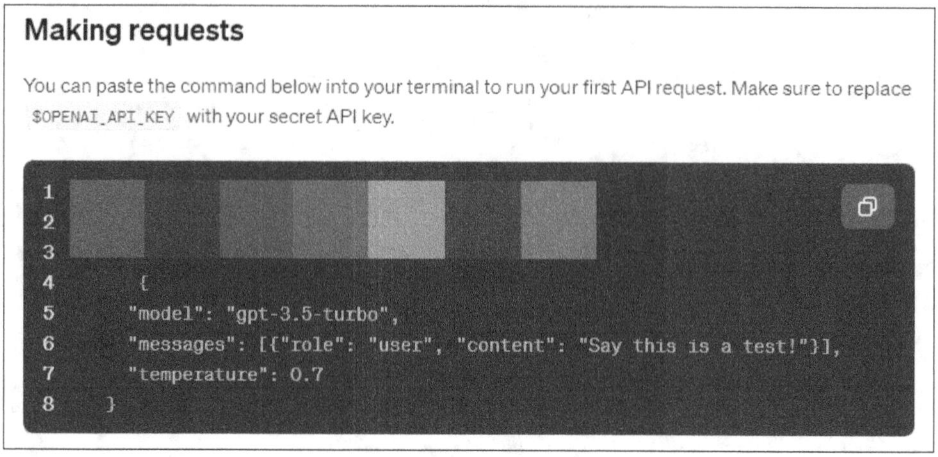

Making requests

You can paste the command below into your terminal to run your first API request. Make sure to replace `$OPENAI_API_KEY` with your secret API key.

```
1
2
3
4    {
5        "model": "gpt-3.5-turbo",
6        "messages": [{"role": "user", "content": "Say this is a test!"}],
7        "temperature": 0.7
8    }
```

Figure 7-15. Model specification code

Where the code says Say this is a test, change it to read **What is the World Data Bank life expectancy metric?** Our Power BI workbook will transmit the question to ChatGPT, which will return an answer for display on the Power BI workbook.

Tokens are the basic unit that OpenAI GPT models use to compute the length of a piece of text. They are groups of characters that sometimes align with words, but not always. The number of characters varies, and the token may include punctuation signs or emojis. In the default example, note that the number of tokens is set to 7. However, we must change the number of tokens to 1,500 to retrieve the entire text from the ChatGPT API call. Therefore, the code should appear as follows:

```
{
    "model": "gpt-3.5-turbo-instruct",
    "prompt": "What is the World Data Bank Life Expectancy metric?",
    "max_tokens": 1500,
    "temperature": 0
}
```

Copy and paste the code into a temporary holding space for now, such as a Notepad file. You will need it shortly. In the next step, we will go back to the Power BI portal and set up a streaming dataset in Power BI to store the code.

Creating a Streaming Power BI Dataset

Log into the Power BI service at *https://www.powerbi.com* to create a streaming Power BI dataset (Figure 7-16). You will need a Premium workspace to do this.

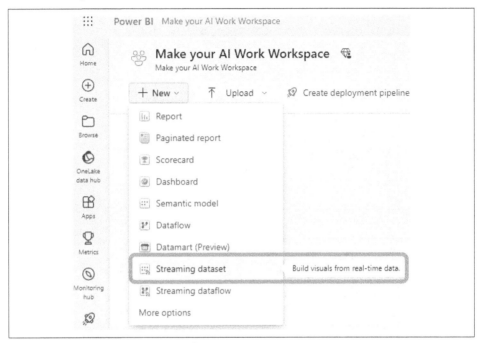

Figure 7-16. Creating a streaming dataset

Select "Streaming dataset" and you will see the options in Figure 7-17.

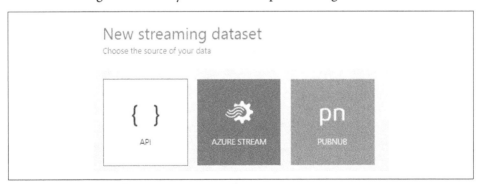

Figure 7-17. Options for a new streaming dataset

Select API and click Next. On the next page, shown in Figure 7-18, first give the dataset a name; here we have called it "ChatGPT dataset."

You will need to add an entry under Values from stream, which we will call ChatGPT Response. It should be in Text format.

Toggle "Historic data analysis" to on so you can keep the history. Then, click Create.

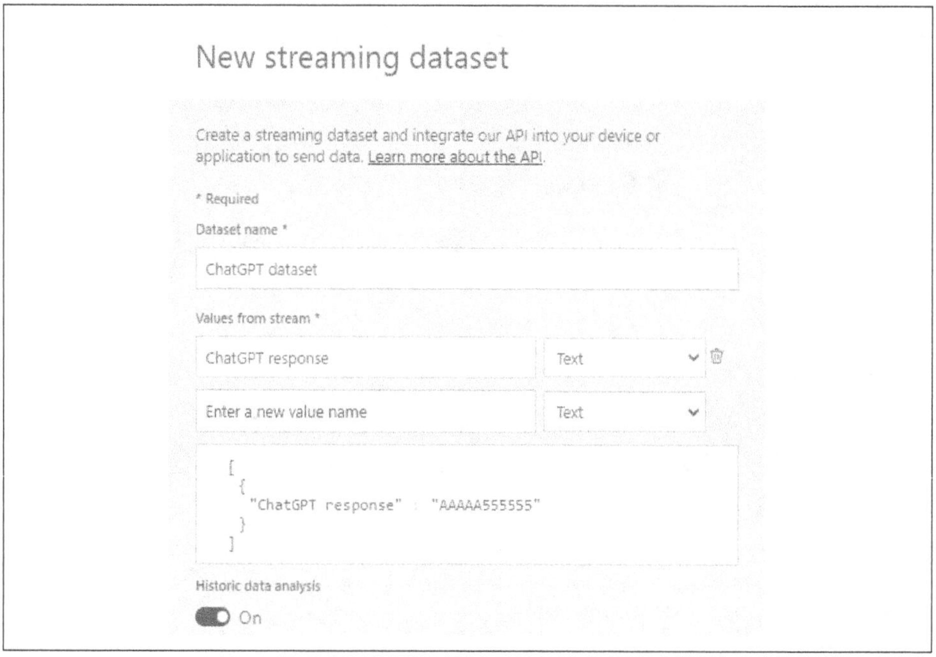

New streaming dataset

Create a streaming dataset and integrate our API into your device or application to send data. Learn more about the API.

* Required
Dataset name *

ChatGPT dataset

Values from stream *

| ChatGPT response | Text | 🗑 |
| Enter a new value name | Text | |

```
[
  {
    "ChatGPT response" : "AAAAA555555"
  }
]
```

Historic data analysis
🔵 On

Figure 7-18. Creating a Power BI streaming dataset for ChatGPT responses

When the streaming dataset is created, you will see a confirmation message (Figure 7-19).

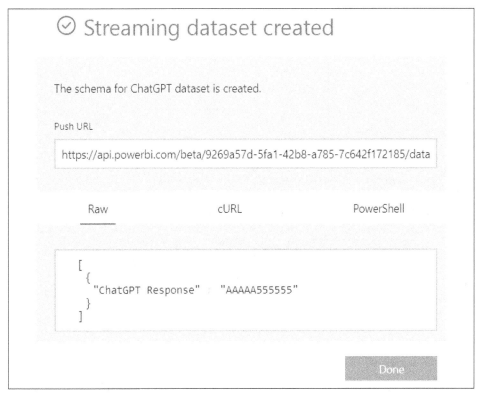

Figure 7-19. Streaming dataset created

Click Done. Power BI now creates our streaming dataset, which is listed in the Power BI workspace (Figure 7-20).

Figure 7-20. Viewing the ChatGPT dataset in the AI workspace

Now that the streaming dataset has been created, we can set up a Power Automate flow. To do this, go back to Power BI and select the Insert bar. From there, click Power Automate (Figure 7-21). Ensure that you are on the Report view.

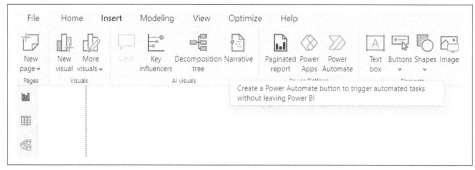

Figure 7-21. Setting up a Power Automate flow in Power BI

The screen in Figure 7-22 appears on the Power BI Desktop window.

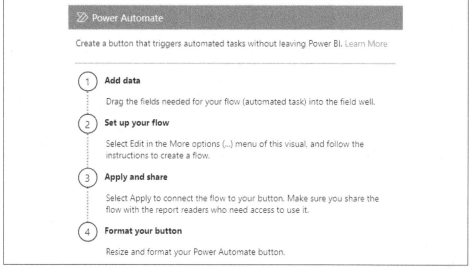

Figure 7-22. Power Automate window in Power BI Desktop

The first step is to add data. For our purposes, we aren't using the data for analysis by ChatGPT. Instead, we request that ChatGPT tell us about the World Bank data source. Power Automate and Power BI will need to transfer data between each solution. Power BI will need to send data to Power Automate so that the data can be sent on to ChatGPT. We need to choose the columns used as dynamic inputs to the Power Automate flow. To do this, click the Power Automate box and select the Countries.Index column so that it appears in the "Power Automate data" Data field in the Visualization pane on the righthand side (Figure 7-23). We only need to add one column of data for the flow to work, so select Countries.Index to give the flow some data to send back and forth. Figure 7-23 is an example of the visualization pane where you can see that the field name is specified as "Power Automate data."

Figure 7-23. "Power Automate data" Data field in the Visualization pane

Altogether, the Power BI Desktop will appear as shown in Figure 7-24.

Figure 7-24. The Power BI Desktop showing the Power Automate screen with data

Once the data is added to Power Automate, you can set up the flow. Click on the three dots at the top of the Power Automate dialog and then select Edit (Figure 7-25).

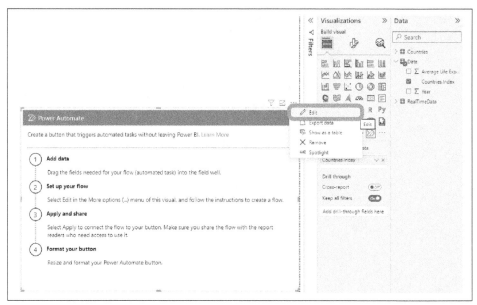

Figure 7-25. Editing the Power Automate button

Click on Edit to set up the Flow. If you have not signed up for Power Automate, then you will see the sign-up screen in Figure 7-26.

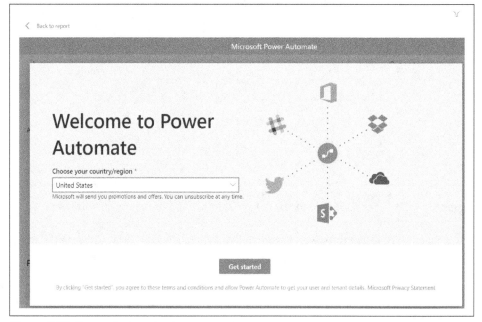

Figure 7-26. Power Automate sign-up screen

In the Power BI Desktop, choose "Instant cloud flow"; you will be taken to the next screen to set up a flow. Next, we will set up an instant cloud flow. To do this, select "Instant cloud flow" from the options list (Figure 7-27).

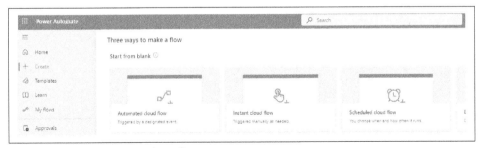

Figure 7-27. Options to make a flow

The first step, "On Power BI button clicked," will appear automatically (Figure 7-28). It is the trigger for the Power Automate flow; when we press the button in the Power BI dashboard, the flow will execute. Select the "New step" button, which appears under the "On Power BI clicked" button.

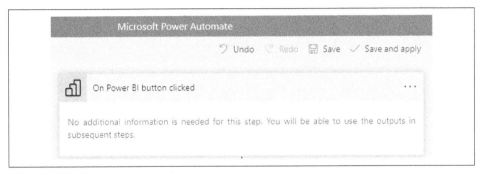

Figure 7-28. Choose "New step" option

Next, give your flow a name and then click the Create button (Figure 7-29).

Once you select this option, Power BI may ask you to sign in again. You can then proceed to the next step, which involves specifying a trigger to start the flow. In our scenario, we will press a button in Power BI to execute the flow and retrieve text that will be displayed on the Power BI canvas. To do this, we scroll down to choose the "Power BI button clicked" option as shown in Figure 7-30. Then click the Create button.

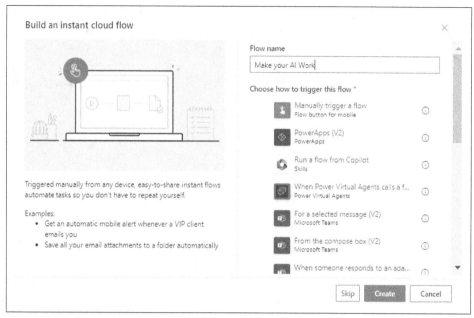

Figure 7-29. Creating an instant cloud flow

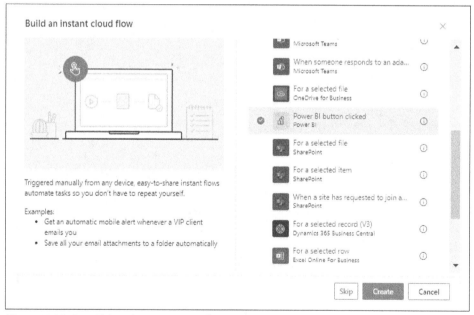

Figure 7-30. Specifying the trigger condition

The Power Automate flow will appear as shown in Figure 7-31.

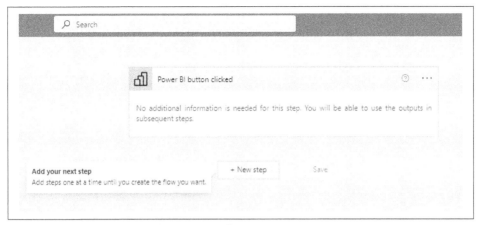

Figure 7-31. Power Automate trigger condition

We have a few more steps to connect Power BI and ChatGPT. Next, select HTTP. Click "New step" and then, in the search bar, enter HTTP. You will see a number of options (Figure 7-32).

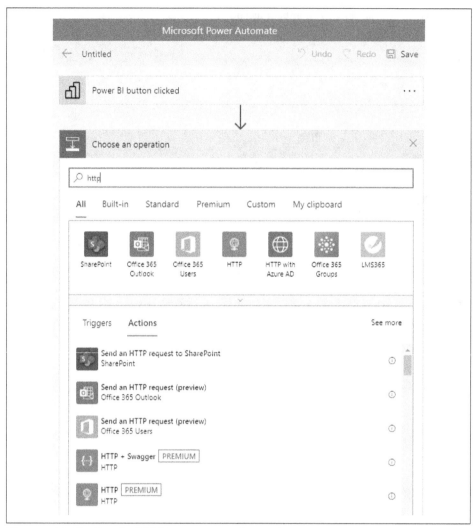

Figure 7-32. Finding the HTTP operation in Power Automate

We need to choose the Select HTTP option to interact directly with the ChatGPT program. You can filter the options by entering HTTP in the search box. We need the HTTP Premium option from the list, shown in Figure 7-33. There are a lot of options—please be sure to choose the right one!

Figure 7-33. HTTP Premium selection

Click "New step." Your screen will look like Figure 7-34.

Figure 7-34. HTTP dialog options

Remember the API key you copied earlier? You will need that now for the HTTP dialog, which should be filled in as shown in Table 7-1.

Table 7-1. HTTP (Premium) settings

Item	Content
Method	POST
URI	*https://api.openai.com/v1/chat/completions*
Content-Type	Bearer <your API key goes here>
| Body | ```
{
    "model": "gpt-3.5-turbo",
    "messages": [
      {
        "role": "user",
        "content": "What is the World Data Bank life expectancy metric?"
      }
    ],
    "temperature": 0.7
}
``` |

Figure 7-35 shows an example of a completed HTTP Premium step.

Figure 7-35. Completed HTTP Premium step
```

The HTTP step will make a call to ChatGPT to get a response. Now, we need to do something with that response so it is ready to use in Power BI. Specifically, we need to parse the data that is returned from ChatGPT. The data comes back in JSON format, so we need to use the Parse JSON step in the Power Automate flow.

Therefore, let's add a new action called Parse JSON.

To add the Parse JSON step, click "Next step" and then select Parse JSON. In the Parse JSON step, you need to do a few things. Click in the Content field, and a dropdown will appear. Look for Body and select it. The screen will appear as shown in Figure 7-36.

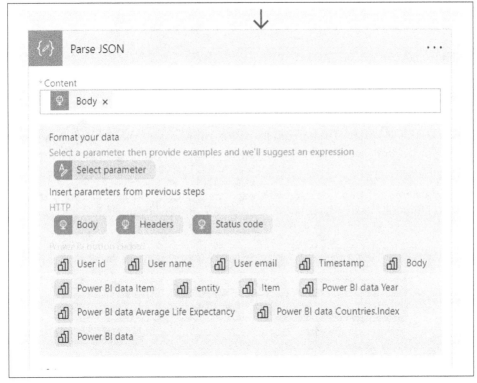

Figure 7-36. Selecting JSON Body content

Next, add the schema, which will be generated from sample data. To do this, click "Generate from sample" (Figure 7-37).

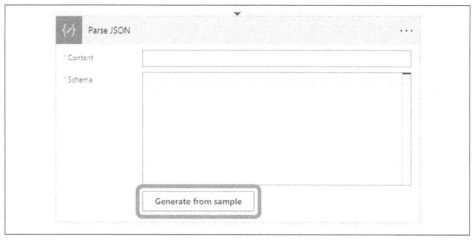

Figure 7-37. Generating a schema from a sample

You can generate the sample on the Getting Started page under the heading Making Request, which is the same page where you copied the code from Figure 7-13 earlier in this chapter. At the time of writing, you can find the code at *https://platform.openai.com/docs/api-reference/making-requests*. For your reference, Figure 7-38 shows the code.

Here is a sample of the code itself when it is copied and pasted. Your code will have different numbers as they have been changed here for privacy reasons.

```
{
    "id": "chatcmpl-abc123",
    "object": "chat.completion",
    "created": 1677858242,
    "model": "gpt-3.5-turbo-0613",
    "usage": {
        "prompt_tokens": 13,
        "completion_tokens": 7,
        "total_tokens": 20
    },
    "choices": [
        {
            "message": {
                "role": "assistant",
                "content": "\n\nThis is a test!"
            },
            "logprobs": null,
            "finish_reason": "stop",
            "index": 0
        }
    ]
}
```

```
 1  {
 2      "id": "chatcmpl-abc123",
 3      "object": "chat.completion",
 4      "created": 1677858242,
 5      "model": "gpt-3.5-turbo-0613",
 6      "usage": {
 7          "prompt_tokens": 13,
 8          "completion_tokens": 7,
 9          "total_tokens": 20
10      },
11      "choices": [
12          {
13              "message": {
14                  "role": "assistant",
15                  "content": "\n\nThis is a test!"
16              },
17              "logprobs": null,
18              "finish_reason": "stop",
19              "index": 0
20          }
21      ]
22  }
```

Figure 7-38. Response code sample from the website

Copy the code from the OpenAI website and then go back to the Power Automate flow in Power BI. Select Schema, shown in Figure 7-39. Copy and paste the sample code into the box that appears and then click Done. The completed Parse JSON box will look like the figure.

Figure 7-39. Completed Parse JSON dialog

The JSON source will serve data into the Power BI ChatGPT streaming dataset. A few more steps and then we are finished—I promise!

Next, select "Add rows to a dataset." First, search for the Power BI options by typing Power BI in the search box. Then, select "Add rows to a dataset" (Figure 7-40).

Then, you need to populate the flow settings. Figure 7-41 shows the "Add rows to a dataset" step.

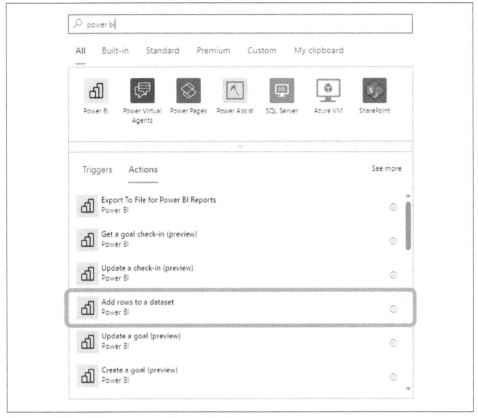

Figure 7-40. Adding rows to a dataset in Power Automate

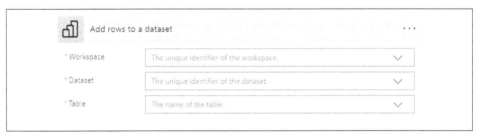

Figure 7-41. Populating the flow settings

Let's fill in the Workspace, Dataset, and Table fields in the flow settings (Figure 7-42). Select your workspace information from the drop-down list. Here, our name is "Make Your AI Work Workspace," but you will most likely have another workspace name.

Then, choose the dataset from the drop-down list. In our example, we used the ChatGPT dataset, but you may have used a different dataset name.

For your table, select RealTimeData.

Figure 7-42. Specify the workspace dataset and table in the flow settings

Click in the text box next to ChatGPT Response, and you will see a range of options. Select "content" (Figure 7-43). You may have to scroll down the list to find it.

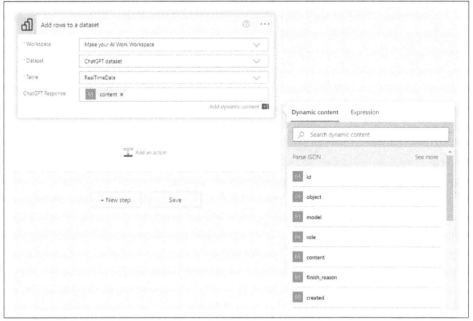

Figure 7-43. Selecting the content option

Your completed Power Automate flow is illustrated in Figure 7-44. It may look somewhat confusing because the last step has now changed to read "Apply to each." This means that every new incoming row of data from ChatGPT will be added to the Power BI dataset.

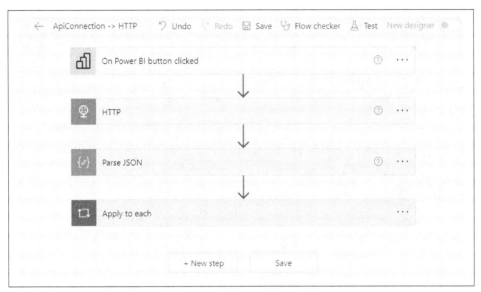

Figure 7-44. Completed Power Automate flow in Power BI

Next, click Save and then "Back to report" (Figure 7-45).

Figure 7-45. Microsoft Power Automate actions panel

For your reference, when the flow is executed, it will land data in the Power BI streaming dataset. You can see the streaming dataset in the Power BI portal in the Power BI workspace. If you access the Power BI workspace by logging in to the portal at *https://www.powerbi.com*, you will see the dataset listed as in Figure 7-46 (here, the streaming dataset is called "ChatGPT dataset").

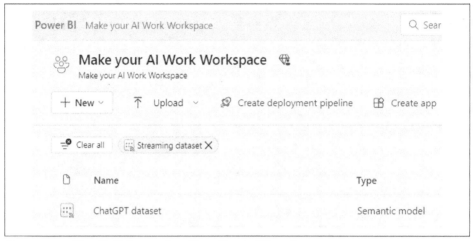

Figure 7-46. ChatGPT dataset listed in a Power BI workspace

In Power BI Desktop, let's connect to the ChatGPT dataset and import the data. Go to the Power BI Desktop Home tab and select the Get Data tab. Then select Dataflows (Figure 7-47).

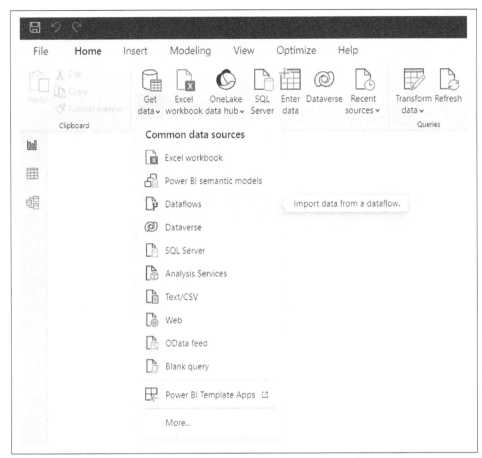

Figure 7-47. Connecting to the ChatGPT dataset in Power BI Desktop

Next, you will be presented with dataset options from the OneLake data hub. You will see the ChatGPT dataset that you created. Select it and click Connect (Figure 7-48).

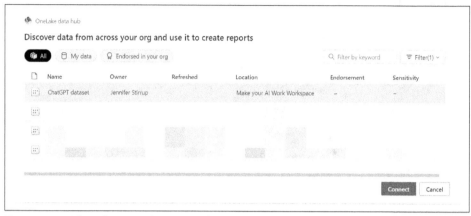

Figure 7-48. The ChatGPT dataset in the OneLake data hub

Power BI Desktop will then present you with options. You may have other datasets in your Workspace already, so you may want to use the Search function to narrow the list. Select the RealTimeData table and click Submit (Figure 7-49).

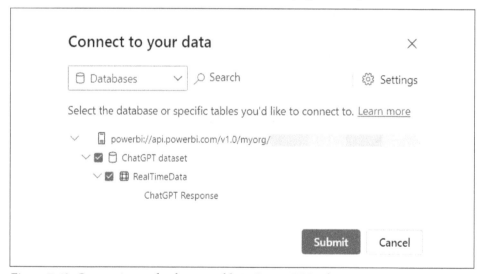

Figure 7-49. Connecting to the dataset table in Power BI Desktop

You may receive a warning about a potential security risk (Figure 7-50).

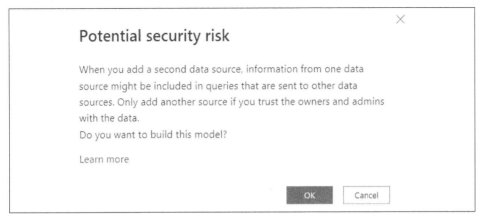

Figure 7-50. Potential security risk

Click OK to proceed.

You will now see the RealTimeData dataset table appear on the Data pane, located on the righthand side of the Power BI desktop. You can see a copy of the Data pane in Figure 7-51.

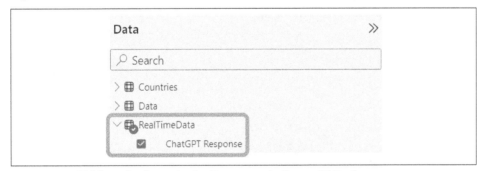

Figure 7-51. Table and column in the Data pane in Power BI Desktop

Now let's add a Table visualization component to the Power BI canvas. To do this, click on the Canvas and select the Table from the Visualizations pane (Figure 7-52).

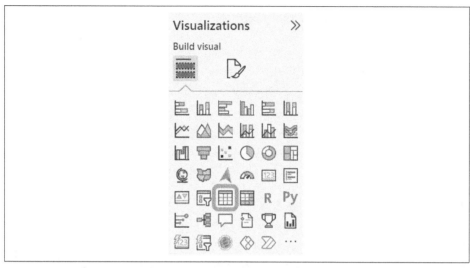

Figure 7-52. Selecting a Table visualization

Power BI will automatically create a table for you. It will recognize the data as Text format. You can see an example in Figure 7-53.

Figure 7-53. The completed data panel

Let's make the dashboard more attractive by adding some more information to the Power BI Desktop canvas, such as a title. You can do this by going to the Insert menu bar and selecting "Text box" (Figure 7-54).

Figure 7-54. Adding a title to the Power BI Desktop canvas

In the text box, type "Average Life Expectancy Over Years by Income Group." Highlight the text and change the font size to 24. Place the title at the top of the canvas.

Now, let's add some text to the Power Automate button so its purpose is clear to the user. Click the Power Automate button and then go to the Visualizations pane. Go to the "Format visual" section and toggle "Button text to On" if it is not already set. In the "Button text" box, type "Tell me about the data source." Figure 7-55 shows these settings for the Power Automate button.

Figure 7-55. Configuring the Power Automate button in Power BI Desktop

So far, your Power BI Desktop canvas looks like Figure 7-56.

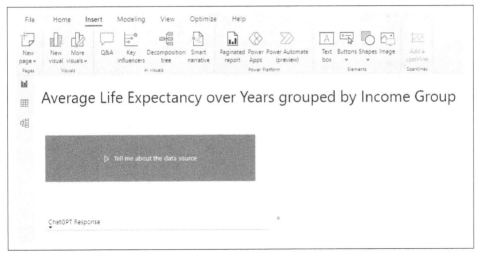

Figure 7-56. Power BI Desktop canvas with title and Power Automate button label

Let's add in a small multiples chart to show the Average Life Expectancy Over Years by Income Group. To do this, click on the Power BI Desktop canvas background and select the Line Chart option in the Visualizations pane.

Let's put the data in the right place. In the "Build visual" pane, drag Year from the Data table into the X-axis option. Drag Average Life Expectancy into the Y-axis option.

Make sure that it will calculate the Average by using the drop-down menu to select the correct calculation (Figure 7-57).

Figure 7-57. Small multiples Visualizations pane checkpoint

You can also rename the field so that its name makes more sense. Using the same drop-down menu as in the previous step, select "Rename for this visual" and change the name to Average Life Expectancy. Then, add Income Group to the "Small multiples" option. The Visualizations pane should look like Figure 7-58.

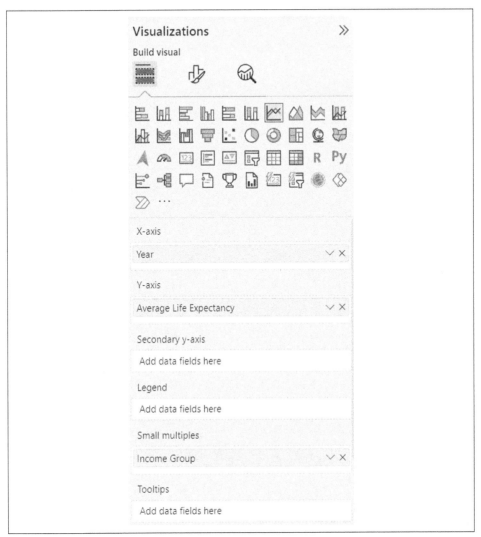

Figure 7-58. Renamed y-axis and Income Group added to "Small multiples" in the Visualizations pane

At this point, the Power BI Desktop canvas will appear as shown in Figure 7-59.

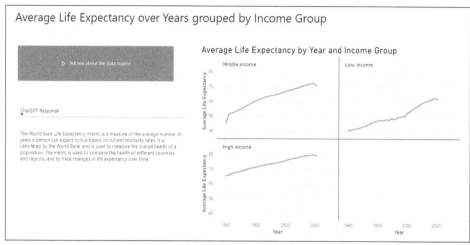

Figure 7-59. Visualization and ChatGPT on the Power BI Desktop canvas

You can rerun the dataflow to see our ChatGPT response in the Power BI Desktop. The Power BI Dataset already has data in it, which was inserted when you pressed Test in the Power Automate dataflow. To rerun the dataflow, hold down Ctrl and click the Power Automate button in the Power BI Desktop. This action will run the dataflow, and the button will show the word Triggered (Figure 7-60).

Figure 7-60. Final dashboard with ChatGPT content

Dashboard Didn't Work?

If your flow didn't work, please check it out in Power Automate. For example, the flow may need to be switched on (Figure 7-61).

You can also see your new flow in the Power Automate portal. To do this, log into the Power Platform portal at *https://portal.office.com*.

It may be that the button was not pressed properly. If the button does not change to read Triggered, then you may need to try clicking on different areas of the button so that it runs properly. For example, it may work when you click on the top-center part of the button.

Figure 7-61. Flow checker

Summary

To summarize, the purpose of adding ChatGPT content to the dashboard is to display more information about the data source next to the data. By adding context, this will help users understand the data better. It is especially useful if the organization uses external data sources, since ChatGPT can help to keep the content updated if information about the data source changes. As a follow-up exercise, you can add other ChatGPT responses to your report. We hope that you have fun!

Creating a Power BI dashboard to display ChatGPT responses could be helpful in a variety of applications. This example has been used to generate a natural language explanation of the data source. If the information changes frequently, the user can easily access up-to-date information on the Power BI dashboard, adjacent to the data itself. ChatGPT could even display the frequency and types of queries, responses, and resolution times. During development of an AI model, a Power BI dashboard could visually present explanatory feedback about the model and its results over time, which could inform efforts to improve the model.

ChatGPT could also explain the data shown in the Power BI dashboard. For example, if a business uses social media to interact with many users on various topics, a user could use a ChatGPT query to ask about trending topics or common questions, and a Power BI dashboard could display the results. Further, a Power BI dashboard could present social media sentiment data.

The key benefit of using AI and Power BI is the ability to query and present data in a visually compelling and easily digestible format, facilitating quicker and more effective decision making to help organizations to become more data-driven.

Text Analytics

What would you do if you had to review over one million technical documents? Well, the professional services company Accenture had that many legal contracts and was adding thousands of new ones each month. This represented a considerable burden on the company, requiring an incredible amount of manual work to individually review and process each document.

That all changed when Accenture developed an AI solution to extract meaning from this ocean of text. The project used text analytics to identify which keywords related to which legal clauses. This automated matching allowed a user to search for a specific legal clause, like "limited liability," even if those specific words never showed up within a contract.[1] Accenture decided to build this intelligent system in-house to have greater control over the outcome. This made sense for the company given the scale of the problem, available resources, and the potential upside of creating a customized system. Other companies facing the same scenario, however, may find it better to outsource production of such an AI model or choose an off-the-shelf solution.

---

1 "Case Study: Unleashing Insights from Accenture's Contracts" (*https://oreil.ly/Ziv-m*), Accenture, accessed January 7, 2024.

Custom Models Versus Pretrained Models

Many organizations face the question of whether to buy or build an AI solution or enlist the help of a partner, and that decision requires understanding the distinction between custom and pretrained models. A *custom machine learning model* is one that is trained from scratch by an individual or organization with their own dataset, often to be applied in a specific use case. Two such examples include AutoML in Power BI (discussed in Chapter 3) and Azure Machine Learning (Chapter 10). Custom machine learning can be beneficial for businesses that need to use internal data to solve a specific problem.

There are also *pretrained machine learning models*, which are trained by another individual or organization for some generic task. They are usually not domain-specific and are designed to make robust predictions in various contexts rather than to solve a known problem. This chapter and the next feature models that were pretrained by Microsoft as part of its Azure AI Services offerings. Features include language detection, key phrase extraction, sentiment analysis, and image tagging. Pretrained models are useful when an organization does not have the skills, data, or compute required to train its own algorithm or when an off-the-shelf algorithm will do just fine.

Finally, there is also a type of model that falls between the custom and pretrained solutions. A *transfer learning model* begins with a pretrained model and then adapts or fine-tunes it with custom data to solve a more specific use case. Models trained from transfer learning can help a business by reducing the amount of time or data required, and they can also perform better if the original model was trained on a larger corpus than what is available for the transfer learning. To illustrate this, imagine you work for a group of contractors that fills out a standard paper invoice by hand and then sends a picture of the complete version to a central location. It would take you too long to individually label a large enough dataset for this task, and maybe a pretrained optical character recognition (OCR) model is not working well to pick up the specifics of the form or construction-specific characters and abbreviations. In this case, you would want to opt for a pretrained OCR model and use transfer learning to incorporate maybe as few as 20 labeled examples from your own business.

Similarly, imagine the same contractor group has a website with a chatbot to assist customers at scale. The company may have purchased a pretrained chatbot but fed it an FAQ list from its own website. This also is an example of transfer learning. The spectrum between pretrained and custom machine learning is very much a continuum, as visualized in Figure 8-1.

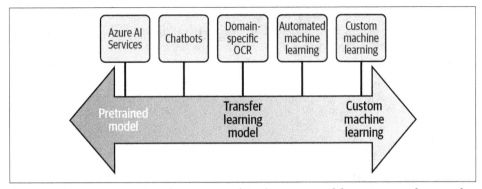

Figure 8-1. The pretrained and custom machine learning model spectrum with examples

Text as Data

Organizations in all sectors and industries are encountering ever-increasing amounts of information in digital formats. Data is now commonly described as large in its *volume* (measured in observations, dimensions, objects, events, or storage size), *variety* (datatypes, degree of structure, or file formats), and *velocity* (speed of data creation, storage, or analysis). The recent scale, diversity, and speed of data presents unique challenges as well as opportunities for organizations to extract meaning beyond just a spreadsheet of numbers. In this chapter, we explore how to best use Power BI with one such datatype: text.

Natural language (i.e., language as it's commonly spoken) is possibly the oldest form of information sharing between people. After spoken communication came writing as a way to store information for later retrieval. In fact, the earliest known writing developed in ancient Sumeria in 3400 B.C.E, as a way to track business records and contracts of agricultural production. Text is now such a ubiquitous form of data that we have *natural language processing* (NLP), which is the subfield of computer science dedicated to the study of how computers can process and analyze spoken and written language.

In order to extract information from text, we need to overcome the challenge of working with messy, semistructured, and highly dimensional data. Humans have the flexibility to say whatever we want, like this very sentence, which is both the power of natural language and the struggle for computers. When data has many possible combinations of values, this is called the *curse of dimensionality* in machine learning. In practice, observations tend to cluster around more similar values. For example, consider a tweet that is 30 words long and written using only vocabulary from the 1,000 most common words in the English language. That one tweet has more permutations than there are atoms in the observable universe, and that's assuming no punctuation or spelling mistakes! However, we are more likely to come across "thank you" than another pair of randomly selected words.

Thankfully, Power BI has different solutions for overcoming the problem of high dimensionality inherent in text data. Each approach utilizes artificial intelligence to extract usable data from text at scale. The methods are part of Microsoft's Azure AI Services (*https://oreil.ly/uQ9b0*), which were discussed in Chapter 7. Here we delve deeper into the three Azure AI features built directly into Power BI that relate to text analytics specifically: Language Detection, Key Phrase Extraction, and Sentiment Analysis.

> The Text Analytics Azure AI features are available in the Power BI service and Power BI Desktop; however, they both require Power BI Premium. See the end of Chapter 1 for details on benefits and costs as well as how to sign up for a free trial.

These three tools are included within Power Query, meaning they can be used to transform data before it is ingested. Only then can the output data be used to build out a new report. We will discuss the abilities and limitations of each Azure AI feature in turn, including step-by-step examples at the end of each section.

> The rest of this chapter discusses the Azure AI features built directly into Power BI. This is distinct from the Azure AI Services discussed in Chapter 7. When reading documentation about the two, be careful that you are aware of which version the author is referring to.

Limitations of Text Analytics

We'll discuss the limitations of each of Power BI's built-in Azure AI features in their respective sections, but here are some general limitations that apply to all three:

- AI insights built into a query can slow down incremental refreshes, causing perforation issues.
- There is currently no support for Direct Query.
- The Azure AI features built into Power BI cannot be customized (i.e., you are not able to add your own training data).
- Microsoft does not document what data was used to build these pretrained models.
- Performance is worse with lower-quality text (e.g., unknown characters, misspellings, short length, mixed language).
- The models are regularly retrained and so may produce different predictions over time.

For these reasons, we recommend against using text analytics for any mission-critical function at your organization. It does, however, provide useful transformations of text data for improved visualizations and insights.

The best way to explore the capabilities and limitations of Power BI's Text Analytics function is to test it out with real-world data. We will try out Language Detection, Key Phrase Extraction, and Sentiment Analysis, but first, we need to gather the data that will be used throughout the chapter's demos. We recommend following along on your own since only so much can be conveyed through static images.

Demo 8-1: Ingest AirBnB Data

In this section, we ingest a custom dataset of over three hundred online reviews from an AirBnB listing in northern Italy (Figure 8-2). The one-bedroom apartment is located in a lakeside resort town in the province of Trentino and receives many international visitors. We will use this multilingual text data to explore the AI insights within Power BI Desktop.

Figure 8-2. An AirBnB listing that receives many international travelers and has an impressive average star rating of 4.95/5

Open a new report in Power BI Desktop and click through the pop-up window. Check that you are signed into your Microsoft account. If not, then you will see the "Sign in" option near the top-right corner (Figure 8-3). Click this and follow the prompts to connect your school or work account with Premium access. Refer to the end of Chapter 1 for details about Power BI Premium and how to enroll in a free trial.

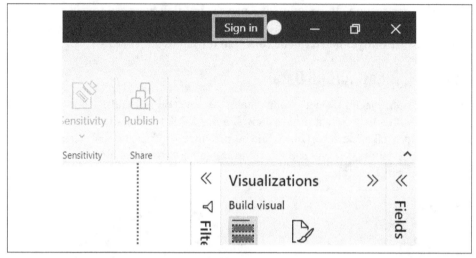

Figure 8-3. Signing in to your Microsoft account in Power BI Desktop

Now it is time to ingest the sample data. In the Home ribbon, select "Get data" and then Web as the source of the data (Figure 8-4).

 You can also ingest the data as a dataflow using an organizational account. Refer to Chapter 1 for instructions and a use case.

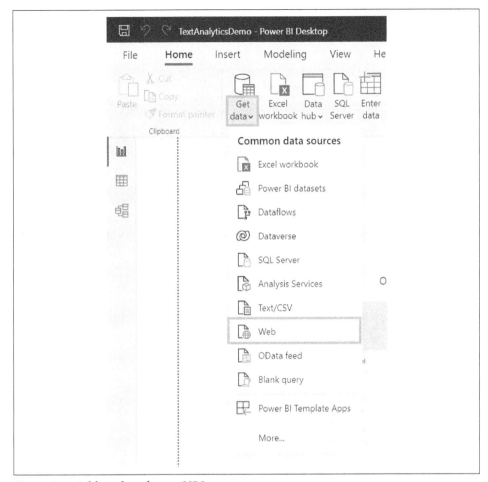

Figure 8-4. Adding data from a URL

If you selected the "Get data" icon instead of the "Get data" text, you will instead see a different pop-up window. If this happens, type "web" in the Search bar, select Web, and then click Connect before proceeding to the next step.

In the new pop-up window, copy this link (*https://raw.githubusercontent.com/tomwei nandy/ai-with-power-bi/main/Chapter8/TrentinoReviews.csv*) and paste it in the box under URL. This is a CSV of the AirBnB reviews hosted on this book's GitHub repository. Click OK (Figure 8-5).

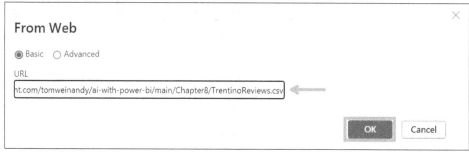

Figure 8-5. Pasting a URL of raw data from GitHub

You will now see a preview of the data that shows the review date, the first name of the reviewer, and the review of the AirBnB. Before loading the data into the Power BI report, we want to augment the data using Power BI's Text Analytics functionality. To do this, select Transform Data (Figure 8-6).

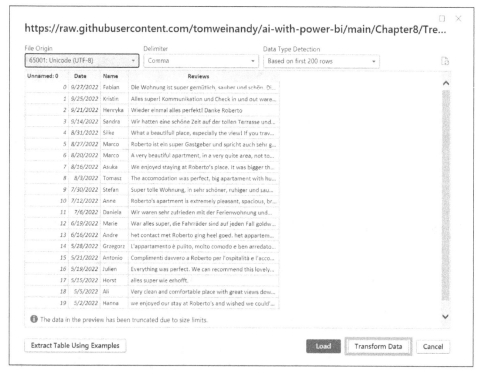

Figure 8-6. Preview of data before transformation

This opens up Power Query Editor to complete the data transformations (Figure 8-7). Note that this is a separate window, so if you get lost, be sure to check whether it is obscured by the Power BI report window.

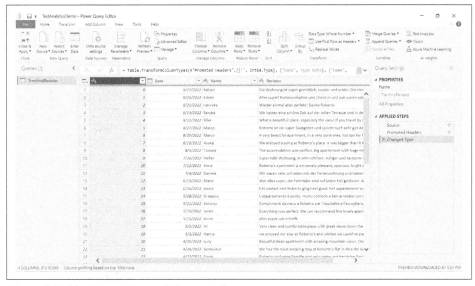

Figure 8-7. The Power Query Editor window

Now is a good time to save the report using the save icon in the upper-left corner or by selecting File and then Save. If prompted, select Apply to apply the changes to the data that occurred from the ingest (Figure 8-8).

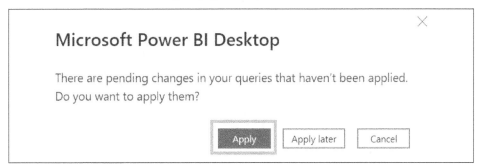

Figure 8-8. Applying changes

Now you are ready for text analytics transformations. Although you can technically skip ahead to any of the demos, we recommend continuing in the order presented to receive the full, intended experience.

Language Detection

The first of the AI insights we'll explore uses *language detection*, which predicts the language a given text is written in. Language detection has many use cases within a business, such as routing emails to the appropriate customer service agent, responding to social media posts in the same language, sorting product reviews, and moderating forum posts.

In Power BI, the Language Detection feature is most useful for tagging text and then using the tagged text for filtering and highlighting. This can be done on the backend to ensure, for example, that a report contains only text from the language spoken by the audience or to build a report where the user has the option to select which language text is displayed.

How It Works

Language Detection takes text data as an input and predicts which language that text most likely is in (Table 8-1). It outputs both the name of the language and its corresponding ISO code. The ISO column can be deleted if you want to minimize memory; however, we recommend keeping the column, as it can be used as an input to speed up the performance for Key Phrase Extraction and Sentiment Analysis (more on this later).

Table 8-1. Sample input and output for Power BI Language Detection

Sample input	Sample output	Sample output
Esta bicicleta es simplemente impresionante. Nunca había tenido uno así.	Spanish	es

 ISO is the short name of the International Organization for Standardization, which has made over 24,000 lists of standards, most commonly in the areas of technology, management, and manufacturing. The ISO code here allows you to easily join this dataset with others using the same code while avoiding the messiness associated with inconsistent languages or country names.

Performance and Limitations

Language Detection supports over 120 languages at the time of this writing, but you can go to Microsoft's website to find the most up-to-date list (*https://oreil.ly/Ajpu5*). It is worth noting that Language Detection will predict only the *single* most probable language. An incorrect label is more common when the input text is ambiguous in some way.

Although there are no strict rules describing when Language Detection works the best, you will find the model performs better when input text:

- Is longer
- Does not rely on emojis or emoticons
- Is in a single language
- Has fewer cognates (e.g., *horrible communication* is English but *communication horrible* is French)

When an input text contains a mix of languages, then the algorithm will return the language that has the highest representation within the input text. This also increases the likelihood of a misattribution.

The strongest recommendation is to provide input text that is long enough that identification is easy. We have found Language Detection within Power BI to be rather accurate. If you notice systematic issues with Language Detection on your own data, make sure that your original data is properly encoded in the text's native script. This is especially true if it is based on a non-Latin alphabet, like the romanized Pinyin Chinese or Franco-Arabic, neither of which is currently supported in Power BI.

Language Detection will return *<unknown>* when it does not have enough information to make a sufficiently confident decision.

Demo 8-2: Language Detection

Demo 8-1 ended with ingesting the AirBnB data into a report but not yet performing any transformations. In this section, we will use Language Detection within Text Analytics to predict which language each review was written in. This can be useful for a business analyzing the AirBnB listing data to understand the background of different customers, identify patterns in reviews by groups of customers, or simply to filter out foreign language reviews in the Power BI report.

If the Power Query Editor window is not already open, then click the "Transform data" icon in the Home ribbon (Figure 8-9).

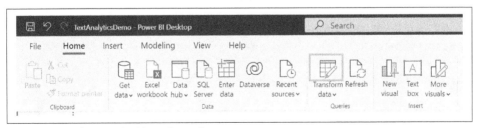

Figure 8-9. Selecting the Transform data icon

Now select Text Analytics under the AI Insights group (Figure 8-10).

Figure 8-10. Selecting the Text Analytics icon

A new window will appear and confirm your access level—this may take as long as a minute. Sign in here if prompted. Your license will be added by default, and if you have Power BI Premium, you will be able to proceed. You may either remain with the default (and do nothing) or select which license you want to use (Figure 8-11).

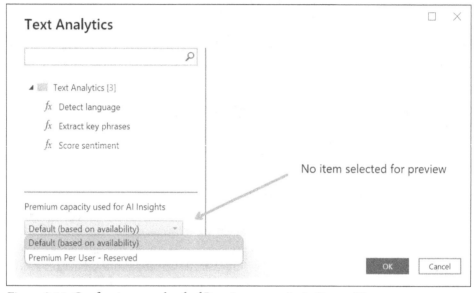

Figure 8-11. Confirming your level of Premium capacity in Power BI

Select "Detect language" from the left pane. Now you need to identify the column of data you wish to run through the algorithm. You could type the column name in the text box on the right pane, but it is easier to instead click the ABC icon and then select Column Name (Figure 8-12).

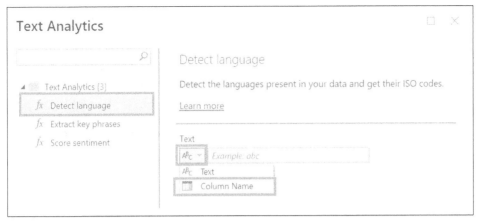

Figure 8-12. Enabling a dropdown of column names in Language Detection

Next, click the drop-down arrow and select Reviews, since that is the column of text whose language we want to predict. Click OK to run the data through the Language Detection algorithm and produce results (Figure 8-13). This may finish in as little as a minute; however, larger amounts of data can take much longer. It is worth noting the amount of time it takes for your use case because this will impact future data refresh durations.

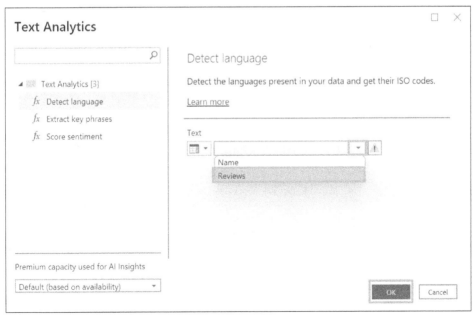

Figure 8-13. Specifying the text column whose language you want to detect

You may now see a warning that must be agreed to before proceeding. This appears because Text Analytics works by sending data to a machine learning algorithm hosted on the cloud before returning results to the Power BI report. Some organizations do not permit certain data to leave their premises, and in that instance, they should not use Text Analytics. Read more about Power's BI's privacy levels in Microsoft's official documentation (*https://oreil.ly/_F-Bs*). You can safely ignore the privacy level for this demo because the AirBnB review data is not sensitive; however, be sure to understand your organization's data policies and use the appropriate privacy level for other reports (Figure 8-14).

Figure 8-14. Warning that appears the first time you use Text Analytics on a new dataset

The transformed data is now visible in the Power Query Editor window as columns newly added at the end of the table (Figure 8-15). (You may need to scroll to the right to see them.) The column Detect language.Detected Language Name contains the full name of the review's language, and the column Detect language.Detected Language ISO Code contains the associated ISO code of that language. The ISO code seems redundant now, but we can use it for other Text Analytics augmentations.

Also note that this transformation was recorded in the Applied Steps well. This shows each data manipulation performed, and the listing of steps is useful for replicating or editing processes as well as diagnosing problems. If you make a mistake, just delete the step!

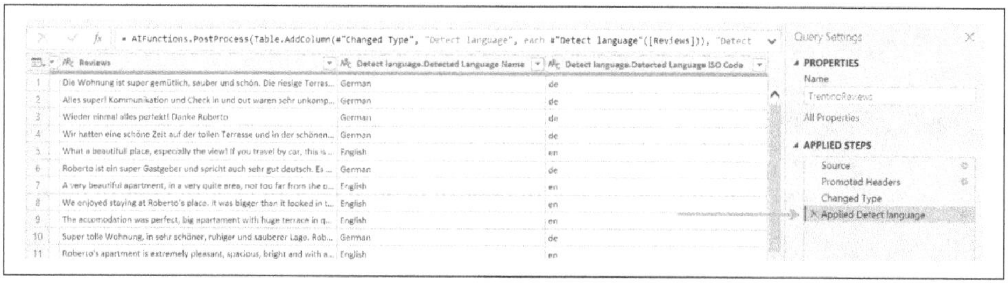

Figure 8-15. The new columns with an applied step added

As a final step, let's change those new column names to something less clunky. Right-click the Detect language.Detected Language Name column header and select Rename. Now replace the header with Language (Figure 8-16).

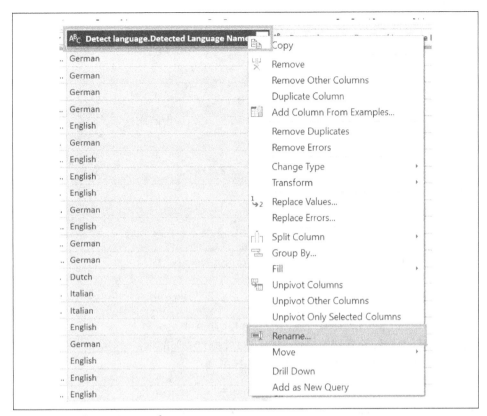

Figure 8-16. Renaming a column

Repeat this action with the last column, calling it ISO. You should now see the shortened header names, as well as seeing Renamed Columns recorded as an applied step (Figure 8-17).

Save your work and apply changes if prompted. The next demo will give you experience using Key Phrase Extraction. If you do not want to perform other transformations, then you may select Close & Apply in the upper-left corner, which will return you to the report window.

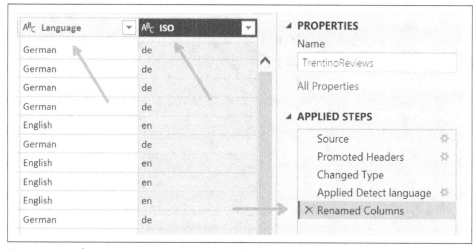

Figure 8-17. The newly renamed columns with associated applied step

Explore the results on your own by considering the following questions:

- How does Language Detection perform for short reviews?
- Care to guess why the German ISO code is not "ge" and why Spanish is not "sp"?
- Who wrote a review in Polish? In Finnish?
- What is the language of origin for the name "Alessandro"?
- Which language was the most common in 2014? In 2022?

If you were not following along on your own in Power BI, you can still explore the augmented data from the transformed data file on this book's GitHub (*https://oreil.ly/ch8_datacsv*).

Key Phrase Extraction

As data becomes cheaper and easier to generate and store, some businesses find themselves having *too much* data instead of *not enough*. It's not that data itself is the problem; instead, those companies are not producing enough meaningful insights from the data to justify its storage cost. This is common with raw text data, especially when there is more than can be practically read by a single person. *Key phrase extraction* is one way to identify the most relevant parts of text by generating a list of which phrases are predicted to be the most significant.

Businesses can use key phrase extraction for a wide array of use cases, such as identifying the topic of an inquiry for routing to the correct customer representative, finding related terms to improve SEO, locating pain points from consumer reviews to help new product development, flagging inappropriate content on a platform, scanning résumés for relevant skills, and extracting key themes in online reviews.

Another common approach to reduce the size of text in natural language processing is to remove stop words. In NLP, *stop words* are the most commonly used words that are either filler within natural language or make only moderate modifications to the main ideas. Common examples in English are *if*, *and*, *um*, and *but*. There is no accepted list of what is or is not a stop word, but we recommend the multi-language lists put together by Ranks NL (*https://www.ranks.nl/stopwords*). For example, the phrase "It was the best of times, it was the worst of times…" would be reduced to "best times worst times." The output may not capture the same meaning of the original, but it provides a useful gist of the original with only a third of the words.

How It Works

Power BI's Key Phrase Extraction functionality uses a related approach to exclude stop words, but its use of AI results in a more sophisticated approach and a greater reduction of text. Note that it extracts *key phrases* and not just *keywords*. For example, Table 8-3 shows the output can include a single word or a phrase, like "great bike."

The Key Phrase Extraction algorithm takes unstructured text as an input with the option of including the ISO language code as a second input. The first column output is a list of all key phrases found within the input text. The second column includes the individual key phrases found within the list.

As seen in the example input and outputs in Tables 8-2 and 8-3, respectively, using Key Phrase Extraction with a single input text will produce new columns when there is more than one key phrase. In other words, this transformation will vertically explode the number of rows according to the length of the key phrases list. Although there is no way to disable this type of transformation, following the steps in the demo will keep the original number of rows by deleting the individual key phrase column and then removing duplicates from the dataset.

Table 8-2. Sample input for the Key Phrase Extraction algorithm

Sample input	Sample input (optional)
Completed 60 mils on this bike, great bike. Gear shifting is smooth and good pace.	en

Table 8-3. Sample output for the Key Phrase Extraction algorithm

Sample output	Sample output
great bike, Gear shifting, good pace, mils	great bike
great bike, Gear shifting, good pace, mils	Gear shifting
great bike, Gear shifting, good pace, mils	good pace
great bike, Gear shifting, good pace, mils	mils

Performance and Limitations

Key Phrase Extraction works best with larger chunks of text, as they are more likely to contain relevant phrases.

You can also specify the ISO language code to speed up performance. At the time of this writing, Microsoft supports 94 languages (*https://oreil.ly/qBnWk*) for Key Phrase Extraction.

Just as with the other text analytics included in Azure AI Services, the output's reliability depends on the quality of the input text. The example in Table 8-3 shows this, with the misspelling *mils* (instead of *miles*) identified as a key phrase with no spelling correction.

Demo 8-3: Key Phrase Extraction

Key Phrase Extraction can be useful in the AirBnB example to find which topics are most frequently discussed about the listing and if any of those are pain points that can be resolved.

This picks up where Demo 8-2 left off, after the language of each review has already been identified. Since the text language is an optional input, you are also welcome to jump here after completing the data ingestion from Demo 8-1.

If the Power Query Editor window is not already open, select Transform Data in the Home ribbon.

Once in the Power Query Editor window, click Text Analytics in the Home ribbon (Figure 8-18).

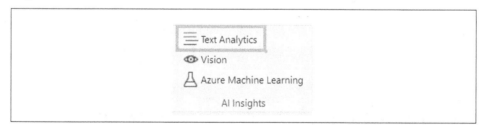

Figure 8-18. The Text Analytics icon

Select "Extract key phrases" in the left pane of the pop-up window. Then click the ABC icon and select Column Name (Figure 8-19).

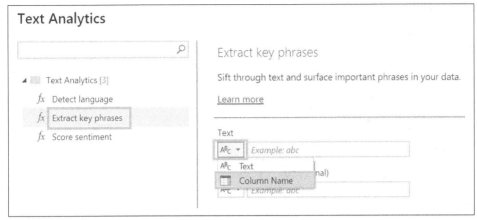

Figure 8-19. *Enabling a dropdown of column names in Key Phrase Extraction*

Now click the drop-down arrow and select the Reviews column. This identifies the input text to extract the key phrases from (Figure 8-20).

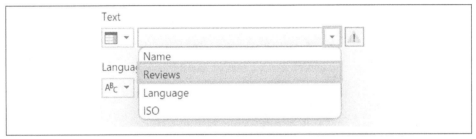

Figure 8-20. *Specifying the text column with key phrases you want to extract*

You can include the language ISO code as an input. This will speed up the results by not requiring the algorithm to also detect the language of the text. It also allows the analyst to fix any mislabeled languages and forces the algorithm to use a given ISO code instead of repeating a mistake.

Change the ABC icon to Column Name and select ISO from the dropdown (Figure 8-21).

Figure 8-21. *Specifying the text column with the detected language ISO code*

Click OK when done.

After Key Phrase Extraction is complete, you will notice there are now multiple rows for the same review. This is because a single review likely contains multiple key phrases. The transformation is designed to explode this data vertically, generating a unique row for each key phrase. For example, notice that the one review from Fabian now has 10 rows (Figure 8-22).

Date	Name	Reviews	Language
9/27/2022	Fabian	Die Wohnung ist super gemütlich, sauber und schön. Die riesige Terras...	German
9/27/2022	Fabian	Die Wohnung ist super gemütlich, sauber und schön. Die riesige Terras...	German
9/27/2022	Fabian	Die Wohnung ist super gemütlich, sauber und schön. Die riesige Terras...	German
9/27/2022	Fabian	Die Wohnung ist super gemütlich, sauber und schön. Die riesige Terras...	German
9/27/2022	Fabian	Die Wohnung ist super gemütlich, sauber und schön. Die riesige Terras...	German
9/27/2022	Fabian	Die Wohnung ist super gemütlich, sauber und schön. Die riesige Terras...	German
9/27/2022	Fabian	Die Wohnung ist super gemütlich, sauber und schön. Die riesige Terras...	German
9/27/2022	Fabian	Die Wohnung ist super gemütlich, sauber und schön. Die riesige Terras...	German
9/27/2022	Fabian	Die Wohnung ist super gemütlich, sauber und schön. Die riesige Terras...	German
9/27/2022	Fabian	Die Wohnung ist super gemütlich, sauber und schön. Die riesige Terras...	German
9/25/2022	Kristin	Alles super! Kommunikation und Check in und out waren sehr unkomp...	German
9/25/2022	Kristin	Alles super! Kommunikation und Check in und out waren sehr unkomp...	German
9/25/2022	Kristin	Alles super! Kommunikation und Check in und out waren sehr unkomp...	German
9/25/2022	Kristin	Alles super! Kommunikation und Check in und out waren sehr unkomp...	German
9/25/2022	Kristin	Alles super! Kommunikation und Check in und out waren sehr unkomp...	German
9/25/2022	Kristin	Alles super! Kommunikation und Check in und out waren sehr unkomp...	German
9/25/2022	Kristin	Alles super! Kommunikation und Check in und out waren sehr unkomp...	German
9/25/2022	Kristin	Alles super! Kommunikation und Check in und out waren sehr unkomp...	German
9/25/2022	Kristin	Alles super! Kommunikation und Check in und out waren sehr unkomp...	German
9/25/2022	Kristin	Alles super! Kommunikation und Check in und out waren sehr unkomp...	German
9/21/2022	Henryka	Wieder einmal alles perfekt! Danke Roberto	German
9/21/2022	Henryka	Wieder einmal alles perfekt! Danke Roberto	German

Figure 8-22. Creation of a new row for each key phrase extracted from the source text column

Personally, we tend to not find these additional rows worth the larger storage size and longer compute times. You can return to the original number of rows by right-clicking the "Extract key phrases.KeyPhrase" column and selecting Remove (Figure 8-23).

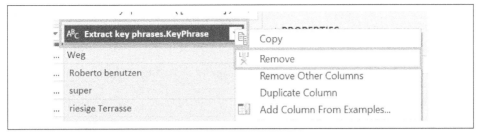

Figure 8-23. Removing the column of individual key phrases

Second, right-click the "Extract key phrases" column and select Remove Duplicates (Figure 8-24). This will drop now-duplicate rows and return to the original review-level dataset.

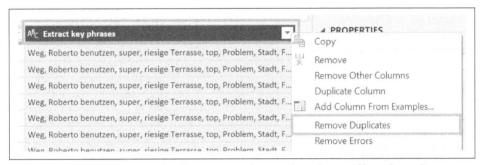

Figure 8-24. De-duplicating the dataset according to the column of key phrase lists

Rename the column by right-clicking the "Extract key phrases" header, selecting Rename, and replacing the column name with "Key phrases."

Now the key phrases for each review are stored as a list. At the end of the chapter, you will see that Power BI can effectively parse a column of lists and use the individual items in insightful ways.

Before we move on, let's look at how the algorithm fared. Below is one review from a guest named Lucy with the identified key phrases *underlined*. Note how "beautiful clean apartment" was identified in the first sentence but then "apartment" alone was appropriately ignored in the third sentence. But the analysis is not perfect; it highlights "issues" in the second sentence when "no issues" would have better captured the meaning of the reviewer.

> *Beautiful clean apartment* with *amazing mountain views*. Check in was easy and we had a *great stay* with no *issues*. Everything you need is in the apartment. *Perfect location* for *Riva*, we will be back! recommend to everyone visiting Riva.

Save your work and apply changes if prompted. The next demo will explore Sentiment Analysis. If you do not want to perform other transformations, then you may select Close & Apply in the upper-left corner to return to the report window.

Explore the results on your own by considering the following questions:

- Are all nouns extracted?
- When are adjectives included in a key phrase, and when are they not?
- Can you find examples of key phrases that should not have been extracted?
- Do you notice any pattern to the algorithm's "mistakes"?
- Are there any languages that work with Language Detection but not with Key Phrase Extraction?

If you were not following along on your own in Power BI, you can still explore the augmented data from the transformed CSV on this book's GitHub (*https://oreil.ly/ch8_datacsv*).

Sentiment Analysis

Sentiment analysis is the process of assigning a sentiment score to text based on how positive or negative it is. This is a common machine learning method to distill a chunk of text into a single number or category. One early example comes from Alfred Cowles, who in 1933 published a paper using sentiment analysis in finance. He reviewed 28 years of articles by the editor of *The Wall Street Journal* and labeled each as "bullish" (positive), "doubtful," or "bearish" (negative). From there, Cowles evaluated an investment strategy based on trading stocks according to the sentiment of articles that mention them.[2]

Sentiment analysis today takes a similar approach but with greater scale and ease. Businesses use these techniques to measure trends in social media sentiment, shape public relations strategy, evaluate how well chatbots interact with customers, and filter product reviews between brand ambassadors and disgruntled customers. Even though many online reviews now include star rating systems, researchers found that using sentiment analysis from online reviews in combination with star ratings makes better predictions of product sales than just using star ratings alone.[3]

---

[2] Alfred Cowles 3rd. "Can Stock Market Forecasters Forecast?" *Econometrica* 1, no. 3 (1933): 309–24. *https://doi.org/10.2307/1907042*.

[3] Li, Xiaolin, Chaojiang Wu, and Feng Mai. "The effect of online reviews on product sales: A joint sentiment-topic analysis." *Information & Management* 56, no. 2 (2019): 172-184.

How It Works

Sentiment Analysis within Power BI is a pretrained machine learning algorithm used to predict whether a chunk of code is positive or negative. In this way it is a classification model; however, it also produces a numeric value of its confidence in the prediction. This numeric value can be interpreted as the degree to which text is predicted to contain positive sentiment, with 1 being completely positive and 0 being completely negative.

The model includes two parts. First, a chunk of text is categorized as to whether it is objective or subjective. Objective text is automatically scored as 0.5 and does not proceed, while subjective text progresses to a scoring stage. The model then passes the text to a sentiment scorer that leverages a variety of text analytics methods, such as word associations, word placement, part-of-speech analysis, and text processing.

Like Key Phrase Extraction, the input includes both a selection of text and the optional ISO language code. The output is then a single column with a sentiment score corresponding to each text chuck, as shown in Table 8-4.

Table 8-4. Sample input and output for Power BI's Sentiment Analysis

Sample input	Sample input (optional)	Sample output
My wife and I both purchased this bike and so far, less than a month, we have been very happy with these bikes.	en	0.813

The final output score can be further modified to the user's liking. Some people find a scale from 0% to 100%, or binning the scores as negative, neutral, or positive, to be more intuitive for a report user. You may also wish to transform the sentiment score to a –1 to 1 scale, where negative and positive numbers correspond to negative and positive sentiment. This can be done by using a transformation of [Sentiment score]*2 - 1.

Recommendations and Limitations

Unlike Language Detection and Key Phrase Extraction, Sentiment Analysis works best with only a modest amount of text. Anything longer than two sentences is more likely to switch between different types of emotion and thus yield an imprecise measurement. It is common in business scenarios to have text with mixed emotions, such as user reviews that discuss both good and bad aspects of a product. Be aware that a score close to 0.5 can represent either neutral text or text that includes a balance of positive and negative elements.

In NLP, text sentiment can be measured in categories (positive versus negative) or on a numeric scale (with –1 to 1 being the most popular), but there is no optimal or universally accepted measure. Indeed, even as intelligent humans, we often misinterpret what other people say and mean. In our experience, we find that measures of sentiment for text are useful at a very high level for identifying patterns. At the same time, we recommend taking any sentiment score of a specific text with a grain of salt. As with any of these Azure AI Services, we suggest that they be used for reporting and visualizing data but not for determining an important outcome for any specific individual.

Microsoft supports 94 languages (*https://oreil.ly/AjUcs*) for Sentiment Analysis at the time of this writing. The algorithm also appears to incorporate emojis in its sentiment predictions, but it is unclear how well they were represented in the model training data. For this reason, we suggest not relying much on scoring text with many emojis or emoticons.

Demo 8-4: Sentiment Analysis

Analyzing our AirBnB reviews with Sentiment Analysis allows us to observe trends over time, by group, or by topic. It quickly creates a meaningful metric from hundreds of online reviews.

This demo picks up where Demo 8-3 left off and assumes the language of each review has already been identified from Demo 8-2. Since the text language is an optional input, you are also welcome to jump here after completing the data ingestion from Demo 8-1.

If the Power Query Editor window is not already open, select Transform Data in the Home ribbon to open it. Once in the Power Query Editor window, click Text Analytics in the Home ribbon (Figure 8-25).

Figure 8-25. The Text Analytics icon

Select "Score sentiment" in the left panel. Then click the ABC icon and select Column Name (Figure 8-26).

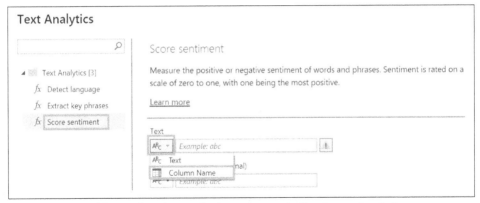

Figure 8-26. Enabling a dropdown of column names in Sentiment Analysis

Now click the drop-down arrow and select Reviews (Figure 8-27). This is the text column of reviews that we want to predict as being positive, neutral, or negative.

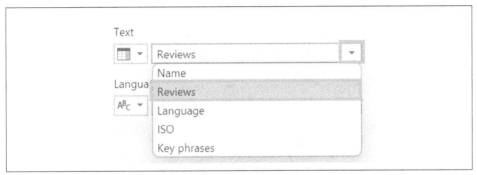

Figure 8-27. Specifying the text column whose sentiment you want to analyze

Repeat this step by filling in "Language ISO code" with the ISO column (Figure 8-28).

Figure 8-28. Specifying the text column with the detected language ISO code

Click OK.

Now you'll see a column added on to the end with a score from 0 (negative) to 1 (positive) corresponding to the predicted sentiment of each review.

The output has a mixed format of integers and text. It needs to be in decimal format before we can proceed to the next step. Click the ABC 123 icon and select Decimal Number (Figure 8-29).

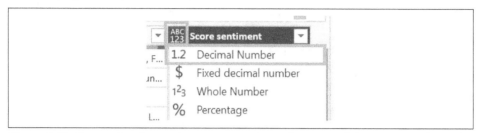

Figure 8-29. Converting the sentiment scores column from mixed data types to decimal number

It may be useful to quantify review sentiment as a single number, but that is not intuitive for the average person. To make a Power BI report that is more user-friendly, let's also categorize each review as positive, neutral, or negative.

Click Add Column to open up a new ribbon and select Conditional Column (Figure 8-30).

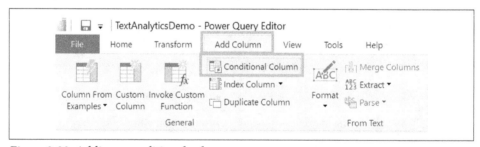

Figure 8-30. Adding a conditional column

There is no best way to determine which numeric scores belong in which sentiment category, but we highly recommend considering the use case when making a decision. The sentiment scores in this dataset skew high because the reviews are overwhelmingly positive, so we will make the threshold higher for binning. Specifically, we will define reviews under 0.6 as negative, equal to or between 0.6 and 0.8 as neutral, and greater than 0.8 as positive.

Complete the Add Conditional Column pop-up as shown in Figure 8-31. Under "New column name" add Sentiment. Then fill out the first condition so it reads, "If Score sentiment is less than 0.6 Then Negative." Click Add Clause and fill in the second condition to read, "Else If Score sentiment is greater than 0.8 Then Positive." Finally, under Else, enter Neutral to complete the logic. Click OK.

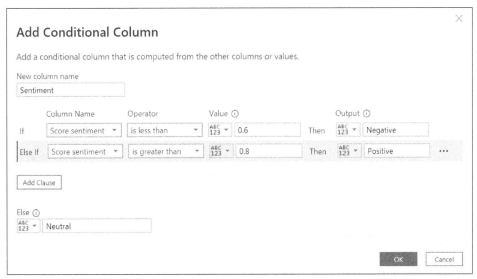

Figure 8-31. Adding a new column denoting sentiment as negative, positive, or neutral

Now you have two columns of sentiment: one defined numerically and the other categorically (Figure 8-32).

1.2 Score sentiment	ABC 123 Sentiment
0.79411763	Neutral
0.743902445	Neutral
1	Positive
0.884615362	Positive
0.999875069	Positive
0.565789461	Negative
0.999969602	Positive
0.999937773	Positive
0.99853915	Positive
0.756410241	Neutral
0.999976695	Positive

Figure 8-32. The numeric sentiment score and the conditional binned rating

We have finished augmenting our data and are ready to return to the report window. Click the Home tab and then the Close & Apply icon (Figure 8-33).

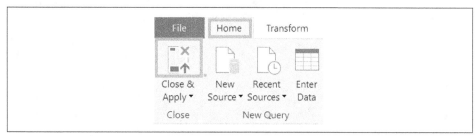

Figure 8-33. Closing the editor

It may take a minute for the data to finish loading. Return to Power BI Desktop and save the report. If prompted, apply changes.

You may still see a yellow bar on the window that remains even after you apply changes. Click "Discard changes" to see what has changed. In this case, it is the privacy levels, which you can disregard because the data will not need to be sent through AI Insights again. Click Discard (Figure 8-34).

Figure 8-34. Discarding changes to the privacy levels

To ensure the data has been correctly loaded, open the rightmost Fields pane and expand the TrentinoReviews table. Check for the following Text Analytics variables: Key phrases, Language, Score sentiment, and Sentiment (Figure 8-35).

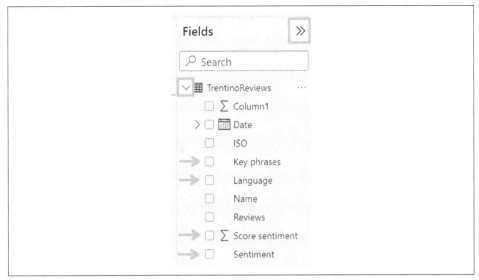

Figure 8-35. The newly created variables in the Fields pane

Now all of the augmented data is in place to build out a new, stunning report. Continue to Demo 8-5 for file links and a completed version of a report using the augmented data.

Explore the results on your own by considering the following questions:

- Do you notice any patterns about the reviews that are perfectly positive (i.e., scored as 1)?
- What review scored the lowest? Which words do you think contributed to the negative score?
- Based on the sentiment score of reviews, is this AirBnB listing a good place to stay?
- Has the listing gotten better or worse over time?
- Are any languages more associated with negative scores? What could be possible explanations for such an association?

If you have not been following along on your own in Power BI, you can still explore the augmented data via the transformed CSV on this book's GitHub (*https://oreil.ly/ch8_datacsv*).

Demo 8-5: Exploring a Report with Text Analytics

In this demo, we will use the transformed data from Demos 8-1 through 8-4 to create a report with AI Insights (Figure 8-36). We will skip the step-by-step process of building out the report and showcase the final result with Text Analytics. You can download your own copy from GitHub (*https://oreil.ly/ch8_result*).

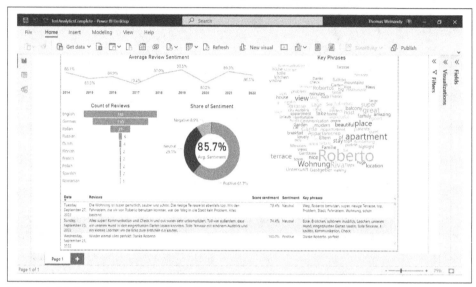

Figure 8-36. Sample report with AirBnB reviews data augmented using Text Analytics

Explore the results on your own by considering the following questions:

- What is the host's name? What is the host's name in Russian?
- What English words are most associated with a negative review?
- What year had the highest number of reviews from different languages?
- Of the reviews written in the top three languages, which ones had the greatest change in sentiment over time?
- What town is this listing in? Do English speakers view the town favorably?

You can also download a blank Power BI file with the transformed data via GitHub (*https://oreil.ly/ch8_transform*) to build the report out yourself.

We recommend considering the Word Cloud visual to represent the key phrases. This is not a standard visual and must be accessed through the AppSource. To do so, click the ellipsis under the Visualizations pane and select "Get more visuals" (Figure 8-37).

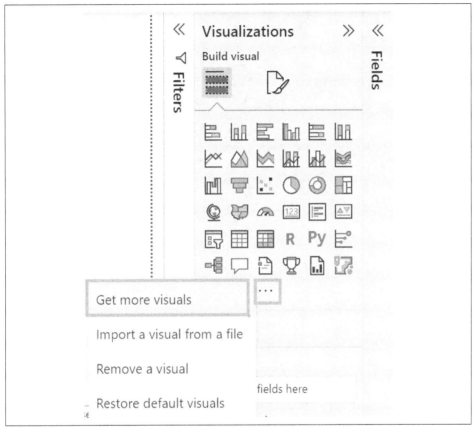

Figure 8-37. Finding a visual from Microsoft AppSource

Use the search bar to find Word Cloud by Microsoft and select it (Figure 8-38). It should now be visible in your Visualizations pane.

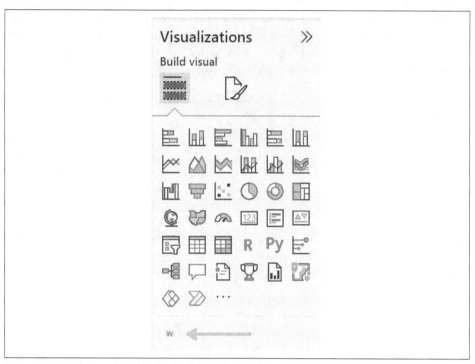

Figure 8-38. The newly added Word Cloud visual

Summary

Text is a common and potentially rich form of data for business decision making. The Text Analytics algorithms showcased in this chapter provide easy-to-use ways to augment datasets within Power BI. The newly transformed data then can help build compelling reports with the assistance of Language Detection, Key Phrase Extraction, and Sentiment Analysis.

In the next chapter, we will explore another tool within AI Insights, Computer Vision, which is used to add tags to images.

Image Tagging

A picture may be worth a thousand words to us humans, but to a computer, a picture provides just a few descriptions, if that. In fairness, image data is incredibly complex to a machine, and it's taken many advances in artificial intelligence to get where we are today. While computers may be lacking in picture recognition, they excel in their speed and scale of analysis. The prevalence of image data means businesses can unlock new insights by leveraging this AI ability.

By the end of this chapter, you will learn the fundamentals of computer vision and its relationship to artificial neural networks. You will also see examples of how organizations leverage object recognition for problem solving and data-driven analytics. Finally, you will be familiar with the benefits and limitations of image tagging within Power BI and confidently apply it to a real-world dataset of AirBnB listings for building a novel report.

Images as Data

We live in a time when data is cheap and getting cheaper each year. In 1956, 1 MB of disk storage cost over $100,000 in today's dollars. Now the same amount of disk storage costs 1/667th of a cent. This massive depreciation has allowed businesses to affordably store large amounts of data either on premises or in the cloud. This includes many different types of data, from numbers and text to more space-intensive formats like audio and video. These multimedia file types provide mind-boggling amounts of data for business use. Statistica forecasts that in just a few years, humanity will create, consume, and store over 25,000 exabytes (EB) of data annually. In comparison, a transcript of all human language ever spoken would fill only 5 EB of data.[1]

Digital photos, at a fundamental level, are nothing more than a table of numbers rendered in a way that produces an image. This can be seen in Figure 9-1, where a photo was converted to a spreadsheet (*https://oreil.ly/UyNUE*) with numbers corresponding to color brightness.

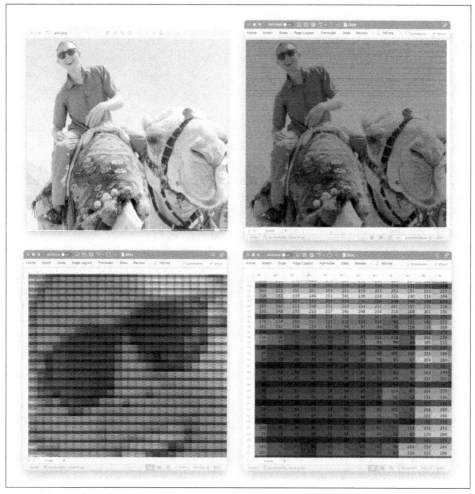

Figure 9-1. A digital image—a matrix of numbers representing color, hue, and position

---

1 An exabyte is equal to one million million megabytes. Storage costs are from John C. McCallum via Our World in Data (*https://oreil.ly/ywpux*), inflation adjustment from the U.S. Inflation Calculator (*https://oreil.ly/Qz84a*), storage forecasts from Statistica (*https://oreil.ly/F7-Wc*), and the exabyte factoid from Roy Williams (*https://oreil.ly/10bDU*) (accessed December 29, 2022).

The alternating rows of red-green-blue hues reveal a detail of me (Thomas) wearing sunglasses (not to be confused with the face on the right in the picture). We can understand a common JPEG file as a structured dataset of pixels defined by color, hue, and position. Now, if we want to identify patterns in structured data, we turn to machine learning for insights.

The field of study that uses AI to extract meaning from images or videos is known as *computer vision*. This is a class of technology that powers anything from content moderation systems to Snapchat filters to driverless cars. Computers, of course, are not capable of sight. Instead, computers take a photo in a digital format (literally, as a collection of digits) and use deep learning to identify patterns within those digits.

Deep Learning

As explained in Chapter 3, machine learning is a class of mathematical algorithms used to identify patterns in data. It is a subset of artificial intelligence, which is any program able to perform tasks that normally require human intelligence. AI is such a widely used term because it includes the most cutting-edge predictive models as well as simple if-then statements used for decision making. For example, the Insights feature, also discussed in Chapter 3, likely uses simple programmatic rules to identify which variables have the largest lift within a visual. On the other hand, Key Phrase Extraction, explored in Chapter 8, likely uses a machine learning model trained on previous data to predict which words belong together as a phrase and which phrases are important.

Deep learning is a subclass of machine learning models that uses artificial neural networks with multiple layers to make predictions. The relationship among artificial intelligence, machine learning, and deep learning is shown in Figure 9-2.

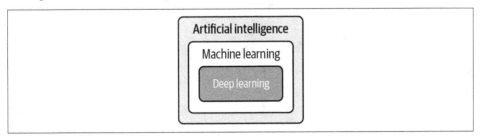

Figure 9-2. AI and its subclasses

An *artificial neural network*, or *neural net* for short, is an algorithm consisting of multiple interconnected series of nodes that produce some output. The neural network structure was inspired by models of the human brain. This is why a node is often called a "neuron." (The brain analogy is far from perfect, but the name has stuck, so we'll keep using it here.) When a neural network has multiple hidden layers, like the one shown in Figure 9-4, then it is called "deep." This is why these machine learning algorithms are referred to as "deep learning."

Neural networks have a rather simple structure, but given a large enough size and enough training data, they can represent incredibly complex relationships. The downside of neural networks is that they can require a significant amount of data and computing power to train. As of now, the most sophisticated algorithms in the world solving the most intricate problems are virtually all some form of artificial neural networks. They are especially good with complicated datatypes, such as text, audio, and—as you may have guessed—images.

For example, the AI system DALL·E 3 (*https://openai.com/dall-e-3*) uses a type of neural network algorithm to turn text prompts into images. Figure 9-3 was generated from the prompt "Photorealistic robot feeling the strain of a 9–5 corporate job keeping himself afloat with coffee. Imagine him performing his work with the attention of someone who's burnt out." Not bad for what is just math!

Figure 9-3. Image generated using DALL·E 3

DALL·E 3 takes text as an input and produces a predicted photo output. Image tagging, on the other hand, takes a photo input and predicts a text output. The results may be different, but they are both based on the power of deep learning.

A Simple Neural Network

Let's walk through a simple example to understand how neural networks work to predict the object in a single image. Recall the photo detail of sunglasses from Figure 9-1, shown as an approximate 20 × 60 table with 1,200 values. We can train a neural network that takes a vector of 1,200 values as an input and then outputs a probability prediction of whether that image contains sunglasses, a dog, or pizza. We can define the structure we want, which can depend on the compute resources available, the amount of training data, model performance, and the complexity of the problem. In this case, we define two hidden layers with five nodes each, shown in Figure 9-4.

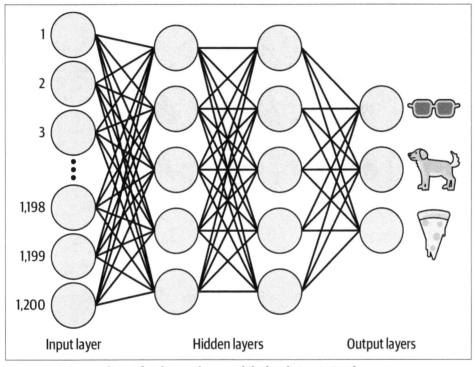

Figure 9-4. A sample artificial neural network before being trained

We now have to train the model using various pictures of sunglasses, dogs, and pizza with a label to signal which is the correct answer. This process assigns values to (1) the nodes in the hidden layers and (2) the weights—the lines that connect all nodes. Often the weights are biased downward, meaning that already-weak signals are dampened or even silenced to reduce noise. This is visualized in Figure 9-5, where line thickness represents weights.

Once the model is trained, we can input to the model a never-before-seen picture of sunglasses formatted as a vector of 1,200 numbers, shown in Figure 9-5 as the input column. The scoring moves from left to right, with the numbers adjusted according to the weights and values of lines and nodes as the score passes through the hidden layers. Then at the output layer, the final score indicates that those 1,200 numbers are predicted to be sunglasses with 89% confidence.

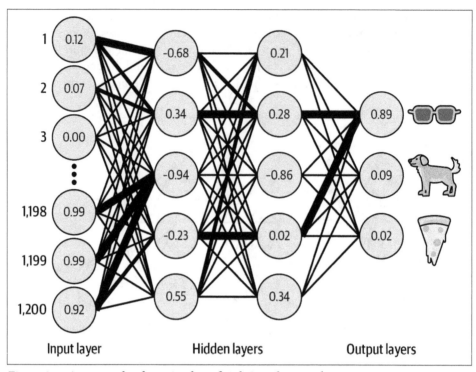

Figure 9-5. An example of a trained artificial neural network scoring an image

Artificial neural networks appear to work like magic, but at the end of the day, it is all just math. To make this more clear, let's imagine what is happening in some of those hidden layers. Each node in the hidden layer takes information from the image and recognizes some small pattern within that image—maybe it is the combination of hues that form the color black or the contrast of light and dark that form a rounded edge. This information then passes into the next hidden layer, which combines the previous information—maybe the combination of colors forms a smooth texture or the pattern of edges forms a rounded shape. Then the nodes representing smooth black circles lead to the prediction of sunglasses because the previous training data followed similar patterns.

To be clear, this is simply an example of what *could* be happening within these hidden layers. The more complex a model is, the more challenging it is to interpret what is happening under the surface. Such a topic is beyond the scope of this book, but those looking to dig into it more should check out *Interpretable Machine Learning* by Christoph Molnar (*https://oreil.ly/vaq0P*).

Image Tagging for Business

There are a wide variety of practical use cases for computer vision and image tagging, which is why we have dedicated an entire chapter to the topic. Facial recognition lets us unlock our phone or computer, while social media sites use it to tag our friends. Manufacturers and consumer packaged goods companies use computer vision for quality control to know when an image reveals a product defect. Retailers use it to track inventory management levels and to understand consumer behavior by watching how shoppers move about a store. Some high-end farm equipment (*https://oreil.ly/v3Tyn*) even has built-in image-tagging capabilities to identify whether a plant is a crop (and should be passed over) or a weed (and should be sprayed with an herbicide).

Probably the most important application of image tagging by data analysts is for image categorization and search. This provides the backbone of a website like Google Photos automatically presents alt text with images, allowing a user to perform various queries of the photo collection, such as "beach," "coffee," or even a specific face. *Alt text*, short for *alternative text*, is a brief text description of an online image often used for accessibility and discovery. In July 2019, Facebook experienced an outage that temporarily prevented pictures from being shown. Instead, and to the surprise of many users, the site displayed the alt text for each image that Facebook had added using image tagging (Figure 9-6).

Figure 9-6. A Facebook image outage revealed this alt text (left) assigned to one photo (right)

Another benefit of alt text is to increase accessibility for people with vision impairments by providing a quick description of an image's contents. Just as with any technology, it is important to consider whether AI is being used in ethical ways (e.g., to provide accessibility) or in unethical applications (e.g., to engage in unwarranted surveillance of individuals).

Image tagging is an effective addition to Power BI that can unlock incredible amounts of information contained within photos—and do so at scale. You can use this to filter pictures by a specific tag, identify trends in user-generated content, and sort incoming image data according to the appropriate audience, to name a few examples. Check out the sample report at the end of the chapter for inspiration.

How It Works

Like the other AI Insights features discussed in Chapter 8, Vision within Power BI leverages Microsoft's Azure AI Services, the catalog of pretrained machine learning models accessible through an API. In this case, the interface to the image-tagging algorithm is built directly into Power BI. It does, however, still securely send data to Microsoft's cloud for scoring. This matters for any organization that restricts what data is allowed to leave its premises.

Vision is available in the Power BI service and Power BI Desktop, yet both require Power BI Premium. See the end of Chapter 1 for details on benefits and costs as well as how to sign up for a free trial.

Also, as with the other AI Insights features described in Chapter 8, Microsoft does not disclose which algorithms are used within these predictive models. It is, however, rather certain that the company uses some form of artificial neural network. The models are also being continuously improved and retrained, so do not be surprised if you get slightly different predictions for the same image over time.

For its input, Power BI's Image Tag can read images as a URL, in raw binary format, or a base-64 encoded string.[2] We recommend using URLs when possible. If you do so, make sure the image URLs are publicly accessible; you can test this by opening the link in a private browsing session. Also in the input, you have the option to specify the ISO code of the language the tag output should be in. Power BI currently supports

---

2 "Base-64 is an encoding format that can represent a binary object as text. For example, paste this base-64 string of over 3,907 characters (*https://oreil.ly/GU9G5*) from GitHub into your browser to find out which emoji it is.

English (en), Spanish (es), Simplified Chinese (zh_chs), Japanese (ja), and Portuguese (pt).

The algorithm will then tag the specified images based on over two thousand objects, living beings, actions, and sceneries. Unlike the tags in other image-tagging programs, the tags here are not defined within any kind of logical hierarchy. This means that a tag could be "dog" but not "animal_dog_puppy."

In the example in Tables 9-1 and 9-2, which uses the image in Figure 9-7, we excluded the ISO language code, and Image Tag automatically defaulted to English tags.

Table 9-1. Sample input for Image Tag

Image	Language ISO code (optional)
https://github.com/tomweinandy/ai-with-power-bi/blob/main/Chapter9/TrentinoExample.jpg	

The output also explodes the number of observations vertically, meaning it creates a new row for each tag in each image. A single image generated four new rows with information about the single tag as well as a list and JSON of the other image tags. See Demo 9-2 for how to reduce the number of rows to the original length of the data.

Also note the confidence column, which states the predicted accuracy for each tag. The confidence level is between 0 and 1; however, the algorithm only returns tags where the confidence is greater than 0.1.

Table 9-2. Sample output from Image Tag

Tag images.Tags	Tag images.Json	Tag images.Tag	Tag images.Error Message	Tag images.Confidence
tree, snow, outdoor, house	{"confidences":[{"name":"tree", "confidence":0.99954599142074585}, {"name":"snow", "confi dence":0.999464213848114}, {"name":"outdoor", "confi dence":0.99440163373947144}, {"name":"house", "confi dence":0.83191853761672974}]}	house		0.8319185376
tree, snow, outdoor, house	{"confidences":[{"name":"tree", "confidence":0.99954599142074585}, {"name":"snow", "confi dence":0.999464213848114}, {"name":"outdoor", "confi dence":0.99440163373947144}, {"name":"house", "confi dence":0.83191853761672974}]}	outdoor		0.9944016337

Tag images.Tags	Tag images.Json	Tag images.Tag	Tag images.Error Message	Tag images.Confidence
tree, snow, outdoor, house	`{"confidences":[{"name":"tree", "confidence":0.99954599142074585}, {"name":"snow", "confi dence":0.999464213848114}, {"name":"outdoor", "confi dence":0.99440163373947144}, {"name":"house", "confi dence":0.83191853761672974}]}`	snow		0.9994642138
tree, snow, outdoor, house	`{"confidences":[{"name":"tree", "confidence":0.99954599142074585}, {"name":"snow", "confi dence":0.999464213848114}, {"name":"outdoor", "confi dence":0.99440163373947144}, {"name":"house", "confi dence":0.83191853761672974}]}`	tree		0.9995459914

Limitations of Vision

The first three limitations listed here are generic to Azure AI Services, while the remaining are specific to the Tag Image function within the Vision AI Insight.

- AI Insights built into a query can slow down incremental refresh, causing performance issues.
- There is currently no support for Direct Query.
- Microsoft does not describe the data used to create these pretrained models.
- Images must be in JPEG, PNG, BMP, or GIF format.
- Report performance is slower with a larger number of photos.
- Objects are often not recognized if . . .
  - They are small (less than 5% of image)
  - The image itself is small (50 × 50)
  - They are stacked or clustered around other objects

The best way to explore the capabilities and limitations of Image Tag is to test it out with real-world data, which we do in Demo 9-1.

Demo 9-1: Ingest AirBnB Data

Previously, an organization with a dataset of images could not do much at scale with that information. Image tagging allows that same organization to extract details hidden in plain sight by augmenting a dataset. This enables greater filtering and pattern recognition to maximize the organization's business intelligence capabilities.

We are continuing our case study from Chapter 8 with data about AirBnB listings from the province of Trentino, Italy. Instead of showing reviews of a single listing, we have details for one hundred listings. This includes the listings' cover images, such as the one shown in Figure 9-7, stored as URLs. In this demonstration, we will show how to tag images within Power BI and then use that data to enhance a report.

Figure 9-7. Photo from an AirBnB listing in northern Italy

Open a new report in Power BI Desktop and click through the pop-up window. Check that you are signed in to your Microsoft account. If not, then you will see the "Sign in" option near the top-right corner (Figure 9-8). Click this and follow the prompts to connect your school or work account with Premium access. Refer to the end of Chapter 1 for details about Power BI Premium and how to claim a free trial.

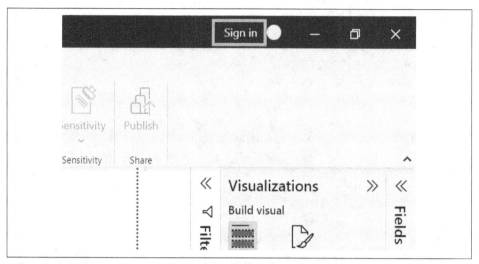

Figure 9-8. Signing into your Microsoft account in Power BI Desktop

Now it is time to ingest the sample data. In the Home ribbon, select "Get data" and then Web as the source of the data (Figure 9-9).

> You can also ingest the data as a dataflow using an organizational account. Refer to the instructions and use case in Chapter 1.

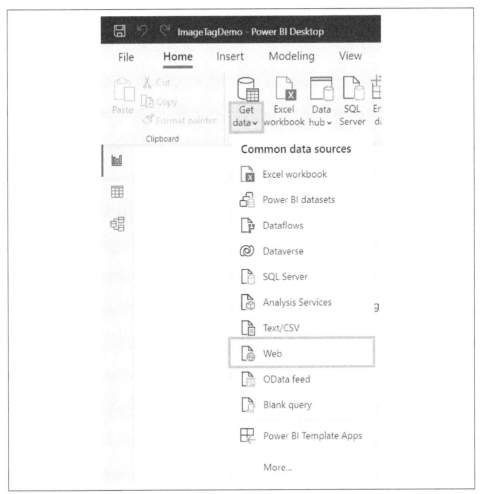

Figure 9-9. Adding data from a URL

If you select the "Get data" icon instead of the "Get data" text, you will instead see a different pop-up window. If this happens, type "web" in the Search bar, select Web, and then click Connect before proceeding to the next step.

In the new pop-up window, copy the link (*https://raw.githubusercontent.com/tomwei nandy/ai-with-power-bi/main/Chapter9/TrentinoListings.csv*) and paste it in the box under URL. This is a CSV of the AirBnB listings hosted on the book's GitHub repository. Click OK (Figure 9-10).

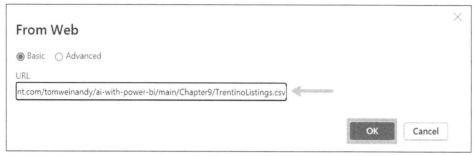

Figure 9-10. Pasting a URL of raw data from GitHub

You'll now see a preview of the data that shows the listing name and description. If you scroll to the right, you'll see an image URL as well as other information about the AirBnB. Before loading the data into the Power BI report, we want to augment the data using AI Insights. To do this, select Transform Data (Figure 9-11).

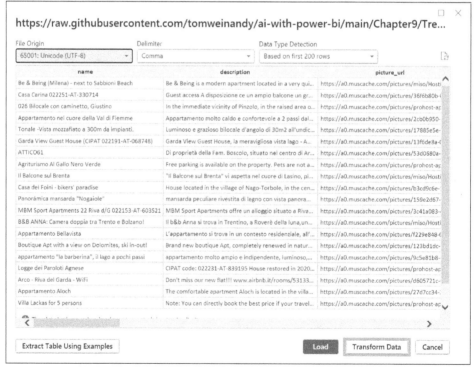

Figure 9-11. Preview of data before transformation

This opens up the Power Query Editor to complete the data transformations (Figure 9-12). Note that this is a separate window, so if you get lost, be sure to check whether it is obscured by the Power BI report window.

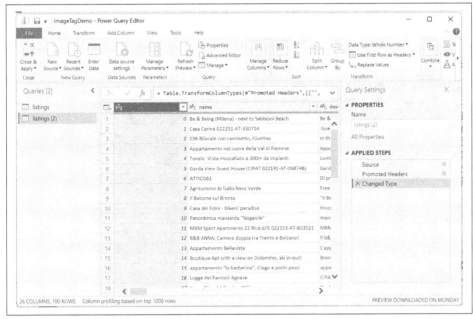

Figure 9-12. The Power Query Editor window

Now is a good time to save the report using the save icon in the upper-left corner or by selecting File and then Save. If prompted, select Apply to apply changes to the data that occurred from the ingest (Figure 9-13).

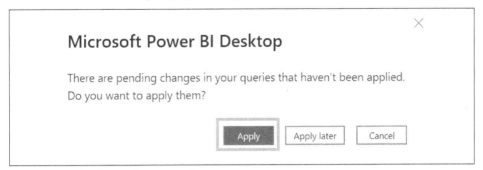

Figure 9-13. Applying changes to the report

The data is now ingested, so we are ready to transform it with Image Tag.

Demo 9-2: Image Tagging

In this section, we will use Image Tag within Vision to predict which objects are present in our AirBnB listings. You can pick up from here if using your own dataset; however, this example will pick up where we left off in Demo 9-1.

If the Power Query Editor window is not already open, then click the "Transform data" icon in the Home ribbon (Figure 9-14).

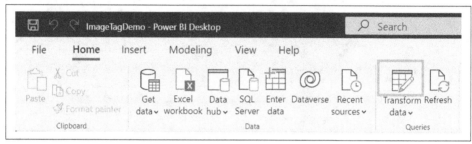

Figure 9-14. Transform data icon

On the Home ribbon, select Vision in the AI Insights group (Figure 9-15).

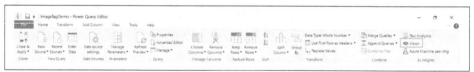

Figure 9-15. Vision icon

A new window will appear and confirm your access level—this may take as long as a minute. Sign in here if prompted. Your license will be automatically added, and if you have a Premium license, you will be able to proceed. You may either remain with the default (and do nothing) or select which Premium capacity you want to use (Figure 9-16).

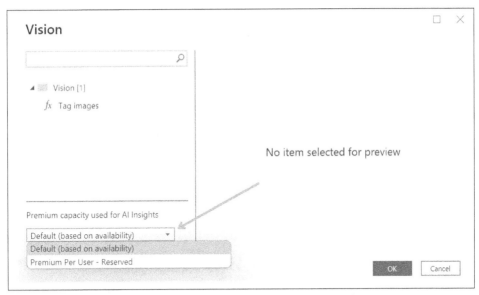

Figure 9-16. Checking your level of Premium capacity in Power BI

Select "Tag images" from the left pane. Next, identify the column of data to run through the algorithm. Select the empty field under "Image (optional)" and then click the variable that holds the images—in this case, picture_url (Figure 9-17).

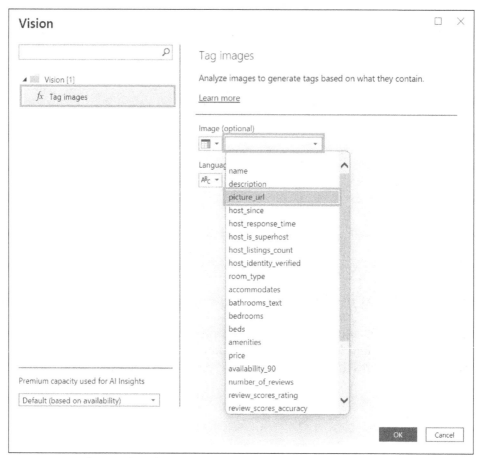

Figure 9-17. Selecting the column with image data

The default language of the image tags is English, so if this is what you intend, proceed by clicking OK (Figure 9-18).

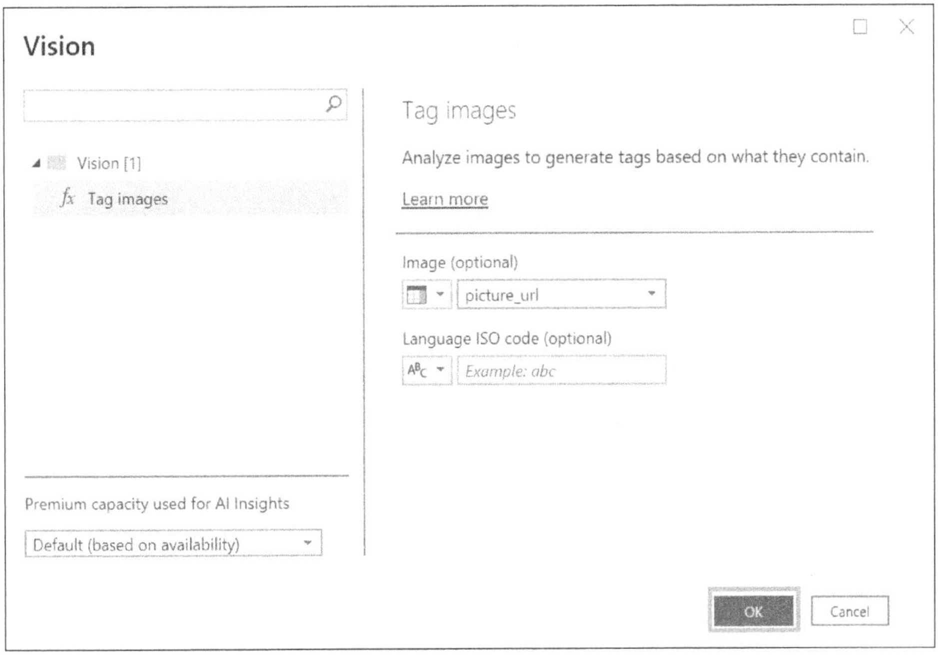

Vision

☐ ✕

🔍

▲ ▥ Vision [1]

   fx Tag images

Tag images

Analyze images to generate tags based on what they contain.

Learn more

Image (optional)

[▥ ▾] picture_url   ▾

Language ISO code (optional)

[ᴬᴮ𝒸 ▾] *Example: abc*

Premium capacity used for AI Insights

Default (based on availability)   ▾

OK   Cancel

Figure 9-18. Beginning image tagging

You may now see a warning pop up that you must agree to before proceeding. This appears because Image Tag sends data to a machine learning algorithm hosted on the cloud before returning results to the Power BI report. Some organizations do not permit certain data to leave the organization. If that is the policy, the organization should not use AI Insights. Read more about Power's BI's privacy levels in Microsoft's official documentation (*https://oreil.ly/_1JRG*). You can safely ignore the privacy level for this demo because the AirBnB listing data is not sensitive; however, be sure to use the appropriate privacy level for other reports (Figure 9-19).

ⓘ Information is required about data privacy.   Continue

Figure 9-19. The warning that appears the first time you use AI Insights on a new dataset

The transformed data is now visible in the Power Query Editor as columns are added on to the end of the table. (You may need to scroll to the right to see them.) We are interested in the new column "Tag images.Tags," but the rest are not relevant for this particular demo. Find this column, right-click it, select Rename, and rename it to "image_tags" (Figure 9-20).

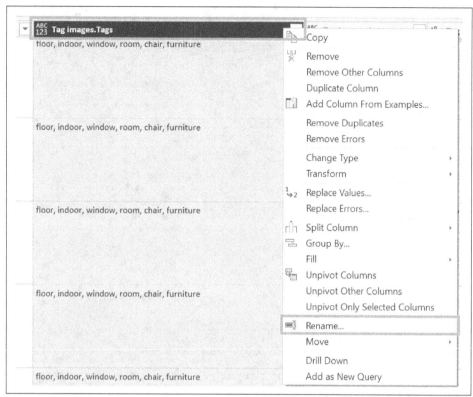

Figure 9-20. Renaming a column

Since you will not need the other new columns, you can delete them to reduce the data load. Highlight the columns "Tag images.Json," "Tag images.Tag," "Tag images.Confidence," and "Tag images.ErrorMessage" and click the Remove Columns icon (Figure 9-21).

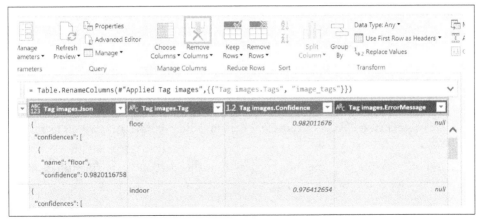

Figure 9-21. Removing the unneeded columns from the data model

You may have noticed that the number of rows has dramatically increased. During the image-tagging step, the dataset exploded vertically, creating a unique row for each object tagged within each image. Now that we have removed the column with a unique tag for each listing, we can deduplicate the rows and return to the original number of observations. Select the Remove Rows option and click Remove Duplicates (Figure 9-22). Note that you still have a column with the list of tags that augments the data.

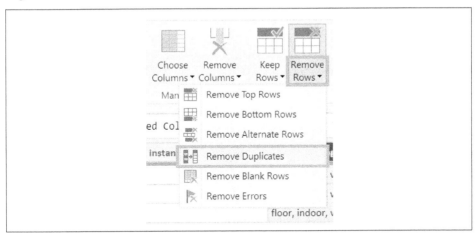

Figure 9-22. Removing duplicate rows from the dataset

Save your work and then click Close & Apply to close out of Power Query Editor.

Explore the results on your own by considering the following questions:

- Which AirBnB listing would be good for a ski trip? Why?
- Does there appear to be some kind of limit on the number of tags allowed for one image?
- What are some of the more common tags identified? The less common?
- The listing named "Al Pescatore for 4 persons" did not have any tags on its image. Why?
- Find an example of something tagged in an image that is not identified as an amenity for that listing.

If you were not following along on your own in Power BI, you can still explore the augmented data from the transformed CSV on this book's GitHub (*https://oreil.ly/ch9_transformcsv*).

We are now ready to build out our report with the tags extracted from the AirBnB listing images. These tags have increased the data available, revealing information previously invisible to Power BI.

Demo 9-3: Exploring a Report with Vision

We will not go step-by-step through how to build a report in Power BI Desktop. Instead, we will highlight two less-common applications: displaying images and creating a word cloud.

First, we will display images of the AirBnB listings in the report itself. Click the Table visual and select the picture_url column so that it populates the Columns well (Figure 9-23).

The problem now is that Power BI is treating the URLs as text and not images. Next, click the "Data view" icon in the left pane to review the data. Select the picture_url column, which will reveal the Column tools ribbon. Next to "Data category," click the dropdown and select Image URL (Figure 9-24).

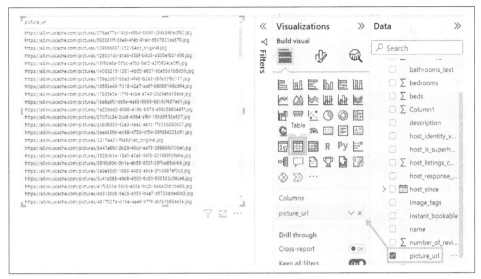

Figure 9-23. Populating a table visual with images

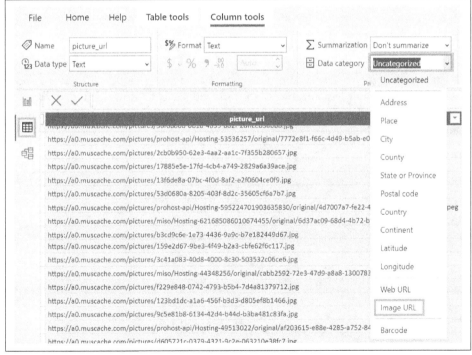

Figure 9-24. Changing the default data category from Uncategorized to Image URL

Return to the Report view by clicking the top icon on the left pane (Figure 9-25). The images of the listings are now displayed; however, they are quite small. To increase the size, select the Table visual already created in the report editor. Then in the Visualizations pane, click the top-middle "Format visual" icon (Figure 9-25). Now you can scroll down to select Image size and increase Height (up to 150). If you cannot find Image size, it is most likely because you do not have the Table visual selected.

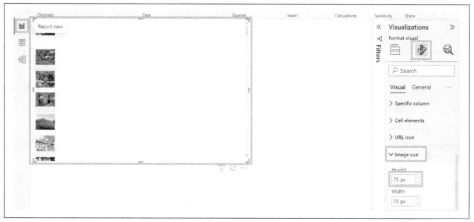

Figure 9-25. Selecting the Table visual in order to change Image size

You may also want to display the image tags as a word cloud. This is not possible with the default visualizations, so you will have to download one through AppSource. Click the ellipsis under the Visualizations pane and select "Get more visuals" (Figure 9-26).

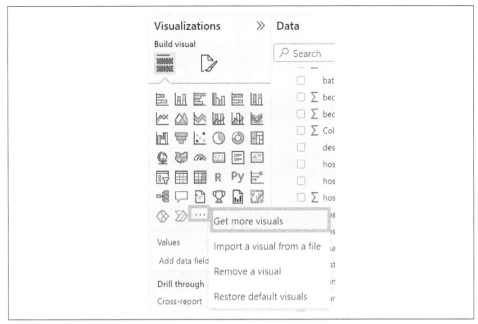

Figure 9-26. Accessing a visual from Microsoft AppSource

Use the search bar to find Word Cloud by Microsoft. Select it and click Add (Figure 9-27).

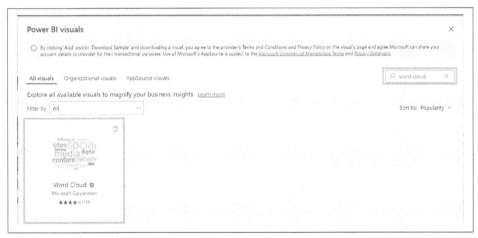

Figure 9-27. Searching for the Word Cloud visual in AppSource

Click OK to proceed. The Word Cloud icon should now be visible in your Visualizations pane (Figure 9-28).

Figure 9-28. How Word Cloud visual displays in the Visualizations pane

We will leave it to you to add the tags column and format the visual to your liking. You can download a completed version of the report for yourself at the book's GitHub page (*https://oreil.ly/ch9_complete*). See the sample in Figure 9-29.

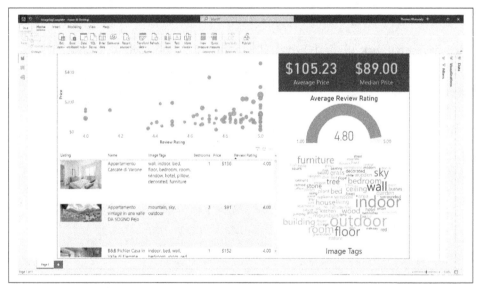

Figure 9-29. Sample Power BI report with image tags that is available for download

Thanks to image tagging, the report has text descriptions that did not exist in the original dataset. A user can even select an individual tag from the word cloud that will cross-filter on all listings with an image of that tag. This creates additional value and usability for Power BI reports with image data.

Explore the results on your own by considering the following questions:

- Do more photos show the inside of the listing or the outside, or are the numbers about the same?
- What's the name of the listing described in Chapter 8? (Hint: it had bushes.)
- Are listings with a picture of nature higher or lower quality? Why do you think that is?
- How would you describe the largest listing? The most expensive listing?
- What is the average price for a 5-star listing? How does that compare to all other listings? (Hint: select multiple points on the scatter plot by holding Ctrl and drawing a rectangle around the points.)

Summary

Thanks to advances in artificial neural networks, computer vision is now more accurate and accessible than ever. Image Tag within Power BI can unlock business insights from data that was previously hidden in plain sight. It is a powerful addition to any dataset that includes pictures, as shown in the example with AirBnB listings. You now have the skills and tools needed to begin augmenting your own reports to create new analyses.

Custom Machine Learning Models

In Chapter 3, we discussed how to train and host a custom machine learning model within Power BI using AutoML. But what if you already have a trained model from a data scientist at your organization? Or you want to specify which algorithm to use? Or you want to more closely monitor and interpret a model? In these cases, you will need another platform that can deploy a custom machine learning model and still connect with Power BI. The solution here is to use Azure Machine Learning (details later on how to get a free trial of this through Azure). We will show you how to train your own custom model in Azure and use it to score data within Power BI.

AI Business Strategy

In 2013, the MD Anderson Cancer Center in Houston, Texas, started an AI project to diagnose and recommend treatments for cancer patients. After four years of development and $62 million in costs, the project was paused before ever being used on patients. At the same time, the center's IT department successfully implemented AI models to make hotel and restaurant recommendations for patients' families, identify patients who needed help to pay bills, and address staffing problems.[1]

The lesson from the story is that smaller-scale applications are often much more successful than moonshot projects. We do not, however, want to deter an organization from being ambitious; instead, a business should start small and scale up—in terms of both project scope and organizational capabilities. It's better to develop an AI strategy and invest in capabilities than to put all your eggs in one basket on a single solution. Companies should understand the strengths and weaknesses behind the various AI

---

1 Thomas H. Davenport and Rajeev Ronanki, "Artificial Intelligence for the Real World," *Harvard Business Review* 96, no. 1 (2018): 108–116.

technologies as well as their own internal strengths and weaknesses to execute on those technologies.

Organizational Learning with AI

So how does an organization scale its artificial intelligence capabilities? Some researchers interested in this question interviewed over three thousand managers and executives to define the path companies take to integrate AI into their business.[2] They identified four such stages, visualized in Figure 10-1. First is *discovering AI*, when an organization applies AI in a targeted area to a narrow set of business problems. In the next stage, the organization begins *building AI* by investing in the data, cloud infrastructure, and hiring necessary to establish AI capabilities. Here the company has data science roles applying AI across multiple departments. Third, the organization is *scaling AI* when it has embedded a suite of AI solutions into a wide array of processes and problems. It is able to more quickly and effectively train, evaluate, deploy, and monitor machine learning models. The final stage is *organizational learning with AI*. Organizations at this point have structured themselves in such a way that humans and algorithms across the company are actively working together, learning from each other, and continuously improving in the process. In this stage, AI is not just a strategic part of the business—it is actively guiding the business's strategy.

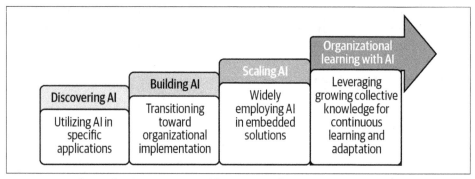

Figure 10-1. The path to organizational learning with AI

The next goal of the research was to determine how AI impacts the bottom line of an organization. Surprisingly, the researchers found that most companies are still not seeing strong returns from investment in AI. Digging deeper into the numbers, they discovered that the level of AI maturity at a company mattered a great deal. The researchers used logistic regression to predict the likelihood that a company

---

2 Sam Ransbotham et al., "Expanding AI's Impact with Organizational Learning," *MIT Sloan Management Review* and Boston Consulting Group, October 2020.

receives significant financial benefits from using AI.[3] They also broke down the results according to the four stages of AI maturity.

As shown in Figure 10-2, organizations discovering AI have a measly 2% chance of significant financial benefits from the "one-and-done" approach of discovering AI, but this increases to 21% when building AI. There is a similar jump to a 39% likelihood of receiving significant financial benefits when the organization is scaling AI; however, the probability jumps more dramatically to 73% by organizational learning with AI.

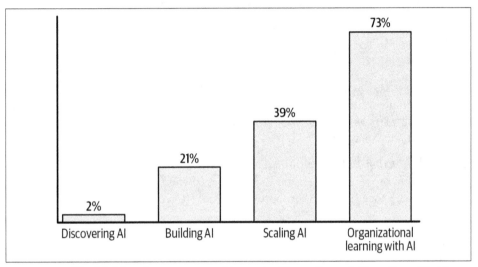

Figure 10-2. The likelihood a company achieves significant financial benefits with AI

We take three lessons from these findings. First is how large returns from AI investments can come from any stage of maturity. There is no magic rule that your company will be transformed after hiring its 10th data scientist. Second, the likelihood of significant financial returns increases as a company moves along the path toward organizational learning with AI. It is still good business strategy to develop AI skills and capabilities (but you already know that as a reader of this book). The third lesson we take from this study is that there is no guarantee an organization will receive a significant financial benefit from AI. Even companies at the final stage have more than a one in four chance of not seeing significant benefits.

---

3 *Logistic regression* is a machine learning algorithm that predicts one of two outcomes, in this case, if a company received significant financial benefits or not. See "Binary Prediction" on page 90 for more details. As defined by the researchers, "significant financial benefits" means a $5 million to $100 million increase in revenue or reduction in costs. The precise threshold varies by the size of the company.

Successful Organizational Behaviors

One limitation of the previous research is that it was more predictive of financial performance than prescriptive for how an organization should behave. Another related study, also using interviews with managers and executives, identified five key behaviors to successfully use AI within an organization:[4]

Integrate AI strategy into business strategy
    Researchers found that 88% of respondents who integrated AI initiatives into their digital strategy reported a positive business impact.

Unify AI initiatives with larger business transformations
    In order for AI initiatives to succeed, managers must create cross-functional collaborations by unlocking data and allowing teams to work together.

Take on large risks that prioritize revenue growth over cost reduction
    Of respondents who saw revenue growth, 72% expected similar results in the next five years, while only 44% of respondents who saw cost reduction expected to see it happen again.

Align AI production with AI consumption
    Successful organizations ensure that business owners, process owners, and developers work together to adopt solutions effectively across the company.

Invest in talent and avoid technological lock-in
    The most effective AI application leverages in-house data and a customized algorithm to solve a specific business problem instead of using off-the-shelf technology. Respondents reported seeing value in 34% of the AI initiatives under the CEO (who is more likely to invest in the process) compared to 17% of the AI initiatives under the CIO (who is more likely to outsource the technology).

The last point emphasizes how important it is for an organization to tailor AI to suit its own business needs. This, not coincidentally, is the topic of the current chapter: how to apply custom algorithms in Power BI using Azure Machine Learning. But before we dive into that topic, it is worth first explaining what we mean by the title and what makes a machine learning model "custom."

Custom Machine Learning

We already covered the difference between pretrained and custom machine learning models in Chapter 8. Now we are going to explore conceptually what it means to train a custom machine learning model.

---

4 Sam Ransbotham et al., "Winning with AI," MIT *Sloan Management Review* and Boston Consulting Group, October 2019.

Machine Learning Versus Typical Programming

A helpful way to understand machine learning is to contrast it with what came before: traditional programming. To write an algorithm with traditional programming, you have to code line by line what the algorithm will do. We show this conceptually in Figure 10-3.

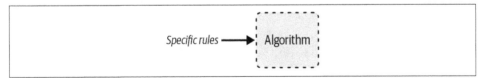

Figure 10-3. Coding an algorithm with traditional programming

For example, imagine you want to create an algorithm for sentiment analysis using traditional programming. You could achieve this by coming up with thousands of specific rules, such as:

- If text contains the word "happy," then label as "positive."
- If text contains the word "sad," then label as "negative."
- If a word is preceded by the word "not," then assign the opposite label.

This method of traditional programming creates an algorithm that is still AI (as it simulates human intelligence); however, it can require a lot of human effort to create and might not provide the most robust of predictions.

Compare this with the process of training a machine learning algorithm, shown in Figure 10-4.

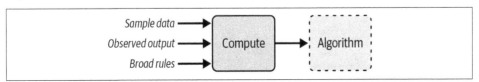

Figure 10-4. Training an algorithm with machine learning

The first requirement is the sample historical data. Some machine learning algorithms can work with a modest amount of data (e.g., ordinary linear regression) while others are much more data intensive (e.g., deep learning).

The second input is observed output. This is the labeled outcomes required in supervised machine learning models. If a problem class is unsupervised machine learning (e.g., clustering, anomaly detection), then there is no observed output.

The third requirement is the broad rules that define what kind of algorithm is being used and, if applicable, its hyperparameters and evaluation metric. For example, you may declare that you would like a decision tree algorithm that is trained on no more than 10 variables and includes no more than 4 branches. These rules are broad because they determine certain aspects like the type of model and how it's tuned, yet they do not code the exact weights that define the shape of the algorithm.

These three inputs are then used to train an algorithm that defines the specific rules for how predictions are made. For example, we could use machine learning to create an algorithm for sentiment analysis. We would need to have a collection of text snippets (the sample data) with labels stating which are positive and which are negative (observed output) and select which sort of algorithm to train (broad rules). The training process then identifies which rules make for the best predictions based on the sample data—maybe the algorithm finds on its own that snippets with the fire emoji ( ) are almost always positive.

The main difference between traditionally programmed algorithms and machine learning algorithms is that the former hardcodes the rules as an input while the latter uses a model-training stage to generate the rules. In other words, the program "learns" from the sample data which specific rules best predict the previously observed output—thus the name "machine learning." Another important distinction with machine learning algorithms is that they require compute for training, which can become expensive for certain types of algorithms, data formats, and scenarios.

The new algorithm, whether traditionally programmed or trained via machine learning, is then ready to be deployed to make predictions, as shown in Figure 10-5.

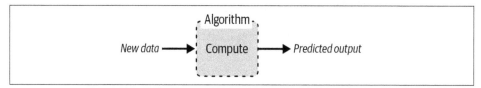

Figure 10-5. Deploying an algorithm for prediction

The power of machine learning is its ability to write the rules of prediction at a speed, scale, and level of sophistication not possible with human programmers alone. Machine learning results are also often better than unassisted humans at identifying underlying patterns in data.

Narrow AI Versus General AI

We have already discussed many different AI tools within Power BI and what they can do, but we have not spent much time covering what these models *cannot* do. That is because the previous examples of machine learning are all narrow AI and can perform only their intended purpose. *Narrow intelligence* refers to AI that is only capable of implementing some predefined task or small set of tasks. For example, a calculator is narrow AI because it can execute only specifically programmed functions. As Pablo

Picasso said about computers, "But they are useless. They can only give you answers." We may not agree that narrow AI is "useless," but Picasso was right to identify its limited intelligence.

Sometimes narrow AI is also referred to as "weak AI"; however, we dislike that term because these algorithms can still be incredibly powerful and sophisticated models. Google Search may be the most highly developed algorithm in human history, even though it "only" retrieves and ranks content on the internet. It just does so very well.

Conversely, *general intelligence* (sometimes referred to as strong AI or artificial general intelligence [AGI]) is the ability to exhibit a wide range of cognitive abilities and functions. You exhibit general intelligence because you can read this book about AI, interpret the pictures inside the book, tell a friend about the book, leave a five-star review of the book, and question if the book's authors are making a joke or just sounding desperate. A narrow AI algorithm may consistently beat you in a game of chess, but it cannot write a post on LinkedIn about an insightful anecdote from *Artificial Intelligence with Microsoft Power BI.*

 AGI has been portrayed in film for nearly a hundred years, often as an antagonist to human characters. This goes at least as far back as the Maschinenmensch in *Metropolis* (1927), followed later by HAL 9000 in *2001: A Space Odyssey* (1968), the T-800 series in *The Terminator* (1984), Agent Smith in *The Matrix* (1999), and the titular Ultron in *Avengers: Age of Ultron* (2015). These movies shaped public perceptions around AI as being general intelligence, when in reality, nearly all of AI today is narrow intelligence.

AI personal assistants like Alexa and Google Home also seem to exhibit general intelligence because they can perform a variety of tasks; however, they are more like a highly architected stack of narrow AI algorithms. For example, when you ask Siri to "open the pod bay door," the algorithm goes through the series of steps described in Figure 10-6. It first uses a model designed to convert audio data to text, then it uses a language understanding model to predict the intention of the text, then it conveys that intention in the form of a question to a model that retrieves an answer, and finally, it converts the text answer into audio that you can hear.

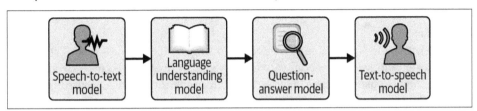

Figure 10-6. AI in a home assistant is a stack of narrow AI models

Large language models (LLMs) are some of the first widely available algorithms that exhibit signs of AGI. Like ChatGPT, explored in Chapter 7, LLMs are highly sophisticated text completion models. What makes them different from narrow AI is that LLMs can perform tasks that they were not specifically trained to do. The developers of ChatGPT did not know what the algorithm would be capable of until after it was trained. We believe we are in the earliest stage of AGI development, because LLMs are capable of a wide variety of tasks but are still limited to text-based input and outputs.

For the remainder of this chapter, we are going to stay in the realm of narrow intelligence as we build machine learning models in Azure Machine Learning and deploy them within Power BI.

Azure Machine Learning

Azure Machine Learning (Azure ML) is a cloud-based service by Microsoft for managing all components of the machine learning lifecycle. It allows users to train, deploy, and monitor machine learning models at scale and with all of the benefits of Microsoft Azure, such as data storage, governance, security, and compliance. The *machine learning lifecycle* is the iterative process of building and deploying machine learning products to continuously improve business goals.

Figure 10-7 visualizes the machine learning lifecycle, describing step-by-step how your organization can repeatedly deploy machine learning to achieve its goals:

1. *Business goal*

    Begin by articulating the specific business problem to solve or the goal to work toward.

2. *Data collection*

    Identify the data needed to reach the business goal and ensure it is in a condition and location to be processed. It may also be necessary in this stage to build a data model.

3. *Data processing*

    Ensure the data is in a usable format, clean it, and define the variables that will be consumed by the machine learning model.

4. *Model training*

    Determine the type of algorithm needed to support the business goal. Then train, evaluate, and select a model. At this stage, there may be feature selection that modifies, drops, or creates new variables from the model. If so, return to Step 3 and incorporate those changes.

5. Model deployment

Deploy the chosen model. Now it can consume new data that has gone through the same preprocessing defined in Step 3. The new data is scored, and those predictions help inform the business goal from Step 1. As an optional addition, the model can be interpreted, and the resulting insights can be used to describe which model features are most important or identify prescriptions for which business levers can be pulled to increase impact.

6. Model monitoring

Machine learning models will inevitably experience technical issues at some point. They also slowly lose their predictive power as the world changes (in a process called *drift*). Either way, the model will have to be monitored over time to see if there are any changes in performance. As a model loses efficacy, it will become necessary to retrain it (Step 4) with more recent data. The model's performance will also impact the business goal, which begins the cycle over again.

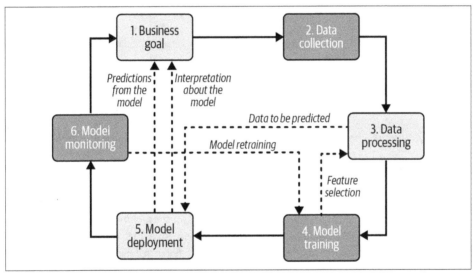

Figure 10-7. The machine learning lifecycle

The operational process of using infrastructure and automation to monitor and maintain machine learning models is known as *MLOps*, short for *machine learning operations*. MLOps is a necessary consideration for any custom machine learning model used in production. Although it is out of scope for this book to go very deep into MLOps, we will point out that all standard MLOps features are available within Azure Machine Learning. For this chapter, however, we will focus on Steps 4 and 5: training and deploying custom machine learning models.

Azure Subscription and Free Trial

You will need to sign up for an account to access the free or paid version of Azure Machine Learning. We recommend starting with the trial version (*https://oreil.ly/ hcE3J*) to take advantage of the $200 in free credit available for your first 30 days. You will need to use your work email and sign up with a credit card (even for the trial version, but you will not be charged). Click the given link and follow the prompts, starting with the welcome screen shown in Figure 10-8.

Figure 10-8. Signing up for a free 30-day trial of Azure

Additionally, you will need a Premium version of Power BI in order to use an Azure Machine Learning model in Power BI. See "Premium, Pro, and Free Power BI" on page 26 for details.

Azure Machine Learning Studio

Although there are more technical ways of accessing Azure Machine Learning, we will exclusively be using the Studio in this chapter. *Azure Machine Learning Studio* is a browser-based UI that provides a centralized location for working with and tracking the artifacts used to build, train, and deploy machine learning models.

Let's explore some of the features of Azure Machine Learning Studio, pictured in Figure 10-9. In order to prevent this chapter from spinning off into its own book, we will focus on 10 components relevant to a Power BI developer who wishes to consume a custom model from Azure Machine Learning.

The screenshots here are of a workspace as it looks after completing the demo at the end of this chapter. This will allow you to see the different components of Azure Machine Learning Studio in use with example assets. For instructions on how to log in and create a workspace, please see the demo.

Figure 10-9. Select features in Azure Machine Learning Studio

1. Home

We begin with the Home screen as it appears when first opening Azure Machine Learning Studio (Figure 10-9). The lefthand side is the navigation pane we will explore in the rest of this section.

The top-right corner shows that we are logged in under a workspace named "vending-machine," also shown at the top of the screen. The tiles within the home page highlight some of the Studio's different offerings.

2. Notebooks

Next on the lefthand pane is the Authoring section, where we see three different ways to train a model in Azure Machine Learning Studio. The authoring service *Notebooks* combines Jupyter Notebooks, cloud file storage, a terminal, and attached compute for collaborative and highly customizable coding. You can create a blank notebook, upload an existing notebook, or (shown in Figure 10-10) begin with one of the tutorial or sample notebooks.

Are you unsure which algorithm to use in your model? We suggest exploring this flowchart for selecting algorithms (*https://oreil.ly/ OlXMp*) with links to documentation from *scikit-learn*, the popular machine learning library in Python.

Figure 10-10. Training a model with Notebooks, including one of the included quick starts

3. Automated ML

Automated ML is another means of training a machine learning model. This utilizes the same methods of AutoML within Power BI (see Chapter 3 for details) but with additional options. In short, *Automated ML* provides a step-by-step guide for defining a problem, training multiple models, and evaluating the best model for the job. This method is ideal if you are looking for a low-code option and require only modest customization.

Figure 10-11 shows the Automated ML page after going through Demo 10-1. Notice the arrow pointing to the trained model that can now be consumed within Power BI.

4. Designer

Designer is a graphic UI where a user can build a pipeline that goes through the entire process of loading data, preprocessing data, training a model, and evaluating a model. It includes a canvas where each step is built with drag-and-drop modules that are linked to create an entire workflow. This is a low-code option for a process with standard data science applications but also includes modules for adding Python and R scripts, making it an ideal solution for teams with varying levels of programming experience. Figure 10-12 shows the Designer page, highlighting some examples of the prebuilt models included.

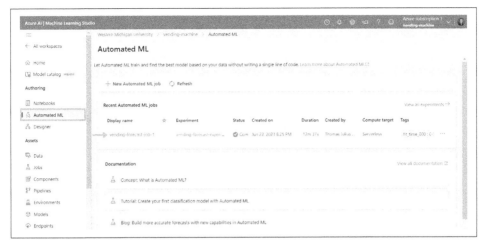

Figure 10-11. Sample model trained using Automated ML

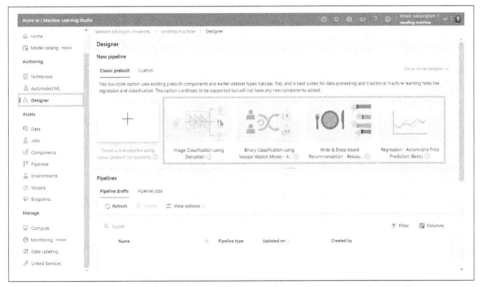

Figure 10-12. Sample workflows for training a model in the drag-and-drop Designer

5. Data

The lefthand pane also collects various assets utilized or produced through the machine learning lifecycle (Figure 10-13). The *Data* page is where you can directly upload data, but in this case, we added the data when training an algorithm elsewhere in the Studio and it was automatically made available here. Clicking the dataset will allow you to view it, track the version history, and perform other labeling.

Figure 10-13. An example data asset used to train a model

6. Jobs

Jobs is where you can track the machine learning training jobs and runs. These can also be organized into groups called *experiments*. For example, Figure 10-14 shows "vending-forecast-job-1," which includes multiple models, each trying to forecast vending machine sales. If we were unhappy with these results, then we could add another job but keep it part of the same experiment (vending-forecast-experiment-1) because it is trying to solve the same problem.

Figure 10-14. An example machine learning job that trained a series of models

7. Models

After a model is trained, it will be automatically added to the Models page. Figure 10-15 shows a single example created from this chapter's demo. *Models* is where you can edit the model's metadata for improved tracking and filtering as well as register additional models from previous training jobs and directly from files. This means you can train a model locally on your laptop, export it as a binary object, and then upload it to Azure Machine Learning for deployment.

Figure 10-15. An example model automatically saved following a completed job

8. Endpoints

Once you identify your preferred model and are ready to put it into action, you can deploy it to start scoring new data with its predictions. Deployed models are tracked in the *Endpoints* section. Figure 10-16 shows one such model that is ready to be consumed by another service, such as Power BI.

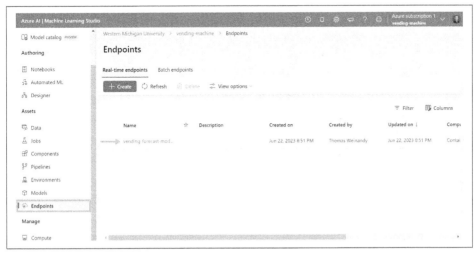

Figure 10-16. An example endpoint for a deployed machine learning model

9. Compute

You will also want to know about the *Compute* page if you will be building solutions that require more sophisticated designs. For example, you will need to spin up compute to power training on a Jupyter Notebook. This section, shown in Figure 10-17, will track which compute resources are running. There is nothing showing in this screenshot because the chapter demo goes through an example with Automated Machine Learning, where compute is automatically spun up for the job and then spun down once complete.

Figure 10-17. The page for tracking compute resources

10. Data Labeling

We wanted to call out one last feature within Automated Machine Learning Studio: *Data Labeling* (Figure 10-18). This section opens a guided wizard for labeling your own set of image, text, or audio data. For example, imagine you're the owner of a restaurant that has pictures of different entrees posted on social media. You can upload these pictures and one by one go through and label what is in each picture. Then you can use that corpus to train an image recognition algorithm that is customized to predict what dishes are present in future posted pictures.

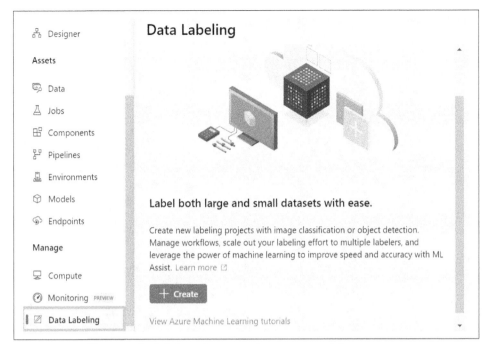

Figure 10-18. The page for labeling data to train custom models

We sadly do not have the space to go further into MLOps and how it applies to Azure Machine Learning. To learn more, we recommend this overview by Microsoft (*https://oreil.ly/foLA0*), or for more in-depth options, you can explore the books available at O'Reilly online learning (*https://oreil.ly/YrnJw*).

Regardless, Azure Machine Learning is a great way for businesses to train and deploy machine learning models in an affordable, collaborative, and secure way. The cloud-based environment allows organizations to immediately scale up or down and only pay for what they use.

Demo 10-1: Forecasting Vending Machine Sales

Let's illustrate how a business can leverage Microsoft Azure to train a custom machine learning model in the cloud using sales data from five vending machines located in New Jersey (Figure 10-19). We will utilize Azure Machine Learning Studio using Automated ML and deploy our model in a web service. This will then let us consume a model in Power BI to score predictions of future vending machine sales.

Figure 10-19. Vending machine snacks

This demo requires an Azure subscription and Power BI Premium to follow along on your own. See "Azure Subscription and Free Trial" on page 330 for details.

You may find this demo to be the most difficult in the book. We understand it covers topics that are different from what the typical data analyst sees on a day-to-day basis, but we encourage you to persevere and follow along. We believe the best way to understand a new tool is with a hands-on approach where you encounter errors and learn how to troubleshoot them. Your grit will be rewarded.

Creating an Azure Machine Learning workspace

Go to *https://portal.azure.com* and sign in to your Microsoft Azure account.

 Your Power BI account will need access to the Azure Machine Learning model you will train and deploy. To avoid having to grant read access to a model, it is easiest to use the same account between Azure and Power BI.

Open Azure Machine Learning on the home page. If you do not see it, use the search bar (Figure 10-20).

Figure 10-20. Searching for the Azure Machine Learning service in the Azure Portal

Our first task is to create a new workspace. A workspace is a directory that contains the components and assets associated with a machine learning project.

Click Create and then select "New workspace," as shown in Figure 10-21.

Figure 10-21. Creating a new Azure Machine Learning workspace

Your Azure subscription will automatically populate. You will have the option of either selecting an existing resource group or creating a new one. A *resource group* in Azure is a virtual container of resources that fall under the same organizational permission and policies. This allows a business to define sharing and rules across the entire collection of resources as well as structure billing based on the project needs. Each resource group is based in a single region of servers where it is maintained. You may select an existing resource group; however, we highly recommend creating a new resource to monitor the costs associated with the demo.

We named our resource group "ai-demo." We then named our workspace "vending-machine." This will automatically populate unique names for the storage account, key vault, and application insights (Figure 10-22).

Select the region nearest to you. In this case, we are using East US.

Keep the container registry as None.

There's no need to further configure the workspace, so click "Review + create" and then Create.

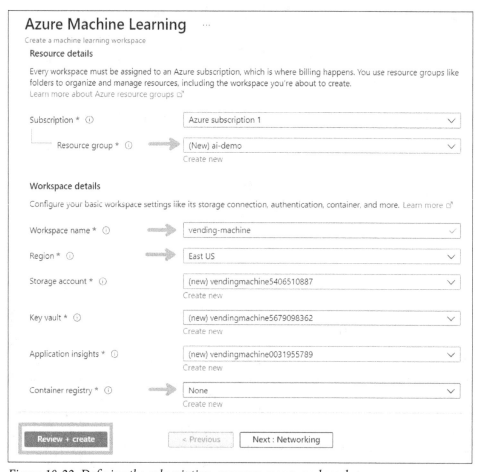

Figure 10-22. Defining the subscription, resource group, and workspace

It will take a minute or two to deploy the resource group. You can see all of the associated resources under "Deployment details," including the Azure Machine Learning workspace (Figure 10-23).

Click "Go to resource."

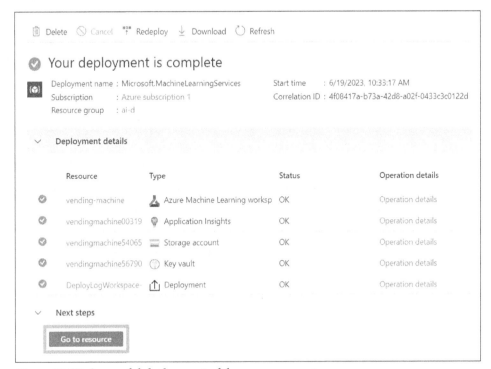

Figure 10-23. Successful deployment of the resource group

You now have a workspace created and populated with the resources needed to train a custom machine learning model.

Training a custom model in Azure Machine Learning Studio

Recall that we want to train a model to forecast vending machine sales. We are interested in finding the best model quickly and are indifferent to the use of any specific algorithm. For this reason, we will use Automated ML.

If you just created a resource group and workspace, click "Launch studio" to open Azure Machine Learning Studio. If instead you are returning to an existing workspace, go to Azure Machine Learning within the Azure portal and select your workspace.

Once inside the workspace, select Automated ML and then click "New Automated ML job," as shown in Figure 10-24.

Figure 10-24. Creating a new Automated ML job

This opens a wizard that guides you through the steps for setting up an Automated ML job. Name the job and experiment related to the problem at hand for easier reference later. We chose "vending-forecast-job-1" and "vending-forecast-experiment-1," respectively. Click Next to proceed (Figure 10-25).

Thoughtful naming is an important practice in data science because often many models are trained before a final one is selected. As a wise person once said, there are only two hard problems in computer science: cache invalidation, naming things, and off-by-one errors.

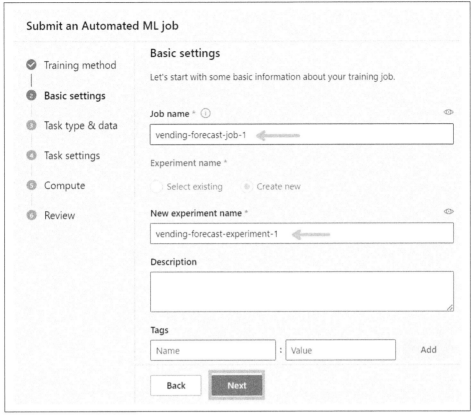

Figure 10-25. Naming the Automated ML job and experiment

Now we have to select which class of algorithm we want and what data it will be trained on.

Under "Select task type," choose "Time series forecasting" from the dropdown (Figure 10-26). You can see there are more options here than in the related AutoML tool within Power BI.

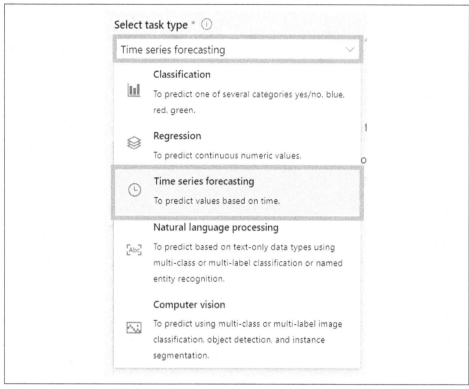

Figure 10-26. Selecting the forecasting option from the list of solutions

The "Select dataset" section shows which data assets, if any, are already uploaded and in a usable format for Automated ML. You'll need to upload a dataset, so click Create (not pictured).

This opens a new wizard to create a data asset. Name it "vending-machine-sales" and keep the type as Tabular. Click Next (Figure 10-27).

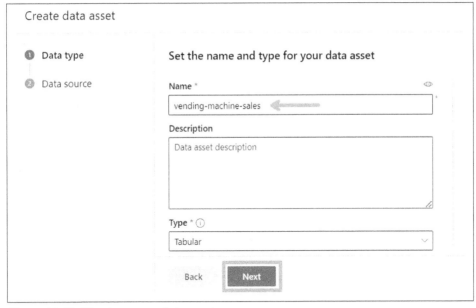

Figure 10-27. Naming a new data asset

Next, select "From web files." Under Web URL, paste *https://raw.githubusercontent.com/tomweinandy/ai-with-power-bi/main/Chapter10/VendingRevenue.csv* in the box. Click Next when done (not pictured).

You now see a preview of the data with weekly vending machine sales from five locations (Figure 10-28). Keep the settings the same and click Next to proceed.

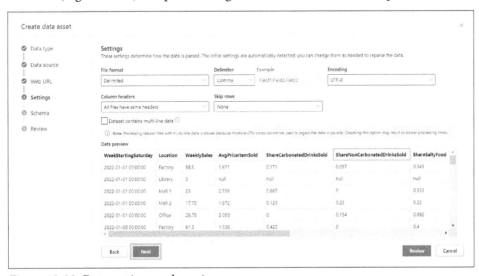

Figure 10-28. Data settings and preview

Next you see the predicted schema of the data and have the option to make edits. For example, the WeekStartingSaturday column was accurately predicted to be a date type, and even the date format is correct. Also note that you can toggle a variable to remove it from the model.

The predicted schema looks good, so we do not have to make any changes. Click Next (Figure 10-29).

Figure 10-29. Showing the predicted schema of the ingested data

A review of the data shows it to be fine, so select Create (not pictured).

You should now return to the previous Automated ML wizard. Make sure "Time series forecasting" is selected as the task type, select the newly created dataset "vending-machine-sales," and click Next (Figure 10-30).

Figure 10-30. Selecting the task type and dataset for an Automated ML job

Now we can specify the details of the forecasting model. Under "Target column," select WeeklySales, as this is the variable we wish to forecast. Then under Time column, select WeekStartingSaturday to define the time interval. Leave the option "autodetect time series identifier(s)" selected (Figure 10-31).

Figure 10-31. Specifying details for training a forecasting model

Uncheck Autodetect forecast horizon and define the horizon as 53. This means you are explicitly saying you would like to forecast 53 weeks into the future.

Immediately under the forecast horizon is an option to enable deep learning. Deep learning models are often more accurate when there are large amounts of data. This, however, comes at the literal cost of requiring more compute to train. Leave this option unchecked for this demo.

Next, select the gear icon next to "View additional configuration settings." This opens up a righthand pane that lets us change the primary metric. The *primary metric* is the objective function by which we evaluate our model. In this case, the "best" model is defined as the one with the lowest normalized root mean squared error. Leave this as is.

Within the "Additional forecasting settings" dropdown, select United States (US) to include American holidays in the model. Click Save.

We now want to limit how long the job will take to run. Although there are many options, we will just limit the number of models it will train and test. Under "Max trials," enter 10 (Figure 10-32).

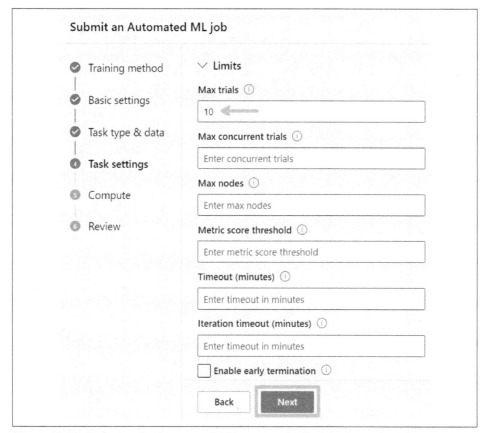

Figure 10-32. Reducing the Automated ML runtime by limiting it to 10 trials

Without limits, the Automated ML run can go for a long time before finishing, especially if you do not properly set the compute to match the size of training data or algorithm complexity. This same example, without any limits, took 43 minutes to finish.

Next, we want to evaluate our model using 5-fold cross-validation. K-fold cross-validation is a way to ensure that a machine learning model is not "overfit" by testing its performance on k-many subsets of its own data. Overfitting occurs when a model has, in a sense, just memorized the training data and does a poor job of predicting new observations.

Under "Number of cross validations," input 5. Click Next (Figure 10-33).

Figure 10-33. Specifying 5-fold cross validation

We are now ready to select the cloud-based computing resources we want to rent in order to train the model. To keep things simple, we will use the default settings. Note in Figure 10-34 that the virtual machine size will cost a modest $0.29 for each hour to use. Not bad!

Click Next.

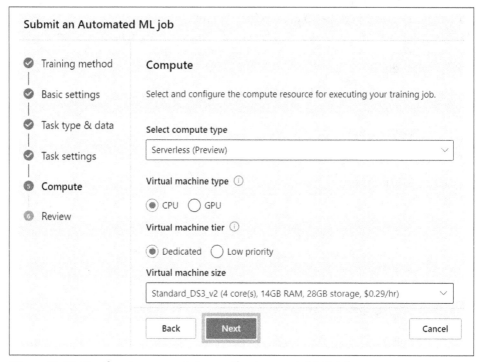

Figure 10-34. Configuring compute to run the Automated ML job

As shown in Figure 10-35, we now see an overview of the run specifications. If you are following along, double-check that your configurations are the same. Then click "Submit training job."

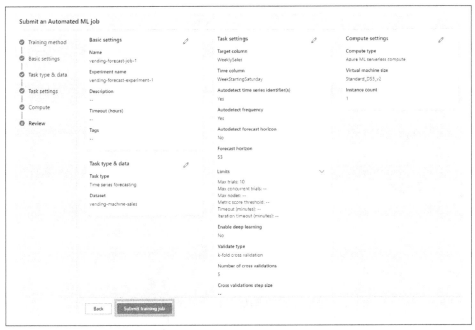

Figure 10-35. Review of the Automated ML job settings

This opens up the Jobs page, where you can now monitor the job status. Click Refresh if there is no change after one minute or if there is no animated processing bar.

Once "Setting up the run" is done and replaced with "Model training," you can select the "Child jobs" tab to watch as individual models are trained and tested (Figure 10-36).

Figure 10-36. The status overview as an Automated ML run completes

It will take some time to train and test 10 different models, so use this moment as a break to walk around and maybe pour yourself some coffee.

When the job finishes, you will see a green checkmark under Status (Figure 10-37). The Duration indicates that the entire job took nearly 13 minutes.

Next, move to the lower-right section describing the best model. It seems that in this instance, the best model was the tree-based algorithm XGBoost with some preprocessing steps included. You can select StandardScalerWrapper, XGBoostRegressor to learn more or explore the associated tuning parameters by clicking "View hyperparameters."

Finally, you can see the primary metric by which this model was selected (normalized root mean squared error of 0.24500) and whether the model has been deployed ("No deployment yet").

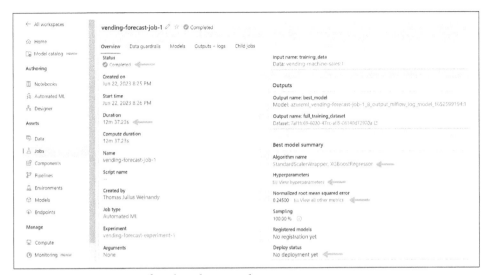

Figure 10-37. Overview after the job is complete

This is the model we want to consume in Power BI, but first, we must deploy it to score new data. We will pick up here in the next section.

Deploying a custom model in Azure Machine Learning

Let's return to Figure 10-37. Under "Algorithm name," select StandardScalerWrapper, XGBoostRegressor.

From here, click Deploy and then select "Web service" (Figure 10-38).

Figure 10-38. Deploying a model as a web service

Give a name to the model, such as "vending-forecast-model-1," and change the Compute type to Azure Container Instance. Click Deploy (Figure 10-39).

Deploy a model ✕

Name * ⓘ   ⦿

vending-forecast-model-1 ⟸━━━━━

Description ⓘ

```
[                                                              ]
[                                                              ]
[                                                              ]
[                                                            ⟋ ]
```

Compute type * ⓘ

Azure Container Instance ⟸━━━━━ ⌄

Models: vendingforecast8

Enable authentication

⬤◯

This model supports no-code deployment. You may **optionally** override the default
environment and driver file.

Use custom deployment assets

☐ Use custom deployment assets

〉 Advanced

[**Deploy**] [Cancel]

Figure 10-39. Configuring the deployment

You should see a green bar confirming that the model was successfully deployed. You
can confirm this, or locate the model later, by selecting Models in the lefthand pane
(Figure 10-40). Note that the model name has changed—this is normal.

Figure 10-40. Confirming the model was deployed

Consuming a custom model in Power BI

Now that we have trained multiple custom machine learning models and deployed the best one as a web service, we are ready to consume it within Power BI Desktop. Begin by signing in to your account in Power BI—the same account where your model resides. Then select "Get data," followed by Web (Figure 10-41).

Figure 10-41. Adding data from the web for scoring

Under URL, paste *https://raw.githubusercontent.com/tomweinandy/ai-with-power-bi/main/Chapter10/VendingRevenueForecast.csv* and click OK (not pictured).

 You will need a Pro, Premium, or Enterprise subscription to Power BI to consume a machine learning model hosted on Azure.

As you can see in Figure 10-42, the data here does not include sales because it represents future observations. Since we trained our forecast model to take other columns of data as inputs (e.g., AvgPriceItemSold), those variables are included as average values by location from the previous year.

We will consume our custom model deployed in Azure Machine Learning and use it to score data within Power Query Editor. Click Transform Data to proceed.

You may notice in Figure 10-42 that the dates and times are a bit off. That's because we are using Power BI Desktop, which automatically converts datetime values to the local time of the user. This poses a problem in this example because the dates need to remain at midnight and not change based on where the user is located.

Skipping this step will throw an error, and the model will not be able to make predictions.

WeekStartingSaturday	Location	WeeklySales	AvgPriceItemSold	ShareCarbonatedDrinksSold	ShareNonCarbonatedDrinksSold	ShareSa
12/30/2022 7:00:00 PM	Factory		1.886611148	0.400229422	0.097012507	0.
12/30/2022 7:00:00 PM	Library		2.044618871	0.13388721	0.174926396	0
12/30/2022 7:00:00 PM	Mall 1		2.028816406	0.237470294	0.186567769	0.
12/30/2022 7:00:00 PM	Mall 2		1.809008102	0.154978034	0.15413249	0.
12/30/2022 7:00:00 PM	Office		1.75892464	0.045588027	0.045914899	0
1/6/2023 7:00:00 PM	Factory		1.886611148	0.400229422	0.097012507	0.
1/6/2023 7:00:00 PM	Library		2.044618871	0.13388721	0.174926396	0
1/6/2023 7:00:00 PM	Mall 1		2.028816406	0.237470294	0.186567769	0.
1/6/2023 7:00:00 PM	Mall 2		1.809008102	0.154978034	0.15413249	0.
1/6/2023 7:00:00 PM	Office		1.75892464	0.045588027	0.045914899	0
1/13/2023 7:00:00 PM	Factory		1.886611148	0.400229422	0.097012507	0.
1/13/2023 7:00:00 PM	Library		2.044618871	0.13388721	0.174926396	0
1/13/2023 7:00:00 PM	Mall 1		2.028816406	0.237470294	0.186567769	0.
1/13/2023 7:00:00 PM	Mall 2		1.809008102	0.154978034	0.15413249	0.
1/13/2023 7:00:00 PM	Office		1.75892464	0.045588027	0.045914899	0
1/20/2023 7:00:00 PM	Factory		1.886611148	0.400229422	0.097012507	0.
1/20/2023 7:00:00 PM	Library		2.044618871	0.13388721	0.174926396	0
1/20/2023 7:00:00 PM	Mall 1		2.028816406	0.237470294	0.186567769	0.
1/20/2023 7:00:00 PM	Mall 2		1.809008102	0.154978034	0.15413249	0.
1/20/2023 7:00:00 PM	Office		1.75892464	0.045588027	0.045914899	0

Figure 10-42. Viewing a sample of the data before transforming it

To fix this, wherever you may live, you will need to add a new column with time in a UTC format. Go to the Add Columns section and click Custom Column (Figure 10-43).

Name the new column WeekStartingSaturdayUtc and add the following M code as the custom column formula: `DateTime.From(DateTimeZone.RemoveZone(DateTimeZone.ToUtc(DateTimeZone.From([WeekStartingSaturday]))))`.

These functions (read from the inside outward) cast the column to a time zone–inclusive format, convert it to UTC, remove the time zone, and then cast it back to datetime format. Click OK when done.

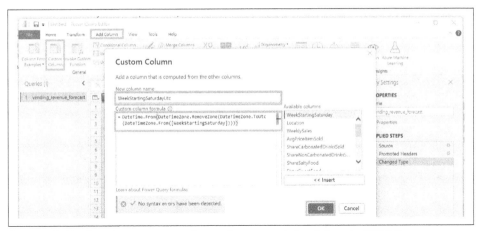

Figure 10-43. Creating a custom column that converts local time to UTC time

In the last step of the conversion to UTC, click the icon within the column header and change it to the datetime icon (with a calendar and clock), as shown in Figure 10-44. If everything worked correctly, then the new column will be in datetime format for midnight of New Year's Eve.

If the time is correct, then click the rightmost Azure Machine Learning tile to find the trained model.

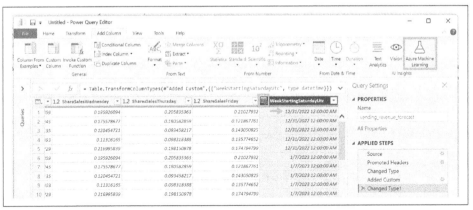

Figure 10-44. Changing the new UTC column to datetime before consuming a machine learning model

Either you will have to use the same Microsoft login in both Power BI and Azure, or you will have to make sure your Power BI account was granted read access to the deployed model.

If you are logged into the right account and if you successfully deployed the machine learning model, then it should appear in the left pane of the pop-up window (Figure 10-45). Select "AzureML.vending-forecast-model-1" and change the target column to WeekStartingSaturdayUtc (note the "Utc" at the end).

The other columns in the new dataset should all match the expected columns specified by the model. Click OK.

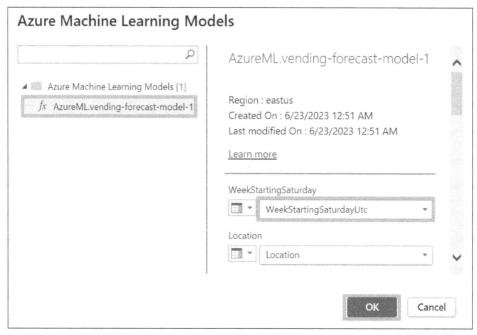

Figure 10-45. Consuming a custom model to score new data in Power BI

If prompted by the privacy warning pictured in Figure 10-46, select Continue, then Ignore Privacy Levels..., and click Save.

Figure 10-46. The privacy warning that appears each session the first time a dataset is sent through Azure AI Services

If successful, then you should see the new column "AzureML.vending-forecast-model-1" (Figure 10-47). Change the datatype to decimal by changing the icon in the column header to the 1.2 icon.

Now we have weekly forecasts for vending machine sales by location for the entire next year! Click Close & Apply when you're finished admiring your work. This will now appear in the data model and can be used to build out a new Power BI report.

 Issues occurring within a deployed model will pass on a brief error message to Power BI; however, these are often not detailed enough to fully express the problem. If you find yourself in this situation, go back to the Endpoint section in Azure Machine Learning Studio (the one pictured in Figure 10-16) to find the deployment logs.

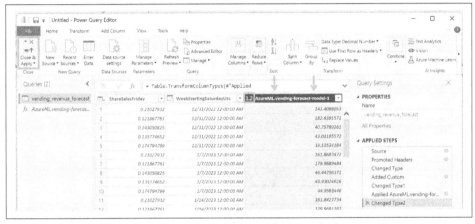

Figure 10-47. Transformed data with weekly sales forecasts by location

Kudos for staying with us to the very end! We hope this demo challenged your skills and widened your perspective on the capabilities of Power BI.

Summary

Now consider what problems you could solve by combining Azure Machine Learning with Power BI. Are you a key decision maker at your organization? If so, recall the five successful organizational behaviors for successfully leveraging AI and identify which is best in terms of level of effort, probability of success, and favorability of outcome.

Or are you a practitioner able to build your own solutions? If so, recall the machine learning lifecycle (Figure 10-7) and walk through the process to train and deploy a working prototype. Be sure to focus on developing a solution that is actionable and provides measurable business value.

Either way, you will find that building custom machine learning models can unlock a new level of problem solving. We hope you see Azure Machine Learning as a valuable addition to Power BI—not just as another way to transform data but as an opportunity for your organization to fully customize AI to meet its own needs.

Data Science Languages: Python and R in Power BI

In 2012, an article came out in the *Harvard Business Review* calling data scientists "the sexiest job of the 21st century." In many ways, the article was predicting the future we live in today—that there would be this occupation of highly educated professionals in business using statistics, programming, and the scientific method to make discoveries from big data. Where the article struggled though was in giving a more precise description of what data scientists actually do. The job title was still new enough that the authors were even compelled to put "data scientist" in quotes, indicating that the term had not yet gained acceptance.[1]

Companies since then have greatly increased hiring for this role. As of 2022, the US Bureau of Labor Statistics reported there were 36,500 data scientists in the United States alone and expected that number to grow by 23% over the next decade.[2] Data scientists today are more prevalent than ever and work across a wide range of industries.

It is still true that data scientists are inherently multidisciplinary and practice a diverse set of skills. What has changed since the *Harvard Business Review* article is that we have gained clarity about their job functions. There is now greater under-standing that data scientists solve problems using machine learning and artificial intelligence (neither of which were mentioned in the article).

---

1 Thomas H. Davenport and D. J. Patil, "Data Scientist: The Sexiest Job of the 21st Century" (*https://oreil.ly/MZaIQ*), *Harvard Business Review* 90, no. 10 (2012): 70–76.

2 "Occupational Outlook Handbook: Computer and Information Research Scientists" (*https://oreil.ly/q0xua*), Bureau of Labor Statistics, US Department of Labor, accessed January 19, 2024.

One common way to describe the field of data science today is as the intersection of three subjects: computer science, statistics, and business/domain knowledge. This is visualized in Figure 11-1, where we see data science at the center of the Venn diagram. We can also see the adjunct disciplines of machine learning as the combination of computer science and statistics, data analysis as the combination of statistics and business/domain knowledge, and traditional programming as the intersection of business/domain knowledge and computer science.

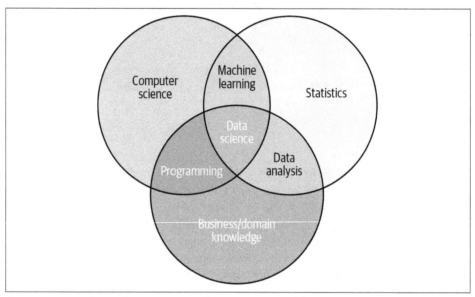

Figure 11-1. Defining data science as the intersection of three disciplines

The diagram shows how successful data scientists are bringing together deep knowledge of a business and its industry, rigorous training in statistics, and the ability to write their own scripts and programs. This also gives credence to why we are dedicating an entire chapter of this book to how to use the two most popular programming languages in data science: Python and R. By using Python and R within Power BI, you will be able to better leverage the data scientist's toolkit to tackle new problems within your organization.

You don't need to be a data scientist in name before you can use the data science toolkit. Indeed, this entire book is dedicated to democratizing artificial intelligence for business users of all kinds. These skills will benefit not only your organization but you as well. According to data from Revelio, jobs requiring AI-related skills earn 5.8% higher salaries than similar jobs at the same company. The study also found that Python and machine learning were the two most commonly requested skills for these

AI jobs.[3] So let's dive into programming within Power BI to unlock your next level of AI expertise!

Python Versus R

The two primary programming languages for data scientists are Python and R. The best way to understand how and where they are applied is to go over their similarities and differences.

How Python and R are similar:

Open source
Both are free, open source programming languages that have extensive online communities supporting their use and wide ecosystems of libraries and tools.

Syntax
Both have a similar syntax and logical structure based on stored variables and functions for building higher levels of abstraction.

Data analysis
Both readily handle data cleaning, transformation, and processing for producing statistical results.

Data visualization
Both have extensive libraries for building compelling, highly customizable data visualizations.

Data science
Both have libraries and ecosystems for developing artificial intelligence, machine learning, and deep learning algorithms.

How Python and R are different:

Primary purpose
Python was built as a general purpose programming language that eventually grew into data analysis and data science. R was built as a programming language specifically for statistical analysis and eventually expanded into other areas.

Interoperability
Python can perform a much wider set of tasks and is overall much better than R at integrating with other systems and languages for more complex architectures.

---

3 Loujaina Abdelwahed and Beyza Arslan, "Revelio Labs X LinkUp: Do AI Skills Pay Off?" (*https://oreil.ly/S40aN*), Revelio Labs, July 18, 2023.

Specialization

R is more specialized for statistical analysis and can often more efficiently execute advanced and niche statistical algorithms.

Communities

Python is more widely used in industry and by computer scientists, while R is more popular in academia and among statisticians.

Ease of learning

Python is more readable and in general can be learned more quickly than R.

One illustrative application of the two is in a paper I (Thomas) wrote to quantify how brand mentions on X (formerly Twitter) impact foot traffic to retail stores of those brands.[4] I found it was better to use Python to connect to the Twitter API, parse the JSON output, and then complete all data processing. Then I used R to perform the hierarchical linear regression, since R had better libraries and resources available for the more technical statistical topic of multilevel analysis.

When it comes to data science tasks, the two programming languages share more similarities than differences. If you are not proficient in either, then we recommend getting started with Python since it is easier to learn and has more resources for beginners. Also, the types of organizations that use Power BI are also more likely to use Python. As you will see later in the chapter, Python has also become more popular than R for machine learning tasks.

 We wrote this chapter for an audience with a wide array of coding skills and familiarity with Python and R. All code is written in highlighted syntax with inline comments to make it more readable. We suggest that even novice programmers review the code (pick either Python or R) to try to understand the various steps and what purpose they serve. A line of code starting with the "#" character is a comment, meaning it is not executed by the program but serves as an explanation of the preceding code section.

There is enough content for each of these languages to fill multiple shelves and hard drives, so this chapter focuses exclusively on their application to Power BI. If you want to learn more about Python, R, or how to use them in data science, check out the many options available through O'Reilly (*https://oreil.ly/wB9P6*). We also highly recommend Ryan Wade's excellent *Advanced Analytics in Power BI with R and Python* (*https://oreil.ly/wb6wI*) (Apress) that is devoted entirely to discussing a topic to which we can dedicate only a single chapter.

---

4 Thomas J. Weinandy et al., "Twitter-Patter: How Social Media Drives Foot Traffic to Retail Stores" (*https://doi.org/10.1057/s41270-023-00209-7*), *Journal of Marketing Analytics* (February 6, 2023): 1–19.

All code is available for download on the book's GitHub page. See the files for the combined Python scripts (*https://oreil.ly/ch11_pyscript*) and the combined R scripts (*https://oreil.ly/ch11_rscript*).

Limitations

You can run Python and R scripts at various stages of building a Power BI report, namely at data ingestion, data transformation, and data visualization. Running these programming languages within Power BI does, however, come with unique limitations:

- Power BI automatically drops duplicates from a dataframe.
- N/A values are automatically converted to null.
- Datatypes may change when a dataframe is ingested or transformed.
- A script run will abort after 30 minutes if it has not finished by then.
- Python and R visuals have no tool tips or on-visual interactions.
- R scripts cannot run in the Power BI service.
- Python scripts can run in the Power BI service, but only if all data sources are set to public (see Microsoft's official documentation (*https://oreil.ly/Chd1L*) for further guidance and troubleshooting of Python integration into Power BI Service).
- Libraries must be installed locally, not within Power BI.
- Error messages within Power BI are not very detailed.

Setup

To address those last two limitations, we recommend writing your Python and R code within an *integrated development environment* (IDE) and then copying it over to Power BI. An IDE is an application for writing, editing, and running code with common features such as versioning, syntax highlighting, and code completion. IDEs usually offer detailed error codes to help with debugging as well as the ability to download software packages that expand the functionality of a language beyond its base code.

If you are a beginner and plan to only use Python, we recommend Google Colab (*https://colab.research.google.com*). This free, browser-based IDE runs everything on the cloud and does not require any installation. If you plan to only use R, then RStudio is the most popular (see details in "Setting Up R" on page 372). Otherwise, IDEs like Visual Studio Code or PyCharm are excellent and support both languages.

Before you can use Python and R within Power BI, or within an IDE application on your desktop, you will have to install the base programs of Python and R. The next two sections show how to get set up, including downloading the necessary libraries and packages used in the examples.

Setting Up Python

We will download Python and set up an environment using the package manager conda. This dedicated environment lets us control the version of Python and packages to use with Power BI while not interfering with other versions of Python that may be running on our computer. It also does not require admin permissions, since some readers may not have access to install packages to their base applications.

Begin by navigating to *https://www.anaconda.com/download* and select Download (Figure 11-2).

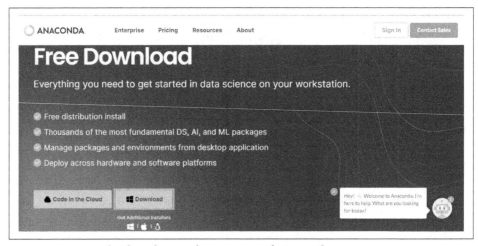

Figure 11-2. Downloading the Windows version of Anaconda

Then open the downloaded file to launch the Anaconda setup wizard, shown in Figure 11-3. Go through all of the steps to complete the installation.

Figure 11-3. The Anaconda setup wizard

Python can operate with its base code, but most data science functions require additional libraries that must be downloaded and attached to the application running Python. We will create a dedicated environment with conda, download Python to that environment, and then use pip to download libraries to that environment.

For example, pandas is a popular library for Python that enables many kinds of dataframe manipulation. This allows a user to perform common data processing tasks like merging tables, handling missing values, creating new columns, and grouping into summary statistics. The pandas package is not included with the base version of Python, but we can install it for free to our environment using pip.

We will be using several libraries for this chapter in a dedicated conda environment of Python version 3.10. To do so, follow these steps:

1. Search for and open the Anaconda Prompt app.

2. Create a conda environment with the name "pbi-demo" and download Python 3.10 to that environment:

   a. In the command line, type out **conda create --name pdi-demo python=3.10**. (Note: As shown in Figure 11-4, we are currently in the "base" environment.)

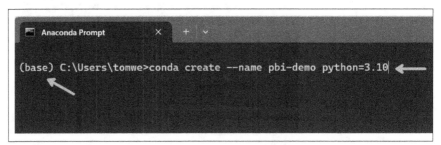

Figure 11-4. Creating a new conda environment with the Anaconda prompt

   b. Press Enter and wait for the install to complete (Figure 11-5).

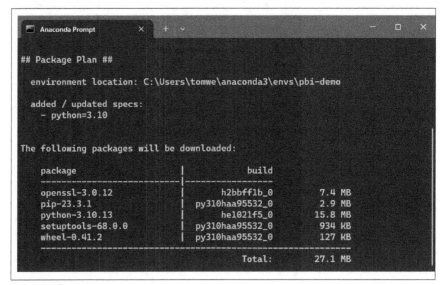

Figure 11-5. Details about the newly created environment with included packages

   c. When asked to proceed, type **y** and press Enter.

3. Move from the base environment to the new environment (Figure 11-6):

   a. Type **conda activate pbi-demo** and press Enter.

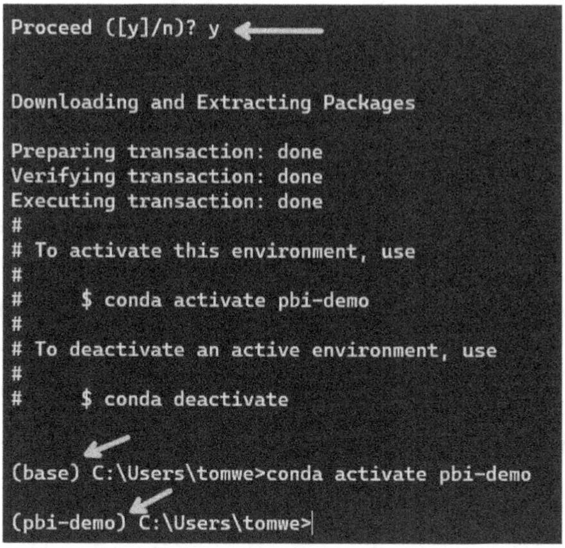

Figure 11-6. Activating the newly created pbi-demo environment

4. To install the pandas library (Figure 11-7):

   a. In the command line, type **pip install pandas**.

   b. Press Enter and wait for the install to complete.

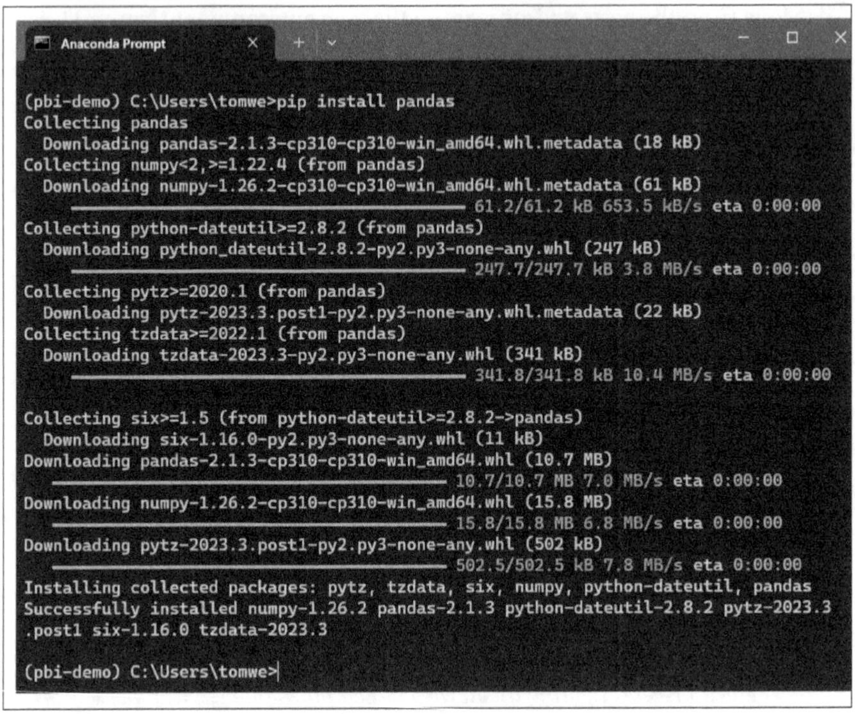

Figure 11-7. Successfully installing the pandas package, which includes other dependent packages

5. Repeat Step 4 with the following lines of code (pressing Enter and waiting after each):

   a. `pip install matplotlib`

   b. `pip install requests`

   c. `pip install tensorflow`

   d. `pip install scikit-learn`

6. Find the location of the conda environment (Figure 11-8):

   a. Type `conda env list` and press Enter.

   b. Copy the path to the conda environment.

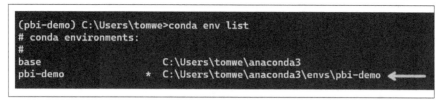

Figure 11-8. Finding the path to the conda environment (asterisk denotes active environment)

7. Set this environment as the home directory in Power BI:

   a. Open Power BI and select File in the upper left.

   b. Navigate to "Options and settings" and then Options (Figure 11-9).

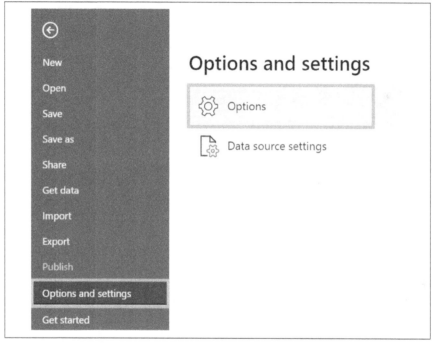

Figure 11-9. Accessing the Python Script Options in Power BI

   c. Select "Python scripting" from the left column.

   d. Set the Detected Python home directories to Other.

   e. Set the Python home directory as the path you copied in Step 6.

   f. Click OK (Figure 11-10).

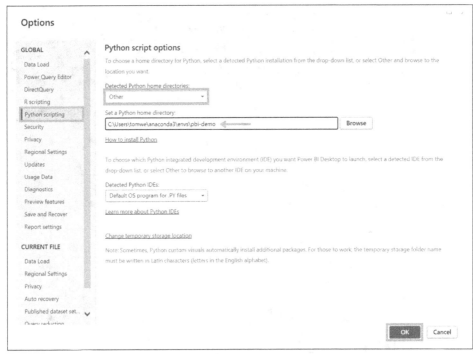

Figure 11-10. Setting the Python home directory in Power BI

You are now ready to begin using your dedicated Python environment with installed packages in Power BI.

Setting Up R

We will navigate to *https://cran.r-project.org/bin/windows/base* to download the latest version of R (Figure 11-11). (Note: It's OK if you are seeing a more recent version than what is shown in the figure.)

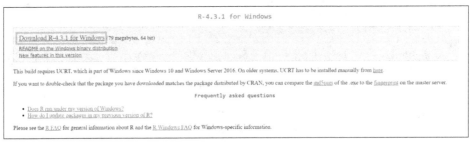

Figure 11-11. Installing R on the local Windows machine

We will save the application and complete the setup wizard to finish installing the base R program.

R can operate with its base package, but most data science functions require additional packages that must be downloaded and attached to the application running R. We will use the IDE RStudio to locally install our R packages; however, this can often be done within your preferred IDE as an alternative.

You can go to *https://posit.co/download/rstudio-desktop* and skip to Step 2 (since you have already installed R), as shown in Figure 11-12.

Figure 11-12. Installing RStudio on the local Windows machine

Complete the setup wizard and launch RStudio. In the lower-right quadrant, select the Packages tab and click Install. A new window will pop up, where you'll type the package name "zoo" and click Install (Figure 11-13).

Figure 11-13. Installing packages in RStudio

Repeat this process to install three more packages: ggplot2, readr, and xgboost.

You are now ready to begin using R in your IDE and Power BI.

Ingestion

The first way to use Python and R in Power BI is for data ingests. Power BI already has various ways to bring in data through Power Query; however, there are times when the default user interface is insufficient and you need some custom code. Here are a few business examples of when Python and R scripts can save the day:

Joins
> The standard approach in Power BI is to ingest multiple datasets and then join them together; however, this can be memory-intensive if the datasets are large, unnecessary if not all of the data is being used, or time-intensive if the scenario involves more complicated joining logic. Scripts can bypass all of these by performing advanced joins within the ingest process.

Masking
> Sometimes datasets include sensitive information that, for privacy and security reasons, should not be brought into Power BI. A business could use Python and R scripts to mask personally identifiable information within the data ingest process. For example, the scripts could include code that uses regular expressions to scrub out any phrase with an "@" (likely emails), 10-digit numbers (possible phone numbers), or 9-digit numbers (possible Social Security numbers).

API
> Python and R scripts also can call APIs as a way to ingest data. A user could even have the script read a local file with saved credentials, use that to call a private API, and parse the responses into a custom dataframe that is ingested into Power BI.

Web scraping
> There are already web-scraping abilities natively built into Power BI (see Chapter 4, but these are not always robust. When they are insufficient, we recommend using a Python or R script to do the trick.

Dynamic text
> You can also use scripts to locate files that have dynamic names, locations, or text. For example, you may have hundreds of files in a single location but only need the one that meets a specific (but changing) criterion. Without scripts, Power BI would have to ingest all of those files before searching for the specific criterion you need.

We will consider the last business scenario to demonstrate the use of Python and R scripts for data ingestion, transformation, and visualization. Imagine we have a folder with multiple CSV files of data, where a new dataset is saved each month with a timestamp added to the filename. Instead of having to replace the source file each month, we can include code that locates the most recent file and ingests only that one into Power BI.

Specifically, our data will track the relative popularity of Python and R over time according to the frequency of online searches that include the application names. We will use Google to compare the two but will need to find a way to isolate interest just in the computer languages. In other words, we need to exclude false positives, such as searches for the letter *r*, the animal *python*, or the television show *Monty Python*. We will therefore exclusively compare the searches for "R machine learning" and "Python machine learning" to see which has more clout among the data science community.

The example is repeated twice—once with Python code and again with R code. We suggest reading only the section about using your preferred language and skipping the other to avoid redundancy.

If you care to follow along, you can download the data (with dates added to the filenames) from this book's GitHub page (*https://oreil.ly/ch11_trenddata*). Just remember to unzip the files and rename the filepath variable in the code to where you save them.

Ingesting Data with Python

Open up Power BI Desktop and select "Get data." From here, search for and select "Python script" (it's within the "Other" section). Next, click Connect, as shown in Figure 11-14.

Figure 11-14. Ingesting data with a Python script

Now a Python script window opens up (Figure 11-15). Take the code that was written and tested in our IDE (shown next) and copy it into this script box. The code allows us to receive the most recent file of Google Trends data we have saved locally. Click OK to run the script in Power BI.

Be sure to change the filepath in the code to where you saved the folder GoogleTrendsData.

```python
# Import packages
import os
import pandas as pd

# Set directory
filepath = "C:/Users/tomwe/Documents/GoogleTrendsData/"
data_folder = os.path.expanduser(filepath)

# Read the list of files in the specified folder
files = os.listdir(data_folder)

# Extract "multiTimeline" files
google_trends_files = [file for file in files if file[0:13] == "multiTimeline"]

# Identify the most recent date
most_recent_file = max(google_trends_files)

# Load data
df = pd.read_csv(filepath + most_recent_file, skiprows=2)
print(df)
```

Figure 11-15. Adding the Python script to load the most recent file

The script successfully identifies the most recent file that begins with "multiTimeline" and loads it into Power BI. Select the dataframe we named "df" from the lefthand panel and click Transform Data (Figure 11-16).

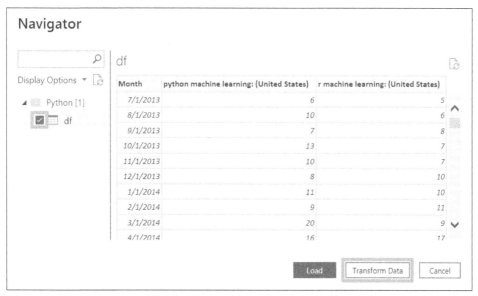

Figure 11-16. A preview of the dataframe ingested with a Python script

We will pick up from here in "Transforming Data with Python" on page 381.

Ingesting Data with R

Open up Power BI Desktop and select "Get data." From here, search for and select "R script" (it's within the "Other" section). Next, click Connect, as shown in Figure 11-17.

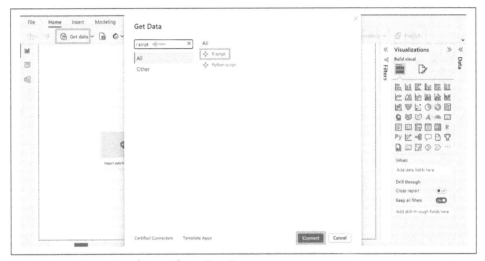

Figure 11-17. Ingesting data with an R script

Now an R script window opens up (Figure 11-18). Take the code written and tested in our IDE (which appears next) and copy it into this script box. This code allows us to receive the most recent file of Google Trends data we have saved locally. Click OK to run the script in Power BI.

Be sure to change the filepath in the code to where you saved the folder GoogleTrendsdata.

```
# Set directory
filepath <- "C:/Users/tomwe/Documents/GoogleTrendsData/"
setwd(filepath)

# Read the list of files in the specified folder
file_list <- list.files()

# Extract "multiTimeline" files
filtered_list <- grep("^multiTimeline", file_list, value=TRUE)

# Identify the most recent date
most_recent_file <- max(filtered_list)

# Load data
full_filepath <- paste(filepath, most_recent_file, sep="")
df <- read.csv(most_recent_file, skip=2)
print(df)
```

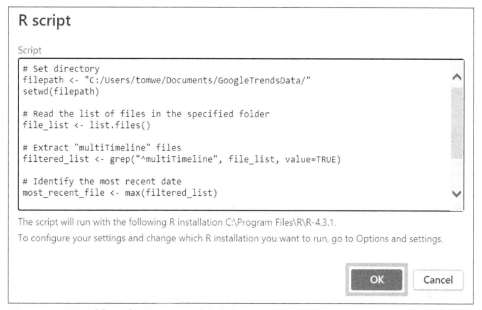

Figure 11-18. Adding the R script to load the most recent file

The script successfully identifies the most recent file that begins with "multiTimeline" and loads it into Power BI. Select the dataframe we named "df" from the lefthand panel and click Transform Data (Figure 11-19).

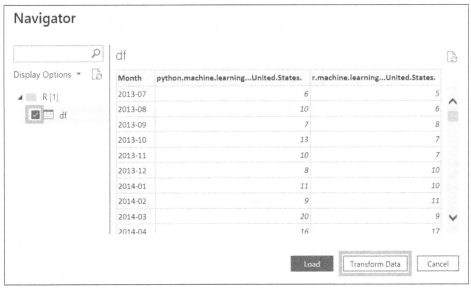

Figure 11-19. A preview of the dataframe ingested with an R script

We will pick up from here in "Transforming Data with R" on page 384.

Transformation

Say you already have a preferred way to ingest data into Power BI without using a Python or an R script. You can also incorporate these languages into the data transformation stage within Power Query Editor. This allows for more advanced forms of data cleaning or feature engineering beyond what can be done with the built-in abilities of Power BI.

For example, you can perform the following transformations that are common in data science preprocessing:

Data cleaning
> Perform more advanced transformations on your data, like renaming a large number of columns at once, dropping observations that meet specific criteria, or filling in missing values with complicated imputation methods.

Normalization/scaling
> Many machine learning algorithms require or perform better when trained on normalized/scaled data.

Calculated columns

Add new columns with more complicated logic. For example, you can use a Python or an R script to convert pairs of latitude and longitude coordinates into haversine distances that measure the great-circle distance between two points.

Outlier detection

Flag or remove outliers from a dataset based on simple identification criteria or more advanced anomaly detection algorithms.

Text analysis

You can use Python and R to perform different kinds of natural language processing on text data, such as sentiment analysis or key phrase extraction. We discussed these examples in Chapter 8. However, those demonstrations used Azure AI Services, which require Power BI Premium. If you are using the free version of Power BI Desktop, you can bypass paid subscriptions by performing the text analytics with Python or R.

Soon we will review how to add Python and R scripts within Power Query Editor for data transformations. We'll use the same dataset of Google Search frequency over time for "Python machine learning" and "R machine learning."

The data transformation examples in this section are meant to show off different ways of using Python and R within Power BI. Since we already used a script to ingest our data, it is better practice to also perform data manipulations within that same script instead of adding a superfluous step here. Do as we say, not as we do.

Transforming Data with Python

Next, we want to use Python within Power BI Editor to transform our Google Trends data. This is a continuation of the example from "Ingesting Data with Python" on page 375. First, notice that the Month column was loaded as a date type (as shown by the calendar icon). We want this data to be text type, so remove the Change Type step from the list of applied steps (Figure 11-20).

Pay attention to the datatypes when using Python or R. Power BI can automatically change datatypes, so code that successfully ran in an IDE may break when run in Power BI.

Figure 11-20. Removing the Change Type step

Now we want to use Python to create two new columns in Power Query Editor that calculate a six-month moving average of the Google Trends search indices. We'll also rename the columns.

Go to the Transform tab and select "Run Python script." A window will appear where you can copy over the following code tested in our IDE. Select OK (Figure 11-21).

There are two elements to call out here. First, note that our previously ingested dataframe was called "df" but now Power BI has changed it to the default "dataset." Second, we are also importing the popular pandas package for dataframe manipulation. If you encounter an error saying that Power BI can't find a package, return to "Setting Up Python" on page 366 and make sure the package was installed.

```python
# Import packages
import pandas as pd

# Add six-month moving average
df_rolling = dataset.set_index("Month")
df_rolling = df_rolling.rolling(6, min_periods=1).mean()
df_rolling = df_rolling.reset_index()

# Rename columns
df_rolling = df_rolling.rename(
    columns={"Month":"month_year",
            "python machine learning: (United States)":"python_moving_average",
            "r machine learning: (United States)": "r_moving_average"})

# Insert original columns to the new dataframe
df_rolling.insert(1, "python_machine_learning",
                dataset["python machine learning: (United States)"])
df_rolling.insert(2, "r_machine_learning",
                dataset["r machine learning: (United States)"])

# Encode date to proper format and insert into dataframe
date_column = pd.to_datetime(df_rolling["month_year"]).dt.date
df_rolling.insert(1, "date", date_column)
```

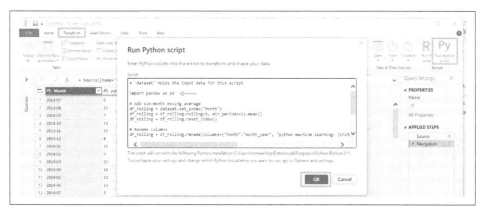

Figure 11-21. Adding a Python script to transform the data

As we see in Figure 11-22, there are now two dataframes: the ingested "dataset" and the new one with the added columns called "df_rolling." Select Table next to "df_rolling" to proceed.

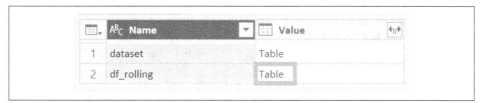

Figure 11-22. Select a dataframe from the two used in the script

You may have noticed that the previous script added a second date column. This will be used later in our data visualization, but first, we need to recast some datatypes.

After deleting the new Change Type step (as shown in Figure 11-20), change the date column to Date type (Figure 11-23).

ABC month_year	ABC date	ABC python_machine_learning	ABC r_machine_learning
1	2013-07	1.2 Decimal Number	5
2	2013-08	$ Fixed decimal number	6
3	2013-09	1²3 Whole Number	8
4	2013-10	% Percentage	7
5	2013-11	Date/Time	7
6	2013-12	Date	10
7	2014-01	Time	10

Figure 11-23. Recasting the date column from text to Date type

As seen in Figure 11-24, we now have one text type column and one date type column. These will both be used in "Visualizing Data with Python" on page 386, where this example picks up. Click Close & Apply before proceeding (not pictured).

Figure 11-24. Preview our data transformed with a Python script

Transforming Data with R

Next we want to use R within Power BI Editor to transform our data. This is a continuation of the example from "Ingesting Data with R" on page 378. You will use R to create two new columns in Power Query Editor that calculate a six-month moving average of the Google Trends search indices. You'll also rename the columns.

Go to the Transform tab and select "Run R script." A window will appear where you can copy over the following code tested in our IDE. Select OK (Figure 11-25).

There are two elements to call out here. First, note that our previously ingested dataframe was called "df" but now Power BI has changed it to the default "dataset." Second, we are also attaching the *zoo* package for manipulating time series data. If you see an error saying that Power BI can't find a package, return to "Setting Up R" on page 372 and make sure the package was installed.

```
# Import packages
library(zoo)

# Rename dataframe
df_rolling <- dataset

# Rename columns
colnames(df_rolling)[colnames(df_rolling )=="Month"] <- "month_year"
col1 <- "python.machine.learning...United.States."
colnames(df_rolling)[colnames(df_rolling )==col1] <- "python_machine_learning"
col2 <- "r.machine.learning...United.States."
colnames(df_rolling)[colnames(df_rolling )==col2] <- "r_machine_learning"

# Add six-month moving average
df_rolling$month_year <- as.Date(paste(df_rolling$month_year, "01", sep = "-"))
```

```
df_rolling$python_moving_average <- rollapply(df_rolling$"python_machine_learning",
    width=6, FUN=mean, align="right", partial=TRUE)
df_rolling$r_moving_average <- rollapply(df_rolling$r_machine_learning,
    width=6, FUN=mean, align="right", partial=TRUE)

# Load data
print(df_rolling)
```

Figure 11-25. Adding an R script to transform the data

Pay attention to the datatypes when using Python or R. Power BI can automatically change datatypes, so code that successfully ran in an IDE may break when run in Power BI.

Click Close & Apply (Figure 11-26) before proceeding to "Visualizing Data with R" on page 390, where this example picks up.

Figure 11-26. Previewing the data transformed by an R script

Visualization

Power BI is known for its beautiful out-of-the-box visuals; however, these are limited in both number and degree of customization. There are additional visuals available for download within the AppSource, but even these may not always meet a business's needs.

This is where Python and R visuals come in. They are both available within the Visualizations pane, and they allow a user to leverage libraries popular among data scientists, like seaborn (Python), matplotlib (Python), and ggplot2 (R).

One downside is that these visuals appear as static images. This means they do not have a hover-over feature (e.g., tool tips), and you cannot click on or select any of their elements (e.g., highlighting). They can, however, respond to cross-filtering from other visuals, in which case the image is rendered again based on the filter criteria. This is explored in the following examples for Python and R.

To create Python or R visuals within Power BI, you will have to enable script visuals. These can be turned on within "Options," but the easier method is to select a Python script visual or an R script visual. The first time you do this in a report, the pop-up in Figure 11-27 will appear, and you can select Enable.

Enable script visuals

You need to enable script visuals to begin creating Python script. Script visuals can execute script code that may contain security or privacy risks.

Enable   Cancel

Figure 11-27. Enabling Python and R script visuals

The following demonstrations are our final examples using Google Trends data to compare the relative online popularity of "Python machine learning" and "R machine learning" using time series analysis.

Visualizing Data with Python

This is a continuation of example in "Transforming Data with Python" on page 381. We previously ingested and transformed data from Google Trends comparing the relative popularity of Python and R for machine learning. Now we want to visualize the difference over time.

Notice in Figure 11-28 that we have our dataframe (now named "df") in the Data pane. Within the Visualizations pane, click on the "Python visual" icon. This opens the visual on the canvas as well as a Python script editor where the code will go.

To call the dataframe columns as variables, we must first bring them into the visual by adding them to the Values well (also shown in Figure 11-28).

Also notice the callout in the Python script editor that Power BI will automatically remove duplicate rows *before any code is run*. If this, in the future, ever affects your data, then return to Power Query Editor and add an index column.

Figure 11-28. Adding a Python visual and populating it with data

Notice in Figure 11-28 that the month_year variable is not part of a hierarchy and does not have "Year," "Quarter," "Month," or "Day" below it. If you see those values, go to the drop-down arrow next to month_year and change Date Hierarchy to month_year; otherwise, you will receive an error message.

You can now add the following code into the Python script editor and click the Run icon in the top-right corner (Figure 11-29).

This code calls our data as "dataset" (again, the default for Power BI) and imports the data visualization package matplotlib. Power BI does not have a way to combine a line plot with a scatter plot, but this is not an issue for matplotlib. We are also able to customize the visual to our precise preferences.

```python
# Import packages
import matplotlib.pyplot as plt

# Format plot
fig = plt.figure(figsize=(16,8), dpi=200)
```

```
plt.title("Change in Programming Language Popularity Over Time", fontsize=20)
plt.ylabel("Google Search Frequency Index", fontsize=16)
plt.yticks(fontsize=16)

# Plot moving averages as a line
plt.plot(dataset["month_year"], dataset["python_moving_average"],
        c="gold", linewidth=3)
plt.plot(dataset["month_year"], dataset["r_moving_average"],
        c="red", linewidth=3)

# Plot monthly observations as a scatter plot
plt.scatter(x=dataset["month_year"], y=dataset["python_machine_learning"],
          c="gold", alpha=0.5)
plt.scatter(x=dataset["month_year"], y=dataset["r_machine_learning"],
          c="red", alpha=0.5)

# Set the x-axis tick positions, labels, and angle
    # [6:] skips the first 6 labels (to start in January)
    # [::12] then selects every 12th label thereafter
xticks = dataset["month_year"][6:][::12]
xtick_labels = [str(i) for i in xticks]
plt.xticks(xticks, xtick_labels, fontsize=20)
plt.xticks(rotation=30)

# Add the legend
plt.legend(["Python machine learning", "R machine learning"],
          fontsize=16, frameon=False)

# Display plot
plt.show()
```

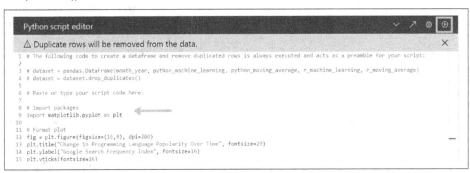

Figure 11-29. Running a Python script to create a custom visual

The result, shown in Figure 11-30, is aesthetically different from other Power BI
visuals but presents a compelling view of our data. The plot shows that the Google
Search frequency indices of "Python machine learning" and "R machine learning"
change over time. Each dot is a single month's observation, while the lines are
six-month moving averages.

We see how the two time series grew in popularity at the same level and rate for the first two years of observations. Then in the middle of 2015, there was a split where searches for "R machine learning" leveled off in relative terms while "Python machine learning" searches continued to climb.

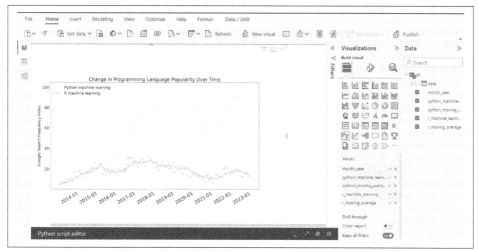

Figure 11-30. A custom Python visual

Furthermore, the visual is responsive to cross-filtering. We demonstrate this by adding a slicer to the canvas and populating it with the date variable (Figure 11-31). This allows us to adjust the date interval, which in real time changes the visual's time horizon.

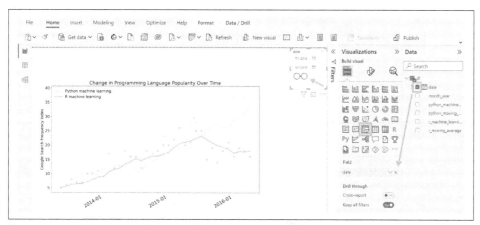

Figure 11-31. Custom Python visuals respond to cross-filtering

This concludes our demonstration of using Python in Power BI with Google Trends data. The next demo, leveraging Python to predict outcomes from a pretrained machine learning model, uses a different dataset and scenario.

Visualizing Data with R

This is a continuation of the example in "Transforming Data with R" on page 384. We previously ingested and transformed data from Google Trends comparing the relative popularity of Python and R for machine learning. Now we want to visualize the difference over time.

Notice in Figure 11-32 that we have our dataframe (now named "df") in the Data pane. Within the Visualizations pane, click on the R visual icon. This opens the visual on the canvas as well as an R script editor where the code will go.

To call the dataframe columns as variables, we must first bring them into the visual by adding them to the Values well (also shown in Figure 11-32). We also change the "month_year" variable from Date Hierarchy to "month_year" since the script is based on its original format.

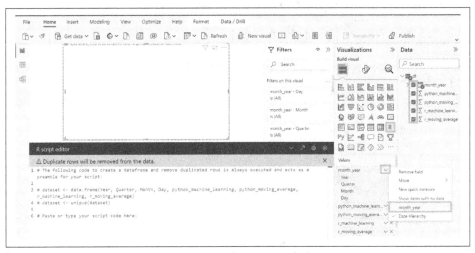

Figure 11-32. Adding an R visual and populating it with data

You can now add the following code into the R script editor and click the Run icon in the top-right corner (Figure 11-33).

 Also notice the callout in the R script editor that Power BI will automatically remove duplicate rows *before any code is run*. If this ever affects your data, then return to Power Query Editor and add an index column.

This code calls our data as "dataset" (again, the default for Power BI) and imports the data visualization package ggplot2. Power BI does not have a way to combine a line plot with a scatter plot, but this is not an issue for ggplot2. We are also able to customize the visual to our precise preferences.

```
# Import packages
library(ggplot2)

# Encode data to proper format (not necessary in R Studio)
dataset$month_year <- as.Date(dataset$month_year)
dataset$python_machine_learing <- as.numeric(dataset$python_machine_learning)
dataset$r_machine_learning <- as.numeric(dataset$r_machine_learning)
dataset$python_moving_average <- as.numeric(dataset$python_moving_average)
dataset$r_moving_average <- as.numeric(dataset$r_moving_average)

# Display plot
ggplot(dataset, aes(x=month_year)) +

  # Add scatter plots
  geom_point(aes(y=python_machine_learning, color="gold"), alpha=0.5, size=4) +
  geom_point(aes(y=r_machine_learning, color="red"), alpha=0.5, size=4) +

  # Add line plots
  geom_line(aes(y=python_moving_average, color="gold"), lwd=2) +
  geom_line(aes(y=r_moving_average, color="red"), lwd=2) +

  # Add labels
  labs(x = "", y = "Google Search Frequency Index") +
  ggtitle("Change in Programming Language Popularity Over Time") +

  # Format
  theme_minimal() +
  theme(text=element_text(size=24)) +
  theme(plot.title = element_text(hjust = 0.5),
        panel.grid = element_blank(),
        panel.border = element_rect(color = "black", fill=NA, size = 0.5),
        legend.position = c(0.15, 0.9),
        legend.background = element_blank()) +

  # Override legend so colors, labels align with plot
  scale_color_identity(name="",
                       breaks=c("gold", "red"),
                       labels=c("Python machine learning", "R machine learning"),
                       guide = "legend")
```

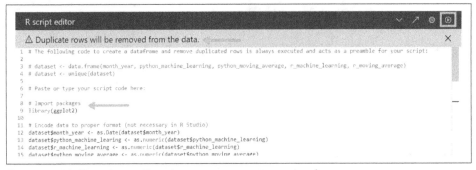

Figure 11-33. Running an R script to create a custom visual

The result, shown in Figure 11-34, is aesthetically different from other Power BI visuals but presents a compelling view of the data. The plot shows that the Google Search frequency index of "Python machine learning" and "R machine learning" changed over time. Each dot is a single month's observation, while the lines are six-month moving averages.

We see how the two time series grew in popularity at the same level and rate for the first two years of observations. Then in the middle of 2015, there was a split where searches for "R machine learning" leveled off in relative terms while "Python machine learning" searches continued to climb.

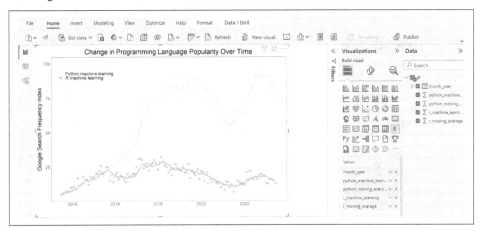

Figure 11-34. A custom R visual

Furthermore, the visual is responsive to cross-filtering. We demonstrate this by adding a slicer to the canvas and populating it with the date variable (Figure 11-35). This allows us to adjust the date interval, which in real time changes the visual's time horizon.

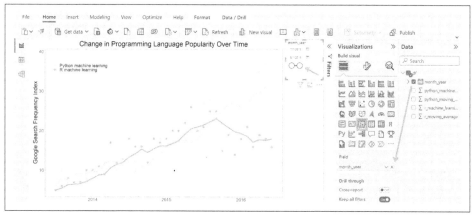

Figure 11-35. Custom R visuals respond to cross-filtering

This concludes our demonstration of using R in Power BI with Google Trends data. The next demo, leveraging R to train and apply a machine learning model to predict outcomes, uses a different dataset and scenario.

Machine Learning

Ingestion, transformation, and visualization are the backbone of applying Python and R in Power BI, but we have not yet covered the purest of data science components within those data science programming languages: machine learning. You can train and/or apply machine learning models using the same approaches we already described within the ingest and transform stages.

In Chapter 3, we covered how to train and deploy an algorithm using the built-in AutoML feature, and then in Chapter 10, we discussed training and deploying algorithms using Azure Machine Learning. Both of those approaches, however, require Power BI Premium. Instead, you can use Python and R with the free Power BI Desktop to train a model or use a pretrained model to score data.

Before we dive into the examples, let's cover two new concepts that will help those of us who are newer to data science. First is overfitting. *Overfitting* is the problem in machine learning when a model gives too much weight to the specificities of the training data and does not perform well when generalizing on out-of-sample data. This is like a student who memorizes the answers to a study guide without actually learning the material, resulting in high performance on the study guide but poor performance on a test with new questions. One common way to reduce the likelihood of overfitting is to train a model on a subset of data and then use a hold-out set of data to evaluate that model.

The second concept introduced in the demonstrations is a *pickle file*. Just as a cucumber can be pickled for later consumption, an algorithm can be saved for later use. *Pickling* is the process of taking a Python object (or group of Python objects) and converting them into a single binary file that can be unpacked later and loaded back into a Python environment. It's a useful way to combine and save AI assets, such as one file that defines an algorithm's structure with another file that defines the parameters of that same algorithm.

With those concepts out of the way, we are ready to see how a business can use Python and R for machine learning within Power BI. The final two examples are distinct from the rest of this chapter because they are performing different tasks. The Python demo shows how to load a pretrained, pickled model in Power BI to transform data that has already been ingested. Then, the R demo shows how to train a model and use it to score data—all within the data ingestion stage of Power BI. We recommend reading both sections, even if you exclusively use one of the languages.

The examples use the same vending machine dataset introduced in Chapter 10. Previously, we used that weekly sales data to forecast future demand to know how much inventory to order. To mix things up, we are going to walk through a different scenario where our data feed is corrupted, erasing the variable that indicates each vending machine's location. We will use AI to see whether we can accurately predict a vending machine's location based on the other supplementary information provided.

Using a Pretrained Model with Python on Transform

Imagine that the scenario described in the previous paragraph occurs, and you now have to add a new column of predicted locations to your data model within Power BI. Luckily, a data scientist on staff sends you a deep learning model as a pickle file to help out. You return to this book (specifically, Chapter 9) to brush up on deep learning and begin.

Although we are showing how to score data within the data transformation stage in Power BI, it is equally possible to do the same within the data ingest stage. We leave it to the reader as a challenge to adapt the sample Python script to score the data on ingest.

We'll load in our base data by clicking the arrow icon next to "Get data" and selecting Web (Figure 11-36).

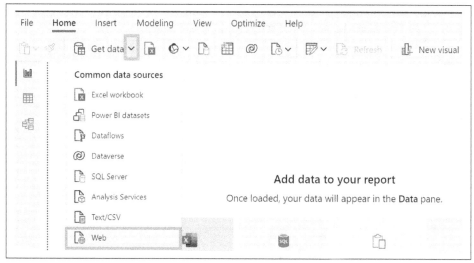

Figure 11-36. Ingesting data from the web

Under URL, we add *https://raw.githubusercontent.com/tomweinandy/ai-with-power-bi/main/Chapter11/VendingRevenue.csv* and click OK (not pictured).

This presents a preview of our data, shown in Figure 11-37. The "Location" column is present (even though our story said otherwise), but it will later let us compare our predictions against the true result.

We now want to score the data to predict location. Note that there are five distinct locations, making this a multi-class classification problem. Click Transform Data to proceed.

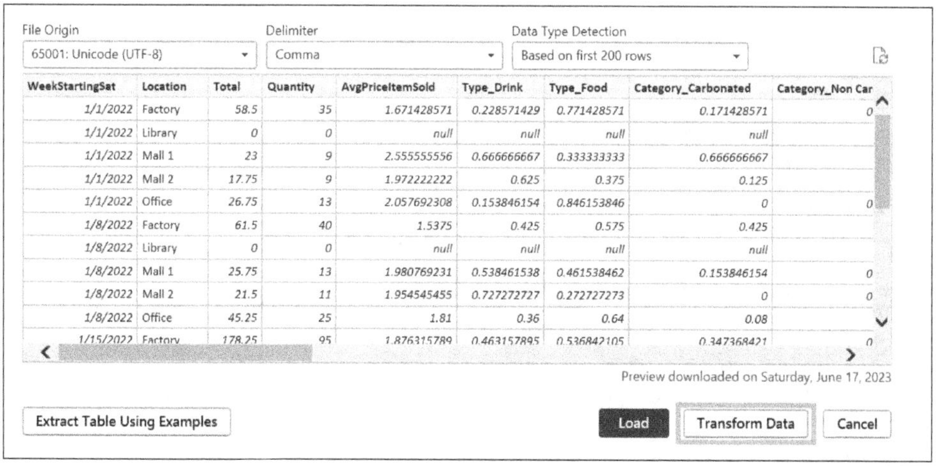

WeekStartingSat	Location	Total	Quantity	AvgPriceItemSold	Type_Drink	Type_Food	Category_Carbonated	Category_Non Car
1/1/2022	Factory	58.5	35	1.671428571	0.228571429	0.771428571	0.171428571	0
1/1/2022	Library	0	0	null	null	null	null	
1/1/2022	Mall 1	23	9	2.555555556	0.666666667	0.333333333	0.666666667	
1/1/2022	Mall 2	17.75	9	1.972222222	0.625	0.375	0.125	
1/1/2022	Office	26.75	13	2.057692308	0.153846154	0.846153846	0	0
1/8/2022	Factory	61.5	40	1.5375	0.425	0.575	0.425	
1/8/2022	Library	0	0	null	null	null	null	
1/8/2022	Mall 1	25.75	13	1.980769231	0.538461538	0.461538462	0.153846154	0
1/8/2022	Mall 2	21.5	11	1.954545455	0.727272727	0.272727273	0	0
1/8/2022	Office	45.25	25	1.81	0.36	0.64	0.08	
1/15/2022	Factory	178.25	95	1.876315789	0.463157895	0.536842105	0.347368421	0

File Origin: 65001: Unicode (UTF-8) Delimiter: Comma Data Type Detection: Based on first 200 rows

Preview downloaded on Saturday, June 17, 2023

Extract Table Using Examples   Load   Transform Data   Cancel

Figure 11-37. Previewing the data to be transformed

Now click the Transform ribbon and select "Run Python script," shown in Figure 11-38. Then paste the following script into the text box and click OK.

 If you receive an error saying that one of the packages is not found, return to "Setting Up Python" on page 366 for a recap of the installation process. Note that sometimes the library you need to install has a different name than the package you import. Search online if you have trouble.

```
# Load packages
import pandas as pd
import pickle
import requests
import tensorflow as tf
from sklearn.preprocessing import LabelEncoder

# Locate pre-trained model from GitHub
algo_url = "https://github.com/tomweinandy/ai-with-power-bi/raw/main/Chapter11/" \
           "vending_model.pickle"

# Clean data
df = dataset
df = df.dropna()
df = df.drop(columns=["WeekStartingSat"])

# Load the pickled deep learning algorithm
response = requests.get(algo_url)
model_info = pickle.loads(response.content)

# Reconstruct the model architecture
loaded_model = tf.keras.models.model_from_json(model_info["architecture"])

# Set the model weights
loaded_model.set_weights(model_info["weights"])

# Preprocess the data
label_encoder = LabelEncoder()

# Encode location labels
df["Location"] = label_encoder.fit_transform(df["Location"])

# Split the data into input features (X)
X = df.drop("Location", axis=1)

# Predict the labels
predictions = loaded_model.predict(X)

# Change predictions to integers between 0 and 4
encoded_labels = [int(min(max(p.round(0), 0), 4)) for p in predictions]
```

```
# Decode the predicted labels
decoded_labels = label_encoder.inverse_transform(encoded_labels)

# Add the predicted labels to the DataFrame
df.insert(0, "Predicted_Location", decoded_labels)

# Decode Location
df["Location"] = label_encoder.inverse_transform(df["Location"])
```

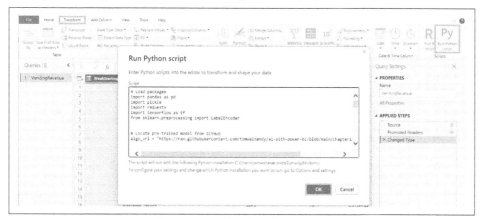

Figure 11-38. Running a Python script to load and apply a machine learning model

The script loaded an algorithm from GitHub saved as a pickle file. You should always ensure you are downloading files from trusted sources—and take additional caution when using pickle files since they may contain unknown and possibly nefarious items.

The run was successful, as shown by the three dataframes from the script seen in Figure 11-39. Select the final result of "df" by clicking the Table link to its right.

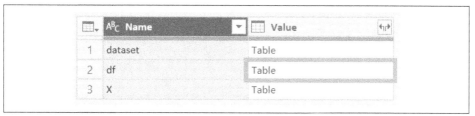

Figure 11-39. Selecting a dataframe from those used in the script

This brings us to Power Query Editor, where we can preview the resulting data. As we see in Figure 11-40, the newly added Predicted_Location column offers predictions that are similar to the actual vending machine location, but they are not perfectly the same. Click Close & Apply to bring the scored data into the Power BI report.

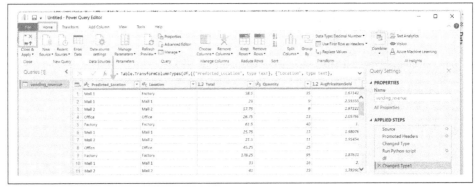

Figure 11-40. Previewing the data that has been transformed and scored by a machine learning model using Python

Training a Model with R on Ingest

The previous example used Python to load a pretrained deep learning algorithm and predict an outcome from sample data. This example will predict the same outcome on the same sample data; however, it will do so with R and by training a new model. Another distinction is that all of this will occur as we ingest the data into Power BI. Let's begin!

First click on "Get data" and then search for and select "R script." Click Connect (Figure 11-41).

Figure 11-41. Ingesting data with an R script

In this demo, we are using the popular xgboost package. This allows us to train a gradient boost model, a class of algorithms with a tree-like structure that in practice have been shown to be relatively efficient when training and very robust when making predictions. Copy the following R script into the Figure 11-42 text box and click OK:

```r
# Load packages
library(readr)
library(xgboost)

# Load CSV from GitHub
repo <- "https://raw.githubusercontent.com/tomweinandy/ai-with-power-bi/"
filepath <- "main/Chapter11/VendingRevenue.csv"
url <- paste(repo, filepath, sep="")
df <- read.csv(url)

# Clean data
df <- na.omit(df)
df <- subset(df, select=-c(WeekStartingSat))
df$Location <- as.factor(df$Location)

# Split the data into training and validation sets
set.seed(24)
train_indices <- sample(1:nrow(df), 0.7*nrow(df))
train_data <- df[train_indices, ]
test_data <- df[-train_indices, ]

# Define the features from the target variable "Location"
features <- setdiff(names(train_data), "Location")

# Convert the data to DMatrix format (an efficient data structure for xgboost)
dtrain <- xgb.DMatrix(data=as.matrix(train_data[, features]),
                      label=train_data$Location)
dtest <- xgb.DMatrix(data=as.matrix(test_data[, features]),
                     label=test_data$Location)

# Set hyperparameters for the xgboost model
params <- list(
  objective="multi:softprob", # For multi-class classification problems
  num_class=length(levels(df$Location)), # Number of classes in target variable
  eta=0.1, # Learning rate
  max_depth=6, # Maximum depth of each tree
  nrounds=100 # Number of boosting rounds
)

# Train the model
model <- xgboost(params, data=dtrain, nrounds=params$nrounds)

# Shuffle and encode original dataset
df_shuffled <- df[sample(1:nrow(df)), ]
df_shuffled_matrix <- xgb.DMatrix(data=as.matrix(df_shuffled[, features]),
                                  label=df_shuffled$Location)
```

```
# Make prediction using trained model
final_predictions <- predict(model, df_shuffled_matrix)

# Convert the predicted probabilities to class labels
final_predicted_ints <- as.integer(round(final_predictions))
location_mapping <- c('Factory', 'Library', 'Mall 1', 'Mall 2', 'Office')
final_predicted_classes <- factor(final_predicted_ints, levels=1:5,
                                  labels=location_mapping)

# Add predicted column to original cleaned dataframe
df_final <- cbind(PredictedLocation=final_predicted_classes, df_shuffled)
```

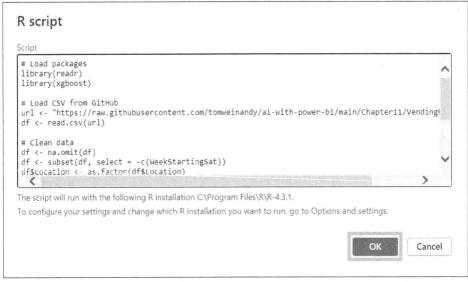

Figure 11-42. Running an R script to load and apply a machine learning model

In this example, we are scoring the same data that was used to train the model itself. This naturally results in overfitting, which artificially inflates how accurate the algorithm actually is. We did this to simplify the demo but still wish to call out that it is not best practice.

Despite going through all of the steps of loading data, preprocessing the data, training an ML model, scoring data, and combining results, the script takes less than a minute to run.

You'll see a window that lists on the lefthand pane the different datasets returned from the script. Select "df_final," which displays the preview shown in Figure 11-43, and then click Load.

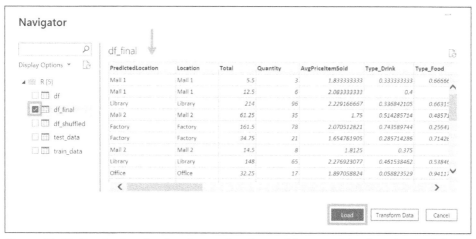

Figure 11-43. Previewing the data ingested and scored by a machine learning model using R

Summary

Python and R are gateways to more advanced applications of Power BI, and true to their status as data science programming languages, they unlock additional ways to incorporate artificial intelligence within Power BI. Businesses benefit from these tools because they allow for:

- Greater complexity of analysis
- More customization
- Opportunities to apply new or existing machine learning models
- The ability to incorporate Power BI into larger data science workflows
- Ways to bypass the paid features restricted to Power BI Premium

As the field of data science continues to mature, we expect integrations between Power BI and programming languages like Python and R will become increasingly valuable to an organization. Whether you are a current data scientist looking to improve your skill at building reports in Power BI or a data analyst looking to expand your programming skills, you too will be well positioned to develop at the intersections of these tools. After all, the common denominator of AI and BI is their "intelligence."

Making Your AI Production-Ready with Power BI

You might wonder whether nontechnical people can help evaluate AI models and prepare them for practical use. In fact, even if business teams do not have a deep knowledge of AI or technology, they can make essential contributions to the evaluation of AI models. For example, businesspeople can offer many insights into why the data is formatted or recorded in a certain way—contextual information that may not be immediately apparent.

As mentioned throughout the book, the business objectives must be explicit from the outset. Throughout the development lifecycle, people's enthusiasm can run away with them, leading them to generate many ideas quickly. It is heartening to see business teams be so engaged with AI. However, if you and your team are tasked with translating all these ideas into action, it may feel overwhelming. The project can be derailed when bubbling-over enthusiasm causes people to change objectives halfway through the project—or more frequently! Stakeholder enthusiasm and the technology team's eagerness to please can result in chaos.

This chapter will explore how businesses can evaluate artificial intelligence models. We will start by looking at strategies to help with the assessment of models. Then you'll apply a model to a dataflow entity, and you'll learn how to use the scored output from the model in a Power BI report. We'll also address some practical ways to evaluate your model from a business perspective.

Strategies to Help Evaluate Models

Business teams can clearly describe key performance indicators (KPIs) for the AI model that align with business goals to ensure that the model's performance positively impacts business success and not just technical metrics. They often have in-depth knowledge of the domain where the AI model will be applied, which is important for ensuring the model solves the correct problems and makes reasonable predictions or decisions from a business perspective.

Let's begin with an example: you work for a company as an analyst and must analyze the relationship between advertising expenditure and sales. The objective is to build a regression model to predict sales based on expenditure. Therefore, you collect media analytics data on advertising budgets, expressed in dollars, and the corresponding sales figures (in units) for various social media campaigns. In this context, *heteroscedasticity* implies that sales variability, as the residuals indicate, is not constant across advertising expenditure levels. How might that occur? Let's look at an example with and without heteroscedasticity.

Scenario Without Heteroscedasticity

Ideally, the residuals would have a consistent spread (variance) for various advertising budgets. For instance, if your model predicts 100 sales units for a campaign with an advertising budget of $10,000 and the actual sales are 105 units, the residual would be −5 units.

Similarly, if your model predicts 500 units for a campaign with an advertising budget of $50,000 and the actual sales are 502 units, the residual would be −2 units. In this case, the spread of residuals is relatively constant across different advertising budgets.

Scenario with Heteroscedasticity

With heteroscedasticity, the spread of residuals changes as the advertising expenditure varies. Continuing with the example, the residuals may exhibit a smaller spread for lower advertising budgets, indicating that the model's predictions are typically closer to the actual sales figures when less is spent on advertising. However, the residuals might have a wider spread for increased advertising budgets, indicating that the model's predictions are less precise when more money is spent on advertising. In this case, the spread of residuals increases as the advertising expenditure increases, implying heteroscedasticity.

In this context, heteroscedasticity is a problem because by breaking the assumption of constant variance of residuals (i.e., homoscedasticity), it can lead to inconsistent predictions, biased coefficient calculations, and invalid statistical inferences.

Several approaches address heteroscedasticity in regression analysis. One standard method is to transform the variables by taking the logarithm of the dependent variable, sales in this example. Alternatively, you can use weighted least squares regression, assigning weights to each observation based on variability. Another option is to explore alternative regression models, such as robust regression techniques.

Detecting and addressing heteroscedasticity in your analysis is crucial to ensure the validity and reliability of your insights and predictions.

How Does Heteroscedasticity Affect AI Models?

In theory, heteroscedasticity does not necessarily lead to bias in the coefficient estimates of a linear regression model. So, on average, the model could produce unbiased estimations. However, in practice, models can produce misleading results if they do not account for heteroscedasticity. This is especially true when using specific model-fitting methods, like ordinary least squares (OLS) linear regression.

The model itself can be inefficient because the estimator's variance isn't at its minimum, and the model needs to fully extract all the information it can from the data. This issue leads to less precise estimates and wider confidence intervals.

Other test statistics, such as t-tests or F-tests, may also be invalid because these tests rely on the assumption of homoscedasticity. If heteroscedasticity is present, these tests may no longer be accurate and thus lead to erroneous inferences. In AI and machine learning, the data is assumed to follow the normal distribution. When this assumption is violated in heteroscedasticity, the model's performance may degrade.

What Can Be Done If Heteroscedasticity Is Suspected?

Data visualization, such as a funnel chart, can deepen an analysis by permitting inspection of the residuals plot for patterns. Graphs can show a more considerable systematic change in spread across the independent variable(s). Additionally, you can use statistical tests like the Breusch–Pagan or White tests to test formally for heteroscedasticity.

If you identify heteroscedasticity in the dataset, several approaches exist to manage it. One standard practice is to transform the variables involved in the analysis. For example, a logarithmic transformation to the dependent or independent variable(s) can stabilize the variance. Another approach is to use weighted least squares (WLS) regression, where the weights are inversely proportional to the variability of the residuals. You could also use models that inherently account for heteroscedasticity, like generalized least squares (GLS) or heteroscedasticity-consistent standard errors. In addition, some machine learning techniques, such as tree-based models, are less sensitive to heteroscedasticity.

Determining acceptable performance levels for AI models involves:

- Understanding the business context
- Setting up relevant performance metrics
- Constantly monitoring the model's performance to ensure it meets the desired business goals

Let's walk through an example. Imagine that you are an analyst for a product retailer. You need to assess an AI model to see if it can predict whether a customer will return a product they've purchased. The goal of the model is to minimize return costs for the organization. The company has decided to optimize the sales process by offering better product recommendations. If it can provide better product recommendations, then the customer will be happier with the recommended product that they purchase and less likely to return it.

Making Your AI Model Ready for the Real World

At some point, you need to make your AI model ready for showtime! In the previous example, defining the acceptable performance for this AI model is crucial. In this case, the goal is to predict returns to minimize costs and provide more accurate recommendations. The business might decide that an acceptable model should correctly predict returns at least 80% of the time. Note that the business teams, not the technical teams, provide direction about performance metrics. This direction establishes the focus for the business and technical teams, and it ensures that both teams direct their efforts toward building a relevant and purposeful AI model. Having the business establish success metrics also supports business adoption of the model. If the business teams do not understand how the model will benefit them, they will not use it.

When considering the deployment of an AI model to production, you need to determine if the model can handle real-world scenarios effectively. It would help if you also did a thorough investigation through robustness testing using various input data, such as with a dataset that has anomalies, errors, and missing data. This strategy will help you to assess how well the model handles variations and edge cases.

In Power BI, fortunately, you have the power of the cloud to help you build scalable and efficient models. The model should be scalable so it can handle any expected workload. You can do infrastructure testing to ensure the model meets latency or throughput requirements.

Ultimately, AI is all about the business, so it is crucial to incorporate business feedback and make revisions based on these insights. If you've ever been part of a software rollout and deployment, you may have come across the concept of user acceptance testing (UAT) as part of the process. In AI programs, we also need to go

---

through UAT, where the technical teams engage domain experts and end users in evaluating the model's usability and effectiveness. The UAT output is feedback on the model's outcomes and user experience.

Once the business and technical teams agree on a direction, the technical teams can work on the data, the model, and the appropriate performance metrics. Choosing the right metric to evaluate the model's performance is crucial, and the choice must be tied back to the overall business success criteria. Suppose we see a business problem as a binary classification problem. In that case, we might use metrics such as accuracy, precision, recall, F-1 score, area under curve (AUC), or the receiver operating characteristic (ROC) curve. For example, the business might prioritize a high recall score because it wants to minimize false negatives. In terms of the previous example of predicting customer returns, a false negative would involve predicting a product will not be returned when, in fact, the customer does send the item back.

It is also helpful to establish a baseline. Many businesses ignore baselines altogether— this is equivalent to trying to run before they can walk! Baselines could involve using a simpler model or an industry standard if one exists. If the new model doesn't significantly exceed the baseline in terms of the insights it adds, it may not be worth deploying.

Assessing the Costs and Benefits to the Business

Business teams are keen on understanding the financial implications of the AI project, including the costs of development, deployment, maintenance, and so on. However, these can be difficult to calculate. Nonetheless, breaking the project down to its known items often yields a good guesstimate. These costs need to be balanced against the anticipated gains in productivity, efficiency, revenue, or cost savings.

Additionally, the teams may worry about whether AI integration may disrupt current business processes or whether it will require fundamental changes to the existing business model. They wonder whether there is, in fact, a need for strategic realignment. The teams may also voice concern about changes to operations, training and retraining, and missing skill sets. Put together, these business changes have cost implications.

How do we ascertain the business cost? For instance, how does an analyst get to the 80% figure mentioned earlier? The business can do a cost-benefit analysis that balances the costs associated with incorrect predictions against the benefits of the insights gained from correct predictions. Wrong predictions include false positives and false negatives. In the example of customer returns, costs might consist of the return postage, merchandise in used condition that cannot be resold, and the labor expense of handling returned goods.

The business teams can ensure that the work is relevant to the organization and its mission by casting the success of the AI model in terms of *return on investment* (ROI). The teams can compare the costs involved in developing, deploying, and maintaining the model to the benefits that the model brings to the business.

The business needs to consider these costs:

- Data collection
- Preparation
- Model development, including the resources required by the technology stack such as computing power and storage, licenses for tools, and personnel costs
- Infrastructure, which may be in the cloud, on-premises, or hybrid
- Hardware and software
- Third-party services or consulting
- Ethical AI considerations
- Operational resource demands once the model is deployed, such as maintenance, updating, monitoring, and potentially the need to retrain the model to maintain its currency
- Integration, if the AI will be interwoven into existing workflows
- Any downtime that occurs

Here's a list of potential direct and indirect benefits to consider:

- Increased revenue
- Reduced costs
- Increased productivity due to solving a challenge, for example, by automating tasks
- Improved efficiency, such as risk management and reduced errors leading to better reputation management
- Improved compliance improvements
- Enhanced customer experience
- Bolstered brand reputation
- Higher employee satisfaction
- Upgraded creativity and innovation
- Greater competitive advantage

Calculating the costs and benefits at a granular level may not be possible, and the calculation is unlikely to be exact. Given the uncertainties and assumptions in projecting

AI costs and benefits, it is a good idea to conduct sensitivity analyses to gauge how changes in key assumptions could impact ROI. This will help you understand the risk profile of the AI project. For example, it is challenging to translate reputational risk into dollars, so you could consider the legal costs if someone filed a claim against the organization.

Here is the basic formula for ROI, expressed as a percent:

ROI = 100 * (Financial benefits − Total investment) / Total investment

The resulting percentage represents the return on every dollar invested. If the result is positive, then the investment is profitable, while a negative ROI projects a loss.

You may also need to take the *time value of money* (TVM) into account. Intuitively, an amount of money is worth more now than the same amount in the future. Future cash flows from the AI system should be discounted back to their present value to reflect the ROI accurately.

Example ROI Calculation

Let's walk through an example of calculating the ROI of a typical AI project in marketing. A company is implementing an AI system to personalize email marketing campaigns, with a goal of increasing sales conversions by sending personalized product recommendations to customers.

We can arrive at the ROI by examining costs versus benefits. We can break down costs into initial investments to develop the project (see Table 12-1) and ongoing expenses once the project is launched (Table 12-2).

Table 12-1. Initial investment costs

Cost	$
Data preparation	10,000
Development	100,000
Cloud infrastructure	5,000
Total investment	**115,000**

Table 12-2. Ongoing costs

Cost	$
Maintenance	10,000
AI model updates post-release	5,000
Marketing campaign	5,000
Total ongoing expenses	**20,000**

Combining the initial investment and post-launch expenses shows that the project cost is estimated to be $115,000 + $20,000 = $135,000.

The project has two main benefits: cost savings and increased revenue. Currently, the average conversion rate from email campaigns is only 1%, with average annual revenue from email marketing of $100,000. It is estimated that personalized recommendations will double the conversion rate to 2%, yielding annual revenue of $200,000. Thus, the project is projected to increase revenue by $100,000.

In addition, the company now uses an external third-party service to generate marketing emails, and the intention is to reduce usage of this service once the AI project is implemented, saving $50,000 in the first year. In total, therefore, estimated benefits will be $150,000.

Table 12-3. Benefits

Benefit	$
Annual revenue	100,000
Reduction in third-party expenses	50,000
Total benefits for year one	**150,000**

To summarize, costs for the first year are estimated to be $135,000 and benefits are estimated to be $150,000.

The calculation is now Total benefits – Total costs, which leaves $15,000. You then divide $15,000 by the Total costs, which are $135,000. Expressed as a percentage, the resulting ROI is 11%. But what does this number mean? It is a positive ROI, meaning that the project will generate more revenue and cost savings than it incurs in costs. Thus, the company can conclude that it is worthwhile to invest in personalizing email marketing campaigns with AI technology. On the other hand, if this had resulted in a negative ROI, then the project would generate more costs than benefits and would not be worthwhile.

Note that this is a simple example to illustrate the ROI calculation. Real-world scenarios may involve more complicated considerations when estimating both direct and indirect benefits. Direct benefits include increased customer lifetime value and brand loyalty. Indirect benefits include items that are difficult to attribute directly to the AI initiative, such as improved customer satisfaction.

Can the Business Teams Have Confidence in the AI Model?

The concerns that business teams express about AI include those about short-term risks and impacts on the organization as well as the longer-term strategic implications of AI technologies for operations, the workforce, and the company's financial position. Business stakeholders may also be concerned about the impact on shareholders or brand reputation. In addition, they may be concerned about the ethics of AI, which is why we have devoted a whole chapter to this fascinating and timely topic.

When delivering an AI project, a common issue is that some business team members are nervous that the AI model is wrong and will cause more problems than it solves. It is easy to dismiss these naysayers as "laggards," but they do pose an interesting and valuable question. It is important to assume good intentions when people ask "what if" questions because they are trying to do their jobs well and to save the company from risk or embarrassment. This section will address how you can manage such concerns and reassure people that the project is being carried out with due diligence.

People do not like surprises regarding IT projects, never mind AI projects! It is always best to be transparent about the limitations of the AI model, potential risks, and the steps being taken to mitigate them. Your integrity will build trust and confidence among the project stakeholders. Timing is everything; it is best to explain the risks when you can also describe the steps you will take to address them.

Is the Model Result Just a Fluke?

When your AI model shows promising results, you are undoubtedly keen to show off to the business teams. However, your sense of achievement and enthusiasm may ebb when you are asked, "Is this just a fluke?" Business teams are naturally interested in whether a model's good performance will repeat consistently. Let's take a look at the testing methodology so you can answer the question fully.

How can we test that the result isn't a fluke? This is where model validation comes to the forefront of making our model production-ready. Before deploying the model, it's essential to validate its performance using a holdout set or cross-validation methods. This ensures that the model's performance is generalized and does not just reflect overfit to the training data.

A *holdout set*, also known as a *validation set* or *test set*, refers to a subset of data held back from the model during the training process. From the model's perspective, it has never seen this data before. The holdout set is used to evaluate the performance and generalization of the prepared model.

When developing a machine learning model, the AI engineer divides the available data into three main subsets: the training set, the holdout set, and the test set:

Training set
This data is used to train the model, adjust its parameters, and optimize its performance.

Holdout set
This data is used to fine-tune the model's hyperparameters and make decisions regarding its architecture, such as selecting the best configuration or comparing different models.

Test set
This data is used to help evaluate the model's performance once all development decisions have been made.

The holdout set is crucial because it provides insight into how the model will perform on unseen data. It helps determine how well the model will generalize to unforeseen real-world examples. This assessment is essential for avoiding overfitting, where the model performs sufficiently on the training data but fails to generalize to unseen examples.

Typically, the holdout set is created by unsystematically partitioning a portion of the available data, ensuring that it is representative of the overall dataset. The size of the holdout set can depend on the quantity of available data. Generally speaking, it should be extensive enough to provide a reliable assessment of performance while still preserving enough data for training and validation.

Assuring Ongoing Model Performance

Once the model has been trained, the job is not over! Even after the AI engineer deploys the model, it's essential to continually monitor its performance to ensure it maintains an acceptable level. If performance degrades, the model may need to be retrained or tuned.

The ultimate measure of model performance is how well it satisfies the agreed-upon business goals. In our hypothetical use case, if the model can invariably and accurately predict returns, showing lower costs and improved customer experience, it performs at an acceptable level. Refining the mode is an iterative process of setting goals, measuring against them, and altering the model to ensure that it is aligned with business goals as necessary.

Now that we have covered some of the business issues in making AI production-ready, let's see how this translates into the real world with Power BI.

Making Your AI Production-Ready in Power BI

Power BI makes it very easy to make your AI production-ready. Picking up from Chapter 3, we will start from the point at which the model has been trained. As a recap, here is an example image of the Power BI portal showing the trained model and some details, such as the name and the date and time it was last refreshed. Under the Actions heading, you can see an ellipsis. If you click on the ellipsis, you can choose the Info option to obtain more information about the model (Figure 12-1).

Figure 12-1. Power BI portal displaying a trained model

You can see an example of the Info page for the Age and Salary Relationship model in Figure 12-2.

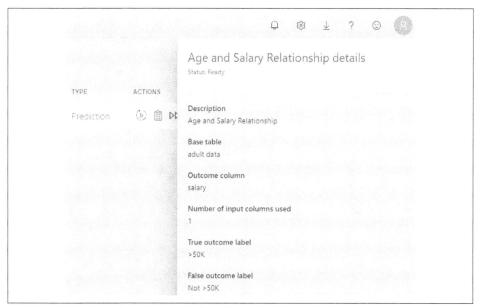

Figure 12-2. Model information on the Info page

You can apply the model from the portal. Figure 12-3 shows the "Apply ML model" button.

Figure 12-3. Applying the model from the portal

In the Apply dialog, you can specify the target entity with the source data you wish to apply the model to (Figure 12-4).

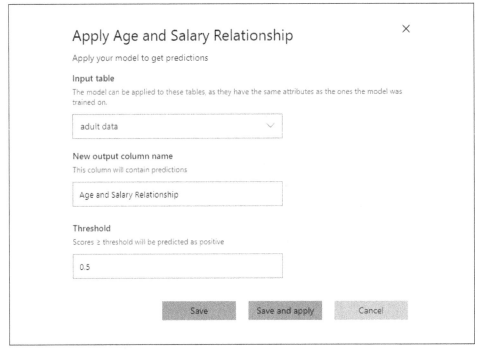

Figure 12-4. Applying the model to data

Then select "Save and apply." Once the model has been applied, Power BI will refresh the data. The Power BI portal will appear as shown in Figure 12-5.

Figure 12-5. Refreshing the data once the model has been applied

Applying the model creates two new tables. You will see that the tables have suffixes: enriched *<model_name>* and enriched *<model_name>* explanations. Figure 12-6 gives an example using the adult data.

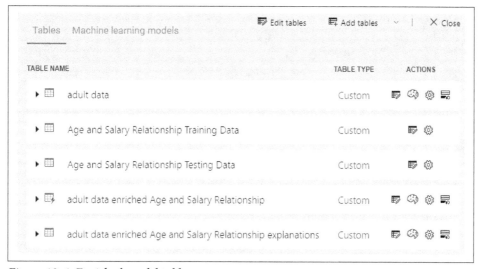

Figure 12-6. Enriched model tables

In our example, applying the model to the adult data table creates:

- Adult data including an enriched age and salary intent prediction, part of which is the model's predicted output
- Adult data including enriched age and salary intent prediction explanations that contain the top record-specific influencers for the prediction

Applying the binary prediction model adds four columns: Outcome, PredictionScore, PredictionExplanation, and ExplanationIndex, each with an Age and Salary Relationship prefix. We assume that older people are likelier to be in the higher salary bracket.

We can also see the tables in the Power BI Portal. Figure 12-7 shows an example of the enrichment table, with the additional columns highlighted.

TABLE NAME	
COLUMN NAME	DATA TYPE
age	Int64
workclass	String
fnlwgt	Int64
education	String
education-num	Int64
marital-status	String
occupation	String
relationship	String
sex	String
capital-gain	Int64
capital-loss	Int64
hours-per-week	Int64
Native-country	String
salary	String
Age and Salary Relationship.Outcome	Boolean
Age and Salary Relationship.PredictionScore	Decimal
Age and Salary Relationship.PredictionExplanation	String
Age and Salary Relationship.ExplanationIndex	Int64

Figure 12-7. Enrichment table with additional columns highlighted

You can also see the Explanation table columns, shown in Figure 12-8.

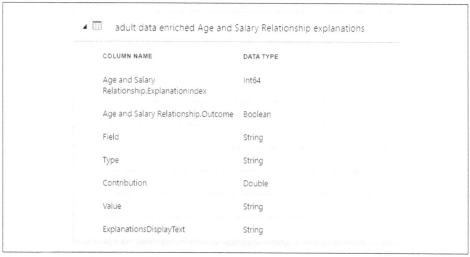

Figure 12-8. Explanation table columns

Once the dataflow refresh completes, you can select the "adult data enriched Age and Salary Relationship" table to view the results (Figure 12-9).

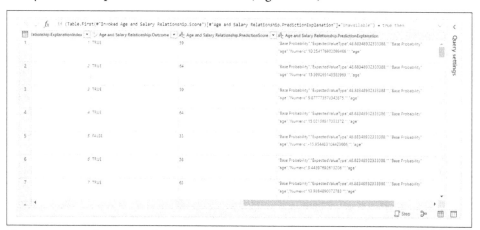

Figure 12-9. Explanation table content

Next, you can invoke the Power BI machine learning model against the test data. To do this, load the test data into the dataflow and go to the AI Insights screen in Power Query (Figure 12-10).

Figure 12-10. Power Query AI Insights tab

You may need to sign in again if you see the dialog in Figure 12-11.

Connect to data source

AzureMLFunctions
AzureMLFunctions

Connection

Create new connection ⌄   ↻

Connection name

Connection

Data gateway

(none)

Authentication kind

Organizational account ⌄

You are not signed in. Please sign in.

Sign in

Connect   Cancel

Figure 12-11. Signing in from the Power Query tab

In the AI Insights dialog, choose the Power BI Machine Learning Models folder from the navigation pane.

The portal will show the machine learning models available to you.

When you open the AI Insights dialog, you will see the input parameters for the machine learning model. These parameters will map automatically as parameters of the corresponding Power Query function. Note, however, that the automatic parameter mapping happens only if the names and datatypes of the parameters are the same.

To invoke a machine learning model, you can choose any of the selected model's columns in the drop-down list as input. In our example, we are going to choose Age. You can specify a constant value to use as input by toggling the column icon next to the input line, but we will leave it blank (Figure 12-12).

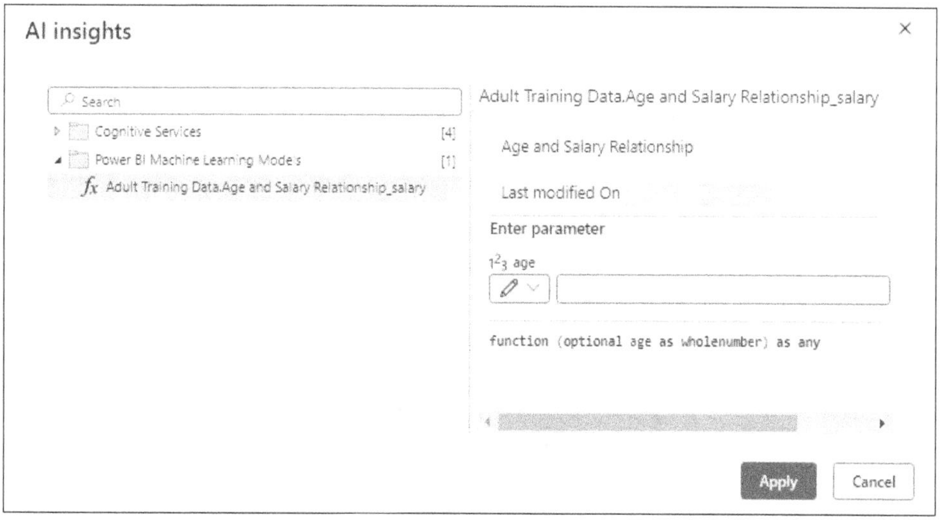

AI insights

Search

▷ Cognitive Services [4]

▲ Power BI Machine Learning Models [1]

fx Adult Training Data.Age and Salary Relationship_salary

Adult Training Data.Age and Salary Relationship_salary

Age and Salary Relationship

Last modified On

Enter parameter

1²₃ age

function (optional age as wholenumber) as any

[Apply] [Cancel]

Figure 12-12. Choosing a machine learning model in the Power BI service

Click Apply to view the preview of the machine learning model output as new columns in the table. You can start to get a feel for the data and the model. In this small example, it is hypothesized that older people are more likely to earn a higher salary than younger people, so you could have an initial view to see whether that bears out. However, as you know by now, you need to do more than simply glance at the model to test it out! You also see the model invocation under Applied steps for the query (Figure 12-13).

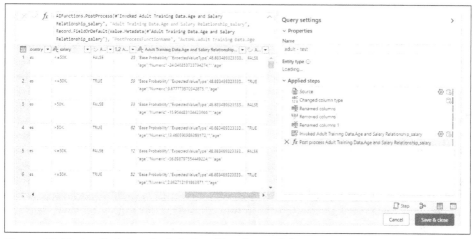

Figure 12-13. Applied steps include invoking the model

After you save your dataflow, the model automatically runs when the dataflow refreshes for any new or updated rows in the entity table.

Data Lineage for the AI Model

You can also use the Lineage view in Power BI to see the tables and functions that make up the Power BI model (Figure 12-14).

Figure 12-14. Lineage view in Power BI

Using the Scored Output from the Model in a Power BI Report

To use the scored output from your machine learning model, you can connect to your dataflow from Power BI Desktop to view the data. This functionality will allow you to share the results with the business teams, helping to ensure that the model is set up to make the data work for the business.

Summary

Congratulations! You can now use the adult data enriched Age by Salary Relationship table to incorporate the predictions from your model in Power BI reports. In this chapter, you reviewed and applied the model to a dataflow entity, and you learned how to use the scored output from the model in a Power BI report. We also addressed some practical ways to evaluate your model from a business perspective.

You can see that everyone, on both technical and nontechnical teams, can appreciably contribute to the evaluation, success, and even profitability of AI models. It can be frustrating when business teams do not show enthusiasm for the technical aspects of the project and raise unvalidated objections. This chapter has provided some ways to help you reassure the teams that the project is worthwhile.

The AI Feedback Loop

AI is poised to have a transformational impact on the scale of earlier general purpose technologies such as blockchain, the cloud, and the internet. Although it is already used in thousands of companies worldwide, most of its big opportunities have yet to be tapped. The effects of AI will be magnified in the coming decade as manufacturing, retailing, transportation, finance, healthcare, law, advertising, insurance, entertainment, education, and virtually every other industry transforms core processes and business models to take advantage of machine learning. The bottlenecks now are in management, implementation, and business imagination. This chapter will look at your next steps once you begin your AI journey.

How Do You Start the Next Project?

The *AI feedback loop* refers to a continuous process in which an artificial intelligence system receives feedback, learns from it, and then improves its performance based on that feedback. The AI feedback loop is an essential part of the training and development of AI models, allowing them to improve their capabilities iteratively over time.

By analyzing feedback over an extended period, developers can follow a model's progress and understand how competently it learns and improves over time. This longitudinal study provides insights into an AI model's overall stability and liabilities in continuous learning.

How Does Feedback Affect the Training and Development of AI Models?

Feedback is crucial for improving AI models because it helps identify their resilience and shortcomings. By analyzing feedback from business users, developers can understand where the model is functioning well and where it's making errors. Based on this information, they can make targeted improvements to enhance the model's implementation.

Feedback is vital in identifying the sources of stability and defects of an AI model by supplying helpful information about its implementation in real-world scenarios. For instance, developers can obtain feedback by identifying errors. Business users are good at providing feedback when the AI model makes mistakes or errors, but ideally, developers should be able to capture this information before the business teams see it. Positive feedback might underline the model's ability to handle specific tasks effectively, while unfavorable feedback can indicate areas where the model needs modification to better meet user expectations. By analyzing this feedback, developers can focus on areas where the model struggles or provides incorrect outputs. As a next step, the developers and testers can take remedial action to correct the model.

Developers can use performance metrics as clues. Performance metrics help them understand the model's strengths and weaknesses and identify how to improve it. Developers can monitor metrics such as accuracy, precision, recall, F-1-score, and others covered in previous chapters.

Reviewing the AI model's output can help to identify biases in the model's results. For instance, if the model consistently prefers or discriminates against particular groups or characteristics, user feedback can expose these biases so that developers can address them appropriately.

AI and Edge Cases in Feedback

In the context of AI and programming, an *edge case* refers to a scenario or input that is atypical, uncommon, or random compared to most of the data or inputs the AI model will encounter during training and operation. Edge cases challenge the typical behavior of a program or algorithm because they present the AI model with rare or extreme values.

In AI and software engineering, edge cases are essential to consider during software development and testing, including the development and training of AI models. Edge cases are welcome because they expose susceptibilities, limitations, or unexpected behavior that might not surface with standard data inputs. Recognizing and managing edge cases properly ensures that the software or AI model is robust, trustworthy, and capable of handling such challenging scenarios.

Ensuring that AI models can address edge cases is essential for their generalization and implementation in real-world applications. In AI, edge cases include infrequent instances or outliers that differ significantly from most training data. When a model does not handle edge cases well, the model might need more representative data to learn from.

How can AI developers handle edge cases? The process involves training and continual testing of AI models. Unfortunately, we can't "set it and forget it" in the world of AI. The model development process involves thorough testing, error analysis, and adjustments to the algorithms or models to make them stronger and more capable of providing accurate outputs in myriad scenarios. User feedback might raise the issue of scenarios or edge cases where the AI model fails to provide accurate or appropriate responses. Analyzing this feedback allows developers to identify areas of the model that require further refinement and fine-tuning.

Sometimes, an increase in the range or the incidence of edge cases tells you that there has been a change in real-world data scenarios that you need to consider. Developers must then retrain the AI model to adapt to new data since the original training datasets may no longer be relevant. Feedback helps identify these novel data instances to determine whether they are edge cases or potentially indicators of a change in the data environment where the AI model lives. Edge cases can reveal whether the model successfully adapts to changing data or struggles to generalize to a change in the data landscape.

Until now, we have been considering how to compare data with data. How do we compare AI models to human performance? For example, let's say that an AI model is required to distinguish wheat seeds from blackgrass seeds in images. Such comparisons could challenge a human expert since distinguishing between the two types of grains is often difficult. Developers can use expert feedback to compare the performance of the AI model with the predictions made by human experts. Blended teams of experts can identify where the AI system outperforms humans, such as speed of identification. The comparison process can also help identify areas where the model falls short, such as accuracy. The process's output can help developers identify areas to focus on, retraining the model to perform better. The experts may also be able to propose edge cases to be considered for the AI process.

Overall, feedback is a valuable source of information that allows developers to assess the real-world performance of an AI model; feedback can support development teams in pinpointing areas for improvement and making data-driven decisions to optimize the model's capabilities and address its weaknesses. Continuous feedback is essential for achieving a highly effective and adaptive AI system.

How Can Feedback Help Fix Errors in an AI Model?

AI models can be high quality but still make mistakes, especially when dealing with complicated and myriad real-world data. Feedback helps pinpoint these errors and provides practical information for correcting them. Developers can use this feedback to retrain and fine-tune the model, reducing the frequency of mistakes in future predictions. Feedback plays a vital role in fixing mistakes in an AI model by supplying information to developers about distinctive issues. It helps identify when and where errors occur in the AI model's result. Business users can point out instances where the model provides erroneous results. This identification of mistakes is essential as it steers developers to the areas that require focus.

One helpful tool is root cause analysis because it identifies the origin or causes of the mistakes. If we know the "why," then it becomes easier to know "how" to improve the model. Root cause analysis feedback often includes context for and explanations of the errors. By understanding why the model made a particular error, developers can devise appropriate solutions to fix it. Say the model invariably misclassifies specific types of inputs. These errors might indicate that the training data needs to be reviewed. Developers can then review and revise the training data to improve the model's performance. The developers might also fine-tune the model's hyperparameters and configurations. Modifying these parameters can significantly influence the model's behavior and improve its precision and reliability. Sometimes, the errors might be too substantial to be fixed through fine-tuning, and the model may need to be retrained on a revised or more extensive dataset.

AI, Bias, and Fairness

As social media sites have become more mainstream, the public has started to become concerned over the use of data with AI. The Netflix documentary *Social Dilemma* (2020) highlighted the ability of AI systems to use our data to manipulate our attention as well as to resell data and data products to the highest bidders. Such use of technology impacts areas such as addiction, propaganda, equity, and education.

Feedback can help uncover bias in the model's outputs. If the AI system exhibits unfair behavior or favors certain groups, developers can use this feedback to implement techniques that promote fairness and mitigate biases. It is essential to address the issue of bias in AI systems to develop fair and ethical machine learning models. There are enterprise and open source initiatives underway to help identify, understand, and alleviate bias in AI. The objective of these tools varies since they target different problems, such as the type of available data and the stage of model development. Technology by itself does not create or solve problems, so there needs to be a careful consideration of the human aspect of AI systems. Businesses can tackle bias in AI models by taking advantage of AI toolkits that can identify bias. It could be asserted that an efficient implementation of AI will combine both a knowledge of ethics and the ability to put them to use when appropriate. Technology companies may experience tension between increasing their profits and avoiding harm, for example. As in other areas of technology, AI has sometimes negatively impacted humans.

The reasoning behind AI's decisions is not always clear, and bias is one area that causes the most confusion as algorithms become increasingly opaque and difficult to understand. Business plans that include AI may lack clarity on how it relates to other technologies, their data, or their customers. It is important to understand clearly what decisions will be based on AI and to what extent, and who is accountable for these decisions. Businesses have an ethical and potentially legal responsibility to create AI models that do not negatively impact individuals or groups of people by incorporating responsible practices into their operations.

Some believe that people's work lives are increasingly shaped by mathematical models and data collection. The "datafication" of the workplace includes one-way data accumulation methods where information is collected with little regard for employee consent or compensation. Algorithms are often opaque, unregulated, and incontestable. Consequently, businesses need to work toward better explainability, fairness, and transparency.

As businesses seek to adopt AI in diverse areas, such as manufacturing, energy, customer services, and health, companies need to have confidence that they understand how the technology is behaving. Businesses may receive legal challenges concerning their use of AI technology. Hence, bias is a crucial factor to include in any assessment of the risks from AI.

Feedback on bias helps align the AI model's performance with user expectations. Developers can use this feedback to prioritize fixes that improve the user experience and ensure that the AI system effectively meets users' needs. Regarding bias, feedback gathered from real-world use is valuable in complementing testing done during development. It helps developers understand how the model behaves in practical scenarios and uncovers errors that might not have been apparent during testing. That said, if the results show a bias toward certain groups of people, then this would ideally be identified before release. If the bias occurs due to an imbalance in the datasets, then the Synthetic Minority Over-sampling TEchnique (SMOTE) can be used. With SMOTE, the larger class is "undersampled" and the smaller class or classes are "oversampled" to bring parity to the AI algorithm.

In summary, feedback is an indispensable tool for identifying errors in an AI model and implementing the necessary fixes. It allows developers to understand the model's limitations, learn from its mistakes, and continuously enhance its performance to provide more accurate and reliable results.

Explainable AI and Feedback

In Douglas Adams's popular 1979 science fiction novel *The Hitchhiker's Guide to the Galaxy*, the supercomputer Deep Thought reveals that the answer to the great question of "life, the universe, and everything" is 42. The novel's characters are frustrated by the vagueness of the answer and don't understand how Deep Thought arrived at that decision. If you have been working with AI, you may find yourself with a similar degree of frustration as you try to understand how and why the algorithm works.

There are a range of initiatives that aim to make AI decision making more transparent and accountable. One initiative is known as Explainable AI, or XAI, which aims to demonstrate the reasoning underpinning AI's decisions. These toolkits provide different perspectives on explainability and fairness by embedding AI's reasoning in distinct points of the end-to-end AI process. Explainability is considered an output of AI processing and output. The idea is that the algorithm's output should be accompanied by an explanation of how the algorithm came to that decision. Ethical toolkits offer practical help from different perspectives on AI decision making. However, the toolkits take different approaches to technology, so their adoption can be confusing for the business and the technical teams.

How Can Members of Organizations Address Ethics and AI?

How can we help people from all parts of the organization understand the importance of thorough testing and fairness in AI models? The value of data capital is enormous and growing. However, AI has implications well beyond the technical considerations.

Often, business leaders have concerns about the transparency and interpretability of AI systems. They are worried about delegating decisions to opaque algorithms that make decisions without clear, understandable rationales. Since they do not understand how the decisions are made, they are not sure if, or how much, they can trust them. It is reasonable for these leaders to consider the worst-case scenario. After all, they are likely to be held accountable if something goes wrong, and it is difficult to implement a quick fix if the business truly does not understand the problem.

The executive leadership may have concerns about compliance and data protection. It can be difficult to understand existing laws and how they may change in the future, so they may fear that any completed work will soon be obsolete and thus a waste of time, energy, and money. These issues can be exacerbated depending on the sector involved. Take, for example, industries with extremely sensitive data, such as healthcare and finance. Consider, too, how a global organization's storage of data in cloud platforms intersects with legal requirements that the data must be held within a given country's borders.

Despite these concerns, businesses can harbor a sense of FOMO, or fear of missing out, because they are anxious about keeping pace with their competitors as AI technologies advance. The potential of data capital to add value is enormous. After all, some of the wealthiest companies in the world, such as Facebook and Google, are built on data capital. Moreover, data is a foundational form of capital that is becoming an everyday part of our lives through smartphones, smart homes, and smart cities. The new normal of device data adds a layer of complexity to ethical considerations because businesses need to think carefully about consent, confidentiality, and care with respect to data.

Companies cannot simply assume good intentions in using AI and data in the workplace, because there are consequences for processes, people, and technology. As a result, companies may have to make difficult choices about undertaking certain projects. The dilemma is that rejecting potentially profitable projects can have a negative financial impact, but adopting an ethically risky project may have legal, financial, reputational, and even physical consequences for the business.

With increasing awareness of ethical concerns around AI, questions often arise about ensuring that AI systems are fair and unbiased. As businesses develop more and more data products, they are struggling to understand how they can prevent the perpetuation of discrimination. The business may also have to review its business processes, which may be out of step with its use of technology.

Following are some ethical toolkits for your review. There will no doubt be many more in the future as businesses recognize their importance.

AEquitas

AEquitas (*https://aequitasresource.org*) is an open source bias audit toolkit. It is intended for policymakers in areas such as criminal justice, education, public health, workforce development, and social services, and it is designed to address bias.[1] It is also intended for use by machine learning developers and analysts to audit machine learning models for bias and to make informed and equitable decisions around developing and deploying predictive risk assessment tools.

Deon

The Deon ethics checklist (*https://deon.drivendata.org*) is a good starting point, and it is easy to integrate into projects from a technical perspective. It is a command-line tool that allows you to easily add an ethics checklist to your

---

1 Pedro Saleiro et al., "Aequitas: A Bias and Fairness Audit Toolkit," *arXiv* (April 29, 2019), *https://doi.org/10.48550/arXiv.1811.05577*.

data science projects. Deon supports creating a new, standalone checklist file or appending a checklist to an existing analysis in many common formats.

Fairness Toolkit (fairkit-learn)

Independent researchers and research institutions have developed the Fairness Toolkit (*fairkit-learn*).[2] This open source Python library integrates with existing machine learning workflows. It provides tools for fairness assessment and mitigation, allowing comparative studies of actions that make AI results increasingly fair or unfair.

Interpret Community SDK

One commonly used package is the open source Interpret Community (*https://oreil.ly/V89Dv*), supported by Microsoft.[3] This is one of the open source toolkits that offer a collection of explainers based on proven and emerging model interpretation algorithms, such as SHapley Additive exPlanations (SHAP) and Local Interpretable Model-Agnostic Explanations (LIME). If developers understand the model better, then they can work toward fairness.

Themis-ml

Developed by independent developers, *themis-ml* is a Python library used to audit models for discrimination and bias, and it includes algorithms for mitigating bias.[4] It works well with the *scikit-learn* library and similar machine learning ecosystems. The *themis-ml* library is aimed at the developer audience.

Model explainers use statistical techniques to calculate feature importance. This enables AI developers to perform *label prediction*, or to quantify the relative influence of each feature in the training dataset on the outcome. Explainers such as SHAP and LIME work by evaluating a test dataset of feature cases and the labels the model predicts for them. They add code to produce explainers as the model is being trained, and the explanation is part of the model's output. They can also generate explanations and predictions from a published model by updating the model to use code that loads the explainer and then returns explanations along with predictions.

At a high level, the models distinguish between global feature importance and local feature importance. *Global feature importance* quantifies the relative importance of each feature in the test dataset as a whole. In contrast, *local feature importance* identifies the influence of each feature value for a specific individual. For example, consider

---

2 Brittany Johnson and Yuriy Brun, "Fairkit-learn: A Fairness Evaluation and Comparison Toolkit," in *Proceedings of the ACM/IEEE 44th International Conference on Software Engineering: Companion Proceedings*, ed. Matthew B. Dwyer (New York: Association for Computing Machinery, 2022), 70–74, *https://dl.acm.org/doi/proceedings/10.1145/3510454*.

3 Find the Interpret Community repository at *https://github.com/interpretml/interpret-community*.

4 Niels Bantilan, "Themis-ml: A Fairness-Aware Machine Learning Interface for End-to-End Discrimination Discovery and Mitigation," *Journal of Technology in Human Services* 36, no. 1 (2018): 15–30.

---

the case where an algorithm identifies the features contributing to the likelihood that someone will pay their credit card balance. In terms of global feature importance, the features may include whether someone is married, their age, and their zip code. In terms of local feature importance, the influence of each feature value for a specific individual prediction may give a different result; for one individual, their marital status, age, and zip code may have less influence than for other people in the dataset.

The result will depend on the type of model being applied. For example, if the outcome is binary, there are only two possible outcomes (0 and 1). The explainer will also aim to show that each feature's support for one class results in a correlatively negative level of support for the other class. A multi-class model will produce different classes as potential outcomes, with each feature getting a local importance value for each possible class. The AI service is deployed with the scoring script, referencing both the predictive model and the explainer. When the downstream application consumes the AI service by sending data to it for processing, the returned results include both the predictions and the associated local feature importance values.

Transparency is a complex area, and selecting informative, discriminating, and independent features is a crucial element of effective AI algorithms. Many areas are relevant, such as pattern recognition, classification, and regression. Transparency also helps to identify bias or unintended correlation in the model.

How is this important to business? AI models are increasingly used to inform decisions that affect people's lives. They can encapsulate unintentional bias that could impact people in both a good and bad way. Therefore, it is crucial to ensure that bias checking is done continuously. While ethical toolkits can help pinpoint and alleviate bias, responsibility for ensuring fairness ultimately rests with the teams developing and deploying AI systems. Businesses should create a collaborative evaluation process to demonstrate a commitment to ethical AI practices. Addressing bias is not a one-and-done job but an ongoing process.

Transfer Learning in Model Training

In the AI feedback loop, feedback can guide developers in applying transfer learning techniques. *Transfer learning* is a machine learning technique that uses knowledge acquired from one task or domain to improve the model's performance in a related job or subject. The model can leverage that knowledge to adapt and perform better on new data. Developers use a pretrained model as a starting point for a new task. This approach benefits the business by saving time and resources while often improving the model's performance in the new learning domain.

Pretrained AI models are widely used in transfer learning across various domains. Developers can use them to jump-start the learning process, where learning begins with a model that the developer previously trained on a large dataset for a related task. The model has already learned to recognize useful features from the data and can extrapolate to other similar tasks.

There are a number of examples of pretrained models being used in transfer learning. One is the ImageNet database, a giant collection of labeled images. The AI developer community uses ImageNet to train image recognition models, forming the basis for models such as VGG, ResNet, and Inception. Developers can then tweak the models for custom, specific image classification tasks, such as pinpointing medical disorders or detecting specific objects in images.

Transfer learning has proven highly effective in various AI applications, including some discussed in this book, such as natural language processing. It allows models to benefit from the knowledge and patterns learned from large datasets and tasks, making AI development more efficient and leading to better-performing models, especially in scenarios where collecting extensive data for each task might be challenging.

How Are Other Organizations Using the AI Feedback Loop?

Many applications use the AI feedback loop. For example, search engines like Google continually use it to improve user search results. Users leave a trail of data breadcrumbs when they engage in internet searches. For instance, users click on search results, spend time reading pages, or open new tabs, and this activity provides data that Google uses to train its search engine algorithms. The company learns from this feedback and uses it to refine its algorithms, constantly improving them to provide a better, more finely tuned set of search results. Similarly, virtual assistants like Siri, Alexa, and Google Assistant rely on the AI feedback loop to understand and respond to user queries better. As users interact with virtual assistants, the AI algorithms learn to recognize speech patterns, understand user intent, and provide more authentic responses to user voice commands.

Social media platforms like Facebook and X (formerly known as Twitter) use the AI feedback loop to personalize users' feeds. As with internet searches, users leave a data breadcrumb trail on social media platforms. Social media companies can analyze users' interactions, such as likes, comments, and shares. The data feeds into AI algorithms to understand user preferences and interests better. The algorithms could also track topics that are trending and use this information to help understand future outliers and trends.

For both internet searches and social media platforms, the data and the feedback help deliver content that is more likely to engage users, keeping them on the platform longer.

Another area of interest is self-driving cars, which use feedback from sensors and devices such as cameras. The goal is to train the AI algorithms to fine-tune their driving behavior while becoming safer.

To summarize, feedback is an essential component for creating effective and adaptive AI models that are useful in the real world. Feedback empowers developers to build AI models that continuously learn from experience. It supports discovering areas for improvement, helping to improve the AI model overall to meet the needs and expectations of users and business stakeholders.

How Can the AI Feedback Loop Help You?

Data visualization is critical in the AI feedback loop by making complex data and patterns more interpretable and actionable. Power BI supports the iterative process of developing and refining AI models; visualization offers clarity at various stages of the process.

Throughout the book, we have shown you how Power BI can help you explore your data through data analysis. Power BI helps you understand the data before starting to think about AI. To have good artificial intelligence, we need good business intelligence. Prior to feeding data into an AI model, Power BI enables us to create insightful visualizations such as histograms, line graphs, and scatter plots to help developers and the business understand the distributions, ranges, and relationships in the data.

Power BI assists AI model development by identifying outliers and anomalies so developers and business teams can decide on a strategy to deal with data points that are unusual, unexpected, or deviate in some way from the rest of the data. It supports efforts to clean the data so that our AI modeling goes more smoothly.

It offers a canvas that will help feature selection. Power BI data visualization can rank and illustrate the significance of various features. This helps both developers and business teams understand the most suitable features and potentially reduce the model's complexity.

Power BI enables us to understand the AI model behavior by visualizing confusion matrices. As a recap, for classification tasks, confusion matrices visually depict true positives, false positives, true negatives, and false negatives. We also covered other visualization techniques such as ROC Curves to visualize the performance of a classification model at various thresholds. Power BI helps to offer a clear picture of model performance, helping to facilitate the process.

In addition, the software makes it easy for users to understand and provide feedback on AI model predictions. Throughout the book, we have given examples of how you can use Power BI to illustrate the data involved in AI, thereby supporting the feedback loop. Business-focused stakeholders without much knowledge of AI may not understand the nuances and intricacies of AI models. Visualization, in the form of charts, graphs, or heatmaps, can provide a common canvas to support communication between developers and stakeholders.

Finally, Power BI facilitates AI adoption by helping the business understand its data, model performance, behavior, and areas of improvement. Data visualization and AI, together, can help to make data work for your business. We look forward to hearing what you achieve with Power BI and AI.

AI and Power BI—Over to You!

To summarize, addressing ethical questions requires strong collaboration and a strategic approach that keeps the business goals in mind. Ultimately, for the AI project to be successful, technical and nontechnical stakeholders must work together to gain a comprehensive understanding of AI's potential risks, benefits, and impact. The soft skills are often the hard skills! As with IT projects, there is a need for transparent and inclusive communication. Diversity, equity, and inclusion mean that everyone has a voice. Additionally, education tailored to the specific business context is key to addressing these concerns effectively. The training should be not just one-time but ongoing as people learn new technology, new processes, and new ways of working.

In Chapter 1, we discussed how to get started. There are a range of options in Power BI dataflows to allow the organization to manage Power BI using the degree of "cloudiness" that it prefers. Ultimately, businesses are trying to find a balance between "silver platter" reports and "self-service," and Power BI dataflows offer both methods while avoiding the "Excel hell" of data puddles that are unmonitored, unmanageable, and unruly pieces of data debt.

In Chapter 8, text is discussed as a common and potentially rich form of data for business decision making. The Text Analytics algorithms showcased in this chapter provide easy-to-use means of augmenting datasets within Power BI. The newly transformed data then can help you build compelling reports with the assistance of Language Detection, Key Phrase Extraction, and Sentiment Analysis.

In Chapter 9, you learned that thanks to advances in artificial neural networks, computer vision is now more accurate and accessible than ever. Image Tag in Power BI can unlock business insights within data that were previously hidden in plain sight. It is a powerful addition to any dataset that includes pictures, as shown in the example with AirBnB listings. You now have the skills and tools needed to begin augmenting your own reports by creating new analyses.

In Chapter 10, you considered what problems you could solve at your organization by combining Azure Machine Learning with Power BI. Are you a key decision maker at your organization? If so, recall the five successful organizational behaviors for successfully leveraging AI and identify which is best in terms of level of effort, probability of success, and favorability of outcome.

Or are you a practitioner who can build your own solutions? If so, recall the machine learning lifecycle (Figure 10-7) and walk through the process to train and deploy a working prototype. Be sure to focus on developing a solution that is actionable and that provides measurable business value.

Whichever direction you decide to take first, you will find that building custom machine learning models can unlock a new level of problem solving. We hope you see Azure Machine Learning as a valuable addition to Power BI—not just another way to transform data but an opportunity for your organization to fully customize AI to meet its own needs.

Index

majority class metrics, 93
many-to-many relationships, 44
marketing personas, 195
masking data for privacy, 374
matplotlib Python library, 386, 387
McAfee, Andrew, 118
MD Anderson Cancer Center, Houston, TX, 321
measures of fact tables, 30, 42
micro-averaged metrics, 92
Microsoft
    licensing URL, 87
    services and devices over local desktop, 18
    SR-CNN model blog post URL, 189
Microsoft Azure (see Azure)
Microsoft Power BI (see Power BI)
MLOps (machine learning operations), 329
    overview by Microsoft URL, 337
model explainers, 430
model performance report in binary prediction demo, 112
modeling data (see data modeling)
models
    AI feedback loop, 423
        AI in Power BI, 433
        biases mitigated, 426
        edge cases, 424
        ethics and transparency in AI, 428-431
        explainable AI, 428
        fixing errors in models, 426
        organizations using feedback, 432
        training and development of models, 424
        transfer learning, 431
    algorithm selection flow chart URL, 331
    business team confidence in model, 411
        is model just a fluke, 411
        model validation, 411
        ongoing model evaluation, 412
    custom models, 262
        AutoML or Azure Machine Learning for, 262
        (see also custom machine learning models)
    ethics and transparency in AI, 428-431
        ethical toolkits, 429
        model explainers, 430
    evaluating
        about, 404

heteroscedasticity effects on AI models, 405
    heteroscedasticity in this context, 404
    managing heteroscedasticity, 405
    scenario with heteroscedasticity, 404
    scenario without heteroscedasticity, 404
Lineage view of data, 420
model made ready for real world, 406
    cost and benefit assessment, 407-409
    making AI production ready demo, 413-419
    return on investment calculation example, 409
    return on investment formula, 409
pretrained, 262
    image tagging, 262
    text analytics, 262
    transfer learning, 262, 431
    validation of, 411
Molnar, Christoph, 298
movies featuring AI, 327
multiclass classification, 90, 93
    (see also classification)

N

narrow versus general intelligence, 326-328
natural language processing (NLP), 263
    stop word removal, 277
    text analytics (see text analytics)
    transfer learning, 432
neural networks, 295
    DALL·E 3, 296
    deep learning, 295
    a simple neural network, 296-298
New York City taxi data (see taxi data from New York City)
NLP (see natural language processing)
noise in time series data, 168
normalization, 199
    of dimension tables, 31
    k-means clustering data, 199
    standardization versus, 199

O

one-to-many relationships, 44
one-to-one relationships, 44
one-versus-all matrices, 92
online resources (see resources online)
OpenAI ChatGPT (see ChatGPT (OpenAI))

volume of data, 263

About the Authors

Jen Stirrup is the founder and CEO of Data Relish, a UK-based AI and business intelligence leadership boutique consultancy delivering data strategy and business-focused solutions. Jen is a recognized leading authority in AI and business intelligence Leadership, a *Fortune* 100 global speaker, and has been named as one of the top 50 global data visionaries, one of the top data scientists to follow on X (formerly Twitter) and one of the most influential top 50 women in technology worldwide. Jen has clients in 24 countries on 5 continents, and her client list includes Microsoft, the National Health Service, the UK and Northern Ireland Governments, the Ashridge Hult Business School, CBS Interactive, O'Reilly, and Virgin Atlantic.

She holds postgraduate degrees in AI and cognitive science. Jen has authored three books on data and artificial intelligence has been featured on CBS Interactive and the BBC, as well as well-known podcasts such as *Digital Disrupted*, *RunAs Radio*, and her own *Make Your Data Work* webinar series.

Jen has given keynotes for colleges and universities and donated her expertise to charities and nonprofits as a nonexecutive director. Jen's keynotes are about AI leadership, diversity and inclusion in technology, digital transformation, and business intelligence. All of Jen's keynotes are based on her two-decades-plus of global experience, dedication, and hard work.

Dr. Thomas J. Weinandy is a research economist at Upside, a digital promotions marketplace that increases the financial power of people and businesses in the real world. There he develops data-driven thought leadership at the intersection of consumer behavior and macroeconomic trends, particularly for the grocery, fuel, and restaurant industries.

He previously worked as a data scientist at BlueGranite, where he integrated machine learning with business intelligence for organizations across various sectors and countries. In addition to his role as a consultant, he hosted the popular *AI in a Day with Power BI* webinar series with over 25,000 online viewers.

Dr. Weinandy received a Ph.D. in applied economics from Western Michigan University, an M.B.A. from Wheeling Jesuit University, and a B.A. in Spanish and social entrepreneurship from John Carroll University. His dissertation, "Applied Microeconomics and Business Intelligence in the Digital Age," analyzed novel instances of digital technology mediating economic activity. He currently resides in Grand Rapids, Michigan, USA.

Colophon

The animal on the cover of *Artificial Intelligence with Microsoft Power BI* is a roan antelope (*Hippotragus equinus*), so named for the reddish-brown roan color of its coat.

Roan antelopes are one of the largest African antelope species, weighing between 510–710 pounds and standing 53–63 inches tall, depending on sex (males are larger than females). They have long, sturdy limbs and a thick neck with a black-tipped mane and a beard. The antelopes' heads are narrow, dark brown or black in color with white markings around the mouth, nose, and eyes. Their horns arch backward from their heads, and can grow up to 39 inches long. Their tails have a black, hairy tip.

Roan antelopes prefer to live in lightly wooded savannas, primarily in West and Central Africa. They can also be found in floodplains and grasslands. As herbivores that spend most of their time grazing for food, they like to have access to open spaces and areas with easily accessible water. While they mostly graze on grass, they will also feed on shrubs, herbs, and acacia tree pods. Roan antelopes live in small herds of 5–15 individuals, with one dominant male (though challenges are common, wherein two males go to their knees and lock horns).

A major factor that impacts roan antelopes is loss of habitat due to human activities, such as agriculture and settlement construction. Illegal poaching is also an issue. Despite these adversities, roan antelope are still considered a species of least concern on endangered species lists. However, many of the animals on O'Reilly covers are endangered; all of them are important to the world.

The cover illustration is by Susan Thompson, based on a black-and-white engraving from *Riverside Natural History*. The series design is by Edie Freedman, Ellie Volckhausen, and Karen Montgomery. The cover fonts are Gilroy Semibold and Guardian Sans. The text font is Adobe Minion Pro; the heading font is Adobe Myriad Condensed; and the code font is Dalton Maag's Ubuntu Mono.

Printed in the USA
CPSIA information can be obtained
at www.ICGtesting.com
JSHW062000170624
64962JS00010B/71

9 781098 112752